An Introduction to the French Poets

By the same author

A SHORT HISTORY OF FRENCH LITERATURE

FRENCH TRAGIC DRAMA IN THE
SIXTEENTH AND SEVENTEENTH CENTURIES
(*forthcoming*)

PRINCIPLES OF TRAGEDY

JEAN RACINE: A CRITICAL BIOGRAPHY

(ed.) THE PENGUIN BOOK OF FRENCH VERSE,
VOLUME II

AN INTRODUCTION TO

THE FRENCH POETS

Villon to the Present Day

GEOFFREY BRERETON

METHUEN & CO LTD
11 New Fetter Lane London EC4

First published in 1956
by Methuen & Co Ltd
11 New Fetter Lane London EC4
Reprinted 1957
First published as a University Paperback 1960
Second edition revised and reset 1973
© 1973 by Geoffrey Brereton
Printed in Great Britain by
Butler & Tanner Ltd
Frome and London

SBN 416 76620 X (hardback)
416 76630 7 (paperback)

Distributed in the USA by
HARPER & ROW PUBLISHERS, INC.
BARNES & NOBLE IMPORT DIVISION

Preface to the Revised Edition

THIS book was originally conceived as a series of introductory studies on the major French poets from Villon's time until today. It was not designed as a consecutive history of French poetry over five centuries, though in the event something of the sort also emerged and will be perceptible in outline. My main concern, however, was to attempt to characterize certain poets as individual writers, to establish for each some kind of literary identity before fitting them into a more general pattern, with all the theories and classifications which that must involve. In that form the book met with a very kind reception from its reviewers and seems to have interested a considerable number of readers since. This revised edition is the same in essentials, with some comparatively minor changes and the addition of some new material described below.

The best and only really valuable approach to literature is through the individual writer, and more particularly if he is a poet. A man who has read only three or four poets with attention, understanding, and some sort of 'enjoyment' may have vast areas of ignorance in the field of poetry as a whole. But if he ever wishes to explore those areas he will be in a better position to do so than one who has a wide knowledge of the history and theory of poetry but is not deeply read in any one poet. The first will at least have a definite starting-point from which he can go on to draw the comparisons and contrasts which are the basis of all true literary studies. From one poet one can proceed to another, either forward or backward in time, but one cannot do this satisfactorily by following a blueprint. The process only becomes illuminating if one moves from one known phenomenon to another, in this way discovering the relationship – or lack of relationship – between them.

How can the individual qualities of a writer be determined? Primarily and basically through a study on his work. This is what matters and is the form in which his 'personality' reaches us. But his biography, when it is recoverable, is not irrelevant. It would be an excess of purism to eliminate every known reference to his social and personal life, his correspondence, the comments of his friends and other contemporaries, and present the naked 'work' as though it were one more chicken taken from some academic deep-freeze. On the contrary, poetry cannot be preserved from contamination by 'life', because that is what it is about.

Of course one can go too far in this direction. To read actual lived experience into every apparent allusion in a poet's work is to misunderstand the creative imagination or, quite often, the poetic conventions of the period. With many poets, particularly before the Romantics, no personal experience is being communicated in any literal way, though a psychological analysis at a much deeper level would never seem unjustified. With certain later poets, such as Nerval, Musset, Rimbaud, some biographical knowledge seems indispensable. Without it the reader is at sea and at the mercy of the opposite excess of computerism.

Poetry, if it is worth reading at all, ought to awaken some personal response. No doubt it can do so, like music, quite anonymously. In music, however, the composer speaks to us through a formidable apparatus of interpretation, in which conductor, musicians and acoustics all play a part. The impact of poetry is more immediate. 'I loathe Baudelaire,' a woman student once said to me, after reading some of his more sadistic poems, 'he must have been a beastly man.' This possible beginning of a hate-relationship struck me as an excellent sign. At least it seemed more likely to bear fruit than a rigorous linguistic analysis.

In short, living poetry is written by living people. The first object of this book is to portray those people, partly as they existed in their time and place, but much more as they present themselves in their work. They have names, just as painters have names, with which this work is signed. It should be possible to go beyond the name and define what it represents, not merely in aesthetic and technical qualities, but in terms of the poetic identity which they themselves were usually engaged in building up.

In doing this it is neither desirable nor possible to ignore the general terminology used in literary history and criticism. Here poets are classed in schools and movements whose titles have become so familiar that to discard them would be a wanton act. They usefully indicate features common to several poets and sometimes the conscious aims of a self-named group such as the Symbolists and the Surrealists. Usually they have historical connotations. They provide undeniably convenient guidelines.

It is when these classifications are overemphasized that they become pernicious. Then they obscure not only important differences but significant resemblances between poets who happen to have been placed in certain categories. Much critical ingenuity has been devoted in the past to tabulating the distinctions between classic and romantic literature, and more recently between classic and baroque. The nineteenth and twentieth centuries offer the apparent sequence of Romanticism, Parnassianism, Symbolism, Surrealism, each of which it becomes imperative to define and, as critical attitudes change, to redefine constantly. It is indisputable that these terms, besides forming a necessary framework to the study of poetry, do correspond to certain broad realities. But broad they are and they should never be taken as absolute. The reasoned classification of such poets as Chénier, Baudelaire, Mallarmé, Claudel under one or other of the well-known headings is no doubt a good critical exercise which can often lead to a better understanding of their work. Undertaken in that spirit, it is not misdirected. It is only when the category is allowed to swallow the poet that it becomes misleading.

These are the guiding principles of the present book. In revising it for a new edition I have added a short chapter on three seventeenth-century poets (Théophile de Viau, Saint-Amant and Tristan L'Hermite) and have recast the last chapter and expanded it into two in order to give a rather fuller picture of modern poetry. The bibliography has also been brought up to date and considerably expanded; it should now point the way towards 'advanced' studies. The original chapters have been retouched in the light of recent research and a few personal second thoughts, but are otherwise unaltered. My response to Victor Hugo might appear as subjective as the woman student's response to Baudelaire, though it has a critical motivation. I have been reading Hugo on and off for many years, always beginning with admiration and even delight and ending each time in disappointment and exasperation. No other major poet in four languages has ever had this effect on me. Musset and Leconte de Lisle are, if anything, even less in favour than when this book first appeared some fifteen years ago. I can still enjoy reading them, though not perhaps as first priorities, and I do not see how it is possible to understand the nature of French Romanticism and its aftermath without some acquaintance with their contrasted work. As for Apollinaire, I still cannot see him as a major poet, for the reasons given in the chapter concerning him. But, like the first aeroplanes, it is undeniable that he started something.

This book has always been intended as an Introduction – that is, a point from which its readers will willingly go on to a further stage. I wrote in the first edition that 'a feeling for English poetry, as diversely based as possible, is the best original equipment for reading poetry in French or any other language'. The more brutal converse of this is: 'If you don't read English poetry, why on earth read French?' Too often the answer will come back: 'For examination purposes.' I never meant to help students to satisfy examiners, whose ways are so often mysterious. But if this book does so, even as a by-product, it will continue to fulfil a certain function, though that is not its main one.

G.B.

January 1972

Chapter 1

François Villon

VILLON was the last of the great French poets of the Middle Ages and one of the few who can now be read without a considerable background knowledge of medieval culture. He loses, of course, something in the process. One may fail to recognize the traditional nature of the themes he is treating, one may miss catching in his comments on life and death echoes going back two hundred years before his lifetime and so not appreciate the interesting twists he gives them. One may, in particular, remain unaware of his masterly use of verse-forms which had been developing during more than three centuries, since the time of the Provençal troubadours. But though he belonged to his age and re-flected its cynicism, its innocent obscenity, its piety, its learning (on a lowish level), and some of its literary conventions, he is more than a merely representative poet. He is both universal and personal enough to carry beyond his age – or, if one prefers it, to carry his age to ours.

If, as modern scholarship tends to show, he is not quite the remark-able special case he was once considered to be, he is none the less the only poet to have expressed the spirit of his time with what *seems* to be a completely personal voice. This, which distinguishes him from all his major contemporaries, is the quality which has ensured his survival and it matters very little whether he was experiencing for the first time the states of mind he communicates. The point is that he communicates them effectively and, to the extent that he does so, makes them his own. Behind the work there is undoubtedly a man. While it would be a mis-take to try to visualize the man too clearly apart from the work, yet something is known of his life from external sources. Scanty though these are, they fit the rest of the picture.

He was born in Paris in 1431, the year when Joan of Arc was burnt at Rouen. His mother, according to his poems, was poor and illiterate. From his father, of whom no mention remains, he presumably took one of his two original names of Montcorbier and Des Loges. In later life he discarded them to adopt the name of a priest who befriended and educated him, Guillaume de Villon. Studying at Paris University,

François Villon took the degrees of Bachelor, *Licencié*, and finally Master of Arts. Even after this, he continued to regard himself as a student, though of an unacademic kind. His first recorded conflict with the law occurred at the age of twenty-four, when he killed a priest called Philippe Chermoye in a brawl and fled from Paris. He returned with a pardon six months later, took part in a successful robbery at the Collège de Navarre and again left the capital, this time for five years. Just before going, he composed his first considerable poem, *Les Lais* (Christmas 1456).

During his wandering in the provinces he visited Orleans, Blois, and probably roved much further afield. He found a temporary patron in Charles, Duke of Orleans – himself a fine poet in the old courtly tradition – who included some of Villon's verses in his own album of poems. He had relations with a gang of malefactors known as *les compagnons de la Coquille* and he continued to fall foul of the law. One of his own compositions suggests that he lay at one time in the Duke of Orleans's prisons under sentence of death but was saved by an amnesty granted to celebrate the birth of the Duke's daughter. He spent the summer of 1461 in prison at Meung-sur-Loire. This time his captor was the Bishop of Orleans. He was released in the autumn of that year to return once more to Paris and write his principal poem, *Le Testament*.

There is no record of the crimes for which Villon suffered these punishments. He may even – though it seems unlikely – have been innocent. But, innocent or guilty, he was by now a marked man in the eyes of the authorities. In November 1462 he was arrested on suspicion of a new robbery. He was about to be released for lack of evidence when his share in the six-year-old affair of the Collège de Navarre was recalled. He was obliged to sign a promise to repay 120 gold crowns before they let him go. When, a few weeks later, he was concerned in a street brawl outside the office of a papal official, his evil reputation nearly destroyed him. He was sentenced to be hanged and it was no doubt while waiting to be executed that he composed the famous *Epitaphe Villon* or *Ballade des pendus*. Meanwhile, he had chanced the desperate throw of an appeal. To his joy, it was granted. He was set free, but under penalty of ten years' banishment from the city and viscounty of Paris. This judgment, rendered on 5 January 1463, is the last authentic mention of François Villon.

Two picturesque anecdotes of his later life were recounted by Rabelais writing some ninety years after. One describes him in banishment in England, chatting with Rabelaisian familiarity to Edward IV. The other depicts him living in his boisterous old age at Saint-Maixantde-Poitou. The interest of the anecdotes, which are certainly inventions, is that already by Rabelais's time Villon had become a legendary figure, famed for his ingenious pranks and his coarse wit. The legend has continued to grow, fed by the abundant material, rich in contrasting pathos and squalor, provided by Villon's own writings. As would be expected, few precise statements of fact can be obtained from such a source. What does emerge is the revelation of a character, drawn with great frankness.

The self-portrayed Villon was a man of some education who drifted into a life of crime and vagabondage through his incurable love of independence. In spite of his obscure parentage, he was not inevitably marked out as a social outcast, for with his benefactor Guillaume Villon and his studies behind him he should have found at least a humble security in some ecclesiastical charge – had he wanted it. On the other hand, he was not a heroic rebel. He became a criminal less from design than from lethargy. He needed money to keep himself alive and to spend on 'taverns and women', and crime appeared the easiest way of obtaining it. Even here, he was not very successful, as his various imprisonments show.

Imprisonment soured him, but brought no repentance. His occasional flashes of regret were for his carefree youth and for the material comforts which had eluded him through his own folly, not for any moral standard from which he had fallen short. He could indulge in self-pity and at the same time cock verbal snooks at the rich and prosperous. Here in fact is the only kind of pride discernible in him; he had kept himself free from the taint of conformism. This was his essential freedom, worth preserving at the cost of many grovellings to the powerful, of many months of captivity in dungeons.

So far we have the makings of a picaresque poet – as handy, because of his peculiar position, with his stabs of satire as he is with his knife – irreverent, racy, slangy, no more respectful of words than of persons so long as they serve his purpose – a highly flavoured 'character', but, on the long view, a minor poet. What raises him to a higher level is his partly traditional preoccupation with two themes which, fundamentally, are one: the shortness of youth, the horror of old age and death. These haunt him, less as poetic commonplaces than as almost tangible realities, to be handled as concretely as Hamlet did Yorick's skull. Over all is his religious seriousness, colouring much that he wrote and giving to some of his verses a solemn tone, though to others – judged by modern standards – a grotesque one. On the whole, however, it would be mistaken to include religion among the motive-forces of Villon's art. He was soaked in the beliefs of his century and he echoed them as unquestioningly as a modern poet might echo, woven into his thought, the main tenets of Freudian psychology.

II

Villon has left some three thousand lines of verse which fall into three main divisions: *Les Lais, Le Testament,* and a small number of miscellaneous pieces. He used two different but related verse-forms which he handled with such ease and mastery that they seem to belong to him as his personal language. The first is an eight-line stanza on three rhymes. The lines are octosyllabic and are used for what might be called the narrative part of *Les Lais* and *Le Testament.* These are the two opening stanzas of *Les Lais*:

> L'an quatre cens cinquante six,
> Je, Françoys Villon, escollier,
> Considerant, de sens rassis,
> Le frain aux dens, franc au collier,
> Qu'on doit ses oeuvres conseillier,
> Comme Vegece le raconte,
> Sage Rommain, grant conseillier,
> Ou autrement on se mesconte –
>
> En ce temps que j'ay dit devant,
> Sur le Noel, morte saison,
> Que les loups se vivent de vent
> Et qu'on se tient en sa maison,
> Pour le frimas, pres du tison,
> Me vint ung vouloir de brisier
> La tres amoureuse prison
> Qui soulait mon cuer debrisier.[1]

Villon's second verse-form is the *ballade*, a more stylized version of the first, with a similar rhyme-pattern. It had been a favourite with medieval French poets ever since it was established in the fourteenth century by Guillaume de Machaut and it was used in English by Machaut's contemporary, Chaucer. Villon writes it in several variations. At its simplest, it consists of three eight-line stanzas and a

[1] In the year 1456, I, François Villon, student, considering with deliberate mind – the bit between my teeth, the collar loose – that one ought to examine one's actions – as Vegetius, that wise Roman and shrewd counsellor, remarks – or otherwise one may go wrong – At the time I have said, at Christmas, in the dead season, when the wolves live on wind and people stay in their houses near the fire because of the hoar-frost, there came to me a desire to break the very amorous yoke which had been tormenting my heart.

four-line *envoi*, as in the well-known *Ballade des dames du temps jadis*, with its refrain 'Mais où sont les neiges d'antan?' – or in the *Ballade des menus propos*, which ends thus:

> Je congnais cheval et mulet,
> Je congnais leur charge et leur somme,
> Je congnais Bietris et Belet,
> Je congnais get qui nombre et somme,
> Je congnais vision et somme,
> Je congnais la faulte des Boesmes,
> Je congnais le povoir de Romme,
> Je congnais tout, fors que moy mesmes.
>
> Prince, je congnais tout en somme,
> Je congnais coulourez et blesmes,
> Je congnais Mort qui tout consomme,
> Je congnais tout, fors que moy mesmes.[1]

The same rhymes recur throughout and the last line of each stanza and of the *envoi* is always the same, making up the refrain. The *envoi* often begins with the word *Prince*, originally addressed to the presiding judge at the medieval literary festivals known as *puys*. More elaborate kinds of *ballade* could be built by increasing the number of stanzas, or the number of lines within the stanza.

In Villon's hands the *ballade* acquires much greater flexibility than its stereotyped form suggests. He uses it for his most impressive pieces – the peaks which suddenly rise above the chirpy running verse of *Le Testament* – but also for poems where dignity would be as incongruous as a horse in the House of Commons. With this limited and traditional technical equipment he wrote almost the whole known body of his poetry.

Les Lais, as he says in the opening stanzas, already quoted, was written at Christmas 1456. He had just taken part in the robbery at the Collège de Navarre and was apparently contemplating a similar coup in the provinces, at Angers. Naturally he does not refer to this, but says that an unhappy love-affair is driving him from Paris. Knowing that he may be gone for some time and that life is uncertain, he makes a number of comic bequests to his friends and enemies. This explains the title of the poem, which is the same as the modern French *legs*,

[1] I know horse and mule, I know their load and their pack, I know Beatrice and Betty, I know counter which numbers and adds, I know vision and dream, I know the Bohemians' heresy, I know the power of Rome: I know all, except myself.
Prince, I know all in short, I know coloured and pale, I know death which finishes everything, I know all except myself.

or legacy. It is sometimes called, less correctly, *Le Petit Testament*. The poem, a relatively short one of some three hundred lines, is a not entirely truthful balance-sheet of Villon's state of mind at the time and a half-mocking, half-serious farewell to his Parisian acquaintances. To his benefactor Guillaume Villon he leaves his reputation, to the woman who has treated him so harshly he leaves his heart, 'pâle, piteux, mort et transi', to his barber he leaves his hair-clippings and to his cobbler his old shoes. Many of his other jokes are topical and local and do not travel well to the reader of today. A few remain surprisingly fresh.

Villon at this point was clearly pleased with himself and life in general. In spite of his protestation that the torments of love have left him 'as dry and black as a sweep's brush', he is still perky, full of an impudent, street-boy wit. He has enjoyed making his mock legacies and is looking forward with some pleasure to the new adventures which await him outside the capital.

Le Testament is a two-thousand-line poem of a more impressive and bitter nature. Five years older than when he wrote *Les Lais*, Villon has just been released, a broken man, from the prison of the Bishop of Orleans. He may have felt that it was literally time to make his will. In any case, while still following very loosely the plan of *Les Lais*, he seems intent on bequeathing in his new poem all the fruits of his pain-fully-acquired experience. Moreover, by encrusting in *Le Testament* poems which he had written earlier, he seeks to give them a more permanent setting and so preserve them. Villon's 'last will and testa-ment' thus has a triple sense. It contains a few mock bequests which ostensibly justify its name; it is his latest word on life; and it represents the body of poetry which he wishes to leave to future generations. The show-pieces in it are certain of the *ballades*, but, although these can be taken out and appreciated in isolation, most of them gain when read in their ingeniously woven context.

Thus the famous *Ballade des dames du temps jadis* is part of a sequence of reflections on the brevity of youth and the inevitable coming of Death the Leveller. Villon leads up to it by a terrifyingly realistic description of the physical changes which death brings – an obsession of the medieval mind which occurs again in the late Renais-sance, then virtually disappears until Baudelaire. He follows it with the deservedly less-known *Ballade des seigneurs du temps jadis*, of which little but the refrain is worth remembering ('Mais où est le preux Charlemagne?'), and then, his pen having become stuck in this groove, with a *ballade* of similar import in pastiched 'Old French'. After this, he works back into the realistic vein of which he was a master and rhymes the regrets of *la belle Heaulmière* for her lost youth. Once beautiful, she is now a hideous old crone, and Villon omits no detail of her decay. And the moral, as she gives it to the younger women who still possess the beauty she has lost, is: Love while you are able, spare no man, take all the profit you can get.

> Prenez a destre et a senestre;
> N'espargnez homme, je vous prie:
> Car vielles n'ont ne cours ne estre,
> Ne que monnoye qu'on descrie.[1]

It should be obvious that there was not a particle of romanticism in Villon's nature. But since many English readers will first have met him in translations of the great *ballades*, they must be warned that some of these translations deform the original by glamourizing it. There is no glamour in Villon. Sex, illness, hunger, cold, poverty, vice, are all described by him in the same flat and precise detail. His only escape from the concrete reality is, not into romanticism, but into humour, which sometimes resembles the cynical, snivelling laugh of the down-and-out. Any translation which makes him express fine sentiments is completely foreign to the original, and represents nothing but its form. There is, however, emotion in Villon, achieved in the hardest way of all: not by rhetoric which is a flourish from above, but by properly rooted pathos, rising from the lowest and grimiest feelings of humanity. His sense of the fundamental brotherhood of mankind, cutting right across distinctions of rank and wealth, is Villon's most positive quality. It saves him from total cynicism and every now and then exalts him above his material and enables him to write some tremendous poem such as the *Epitaphe Villon*, in which he imagines himself to be dangling from the gallows among other hanged criminals:

> Freres humains qui après nous vivez,
> N'ayez les cuers contre nous endurcis,
> Car, se pitié de nous povres avez,
> Dieu en aura plus tost de vous mercis.
> Vous nous voiez cy attachez cinq, six:
> Quant de la chair, que trop avons nourrie,
> Elle est pieça devorée et pourrie,
> Et nous, les os, devenons cendre et pouldre.
> De nostre mal personne ne s'en rie;
> Mais priez Dieu que tous nous vueille absouldre.

---

[1] Take with right hand and with left. Spare no man, I tell you. For old women have no more currency or existence than debased coinage.

Se freres vous clamons, pas n'en devez
Avoir desdaing, quoy que fusmes occis
Par justice. Toutefois, vous sçavez
Que tous les hommes n'ont pas bon sens rassis;
Excusez nous, puis que sommes transsis,
Envers le fils de la Vierge Marie,
Que sa grace ne soit pour nous tarie,
Nous preservant de l'infernale fouldre.
Nous sommes mors, ame ne nous harie;
Mais priez Dieu que tous nous vueille absouldre.

La pluye nous a debuez et lavez,
Et le soleil dessechiez et noircis;
Pies, corbeaulx, nous ont les yeux cavez,
Et arrachié la barbe et les sourcis.
Jamais nul temps nous ne sommes assis;
Puis ça, puis la, comme le vent varie,
A son plaisir sans cesser nous charie,
Plus becquetez d'oiseaulx que dez a couldre.
Ne soiez donc de notre confrairie;
Mais priez Dieu que tous nous vueille absouldre.

Prince Jhesus, qui sur tous a maistrie,
Garde qu'Enfer n'ait de nous seigneurie:
A luy n'ayons que faire ne que souldre.
Hommes, icy n'a point de mocquerie;
Mais priez Dieu que tous nous vueille absouldre.[1]

With this poem, we are outside *Le Testament.* It is one of a score of
pieces written on various occasions which do not fit into the frame-

---

[1] Brother men who live after us, do not harden your hearts against us, for if you have pity
on us poor sinners, God will sooner have mercy on you. You see us hanging here, five,
six; as for the flesh, which we fed too well, it has long ago been eaten and rotted, and
we, the bones, are becoming powder and dust. Let no one laugh at our affliction, but pray
to God that he should absolve us all.

If we call you brothers, you should not be scornful, although we were put to death
by the law. Yet you know that not all men are sane and sensible. Pray for us, since
we are stiff and dead, to the Son of the Virgin Mary, that his grace should not run
dry for us, preserving us from the flames of Hell. We are dead, let no man trouble
us; but pray to God that he should absolve us all.

The rain has scoured and washed us, and the sun dried and blackened us, magpies and
crows have pecked out our eyes and torn off the beards and the eyebrows. Never a moment
are we at rest; this way and that, as the wind changes, it swings us ceaselessly at its will,
more riddled by birds than thimbles (are with holes). Do not be of our brotherhood, but
pray to God that he should absolve us all.

Prince Jesus, who are lord of all men, grant that Hell should not have power over us:
let us have no truck nor dealing with it. Men, there is no place for mockery here; but
pray to God that he should absolve us all.

work of the longer poem. To show how these pieces came to be composed, it is interesting to recall that the *Epitaphe*, written when he expected to be hanged, was followed by a *ballade* of ecstatic gratitude to the judges who reprieved him (ending, typically, with a further request for three days' grace before the sentence of banishment should take effect); and then by a cheerful little *ballade* addressed to his gaoler, who had evidently taken a gloomy view of Villon's chances. 'What do you think now of my appeal?' he asks him. 'Was I wise or mad to try to save my skin?' And with that perky question François Villon disappears from the scene.

III

Because of his archaic though direct language and his remote period, Villon might appear to be isolated from the other poets with whom this book is concerned. His work, as it reads today, has a strongly individualized flavour and nothing quite like it could be expected to occur again. He himself and his immediate material world were the centre of his poetry. His best writing seems to spring straight from experience, for his book-learning was undigested and always remained a surface feature. The main trend of the fifteenth century was still that of courtly poetry, renewed by Alain Chartier (who died at about the time when Villon was born) and continued by Charles d'Orléans and by the 'rhetorical' poets who flourished at the court of Burgundy. When these write of their personal experience, they do so in a discreet and generalized way, subordinating the individual note to an art ruled by elaborate and sometimes exquisite conventions. Moreover, up to Charles d'Orléans, they are often writing for music, in the old troubadour tradition. Villon's verse, on the contrary, was not intended to be sung. Artistic considerations, in the narrower sense, do not influence him. He writes for the broad or knowing laugh, for the gasp of surprise or emotion, rather than for the more subtle reactions of the educated connoisseur. This leads him to put down everything, however trivial, however unflattering to himself, and to put it down raw. The only concealment which he attempted was of facts which might involve him with the law – a practical rather than an aesthetic consideration.

It has already been observed that Villon was no Romantic. If he is sometimes represented as one in popular works, the ultimate blame lies with Sir Walter Scott who *was* a Romantic and whose reconstructions of the Middle Ages have much to answer for. The real Romantic poet, as he appeared in the nineteenth century, is always an arranged figure even in his most intimate self-revelations. He cannot help being conscious of the contrast between himself and his environment. Villon seems to have lacked this self-consciousness. He accepts the environment as inevitable and, within it, remains unstudiedly himself. When he whines, it is not in revolt or in any exhibitionist spirit. It is a spontaneous abject whine forced out of him by misery. He is thus an example of that very rare writer, the subjective realist. His lyricism springs straight from his sensations. He seems unaware of more sophisticated conventions. Ultimately the difference between a poet of the fifteenth century and one of the nineteenth century lies in a changed attitude of society towards the writer. The good writer of any period always does what is expected of him. The great writer, like Villon, manages to exceed expectations.

But if Villon has no equivalent in French literature, it is possible to find him certain affinities, particularly in Baudelaire and Verlaine. He is an early example – to use a much abused word – of the Bohemian poet. He is also – in France the two things have usually gone together – the first good Parisian poet, the first man to find all his material in the streets, the taverns, the personalities and transient happenings of that city. Others after him were inspired by the Paris of their time, but none absorbed its life more thoroughly than he did.

The intense local flavour of much of his work makes it at once more lively and less accessible to the modern reader. It is here, rather than in any fundamental difference between the medieval and the modern mentality, that the chief obstacle to appreciation may lie. But anyone who has the time and opportunity to study Villon's language and environment will be well rewarded. To read *Le Testament* in full is a lasting experience, and one which it is a pity to abandon to the specialist. Meanwhile the great *ballades*, which are admittedly the cream, can be enjoyed with the help of a few footnotes.

Chapter 2

Pierre de Ronsard

BETWEEN Villon and Ronsard lie almost a hundred years – a hundred years of considerable interest since they were a time of transition between the Middle Ages and the Renaissance. On the one hand there was the last elaborate flowering of the medieval scholastic tradition in the Burgundian *Rhétoriqueurs*; on the other, the first signs of the Italian influences which were to revolutionize French poetry appeared in various poets. Among these were Jean Lemaire de Belges, a *Rhétoriqueur* also, but one interested in new experiments; Clément Marot, who had retained something of the medieval popular spirit found also in his contemporary Rabelais and whose sympathy for Villon was shown by the important edition of his work which Marot published; and Maurice Scève, the leader of the Lyons group, whose verse is the earliest reflection of Neoplatonic and Petrarchan influences in sixteenth-century French poetry. Marot and Scève were considerable figures in their different ways and are described in another chapter. Yet it is fair to say that neither quite achieves the stature of a supremely great poet. If one looks at this period from a certain distance, it can be seen as a time of preparation during which the poets of France were waiting in some uncertainty for the high tide of the Renaissance to sweep upon them.

It came in its full splendour with Ronsard and his companions in letters. Never, until the Romantics, was a young movement more deliberately and arrogantly launched. Rarely have a group of writers broken more confidently with a tradition or been more certain that they were setting up a better thing in its place.

Briefly, the aim of the young poets of the Pléiade was to reject everything which characterized medieval French poetry – its verse-forms, its idiom, its subject-matter – and to go straight back for inspiration to the writers of Greece and Rome. Looking on these as their models and elder brothers, they set out to create a literature not so much of imitation as of equal standing. The French tongue, as Du Bellay claimed in the *Deffence et illustration de la langue françoise*, was as rich potentially as the ancient tongues. Given intense study (the first requisite), art and ingenuity, it could be used to produce poetry of the highest kind. Their programme, launched in reaction against their tottering elders, was too absolute to be carried out to the letter. On the one hand, a good deal of their verse was imitative after all and owed more to the intermediary influence of Italian scholars and poets than they admitted openly. On the other hand, the French could not break entirely with the earlier poets of their own country. However much the forms were changed, the spirit of these still persisted in them. Yet in a great measure the poets of the Pléiade did succeed in practising what they preached. Their ideas, in harmony with the larger movement of renewal through humanist scholarship which had spread from Italy through Europe, quickly triumphed over weak opposition. From them, writing in the mid-sixteenth century, modern French poetry may be said to date.

Pierre de Ronsard was early marked out as the leader of the new group. His talent, his energy and the circumstances of his life all fitted him for the place. He was born in 1524 of a family of some distinction which possessed a manor-house in the Vendômois, one of the provinces of the lower Loire. His parents originally intended him for a career of arms and diplomacy and, after a short schooling at the Collège de Navarre (the same that Villon had once burgled), he was attached to the court as a young page.

He followed a princess of France to Scotland when she married James V, then was attached to French embassies in the Netherlands, Scotland again, and Alsace. At eighteen, he experienced a serious illness which left him partly deaf. The objective of his ambitions changed. He flung himself into a new life of intense study under the humanist teacher Dorat, who soon after was appointed head of the Collège de Coqueret. Here Ronsard, together with his friends Jean-Antoine de Baïf and Du Bellay, explored the treasures of classical literature which Dorat opened up to them. After a long apprenticeship they were ready to go out and preach the new doctrine. Du Bellay launched their first manifesto. Joining forces with other young poets and students, they formed a group which they called *La Brigade*. Later, modified in its composition, it became the Pléiade – a name suggested by the seven stars of the Pleiades. This title, launched but never formally adopted by Ronsard, has been used by later historians as the standard term by which the movement is known. Its members rapidly claimed and took their place as the leaders of French poetry, with Ronsard always at their head.

Materially, Ronsard was fortunate to have already formed useful connections at court. Recognition and honours quickly came his way.

He became the official poet and friend of three kings in turn, the favourite poet of princesses – Marguerite de France and the unhappy Mary Stuart. For a quarter of a century he enjoyed a worldly position at least as prominent as it could have been if he had escaped illness and had become a brilliant cavalier-diplomat. But on the death of his last royal patron, Charles IX, he began to find the atmosphere of the court less congenial. He spent the last years of his life, from the age of fifty onwards, in half-retirement in the priories which he had been granted in Touraine and his native Vendômois. When he visited the capital he stayed for preference with his friends in the university rather than at the Louvre. He died tormented by arthritis, at the age of sixty-one, having enjoyed a full but outwardly uneventful life.

II

From the viewpoint of the literary historian, nearly all Ronsard's work is important. His large output, the result of thirty years of prolific writing, reflects in its different phases a mind eager to inquire and experiment; and many of his experiments left a permanent mark on French poetry. Although we are concerned here rather less with tendencies and influences than with that smaller body of poetry which has a permanent appeal, it is impossible to appreciate Ronsard's achievement without tracing at least the outline of his work as a whole. In order to do this, a certain simplification is necessary. Ronsard – a perfectionist in spite of his fluency – was constantly going back to add new poems to his old collections or to repolish existing poems. Because of this practice, his different 'manners' overlap; sometimes he returns to an earlier style years after he appears to have abandoned it. It is therefore not entirely accurate to speak of clear-cut developments in his poetic art. With this reservation – which concerns the detail rather than the general design – it is possible to make a broad classification of his work.

He began with a collection of *Odes*, published in five books between 1550 and 1552, reflecting his study of classical models. His masters were Pindar, Horace and, a little later, Anacreon. Pindar's odes had been written to praise the prize-winners at athletic contests in ancient Greece, or the victors in war, while Horace and Anacreon had applied the ode to more personal and familiar themes. In imitating Pindar, Ronsard failed to acclimatize his model; his adaptations are stiff and self-conscious in their French dress. But with the other two his relations are easier and many of the results can still be read with pleasure for their simple invitations to drink and love. But the main importance of these experiments lay less in the themes than in the form. The odes written by Ronsard and his contemporaries gave French poetry a verse-form no longer limited to a fixed length or rhyme-scheme, as the medieval *ballade* and *rondeau* had been. It could be of any length, though usually it was shortish. The disposition of the rhymes, like the metre, was at the poet's own choice – on the wisdom of which might depend the success of his poem. This new flexibility was an important step in the development of lyric poetry, since the frame could now be fitted to the emotion rather than the contrary. In practice, the ode was at first used chiefly for light love-lyrics, addresses to friends, and nature-poetry. At the other extreme, it came to be used later, by Malherbe, for themes of pomp and circumstance, based sometimes on national events. It reappeared in both veins in the eighteenth century, while many of the medium-length poems of the nineteenth century are in effect odes, though in French poetry the actual term fell out of use. In short, the practice of the ode by Renaissance poets had a liberating influence comparable to the introduction of *vers libres* by the Symbolists.

Without transition, the young Ronsard turned from the Greeks and Latins to Petrarch, under whose influence he wrote the *Amours de Cassandre*, a collection of love-poems addressed to a platonic mistress. Some of these also were short odes, in imitation of Petrarch's use of the form, but the majority were sonnets. The discipline of the sonnet (which was yet more flexible than the *ballade* or *rondeau*) counterbalanced the irregularity of the ode in Rennaissance versification and supplied a check to over-looseness which does not exist in the case of modern free verse. Ronsard's *Amours de Cassandre*, coming three years after Du Bellay's *Olive*, definitely established the sonnet in France and helped to fix its form. Neither Ronsard nor Du Bellay, however, was its introducer. The credit for that goes to older poets whom they at first despised, Marot and Mellin de Saint-Gelais.

A little later, in *Les Amours de Marie* (1555–6), Ronsard showed that his brilliant apprenticeship was completed and that, having assimilated several different manners, he was ready to strike out on his own line. In these more frankly sensual poems he was not afraid to go back at times to the native French tradition which he had originally rejected. In his poetic development the *Amours de Marie* represents a first maturity, the flowering of a talent now sufficiently sure of itself to write directly from personal feeling. These poems are also notable for being written almost exclusively in twelve-syllable lines, whereas the sonnets of the *Amours de Cassandre* had been written in decasyllables; it was the first sustained use of the alexandrine.

By this time Ronsard was famous, and his awareness of his high standing prompted him to move on to a different kind of verse. He began in his *Hymnes* (1555-6) to address 'official' poems to his friends and to the great. A few years later, in his *Discours* (1561-5), he wrote of high political themes and particularly of the fractricidal wars of religion which were tearing France apart. A certain majestic indignation appears in these poems, which were composed from the point of view of the ardent Catholic patriot. To suit his serious matter, Ronsard developed a new manner: he took the alexandrine, with which he had experimented in *Les Amours de Marie*, and, by rhyming it in solemn couplets, launched it as the standard metre of French poetry. His demonstration that the alexandrine was suitable for dignified themes set a precedent of incalculable importance to every French poet and dramatist who came afterwards. It provided them with a means of expression in harmony with the genius of the language, as 'natural' a metre as blank verse – which was developed in this country at much the same date – has become for English poets. Here again, as with the sonnet, Ronsard was not the inventor. The alexandrine had appeared as early as the twelfth century and probably took its name from the medieval *Roman d'Alexandre*, but later poets had neglected it almost entirely in favour of the eight- and ten-syllable line, as in Villon. Among Ronsard's contemporaries, Jean-Antoine de Baïf, the boldest metrical experimenter of the Pléiade, had taken it up a little before he did. Yet without Ronsard's prestige, and above all his mastery in handling the new metre, it would hardly have won such general acceptance. He can fairly be called the father of the alexandrine even though he was not its discoverer. By using it once again to render the grave and restrained sensuality of the *Sonnets pour Hélène*, Ronsard gave further proof of his capacities and at the same time crowned his life's work.

In comparison, his last considerable 'official' poem, *La Franciade*, was a deserved failure. It was planned under the patronage of Charles IX as an epic describing the foundation of the French monarchy by an invented hero Francus, who had wandered to Gaul, like Aeneas to Italy, after the fall of Troy. The legend was a fabricated one, with no real roots in national tradition. The poem was made still more artificial by the mythological machinery, borrowed directly from Virgil, with which Ronsard provided it. He further handicapped himself by using – on the insistence of his royal patron – not the alexandrine which he seemed to have perfected for just such a purpose, but the decasyllabic metre of older poets. It is not surprising that only four books were completed of the twenty-four he had originally announced.

No doubt it would be wrong to attach much significance to *La Franciade*. Most great poets have been tempted on some occasion into unsuccessful concoctions. But it does at least illustrate the uncanny fascination which the epic has exercised on French poets from Ronsard's time until today. Among the partial successes can be set d'Aubigné's *Tragiques*, Chateaubriand's *Martyrs* (but it is in prose), Hugo's *Légende des siècles* (subdivided though it is) and Pierre Emmanuel's *Babel* (1953). Among the partial to total failures are Du Bartas's *Semaine*, a dozen forgotten examples in the seventeenth century, Voltaire's *Henriade* and Lamartine's unfinished *Visions*. Looking first to the Italian Ariosto, then to the Englishman Milton, and fairly constantly to Virgil and Homer, French poets have failed to equal them or to produce a native variation. This is surprising in the country which invented the medieval epic in the twelfth-century *chansons de geste*. But whatever the reasons, the French poetic genius since the Renaissance has been at its best in either the drama or the lyric. The impersonal and narrative talent demanded by the epic has been lacking, or rather has expressed itself in prose. More than other nations, French poets have responded to the stimulus of a personal emotion. Their favourite themes are the joys and sufferings of the individual.

This was where Ronsard, in spite of his immense prestige as an official poet, excelled. And if we must choose, we have little hesitation in naming as his best work his three great collections of love-poems. To do that is not to forget the charm of other scattered poems written to other real or imagined mistresses (biographers have never quite solved the detective problem of their physical existences), nor yet the range and variety of the rest of his work. Besides the titles which have been given, much pleasant verse – some licentious, some ingenious, some descriptive – is to be found in his *Folastries* (1553), his *Bocage* (1554), his *Églogues* (1560–7), his *Bergerie* (1565, dedicated to Queen Elizabeth of England) and several other occasional collections which he published in the course of his long poetic career. But none of these reaches the consistently high standard of the three books of poems for Cassandre, Marie and Hélène.

III

These three women evidently existed, though the first two may have been considerably idealized by Ronsard for the purposes of his art.

Their differing personalities, as depicted by him, help to characterize the verses assembled round their names.

Cassandre Salviati was a young girl of fifteen when Ronsard first met her at a ball at Blois. He worshipped her romantically and continued his adoration after her early marriage to a country gentleman. No doubt her Italian parentage strengthened in his mind the conscious parallel between his love for her and Petrarch's love for Laura. To Cassandre, or to her poetic image, he addressed the delicate invitation of *Mignonne, allons voir si la rose* ... She inspired such deceptively simple sonnets as *Prends cette rose, aimable comme toi* and *Qui voudra voir comme amour me surmonte*, the proud flourish of

> Ville de Blois, naissance de ma dame,
> Séjour des Rois et de ma volonté,

and the learned voluptuousness of

> Ha! je voudrais, richement jaunissant,
> En pluie d'or goutte à goutte descendre
> Dans le giron de ma belle Cassandre
> Lorsqu'en ses yeux le somme va glissant.[1]

The fact that many of these poems are a little stiff is not a defect, but a quality which increases their charm. Ronsard is proudly conscious of his virtuosity. He mingles deliberately an eager tenderness with a glittering display of classical allusions and verbal skill. He is the cock-bird pirouetting before the hen. The total impression is of a young lover surrounding his mistress with marks of slightly formalized courtesy and then, when both have become absorbed in the courtly game, rising to an occasional crescendo of passionate pleading which he hardly hopes will be accepted.

In *Les Amours de Marie*, his approach is more direct. Traditionally, Marie was a country girl from Bourgueil in Anjou, who, like Cassandre, was fifteen when Ronsard, then thirty, first met her. Unlike Cassandre, she became his mistress and died at the age of twenty-one. These circumstances, whether literally true or partly invented, lend to the poems addressed to her a freer and more openly sensual note. To her he writes in a tone of emotional equality which is absent from *Les Amours de Cassandre*. He can also afford to be less literary: the result is such delightful sonnets as *Marie, levez-vous, vous êtes paresseuse*, and *Douce, belle, gentille et bienfleurante rose*. Marie's early death inspired a number of poems of tender grief which, in their kind, have

---

[1] We have modernized the spelling in all quotations from sixteenth-century and later poets.

hardly been surpassed in French. Among them are the lovely sonnet beginning:

> Comme on voit sur la branche, au mois de mai, la rose
> En sa belle jeunesse, en sa première fleur . . .

and the more sombre:

> Je songeais, sous l'obscur de la nuit endormie,
> Qu'un sépulcre entr'ouvert s'apparaissait à moi . . .

with its perfect end-line:

> Mes pieds avec les siens ont fait même chemin.

There is artifice in all poetry and a poet is not necessarily more sincere when he is using simpler language. In fact, simplicity is often the fruit of intense cultivation. It may have been so here, since the poems in which Ronsard mourns the death of Marie were not published until some eighteen years after her death must be supposed to have taken place. Moreover, according to a persuasive theory these moving obituary poems were not inspired by Ronsard's Marie at all, but were written to order as a tribute to Marie de Clèves, the young mistress of Henri III, who died in 1574. They were attached to the earlier Marie poems in order not to proclaim the King's sentiments too publicly. All that can be said about this is that the case is not quite proven.

Without, then, claiming to measure the depth of Ronsard's feeling for Marie by the style of the poems he wrote for whoever she may have been, we can at least say that he succeeds admirably in suggesting a passionate but uncomplicated relationship, lived out in full summer among the meadows and river-banks of a discreetly idealized Anjou.

With the *Sonnets pour Hélène* the style tightens; the expressions of passion becomes grave, sometimes melancholy. This is the restrained passion of a man of fifty for a young woman of high breeding from whom he scarcely hopes for more than friendship. It was also perhaps – though for enjoyment of the poems it makes no difference – a deliberate demonstration by the middle-aged poet laureate that he could write verses in a new fashion better than his younger rivals. Hélène de Surgères, maid-of-honour to Catherine de Medici, was a famous beauty to whom other poets also dedicated their verses. But Ronsard's, as he boasted, alone gave her immortality. In them we see her moving gracefully about the court, saluting him with just a perceptible wave of the hand as she passes; or, seated demurely in her stiff flowered dress near the bank of the Seine, giving him the equivalent of the modern well-bred cut:

> Toi, comme paresseuse et pleine de sommeil,
> D'un seul petit regard tu ne m'estimas digne.
> Tu t'entretenais seule au visage abaissé,
> Pensive toute à toi, n'aimant rien que toi-même,
> Dédaignant un chacun d'un sourcil ramassé.

Again, in a more accessible mood, she sits with him at a window of the Louvre and looks longingly towards the peaceful fields and convents of Montmartre:

> Vous me dîtes, maîtresse, étant à la fenêtre,
> Regardant vers Montmartre et les champs d'alentour:
> 'La solitaire vie et le désert séjour
> Valent mieux que la cour; je voudrais bien y être.'

These familiar touches are not everywhere in the *Sonnets pour Hélène*, but when they appear, as they do most effectively in the famous:

> Quand vous serez bien vieille, au soir, à la chandelle,
> Assise auprès du feu, dévidant et filant,
> Direz, chantant mes vers, en vous émerveillant:
> 'Ronsard me célébrait du temps que j'étais belle.' . . .

they give a physical body to Hélène de Surgères which Cassandre did not have and which in Marie might have been that of any attractive young girl. Hélène is more particularized; her small gestures and mannerisms are better observed. If the other two are perhaps synthetic characters, she is undoubtedly real. The occasional concrete detail makes of the *Sonnets pour Hélène* the finest of Ronsard's love-poems, hence the finest of all his poetry. They also show him at his most characteristic, the assured master of that peculiar blend of the familiar phrase and the classical allusion which marks him out from other French poets.

IV

Ronsard's personal formation, conditioned by the intellectual current of his age, tended to make him a 'literary', even a pedantic poet. He and his contemporaries looked for instruction to the literatures of the past, not to the human scene around them. Yet, in spite of his eager submission to classical and foreign models, he became something different from a French Anacreon or Petrarch. He projected – it would almost seem, in spite of himself – an image of his own century. What saved him, in the final analysis, was a temperamental incompatibility with the ancient writers whom he so much admired. He could never get truly into their skins, and it was partly the spectacle of his French muse straining too obviously to speak Greek and Latin which so irritated the classicists of the next century and caused his work to fall into undeserved neglect. Our view of the classical cultures differs from that of both the sixteenth and seventeenth centuries, though, if any-thing, we are nearer to the first. What Boileau and his contemporaries took for a defect, we consider a saving grace. It was precisely Ronsard's inability either to assimilate his models or to forget them which gave his work its character. A more supple mind would have merged itself in the past and have been lost. A more complicated personality would have become involved in the maze of a learned variety of Marinism, from which he would have been extricated every hundred years or so by a small band of admirers attracted by his inaccessibility.

But Ronsard was a simple character for all his learning. His view of human relationships is the best proof of this. As (in this respect) an average Frenchman of his time, he looked to men for honest friendship, to women for a delicately sensual love. As for himself, he was the never completely satisfied lover – that was the whole extent of his intro-spection. His deepest feeling was a commonplace, beautifully expressed in many different ways, yet fundamentally unvaried: Youth and beauty are short-lived; make the most of them while they last. This was the same theme on which Villon had brooded, but so differently, with a darker and more labyrinthine imagination.

The robustness which kept Ronsard from falling into obscurity or pendantry carried a penalty too. His sensibility was too normal for the richness of his technical powers. He is one of the great poets who have endangered their reputation by writing too much. Not that his verse is empty, but it is repetitive from poem to poem. He achieves the same effect again and again, and in the end such monotonous mastery cloys. There are, for example, sixteen sonnets on the death of Marie. Half a dozen are so good that it is difficult to choose between them. But the reader resents having to choose – the poet should have done that before publication. Otherwise the suspicion creeps in that it is all a virtuoso exercise, again suggested by Petrarch.

It is true that the theme of poetry matters far less than the treatment, and no one quarrels with poets like Mallarmé or Valéry for working for years over comparatively short poems. But the result of their conscious art is an increase in depth and subtlety. With Ronsard, the increase is chiefly in volume, and whatever variety is achieved is verbal only. To read the whole of his work (even excluding *La Franciade* and a number of the flatter poems) is a task to daunt the most enthusiastic. But a hundred or so pieces, skilfully chosen, almost justify his title of 'The Prince of Poets'.

Because Ronsard started from Greek and Latin models, his poetry is sometimes described as 'pagan'. But in this context the word has little meaning. Ronsard was a conventionally devout Catholic, but he wrote of human love as most other non-mystic Christian poets, writing honestly, have also done. That is, he separated religion and love. Any labelling of his poetry as 'pagan', in distinction to the poetry of, say, Villon or Baudelaire, is too misleading to be of much service. It is more reasonable to say that Ronsard was sensual, but non-realistically so; to notice that much of his verse appears to have been written in a garden, as indeed it probably was; and to remember the two factors which saved him, in his best verse, from becoming over-literary. The first was his delight in nature, with which he never lost contact. He constantly returned both in body and spirit to the Loire provinces where his childhood had been spent. Although he sometimes peopled them with nymphs, fauns and mock shepherdesses, the real flowers and birds were there too. He names and describes them with a naturalist's precision. Secondly, an important technical consideration prevented him from overloading his verse. Much of it was written to be set to music, as was still the practice in the Renaissance courts. All his early *Odes* and many of the sonnets and later short poems were conceived less as poems than as songs. This goes far to explain the lack of intricacy in the thought, the relative plainness and diffuseness of the metaphors, the apparent thinness of some of his poems as they stand on the printed page. The inward ear of the modern reader is an inadequate substitute for the singing voice accompanied – literally – by the harpsichord or the lute.

Yet even without this enrichment Ronsard's rhythms stand up to the test of plain reading. At their best, the sense and harmony of his words alone are completely satisfying. He was a good song-writer, but he was also a true poet – with an all too human personality of which he was fully aware:

> Je suis opiniâtre, indiscret, fantastique,
> Farouche, soupçonneux, triste et mélancolique,
> Content et non content, malpropre et mal courtois:
> Au reste, craignant Dieu, les Princes et les lois,

Né d'assez bon esprit, de nature assez bonne,
Qui pour rien ne voudrais avoir fâché personne:
Voilà mon naturel, mon Grévin, et je crois
Que tous ceux de mon art ont tel vice que moi . . .[1]

[1] *Élégie à Jacques Grévin.*

Chapter 3

Joachim Du Bellay

JOACHIM DU BELLAY, who came of a poor branch of a powerful family, was born in 1522 near the little town of Liré in Anjou, and so was almost a compatriot of Ronsard. Tradition has it that the two poets first met by chance at an inn near Poitiers, where Du Bellay was studying law at the university. Ronsard easily persuaded his new friend to join him in Paris, and it is at least certain that from 1547 Du Bellay shared his studies at the Collège de Coqueret and became fired with the same ideas of renewing French poetry and the language itself by emulating the great classical writers. But while Ronsard and their master Dorat were more interested in Greek, Du Bellay was primarily a Latinist.

Du Bellay was thus one of the earliest and most enthusiastic members of the Pléiade group and it was he who, in 1549, published their manifesto, *La Deffence et illustration de la langue françoise*. This ringing attack on pre-Renaissance poetry and bold declaration of new principles has a historic importance which is hardly diminished by the fact that some of its most telling passages were borrowed piecemeal from Latin and Italian authors. Even if the arguments were not all original, the general tenor and timing were. Nor should too much be made of the suggestion that Ronsard and perhaps other members of the group had a hand in writing *La Deffence et illustration*. This suggestion arose because Ronsard and not Du Bellay was the leader of the Pléiade and because within a few years his reputation had overshadowed Du Bellay's. But there is no sound reason to deny Du Bellay the sole authorship of the book or to doubt that the force, and indeed violence, of the manifesto should be credited to him. He was merely a little before Ronsard in raising his voice publicly. He kept his lead by publishing, in the same year as the *Deffence et illustration*, the first sonnet-sequence to appear in French, *L'Olive*. At the end of the fifty sonnets which figure in the first edition, Du Bellay printed his *Vers lyriques* – thirteen odes imitated from Horace, which thus appeared before Ronsard's first published *Odes*.

It would be unjustifiable to speak of a rivalry between the two men, but there was certainly a contrast which began to grow apparent from about this period. While Ronsard easily won success by the attractive character both of his verse and of his personality, Du Bellay was of a more morose temperament. His somewhat stiff and introspective nature handicapped him at court, and particularly in his dealings with his influential relatives. He was ill-equipped to shine in the role of poor relation which he was forced to adopt. When, after a serious illness, he set out for Rome in the suite of his father's cousin, Cardinal Jean Du Bellay (who had also been Rabelais's patron) disaster lay ahead of him.

At first, however, the sight of Rome intoxicated him. This, as much as Hellas, was the cradle of the classical culture which had occupied his mind for so many years. But gradually the contrast between ancient Rome and its modern inhabitants was borne in upon him. He woke from his scholar's dream to find himself among a mob of usurers, pimps and intriguing courtiers. The courtiers in particular – whether they were Italians or Italianate French – sickened him, for he was thrown against them in his daily life. He was too slow and too honest to compete effectively with these smart materialists. Nor could he manage to satisfy his patron the Cardinal, who had inappropriately made him his steward and expected him to cope with money-lenders and creditors.

Je suis né pour la Muse, on me fait ménager![1]

Sick at heart, his thoughts turned back to France – to his friends in Paris and to his native province of Anjou. The result of his unhappiness was a number of poems of considerable poignancy which went considerably deeper than anything that the more robust Ronsard wrote. Du Bellay returned home after five years to publish them and out of misery to make his name as a poet. It rests securely on two books of sonnets, *Les Antiquités de Rome* and *Les Regrets*, both published in 1558. A book of lighter verses, *Les Jeux rustiques*, also written in Rome, appeared in the same year and completes the main part of his poetic production.

The ill-fortune which he experienced in Rome seems to have followed him back to France. He did not obtain another post. His health broke down again and he died on 1 January 1560 at the age of thirty-seven.

---

[1] *Ménager*: housekeeper, steward.

II

Du Bellay takes his place in French poetry as the first master of the sonnet. Although others had written occasional sonnets before him and although Ronsard, coming very closely after him in the same field, did much to establish it in France, no poet – not even Baudelaire, Mallarmé or Heredia in the nineteenth century – made it so much his natural medium of expression. He used, of course, other forms also, and a few of the short poems of the *Jeux rustiques* in particular have a lightness and grace unsurpassed by any other member of the Pléiade group. But they are, when analysed, successful metrical exercises based on Latin or Italian models of which some are translations or close adaptations. In spite of their easy and natural style, they are rarely in the same class as his sonnets.

He had begun, in *L'Olive*, as a disciple of Petrarch, echoing agreeably enough the elaborately idealistic love-poems of the Italian master and serving an indispensable apprenticeship. He needed time to learn the language of the sonnet. When he went to Rome he had assimilated it so thoroughly that it seemed native to him: he had reached the point which every good poet reaches at some time when word and thought are co-created.

By a fortunate chance – but it was enough to make the difference between minor and major poetry – Du Bellay attained the mastery of his medium at the moment when he had something entirely appropriate to say in it. The grave, delicate melancholy which hung over his Roman years was well-suited to the sonnet. If it was less light and artificial than Ronsard's 'suffering' in some of his love-poems seems to have been, it had not the violent, spasmodic quality which Musset apparently experienced when he wrote *Les Nuits*. For grief of this latter kind the sonnet is too formal. The poet seeks relief in a freer, more clamorous kind of verse. But for a dull, persistent pain – never so unbearable as to interfere with the ordinary business of life, yet never relaxing sufficiently to be forgotten, the sonnet is the ideal form of expression. As Du Bellay handled it, it also served to paint the outward scene as he observed it from day to day, to note down his rueful or ironical reflections, and to speak, on occasion, familiarly.

It is possible that Du Bellay's condition, both psychological and physical, was graver than he realized. It is only known that his parents died when he was a child and that he was brought up neglectfully by an elder brother. He may have suffered from some disease. The first serious illness, in his twenties, left him deaf, like Ronsard. The second killed him in his thirty-eighth year. Clearer knowledge of its nature might lead to a fuller understanding of his sombre attitude towards life. But since the fundamental causes are hidden, we are left only with the symptoms as they appear in his poems.

Homesick and spiritually isolated in Rome, he remembered sadly the happier days of his youth:

> C'était ores,[1] c'était qu'à moi je devais vivre,
> Sans vouloir être plus que cela que je suis . . .
> Mais il n'a plu aux dieux me permettre de suivre
> Ma jeune liberté.

Secondly, he mourned over the vanished greatness of Rome, seeking beneath the ruins some trace of the ghosts which, he fancied, might still linger there:

> Pâles esprits, et vous, Ombres poudreuses,
> Qui, jouissant de la clarté du jour,
> Fîtes sortir[2] cet orgueilleux séjour
> Dont nous voyons les reliques cendreuses:
>
> Dites, Esprits (ainsi[3] les ténébreuses
> Rives de Styx non passable au retour,
> Vous enlaçant d'un trois fois triple tour,
> N'enferment point vos images ombreuses!)
>
> Dites-moi donc (car quelqu'une de vous,
> Possible encor, se cache ici dessous),
> Ne sentez-vous augmenter votre peine
>
> Quand quelquefois de ces coteaux romains
> Vous contemplez[4] l'ouvrage de vos mains
> N'être plus rien qu'une poudreuse plaine?

The two searches for the lost glory of a civilization and for a lost personal happiness were in reality the same and were equally fruitless. In his *dépaysement* the poet was looking vainly for the familiar. Sometimes it took the form of his childhood home at Liré, sometimes of the Rome that had been built in his imagination during the enthusiastic years at the Collège de Coqueret. Finding neither, he felt doubly an exile.

Du Bellay's tragedy can be defined in modern terms as one of maladjustment. Before it was defined, its capacity to act as a slow

---

[1] *Ores:* then.   [2] *Fîtes sortir:* raised.   [3] *Ainsi:* provided that.
[4] *Vous contemplez:* you see.

poison was easily underestimated. Other types of suffering, more
rapid in their effect and more dramatic in their manifestation, were held
to be stronger. In French poetry particularly – and this went back to
the troubadours – there was required a sense of sexual deprivation to
reinforce, or at least focus, the more diffused feeling of separation from
life. A basic maladjustment, not pointed by a longing for any specific
person, seemed to warrant only restrained expression in verse. Du
Bellay speaks of 'regrets' and 'exile'. He would have hesitated to
complain that he was in torment – though on one occasion he does so
– when according to the ideas of his century he was merely uncom-
fortable. Hence the sonnets, short, reserved and quietly regretful, perfectly fitted his own conception of his feelings.

His emotional range seems narrow, since he had only one big theme:
nostalgia. His love-poetry, in the early *Olive* and elsewhere, is plainly
derivative. In Rome he seems to have fallen genuinely in love with a
woman he calls Faustine, but his poems to her are in Latin (the *Amores*),
so that what are heard are echoes of Catullus and Ovid rather than his
personal voice. Still, the implications of nostalgia are vast enough in
themselves. They include the Neoplatonic conception of the human
soul in exile from heaven, so long as it remains in the body. Earthly
objects of particular loveliness remind it of the heavenly home to
which it aspires to return. Du Bellay shared this conception, movingly
expressed in one of the sonnets of *L'Olive*:

> Si notre vie est moins qu'une journée
> En l'éternel, si l'an qui fait le tour
> Chasse nos jours sans espoir de retour,
> Si périssable est toute chose née,
>
> Que songes-tu, mon âme emprisonnée?
> Pourquoi te plaît l'obscur de notre jour,
> Si pour voler en un plus clair séjour
> Tu as au dos l'aile bien empanée?[1]
>
> Là est le bien que tout esprit désire,
> Là le repos où tout le monde aspire,
> Là est l'amour, là le plaisir encore.
>
> Là, ô mon âme, au plus haut ciel guidée,
> Tu y pourras reconnaître l'Idée
> De la beauté qu'en ce monde j'adore.

[1] *Empanée*: feathered.

Du Bellay's mature style is distinctive for a feature which other contemporary poets also possessed, but none in so marked a degree. It is a note not easy to define, but unmistakable. After the mid-seventeenth century it disappeared from French poetry, apparently for good. It can best be described as a restrained flourish, as in:

> Telle que dans son char la Bérécynthienne,
> Couronnée de tours, et joyeuse d'avoir
> Enfanté tant de dieux, telle se faisait voir
> En ses jours plus heureux, cette ville ancienne . . .

or in:

> Entre les loups cruels j'erre parmi la plaine,
> Je sens venir l'hiver, de qui la froide haleine
> D'une tremblante horreur fait hérisser ma peau . . .

or, at its simplest, in:

> Cependant que Magny suit son grand Avanson,
> Panjas son Cardinal, et moi le mien encore . . .

This is not the pompous rhetoric of some later French poets, nor is it the tumbling word-flood of certain Elizabethans. While it is almost as far removed from 'natural' speech as either of those, it has a firmness, a virile resonance which they both lack. It suggests rather the Castilian hauteur, but this could not have been a literary influence upon Du Bellay. The origin must be sought in the general tone of the age rather than in any particular place. It is possible to imagine a noble at some ceremony, or a captain among his soldiers, speaking in just such a way. The declamatory intention is there, but the voice is not the professional voice of the actor or the advocate. Behind the words is always the personality of the speaker – proud, stiff, a little distant from his audience in spite of his desire to impress them. It is not difficult – remembering that Montaigne's prose has a comparable flavour – to recognize the voice of the aristocratic amateur, uninfluenced as yet by feminine salon-society. This would explain why, after the sixteenth century, it rapidly became extinct in French literature.

Chapter 4

Other Sixteenth-Century Poets

OF THE POETS whose work became old-fashioned on the advent of the Pléiade, the most vigorous was Clément Marot (1496–1544). A man of whimsical and turbulent character, he was a favourite court poet at one period, like Ronsard after him. But his adventures into heresy – as much the result of carelessness as of deliberate revolt – brought him more than one term of imprisonment and he finally fled to Geneva, then moved on to Turin, where he died. His work, like his life, was lively and inconsequential. He had begun as a disciple of the *Rhétoriqueurs*, of whom his father, Jean Marot, was one, and he was thoroughly grounded in those ingenious verse-forms which Du Bellay contemptuously dismissed as 'confectionery' – the *rondeau* and the *ballade*. Moving with the times, he became attracted by the new humanism and wrote eight of the earliest sonnets in French (six of them translated directly from Petrarch), but he was never a profound classical scholar nor a true Italianist. His real voice is heard in his religious poems, including his metrical version of the Psalms which was adopted by the French Reformed Church; then, by way of contrast, in his broad and racy *Épigrammes* and *Épîtres*, prompted – like some of Villon's *ballades* – by various happenings in his own life; and, most of all, in the *rondeaux* and *chansons* which he took over from medieval tradition and gave a certain graceful and playful twist of his own. The naïve ingenuity of these always gives pleasure, as in:

> Ma Dame ne m'a pas vendu,
> Elle m'a seulement changé:
> Mais elle a au change perdu,
> Dont je me tiens pour bien vengé:
> Car un loyal a étrangé
> Pour un autre qui la diffame.[1]
> N'est-elle pas légère femme?

[1] For she has estranged a faithful lover for another who slanders her.

As Marot handled them, these songs show that there was still life in the old forms, if a superficial life. In the impossible event of there having been no Italian influence, it would have been wonderfully interesting to see whether poets of the calibre of Ronsard would have been capable of expanding the native tradition until it was wide and deep enough to carry the new sensibility, including its borrowings from Greece and Rome. This is pure speculation, which became idle as soon as that most welcome of cuckoos, the sonnet, was hatched and grown. But Frenchmen for a long time after, and even today, have felt a lingering regret for the sly, light-fingered manner of Marot, while recognizing, if really put to it, that verse of that kind could never have withstood the enormous emotional pressure which great poetry must be able to contain.

II

With Maurice Scève (c. 1501–c. 1563), Petrarch's influence enters France, though without entirely expelling the old spirit of the *Rhétoriqueurs*. Scève practised poetry as a 'closed' art, perhaps even as a magic art, as will be seen below. But this is not his most important feature. He stands out as the most considerable of the Lyons poets at a time when Lyons was an active cultural centre by reason of its proximity to Italy. Armies, embassies and scholars came and went through it; it had some of the earliest printing presses. To the north lay the Calvinist territory of Geneva. To the south was Provence, with its ancient cultural traditions and its once equally strong Italian associations. Petrarch had spent part of his life at Avignon, and in a chapel there belonging to the de Sade family Scève claimed to have discovered the tomb of Laura de Noves, who had died in that city nearly two centuries before.

The discovery was not authentic – and indeed it is not certain who the original of Petrarch's Laura was – but Scève probably believed in it and it showed at least where his interests lay. In 1544 he published his chief work, *Délie, Objet de plus haute vertu*, consisting of a long series of *dizains* or ten-line stanzas telling of his faithful but unsatisfied love for his mistress, analysing their relationship and his own feelings, and showing a gradual purification of passion up to the point when it becomes a conductor to 'the highest virtue'. This was the Petrarchan pattern of love and it contrasts obviously with the easy-going and promiscuous sensuality of Marot. In the detail, Scève uses a careful, stiff and complex technique based partly on classical allusions but more on what has been called the 'learned ignorance' of the late medieval scholastics. The 'magic' element first appears in the fifty 'emblems' or symbolical signs with which he headed the different divisions of his poem and in the numerological significance of its length. *Délie* consists of one eight-line stanza and 449 *dizains*. Of the *dizains*, the first five are introductory, while the last three wind up the series. The total may thus be broken down into the formula: $449 = 5 + (9 \times 49) + 3$. Now the figure 5 represented man, the final 3 the Trinity. Nine symbolized the ultimate reintegration of the human with the divine. Forty-nine are the stages of initiation required before enlightenment is reached. Other hidden meanings can also be found in the formula, or read into it. Thus 9 and 49 are the squares of 3 and 7 – numbers whose mystic associations are immemorial.

This is only one example of Scève's desire to relate his personal experience of life to the cosmos as he conceived it. There also appears in *Délie* the symbolism of the moon-goddess – the three-faced symbol of the feminine: chaste and untamed as Diana, serene and light-giving as Selene, cruel and baneful as Hecate. While such 'keys' are not essential to an appreciation of the poetry (which must have other qualities to be worth reading at all), they perhaps help one to understand Scève. First, he saw the poet as a kind of Magus, weaving spells to conjure his own psychological difficulties and to lead him by their special power to a final 'illumination'. Then the reader is expected to be an initiate before he can share fully in the experience of the poem. It has secret meanings which will be missed by the profane – and are intended to be missed whenever the poet regards himself as a priest forbidden to reveal the Mysteries to all and sundry.[1]

This said, with the implied warning that Scève is a difficult poet, it should be added that he can nevertheless be keenly enjoyed without the inside knowledge which few modern readers would be likely to possess. One can enjoy T. S. Eliot's *Waste Land* without the notes, or a ballet while ignorant of the dancer's technique, simply through receiving a general impression of the beauty and precision of the movements. Nothing more than that is needed to appreciate such verses as Scève's *dizain* on the Salamander, the fabulous animal which fed on fire, as the

---

[1] Poetry, particularly sixteenth-century poetry, containing references to occult systems is known as Hermetic poetry – from Hermes Trismegetus ('Thrice-great Hermes'), identified by the Greeks with the Egyptian god of the dead. A body of theological and scientific writings was attributed in early Christian times to his authorship. This knowledge was 'hermetically' closed to all but initiates. In general, magic is dead religion which, however, a great enough poet may be able to resurrect.

poet's mistress lives in and feeds on the fire of his passion without being burnt by it:

> Sans lésion le Serpent Royal vit
> Dedans le chaud de la flamme luisante:
> Et en l'ardeur, qui à toi me ravit,
> Tu te nourris sans offense cuisante:
> Et bien que soit sa qualité nuisante,
> Tu t'y complais, comme en ta nourriture.
>   O fusses-tu par ta froide nature
> La Salamandre en mon feu résidente:
> Tu y aurais délectable pâture,
> Et éteindrais ma passion ardente.

The *dizain* on four rhymes (here, exceptionally, on three) was a form taken over from the *Rhétoriqueurs* and used also by Marot. Had Scève practised the sonnet he might have had a greater influence on his age. As it was, he was respected by the Pléiade poets but quickly forgotten. Interest in him was not renewed until the present century. He may be compared to Gérard de Nerval, who achieved rather similar results in the nineteenth century by his use of the hidden allusion.

While there are several planes of intention and emotion in *Délie*, a living person was at least partly represented in the poem. This was a young married woman, Pernette Du Guillet (*c.* 1520–45), herself a poetess of distinction, who replied to Scève in her own verse. She is a sociable Neoplatonist, something of an unintentional coquette, concerned with *parfaite amitié* rather than with passion and very ready to argue the point in a learned yet human way. Her poems were published after her early death on the initiative of her husband, whose hand should surely be seen in the adjectives used in the volume's title: *Rymes de Gentile et Vertueuse Dame Pernette Du Guillet, Lyonnoise.*

The same adjectives are less applicable to the second of the Lyons poetesses, Louise Labé (*c.* 1525–65), in whose short collection of poems (elegies and sonnets) a sensual passion speaks frankly and ardently, though purely. She bitterly regrets the absence of her lover, whose desertion of her causes literal torment. Though Petrarchan in form, this is poetry straight from the natural feelings.

III

Her unfaithful lover was probably Olivier de Magny (*c.* 1529–61). He met her when he passed through Lyons with the French Ambassador, Jean d'Avanson, whom he served as secretary. In Rome he found Du Bellay similarly employed in the suite of his Cardinal and the two poets worked as comrades in composing verses on the same themes. De Magny's *Soupirs* (1557) appeared a year before Du Bellay's *Regrets*, but was overshadowed by it. His earlier *Gaîtés* and *Odes* imitated Ronsard, and his reputation as an original poet does not stand high. The most one can say is that, if he had lived longer and developed, he might well have figured in the Pléiade group.

The poets whose names Ronsard finally saw fit to associate publicly with his own included, besides Du Bellay, four others who each offer their particular points of interest.

The oldest of them, Pontus de Tyard (1521–1605), provides a direct link between the Lyons poets and Ronsard's group. It was as a disciple of Scève that he published his first *Erreurs amoureuses* (1549), consisting of sonnets and other short poems in the Petrarchan tradition. He went on to be the most spiritual and ingenious of the Neoplatonic poets, but his subtlety often appears tedious in a way that Scève's does not. His philosophical refinements are thin in human content. He became a bishop and an important local figure in Burgundy and no doubt this was the best solution to his career.

Étienne Jodelle (1532–73) is best known for his dramatic works. His youthful *Cléopâtre captive* (1552) was the first original 'regular' tragedy in French and was followed by further experiments in both tragedy and comedy. Much of his poetry was hurriedly written for the requirements of the court, but the sonnets of his *Amours* are interesting for their vigour and for another use of the 'magical' background which we have already observed in Scève. The following rapid-moving sonnet invokes the moon-goddess in her threefold aspect of queen of heaven, earth and hell – a motif which is echoed, or rather executed, in the verbal structure. The recurrent triple groupings suggest the weaving of a spell up to the climax, while the echoings of similar sounds (as *rais*, *rets* and *éprise*, *prise* in lines 9 and 10) contribute to the incantatory effect. There is also the strong suggestion (principally rhythmic) of a fantastic hunt by moonlight. At the same time, the invocation is addressed to the poet's mistress, who is compared to the goddess (lines 5 and 6), then increasingly identified with her, until there is a complete merging in the final tercet:

> Des astres, des forêts et d'Achéron l'honneur,
> Diane au monde haut, moyen et bas préside,
> Et ses chevaux, ses chiens, ses Euménides guide
> Pour éclairer, chasser, donner mort et horreur.

Tel est le lustre grand, la chasse, et la frayeur
Qu'on sent sous ta beauté claire, prompte, homicide,
Que le haut Jupiter, Phébus, et Pluton cuide
Son foudre moins pouvoir, son arc, et sa terreur.[1]

Ta beauté par ses rais, par son rets, par la crainte
Rend l'âme éprise, prise, et au martyre étreinte:
Luis-moi, prends-moi, tiens-moi, mais, hélas, ne me perds

Des flambeaux forts et griefs, feux, filets et encombres,
Lune, Diane, Hécate, aux cieux, terre, et enfers
Ornant, quêtant, gênant, nos Dieux, nous, et nos ombres.[2]

In Rémy Belleau (1528–77), the magic element has no taste of the supernatural. It is rather a half-serious application of those classical and medieval recipes which were indistinct from natural science, as witch-doctoring among primitives is indistinct from medicine – at the most, white magic. In his best work, the *Amours et nouveaux échanges des pierres précieuses*, Belleau describes the fabulous origin and properties of various gems, following the traditional explanations of the earlier lapidaries. Thus, the pearl is born of the marriage of the oyster with the dawn dews. Powdered, it cures catarrh, migraine, lung and liver diseases and purges the melancholy humours. The diamond wins a well-chosen mistress and ensures her fidelity (hence, no doubt, its use in engagement-rings). The ruby combats night fears and pestilential vapours; coral guards against vegetable pests, vermin and shipwreck; the emerald against snake-bite, beryl against the hiccups and marital misconduct. The charm of these comparatively minor poems is in Belleau's descriptive skill – his success in rendering both the appearance and the 'soul' of his delicate and precious models. He showed similar skill in his earlier *Petites inventions*, which describe natural objects such as the snail, the glow-worm, the hour, the shade. He is a miniaturist who well repays discovery, although the modern reader can hardly help adding a quality of quaintness which was not in the original intention. Belleau was also the first French translator of Anacreon and the author of a *Bergerie* – a pastoral medley containing

---

[1] *Cuide . . . terreur*: Thinks his thunder can do less (Jupiter), his bow (Apollo), his terror (Pluto).

[2] In the sestet, *rais* = rays. *Rets* = net. *Luis-moi* = shine on me. *Griefs* = painful (grievous). *Encombres* = traps. *Quêtant* = hunting. *Gênant* = torturing.

The ternary structure adopted here occurs also in other sixteenth-century sonnets, notably in Sponde's 'Tout s'enfle contre moi, tout m'assaut, tout me tente. . .' (*Sonnets de la mort*).

further varied descriptions, love-songs and funeral dirges. He can be browsed through endlessly.

Perhaps the most inventive member of the Pléiade was Ronsard's college friend, Jean-Antoine de Baïf (1532–89). His inventions were partly forced on him by his failure to make an impression with his more orthodox verse. He became interested in eccentric metrical innovations and produced a fifteen-syllable line[1] which he named the *Baïfin*:

> Muse, reine d'Hélicon, fille de Mémoire, ô déesse!

He tried to apply the Latin system of quantitative scanning (without rhymes) to French verse and wrote a number of pieces (*Chansonnettes mesurées*, 1586) which were successfully set to music. But though the skilful placing of long and short syllables makes excellent sense for the composer and can be fixed by musical notation, for the speaking voice the differences are too slight or too variable in French. A rhythmic system borrowed from so different a language as classical Latin could not be fitted to French, and although others besides Baïf made similar experiments, rhyme and a regular syllable-count not dependent on the *duration* of the vowel-sounds prevailed. It is unfortunate that Baïf and his contemporaries were hypnotized by Greek and Latin poetry, for there exist native French rhythms – such as those of oratory and of colloquial speech – which can be harnessed to poetic uses if not to 'regular' poetry. These only began to be explored in the nineteenth century by the writers of prose-poems and in the twentieth by – outstandingly – Claudel. But for the obsession with classical prosody, some such discovery in keeping with the genius of the language might well have been made earlier.

Before the *Chansonnettes mesurées*, Baïf had made a version of the Psalms in quantitative verse (unpublished) and had written the short poems of his *Étrènes de poéҳie fransoèҳe an vers meҳurés* (1574). The semi-phonetic spelling used throughout this volume was another innovation inspired by his interest in the aural and musical qualities of language. Sixteenth-century spelling was, if not chaotic, highly unstandardized, and several besides Baïf advocated reform. Among them was a Marseille schoolmaster, Honorat Rambaud, who confessed that after thirty-eight years of flogging children for spelling mistakes he

---

[1] The longest in French verse until Verlaine produced one of seventeen syllables, only to point out that it consisted of *two* lines, the first of seven, the second of ten feet:

Je prendrais l'oiseau léger, laissant le lourd crapaud dans sa piscine. (See **Verlaine**: *Épigrammes* III and IV.)

had come to long for an easier method. When, in the next century, a fair degree of standardization was attained, it was not through Baïf's simple phonetic system. Here again he had committed himself to a lost cause.

The Pléiade tradition was continued, broadly, to the end of the sixteenth century by Philippe Desportes (1546–1606), who succeeded Ronsard as the reigning poet at the Valois court. Though unoriginal in themes and feeling, Desportes was facile, fluent and capable of delighting his brilliant but superficial public with conceits borrowed from such Italian poets as Bembo, who had renewed Petrarch in more artificial terms. Desportes lacks the learning as well as the occasional clumsiness of Ronsard and writes with a smoothness not divorced from a great mastery of versification. But the *préciosité* of the seventeenth century is already latent in his work, which only needs to be scaled down a little to resemble the elegant language of the salon poets. As here:

> Quand j'éprouve en aimant les rigueurs d'une Dame
> Qui jeune et sans amour se moque de ma flamme,[1]
> Et demeure cruelle au son de mes douleurs,
> Ferme je continue, et souffre en patience,
> Espérant à la fin par ma persévérance
> Caver son cœur de roche amolli par mes pleurs.

IV

In violent contrast are the great religious poets of the latter part of the century. It is true that Desportes, like Marot and others, rhymed his version of the Psalms, and that Ronsard wrote in defence of the Catholic religion in some of his *Discours*. But with those exceptions almost the whole work of all the poets so far named could be read without a hint that this was the century, not only of the Renaissance, but of the Reformation; or that during its last forty years France was torn by religious wars provoked by a deep disturbance in the national conscience.

The reminder that this was so comes with most force from the Protestant poets, whose culture was based on the Bible rather than on the 'pagan' literature admired by the Pléiade, and who were centred not on Paris, but on the rougher and more militant court of Henri de Navarre. It was an atmosphere which bred fanatics and eccentrics and fostered a

---

[1] Compare this conventional figure with Scève's handling of the 'flame' metaphor on p. 32.

literature which helps to prove that most good poetry is a product of deformation.

Guillaume de Salluste Du Bartas (1544–90) was a Gascon gentleman contemporary with Montaigne and belonging to the same region of France and the same social class (a merchant family recently risen into the landed gentry). He served Henri de Navarre as a soldier and diplomat and visited Scotland and Denmark on official missions. As a poet, he had immense designs and a verbal flow of corresponding magnitude. He is garrulous beyond nature. The Gascon stands to the French in much the same relationship as the Irishman to the English (compare James Joyce). Also, like Claudel in our own day, he felt divinely inspired and so was not much troubled by questions of literary taste. He worked himself in with three long didactic and biblical poems (*Uranie*, *Le Triomphe de la foi* and *Judith*), then turned to his main task of describing the whole of creation and all subsequent history. The seven days of creation, as outlined in Genesis, were the subject of *La Semaine* (1578), his chief work. This was followed by a second *Semaine*, retracing the story of humanity as told in the Bible, and left unfinished at his death.

Into his narrative Du Bartas packs an excess of now outdated and even grotesque erudition, much original observation which would escape a city-trained eye, and a verbal inventiveness which must either be admired or derided. Long passages of his uneven poem heave and swell with a magnificent movement, while his 'ill-chosen' but daring images are a proof of his originality as a poet. He appears at his most typical in certain parts of the Fifth Day of *La Semaine*, describing the creation of the birds.

The first of all birds – the phoenix – takes the air, to be followed by an immense multitude of different species:

> L'unique oiseau ramant par des sentes nouvelles,[1]
> Se voit bientôt suivi d'une infinité d'ailes,
> Diverses en grandeur, couleur et mouvement,
> Ailes que l'Éternel engendre en un moment.

The swallow:

> La flairante Arondelle à toutes mains bricole,
> Tournoie, virevolte, et plus raide s'envole
> Que la flèche d'un Turc, qui voulant décocher,
> Fait la corde au tétin et l'arc au fer toucher.

[1] Floating (rowing) down new paths.

The lark:

> La gentille Alouette avec son tire-lire,
> Tire l'ire à l'iré, et tire-lirant tire
> Vers la voûte du ciel; puis son vol vers ce lieu
> Vire, et désire dire: adieu Dieu, adieu Dieu.[1]

The bullfinch, the nightingale, the pheasant, the crow, the pelican and many other birds including the Indian gryphon with its flashing eyes take wing before a flight of cranes in triangular military formation and with queer military habits passes across the sky:

> Si je ne suis trompé, j'entends crier la Grue
> Qui jà déjà voudrait écrire dans la nue
> Le fourchu caractère,[2] et montrer aux soldars
> Par son beau règlement le dur métier de Mars.
> Car lors que les troupeaux des Grues abandonnent
> Le froidureux Strymon, et qu'en automne ils donnent
> Trèves aux nains du Nord,[3] pour s'en aller trouver
> Sous le Libyque Autun un plus clément hiver,
> Un capitaine vole, au front de chaque troupe,
> Qui les cieux aisément de sa pointe entrecoupe;
> Un couple de sergents de longtemps aguerris,
> Les tenant en bataille, avance de ses cris
> Leur trop lente démarche; et puis, quand dans leurs veines
> Glisse plus doux que le miel le somme charme-peines,
> L'une se met en garde, et fait soigneusement
> Et mainte et mainte ronde autour du camp dormant:
> Tenant en l'un des pieds, que le sommeil jà presse,
> Un caillou qui, tombant, accuse sa paresse.
> Autant en fait une autre, une autre après la suit,
> Départant justement les heures de la nuit.

The peacock follows. And finally the cock and the earthbound, iron-digesting ostrich:

---

[1] The meaning, though of secondary importance, is: The pretty lark with its carolling draws the wrath from the wrathful and carolling draws towards the vault of heaven; then turns its flight towards this earth and tries to say: Goodbye God, goodbye God.

[2] *Jà déjà*: now already. The metaphor reappears in the *Soledades* (1612) of the Spanish poet Góngora. 'A flight of cranes is described as an arc, "waxing and waning like moons and *writing winged characters* on the diaphanous paper of the sky".' G. Brenan, *Literature of the Spanish People* (Cambridge, 1951).

[3] Cf. Milton:

> . . . that small infantry
> Warr'd on by cranes.

> (*Paradise Lost*, I, 575.)

A son flanc j'aperçois le Coq audacieux,
Sûr réveille-matin, véritable astrologue,
Horloge du paysan, frayeur du Lion rogue,
Fidèle annonce-jour, Roi du peuple crêté,
Roi qui se lève et couche avecque la clarté
Qui dore l'univers. J'aperçois dans la plaine
L'oiseau digère-fer, qui vainement se peine
De se guinder en haut pour, gaillard, se mêler
Parmi tant d'escadrons qui voltigent en l'air.

Famous in his day well beyond the frontiers of France, Du Bartas
was naturally enough ignored by the seventeenth-century classicists,
to whom he could only appear as a barbarous curiosity, and he has
never regained his once eminent place. For long stretches he can be
boring or laughable. He has no sense whatever of proportion. Yet his
verse moves, as do his images and concepts. It is the only French verse
which, in its more serious-minded way, provides anything approaching a counterpart to the prose of Rabelais.

V

His fellow Protestant now possesses a more solid reputation, and on
the whole deserves it. Agrippa d'Aubigné (1552–1630) came of a
militant Reformist family and was the companion and outspoken
counsellor of Henri de Navarre – in whose service, he says, he was
wounded twelve times. He escaped the massacre of St Bartholomew's
Day, though he might well have been in Paris at the time. It seems that
he had just fought a duel and had left the capital temporarily to escape
the judicial consequences. Though disgusted by his leader's ultimate
conversion to Catholicism which secured him the throne, he remained
in France until after Henri's death, growing more and more intractable
whenever he visited the court. Finally, he exiled himself to Geneva
where he spent the last ten years of his life. He was the grandfather of
Madame de Maintenon.

This iron-principled and tumultuous man began by writing, in imitation of Ronsard, a youthful collection of songs and sonnets, later
entitled *Le Printemps du Sieur d'Aubigné*. The lady to whom they were
addressed was Diane Salviati, the niece of Ronsard's Cassandre. In the
second book of the *Printemps*, written in 1573–7, d'Aubigné went,
however, a long way beyond Ronsard. His attitude towards his mistress, who by then had rejected him, became at once sadistic and
masochistic, as in the passage in which he describes the painting on his

bedroom wall (whether real or imagined) of Diane's portrait sur-
rounded by death's-heads and the bones of *une anatomie* (a skeleton):

> Le lieu de mon repos est une chambre peinte
> De mille os blanchissants et de têtes de morts.
> ... Je mire en adorant dans une anatomie
> Le portrait de Diane entre les os, afin
> Que voyant sa beauté, ma fortune ennemie
> L'environne partout de ma cruelle fin:
> Dans le corps de la mort j'ai enfermé ma vie,
> Et ma beauté paraît horrible dans les os.

Later he imagines that, having died, he will return in nightmare
shapes to haunt his mistress:

> Je briserai, la nuit, les rideaux de sa couche,
> Assiégeant des trois Sœurs infernales son lit,
> Portant le feu, la plainte et le sang en ma bouche.

The first of these conceptions is reminiscent of the medieval juxtaposition of death and love, the skeleton and the healthy body (as in
Villon). Both conceptions point forward strikingly to several of
Baudelaire's poems. In their own period they typify the obsession with
the more sombre aspects of death which is found in several religious
poets of the time, and they are, of course, by the same man who later
described the cruelties and martyrdoms of *Les Tragiques*. With other
passages of *Le Printemps*, they have been seen as one of the earliest
examples in French poetry of the baroque, which is considered in the
next chapter.[1]

Such were the verses of d'Aubigné's youth. At the other end of life,
from his fifties to his seventies, he produced a number of mordant
prose pamphlets, a book of memoirs (*Sa vie à ses enfants*) and his
long *Histoire universelle*, which related the Protestant struggle against
the Catholics from 1553 (the birth-date of Henri IV) until the early
seventeenth century. The whole of his middle life was taken up with
his great work, *Les Tragiques*. He conceived it when lying wounded
after an attempt on his life, began it in 1577, and published it only in
1616. Because this and his other writings did not appear until some time
after the events which inspired them, when both public interests and
literary standards had changed, his importance was long overlooked. 'I
left him out because I could not see where to place him,' remarked the
critic Brunetière when challenged for having omitted d'Aubigné from

---

[1] For *Le Printemps* see particularly: M. Raymond, *Génies de France* (Neuchâtel, 1942).
Also books by O. de Mourgues and J. Rousset in our bibliography.

his *History of Seventeenth-Century Literature*. One can understand his difficulty, because d'Aubigné really does not belong to that period, and a poem published nearly forty years after it was begun tends to seem out of touch when at last it appears. Nevertheless, *Les Tragiques* can be seen in retrospect as the great epic poem of the Wars of Religion. It is, of course, the epic of a sect – but so, to a certain degree, was *Paradise Lost* – and if the general design is less grand and less clear than in Milton, there are some passages of equal height and many others of a burning energy which was not in the English poet's more majestic temperament. As would be expected in a sixteenth-century Huguenot, d'Aubigné owed much to the Bible. Its language and imagery help to fashion his principal work and distinguish him from the poets of Ronsard's school, whose culture was predominantly classical.

Les Tragiques consists of seven books, developed less as narrative than as *tableaux*. The first depicts the general miseries of France, ravaged by war and governed by incapable kings. The next two are filled with invective and satire against the corrupt court of the Valois princes as the puritan saw it and against the iniquitous judges of the Paris *parlement*. Then comes a long evocation of the sufferings of the Protestant martyrs in Europe and in England from Huss of Bohemia to d'Aubigné's own time. The Wars of Religion follow in detail, with a tremendous evocation of the St Bartholomew's Night massacre – of which, it will be remembered, d'Aubigné was not an eye-witness. The last two books, entitled *Vengeances* and *Jugement*, show God's punishments of the enemies of his Church, from Cain onwards, and contain an apocalyptic vision of the final Day of Judgement. When that day dawns, the dead will rise irresistibly from wherever they happen to be lying, to be held to account for their actions:

> Mais quoi! c'est trop chanté, il faut tourner les yeux,
> Éblouis de rayons, dans le chemin des cieux:
> C'est fait: Dieu vient régner; de toute prophétie
> Se voit la période à ce point accomplie.
> La terre ouvre son sein, du ventre des tombeaux
> Naissent des enterrés les visages nouveaux:
> Du pré, du bois, du champ, presque de toutes places
> Sortent les corps nouveaux et les nouvelles faces.
> Ici, les fondements des châteaux rehaussés
> Par les ressuscitants promptement sont percés;
> Ici, un arbre sent des bras de sa racine
> Grouiller un chef[1] vivant, sortir une poitrine;

[1] *Chef*: head.

Là, l'eau trouble bouillonne et puis, s'éparpillant,
Sent en soi des cheveux et un chef[1] s'éveillant.
Comme un nageur venant du profond de son plonge,
Tous sortent de la mort comme l'on sort d'un songe.

The faults of *Les Tragiques* were in its author's character. His alexandrines tumble out impetuously. He is violently insistent, sometimes without necessity. He is entirely extroverted and has no subtlety, metaphysical or theological. But that would only be weakness in an epic – which this hard-riding, hammering poem certainly is.

VI

The most noticeable gap in French poetry had seemed until recently to consist in the lack both of religious mystics such as Spain produced and of the quieter kind of metaphysical poets who enriched English seventeenth-century literature. Neither the didactic Du Bartas nor the militant visionary d'Aubigné quite met the case. But it is now clear that France is not the unaccountable exception she once seemed. She had her introverted religious poets, but their work had lain unknown or neglected. Either it was written by obscure clergy in the provinces, or it became in effect 'provincial' because the mainstream of French poetry turned another way. It would be too much to hope that a St John of the Cross or a Donne is still awaiting rediscovery, but interesting minor finds will certainly be made. Meanwhile, enough good poetry has already been brought to light to prove that Frenchmen of the late Renaissance were also expressing their passionate religious meditations in verse.

Jean de Sponde (1557–95) offers the most striking case. He owes his rehabilitation to an Englishman, Professor Alan Boase, who was the first to call attention to him[2] and has since edited his works. These consist of his youthful love-poems, which are more mannered than d'Aubigné's, and of his *Essai de quelques poèmes chrétiens* (1588), which are concerned almost exclusively with the theme of death. He starts from the theological (and also Neoplatonic) duality of body and spirit, the first wedded to life and its sinful diversions, the second aspiring to break free from their dangerous charm. The ensuing struggle is expressed in verse full of vigorous images:

Ne crains point, mon Esprit, d'entrer en cette lice,[3]
Car la chair ne combat ta puissante justice

[1] *Chef*: head.   [2] In an article in *The Criterion*, January 1930.
[3] *Lice*: lists, battle-ground.

Que d'un bouclier de verre et d'un bras de roseau:
Dieu t'armera de fer pour piler ce beau verre,
Pour casser ce roseau, et la fin de la guerre
Sera pour toi la Vie, et pour elle un Tombeau.

The body, with its shield of glass and its feeble, reed-like arm, has ceased to be the thing of beauty whose transient existence Ronsard had soberly lamented. For the most Christian Sponde, writing when the century had grown old and dark with religious conflict, it was a mere encumbrance to salvation, a time-bound creature which compromised eternity – no longer a rose but a rat:

C'est assez enduré que de cette vermine
La superbe insolence à ta [*the soul's*] grandeur domine.
Tu lui dois commander, cependant tu lui sers:
Tu dois purger la chair, et cette chair te souille.

Sponde expresses this one idea in a few sonnets and three longer poems. He has little variety or subtlety – but neither is he an ordinary moralist. He is expressing an anguish which no doubt he felt personally, to judge by his abrupt, often colloquial style and the concrete slant he gives to what would otherwise be conventional imagery. This is less the voice of a preacher than of a participant in a literal struggle between life and death. His own unquiet life supports that impression. A follower of Henri de Navarre, like d'Aubigné, he seems to have been unsuccessful in the difficult posts he was given. He twice fell into the hands of the Catholics and was imprisoned. Finally, following Henri's example, he abjured his Protestantism, but his conversion brought him no goodwill and he died in poverty and misery.

A second religious poet is also a comparatively new discovery. Jean de La Ceppède (*c.* 1548–1623) was, however, a Catholic throughout his life. His work, consisting of over five hundred sonnets entitled *Théorèmes sur le sacré mystère de notre rédemption,* is much richer in theological dogma and sometimes rises to what is usually understood as mystical feeling and symbolism. His symbolism is in fact biblical and doctrinal, and occasionally classical. One needs to know the 'keys' (which La Ceppède himself provided in prose commentaries) in order to understand him fully. The effect of this special – but not secret – language is sometimes similar to that of Scève's verse. The following sonnet may be compared to Scève's *dizain* on the Salamander quoted on p. 32.

L'Oiseau dont l'Arabie a fait si grande fête
Est de ce grand Héros le symbole assuré.

Le Phénix est tout seul. Le Christ est figuré
Seul libre entre les morts par son Royal Prophète.

Le Phénix courageux se porte à sa défaite
Sur du bois parfumé: l'Amour démesuré
Fait que Christ a la mort sur ce bois enduré,
Qui parfume le ciel d'une odeur très-parfaite.

De sa mouëlle[1] après le Phénix renaissant
Enlève tout son bois et l'emporte puissant
Sur un autel voisin des arènes brûlées.

Par sa divinité le Christ ressuscitant,
Sur l'azuré lambris des voûtes étoilées
Élévera son bois de rayons éclatant.

Christ, divinely resurrected after his death on the wood of the cross
('tree' is the English equivalent), is compared to the phoenix of classical
legend – the 'Arabian bird' of which only one specimen existed.[2] To
renew itself, the phoenix would build a pyre of sandalwood in the
desert, allow itself to be destroyed in the flames, and be reborn from
the ashes. La Ceppède links this profound pagan myth of rebirth
through suffering with the Christian act in which the Deity himself
sets an example of more immediately obvious significance to humanity.
Most of La Ceppède's *Théorèmes* were 'demonstrations' of this kind,
carried out with the help of similar symbols. Since his main business is
to explore and expound, he appears less personally involved than
Sponde and has not the same note of urgency. Just occasionally, however, the ecstatic note of the true mystic rings out.

Such poets – to whom might be added Gabrielle de Coignard of
Toulouse, Jean-Baptiste Chassignet of Besançon and several others
– show that the France of the Counter-Reformation was rich enough
in religious lyricism. Sometimes it is didactic, sometimes quietly con-
templative, but often there is a general spiritual anguish in it. By ignoring it until recently, French criticism was certainly unjust to the
national heritage – an error which is now being generously repaired.
There is an English parallel in the discovery, towards 1900, of the
seventeenth-century mystical poet Traherne, who had been unknown
until then. But this was an isolated case, whereas in France a whole
generation had been overlooked.

---

[1] *Mouëlle*: marrow (ashes).   [2] Du Bartas's 'unique oiseau'. See p. 37.

Chapter 5

François Malherbe: the Baroque
and the Classic

EVERY now and then in the history of literature some absolute, cross-grained figure jams himself by sheer persistence across the current of poetry and diverts, even if slightly, its course. Such was François Malherbe (1555–1628) who, after a long and hard search for patrons and recognition, found himself at the age of fifty in the position of official court poet to Henri IV. The rewards were still not lavish and his frugality became legendary, though the stories of his poverty may be exaggerated. Those who visited his lodgings at an hour when the seven chairs were occupied had to wait outside or sit on the floor. In this room the reputation of Desportes, whose work represented a decadent extension of the Pléiade tradition with a strong injection of Italian influences, was ruthlessly pulled to pieces. Ronsard's works stood on a table, page after page of them covered with corrections in Malherbe's hand. Asked whether he approved of some of the poems he had not corrected, Malherbe is said to have replied that his time and patience were not endless, and to have scrawled a general 'delete' over the rest. This was not criticism: this was war.

But it was also an act of penance. If Malherbe was naturally hostile to Desportes, whom he had succeeded as the reigning poet, he had sinned in his own youth by attempting to imitate Ronsard in execrably minor love-poetry. In renouncing the master, he was shedding his old self. More than that, he literally drew his pen through an early poem of his own, *Les Larmes de Saint Pierre*, a curious work which had come to represent another facet of his misguided past. It was an imitation from the Italian of Luigi Tansillo.[1]

In this discarded poem, critics have seen evidence of the baroque and even of the *précieux*. From those early characteristics, they say, Malherbe moved forward to classicism, which he was the first to advocate consciously. In following such an evolution, he represented in his own

[1] *Le lagrime di San Pietro* (1560).

work the transition from sixteenth-century to seventeenth-century poetry – a transition, moreover, which he was instrumental in bringing about.

Such statements do convey very baldly what in fact occurred. But they require considerable qualification, as do the terms 'baroque' and 'classic', before they acquire a critical validity. The best starting-point will be the actual poem *Les Larmes de Saint Pierre*, which Malherbe published in 1587, at about the time when Du Bartas and Sponde (and also Desportes) were writing.

The subject is the remorse of St Peter when he has denied being a follower of Christ, just after his master has been condemned to death by the Sanhedrin. The saint wanders distractedly through the night, accusing himself and recollecting. The poem is as aimless in its structure as the thoughts it expresses. It evokes the massacre of the Holy Innocents, who were fortunate to die while they were still sinless; the feet of Christ when He walked on the water and saved Peter from drowning; the storm which rumbles symbolically on the horizon; the endless, disjointed imprecations of Peter against life and his own cowardice. The style is marked by strained antitheses, by imagery flowery sometimes to the point of absurdity.

In the first shock of remorse, Peter can only 'cover his burning shame with the ashes of grief' – his blushes turn to a livid pallor:

> Voulant faire beaucoup il ne peut davantage
> Que soupirer tout bas et se mettre au visage
> Sur le feu de sa honte une cendre d'ennui.

The Holy Innocents were lilies incarnadined by the murderers' knives – or rather, as Malherbe phrases it, 'the murderous knife':

> Ce furent de beaux lis, qui mieux que la nature,
> Mêlant à leur blancheur l'incarnate peinture
> Que tira de leur sein le couteau criminel . . .

The poem ends with a personification of the Dawn, who comes out from the doors of night holding a vase of withered flowers in one hand and a pitcher of tears (dew) in the other – an extreme and over-concrete example of the pathetic fallacy sometimes ascribed only to Romantic writers:

> L'Aurore d'une main, en sortant de ses portes,
> Tient un vase de fleurs languissantes et mortes;
> Elle verse de l'autre une cruche de pleurs,

Et d'un voile tissu de vapeur et d'orage
Couvrant ses cheveux d'or,[1] découvre en son visage
Tout ce qu'une âme sent de cruelles douleurs.

II

Even if Malherbe's manner had not changed, he would have done well to forget this immature poem, since those parts of it which might be called baroque are very bad baroque. But his condemnation bore also, or has been taken to bear, on other poets, who used similar conventions with incomparably greater skill. Such poets, running from Agrippa d'Aubigné to Saint-Amant, who lived until 1661, were once classified by the critic Lanson as *attardés et égarés* – stragglers and strayers. Lanson's manual of literature, first published in 1894, fairly represented then and for some time after the orthodox French critical view. Except for the recognition of Ronsard and the other Pléiade poets, whom the Romantics had rehabilitated, this view had not changed much since the days of Boileau. In the eyes of Lanson's generation the main tradition, the typically French tradition, was that of Ronsard (but gropingly), then of the mature Malherbe and Boileau, with, of course, Corneille (but who, again, was groping towards perfection), Racine and La Fontaine. Whoever resisted or eluded the march down the straight and luminous road to classicism, whose philosopher was Descartes, was dismissed as marginal. A secondary consequence of this attitude was that not only were known poets like Du Bartas neglected, but that poets like Sponde and La Ceppède lay entirely forgotten, because there was no research in their direction.

In the early 1940s French criticism came to recognize that classicism was not the only, or perhaps the principal, current. The *attardés et égarés* were now seen to represent a tendency which was equally French, equally fruitful and, until a late date, equally important.

This was both admirable and true. But in the thrill of rediscovering both the post-Renaissance and a submerged seventeenth century, French criticism again yielded to its besetting fondness for general classifications and labelled the whole rehabilitated trend 'baroque'. The consequences were inevitable. Specialized opinion was divided on the exact significance of the term, on its application to certain

[1] Cf. the infinitely more skilful use of such devices by Shelley in the *Ode to the West Wind*:

> . . . there are spread
> . . . even from the dim verge
> Of the horizon to the zenith's height,
> The locks of the approaching storm.

authors, on the historical frontiers of the baroque and its relation to other tendencies such as *préciosité*. Putting aside the comprehensive view which sees most of world art and literature as baroque, with rare and short interludes of classicism – and which therefore attaches Romanticism, Impressionism and even Surrealism to the baroque – we were left with discussions as to where (in French literature) post-Renaissance baroque begins and ends; whether, indeed, going back earlier than d'Aubigné's *Printemps*, it is not detectable in Ronsard; whether Malherbe's *Larmes de Saint Pierre* is baroque or *précieux*; how far Corneille is baroque; whether Bossuet, once considered as the citadel of classicism, is not baroque at least in his early sermons. Individual authors were subdivided in terms of general classifications. 'The *versatile* Tristan L'Hermite,' a critic was led to write, in a study whose general tone was intelligently non-dogmatic,[1] 'who when he is neither baroque nor *précieux*, is already a classicist poet.'

Another critic classed Sponde as baroque and pointed to his passionate awareness of the antagonism between the mobile, the transient and the physical on the one hand, and on the other the unchanging, the eternal, the spiritual. But in the same study[2] Malherbe is anti-baroque for the same qualities: he prefers repose to movement, the eternal stability of the divine to 'our unhappy love of change which he experiences with a kind of anxious horror'. The test-case, Pascal, can obviously be studied from this point of view as baroque (he has been), or considered as classical in his desperate search for permanent truths. Philosophically, of course, the intense experience of 'anguish' is a baroque characteristic, while its resolution in a final certainty is classical. That is what the classifying critics meant, but for the simplest of reasons they could not say so: a writer might spend his whole life in a state of inner conflict and in his last hour – the time to write a paragraph or a few lines of verse – attain the serene certainty towards which his whole work would then be seen to have been a progression. Until the eleventh hour he is an incipient classic struggling to reject the baroque; at midnight he has done so. But suppose he writes down nothing, or what he writes is lost, what is his category then? One cannot base serious literary distinctions on amateur philosophy.[3] One cannot generalize and hope to attain more than approximate truths.

The discussion on the limits of the classic and the baroque, with the drawing of finer distinctions between baroque, *précieux* and meta-

---

[1] Odette de Mourgues, *Metaphysical, Baroque and Précieux Poetry* (Oxford, 1953).
[2] Jean Rousset, *La Littérature de l'âge baroque en France* (Corti, 1953).
[3] Nor, probably, on professional philosophy.

physical, embarked critics on a hopeless though not fruitless attempt to define the terms wished upon them. Almost incidentally, it led to a re-examination of neglected poets and threw new light on their works. Valuable for this (though it has often entailed arguing from the general to the particular), it has nevertheless accumulated a rich store of confusion for the student. The intelligent debate, conducted at a high level of knowledge and perception by experts who frame their theories and definitions only tentatively, hedging them with the most delicate reservations, becomes frozen into solid dogma in manuals and textbooks. Hundreds of ordinary teachers, who assume not unreasonably that what they learnt during their degree courses was authoritative – and who, moreover, feel a duty to align their own teaching with what appears to be university opinion, if only for examination purposes – are soon instructing thousands of pupils in the six characteristics of baroque writing. Or it may be five. Or instead of baroque it will be some other category of literature. And while this circular process goes on, the important distinctions – as that the poetry of d'Aubigné differs totally from that of Saint-Amant and both from that of, say, Góngora – are scarcely touched upon. Yet they are apparent to any reader with the least natural nose for literature. It is this sense which should be developed, leaving those who do not possess it to get on as best they may. And they are not so numerous as the French academic system, with its fundamentally cynical view of the imaginative capacities of the nation, has traditionally held.

'Baroque' is an accepted (though variously defined) term in architecture, painting and decoration, from which it extends legitimately to the stage décor of the court masque and the work of the Italians who designed scenery for spectacular plays and operas in seventeenth-century France. From here it spreads to the texts of the spectacles themselves (when there is one) and gains a footing in literature. Since France certainly had a baroque theatre, it seems impossible to refuse her a baroque drama, and from the overall point of view of the spectacular plays of Corneille, such as *La Toison d'or*, his comedies (as *L'Illusion comique*, *Le Menteur*) and, by contamination, most of his tragedies, fall under this heading. But when a word originally associated with the flowing canvases of Rubens and the mobile statuary of Bernini is applied to the detail of non-dramatic poetry, the analogy becomes strained. Regrettable though it is, 'baroque' has, however, now entered the language of French literary criticism and covers, broadly, the following characteristics:

The metaphysical anguish of men in an unstable world, conscious of the impermanence of everything around them. (This fits much of the religious poetry of the late and post-Renaissance and also the obsession with the theme of death. It does not fit Du Bartas, who had full confidence in his absurd universe, nor the later, non-religious, poets. These latter have to be classed as *précieux* or on the way to *préciosité*, whereas it might be better to see them as examples of a small-scale – pastoral or drawing-room – baroque.)

The attempt to render the sense of impermanence in changing, broken and uncentralized forms and metres. (The analogy with baroque architecture. One can follow it out a certain distance by speaking quite pertinently of the 'structure' of verse, but a point is reached at which the analogy no longer holds.)

The use of imagery to convey the same sense of mobility. Imagery, indeed, acquires an exaggerated importance in a poetry which does not admit the intellectual restraint of reason. The images used are compressed and rapid in themselves and are multiplied rapidly in accordance with the kaleidoscopic impression which the outer world makes on the poet.[1] There is no steady focus on a single concept developed through one, possibly majestic, image and its prolongations – for that is not the way to catch the flame, the running stream, the butterfly, or the transitory essence of human life.

Finally, the use of the free-ranging metaphor mainly or wholly as an ornament. A love of decoration, more or less well integrated with the structure, is a feature of baroque art, and can become one of baroque poetry. According to the particular poet, it varies from the plumes on the hearse – the hyperbole:

> Underneath this marble hearse
> Lies the subject of all verse,
> Sidney's sister, Pembroke's mother;
> Death, ere thou hast slain another
> Fair and learned and good as she,
> Time shall throw a dart at thee . . .

to the feather in the cap – the conceit:

> The feathered fishes of the aery sea,
> Winged poets and woodland musicians.[2]

[1] As in Du Bartas's description of the cock, already quoted – though here at least three of the images cover the same concept of the alarm-clock:

> Sur réveille-matin, véritable astrologue,
> Horloge du paysan, frayeur du Lion rogue,
> Fidèle annonce-jour, Roi du peuple crêté.

[2] i.e. the birds. From the Italian of Marino, quoted Jean Rousset, op. cit., p. 188.

Occasionally it is so well imagined that it really replaces the thing described, as in the Spaniard Góngora's evocation of two hunting-falcons:

> Complainingly they came, perched upon the glove,
> The impetuous whirlwinds of Norway.[1]

In 'classical' art and literature, on the contrary, the centre is fixed because the artist's view of the world is constant. Philosophically stable, he constructs his work with balance and proportion on 'linear' principles. The development (in the case of a poem) is progressive and rational, while the imagery is subordinated to it. No more extravagant flights for the metaphor, since they might trouble the clarity of the unified vision. The metaphor itself is devitalized to ensure its compliance.

Such are the theoretical distinctions – valid, it must be repeated, on broad general lines, but much more questionable when one comes to consider closely the work of particular writers.[2]

III

If we now return to the convenient Malherbe, we find him towards the year 1600 beginning to write dignified 'official' verse for his royal patrons and religious verse of an entirely different kind from the earlier *Larmes de Saint Pierre*. He was now making stately rhymed versions of the Psalms. It may be said of this laborious and unimaginative writer that he had at last found where his true gift lay and was fortunate that it coincided with the new desire for harmony and stability which characterized the France of Henri IV immediately after the long-drawn horror of the religious wars. Malherbe belonged to his time and was by no means a solitary pioneer. Even forgetting the grave and noble poetry of the *Discours* which the despised Ronsard had written in the 1560s and which was the ultimate source of the Malherbian alexandrine, two of Malherbe's contemporaries had written in the same vein. These were Bertaut and Du Perron. The first became a bishop,

---

[1] Quoted by Gerald Brenan, *The Literature of the Spanish People* (1951).

[2] What has been said here applies only to French literature. Historians of German and Italian literature call the whole of their seventeenth centuries baroque periods. The term is also established for Spanish literature. In each of these countries the interpretation is somewhat different, but it corresponds to a more fundamental exuberance than is found in France and is justified by usage and convenience. In English criticism it is hardly current, and one hopes it will be resisted stoutly if it should threaten to become so. The natural allergy of the English to general ideas should in any case prove a sufficient deterrent.

the second an archbishop, and their later verse, at least, is of an impeccable solemnity.

In the campaign which was opening against exuberant imagery (and one understands how nauseating it could become in unskilful hands) Du Perron well expressed what would become the 'classical' attitude. He condemned the 'corrupt and ignoble' metaphor, like one he had heard used by a preacher: 'Lord, wipe my beak clean with the napkin of thy love.' He went on to state a view which, by and large, would be law for the next two hundred years:

> In using metaphors, one should never allow them to descend from the general to the particular. One can say 'the flames of love', but not 'the brands', 'the lantern', or 'the wick'. None of our writers today seems able to avoid this fault. The metaphor is a small simile – an abridged simile – it ought to pass quickly, one should not dwell on it. When it is too prolonged, it is corrupt [*vicieux*] and degenerates into a riddle.

Though not 'prolonged', Marino's *feathered fishes = birds* is obviously of this last type.

Later in the century, the erudite critic Rapin, a contemporary of Racine and Boileau, would write more dogmatically:

> There are metaphors authorized by usage, which poetry could not do without. The poet's duty is to use them prudently, never shocking the modesty of the [French] language.

Though Malherbe is not yet restricted to the purely conventional metaphor and though something of his 'baroque' past still clings about him, his imagery is 'prudent' – that is to say, general – to a considerable degree. He no longer enters into the detail with which he once elaborated his picture of the Dawn. If he personifies Death, or Fate, it is vaguely, so that they become less than allegorical figures and little more than named forces. And in other ways he tones down the particular and the concrete, carefully draping them in a conjurer's cloak of rhetoric. This can be illustrated by comparing the eighth Psalm as rendered by the English translators of the Authorized Version of 1611 with Malherbe's verse paraphrase (admittedly a paraphrase) of the same psalm.

The directness of the Authorized Version:

> When I consider *thy heavens, the work of thy fingers, the moon and the stars,* which thou hast ordained:
> What is man, that thou art mindful of him, and the son of man, *that thou visitest him?*

is in contrast to:

> De moi, toutes les fois que j'arrête les yeux
> A voir *les ornements dont tu pares les cieux*,
> Tu me sembles si grand, et nous si peu de chose,
> > Que mon entendement
> Ne peut s'imaginer quelle amour te dispose
> A nous *favoriser d'un regard seulement.*

Two verses later:

> Thou hast put all things under his feet: All sheep and oxen, yea, and the beasts of the field; The fowl of the air and the fish of the sea, and whatsoever passeth through the paths of the seas;

is in Malherbe:

> Sitôt que le besoin excite son désir,
> Qu'est-ce qu'en ta largesse il ne trouve à choisir?
> Et par ton règlement *l'air, la mer et la terre*
> > N'entretiennent-ils pas
> Une secrète loi de se faire la guerre,
> A qui de plus de mets fournira ses repas?

Not only has much padding been added, but the enumeration of beasts, fowl and fish has been generalized into the elements which contain them: *l'air, la mer et la terre.*

Such parallels do not prove any rule regarding English and French poetic diction. They merely show that *at that date* there was a divergence. For Malherbe, the English translators would have seemed some thirty years out of date, but it would have been easy enough to match their tone in Du Bartas's generation.

For Malherbe's contemporaries, however, there was a growing feeling – often expressed during the seventeenth century – that the concrete and the particular did not suit the genius of the French language. What might be effective in Italian and Spanish (English and German were little known) was at best second-rate in French. Today, in the light of the poetry of the nineteenth and twentieth centuries, we know better. But in 1600 this view was understandable. The French 'baroque' poets do not equal the greatest of their contemporaries in other countries. All that modern research has so far discovered is that they are more interesting than most of the 'classical' poets.

IV

The trend against 'corrupt and ignoble' imagery naturally extended beyond imagery to the whole vocabulary of poetry. In reaction particularly against Italian influence, Malherbe condemned foreign importations, but also those local, technical and popular terms which give literature its body and savour. A kind of class distinction began to be drawn between words which were fit for the poet's pen and words which were not. As a consequence, 'literary' poetry diverged from 'popular' poetry and the type of free-and-easy song that Marot had once written lost caste altogether. There is a place for grandeur in poetry. *Paradise Lost* and one of the best-loved poems in the English language, Gray's *Elegy*, amply prove it. Certain poems of Malherbe's also justify themselves. But too long a separation from the common language produces sterile or over-inflated verse, and this was the danger that lay ahead. On this count, too, Malherbe's 'reforms' were predominantly negative.

His most positive contribution – though this also, in time, would become mere mechanism – was in the metrical field. Following the architectural analogy, one can say that Malherbe's poems, and within the poems each stanza, are constructed symmetrically round a fixed centre. The firmness and regularity of this *structure* shows in the verses quoted above (p. 53), or in:

> N'espérons plus, mon âme, / aux promesses du monde,
> Sa lumière est un verre, / et sa faveur une onde,
> Que toujours quelque vent / empêche de calmer.
> Quittons ces vanités, / lassons-nous de les suivre:
>> C'est Dieu qui nous fait vivre,
>> C'est Dieu qu'il faut aimer.

With a solid competence, but also with a certain complacency, the well-made lines are placed in position one after another. Each alexandrine is exactly balanced on its central caesura or sense-pause. The last two lines of six syllables (half-alexandrines), with their parallel wording, are laid with a sense of slow inevitability on the square little structure, completing it absolutely. The masculine rhyme *aimer* rings like a last hammer-tap. But there is no resonance, of sense or of sound, no prolongation or the suggestion of one. The good workman can walk away from his self-contained work, certain that it will neither collapse nor move in any other way, and proceed to build another exactly like it. Its structure has another feature. The first three lines, with their discreet and dignified metaphor, set out a proposition: the world is vanity. The second half of the stanza immediately and dogmatically draws the moral conclusion: turn away from the world and love God. There is no hesitation, no confusion, no conflict, any more than there is conflict between the two halves of a sandwich. The ordered and stable form reflects a corresponding state of mind.

In order to achieve such effects, Malherbe or his followers established precise rules – as that the alexandrine should always divide into two equal hemistichs, that masculine and feminine rhymes (those ending in a mute *e*) should alternate (though this had always been common practice), and that the rhymes should be as 'rich' as possible, in order to mark the line-endings more strongly. (A 'rich' rhymes involves the final consonant, as the *m* in *calmer-aimer*. But *parler-aimer* would be a 'poor' rhyme. Obviously this was an aspiration more than an absolute rule.) Finally, hiatus, involving certain sequences of vowels which even Ronsard had sometimes used to good effect, was barred on grounds of euphony. It became, in theory, incorrect to write 'joyeux *et é*baudi', as Marot had done, or 'Je répondrai *que oui*', as La Fontaine was to do.

These prescriptions, in themselves sometimes pedantic, were dictated by a growing desire for regularity and sonority and had a basis in 'nature' – but the nature of the disciplinarian, which for others is anti-nature.

V

Malherbe was less dry than his doctrine. In his own field he is perfectly defensible and even admirable, so long as it is not taken for the whole field of poetry. Moreover, he would not by himself have eclipsed the freer kinds of poetry – nor, in fact, did he. Years after his death poets like Saint-Amant, frolicking happily with the Muse and the wineglass, appeared still not to have heard of the new canons of taste. But Fate, in the person of Boileau, was waiting to put an end to such innocent pursuits and, by canonizing Malherbe, to underline his inadequacies.

Boileau's *Art poétique*, published in 1674, contains the famous passage beginning: 'At last Malherbe came.' The first lines, if they claim too much, are still a good characterization of the poet, apart from the reference to 'grace':

> Enfin Malherbe vint et, le premier en France,
> Fit sentir dans les vers une juste cadence:
> D'un mot mis à sa place enseigna le pouvoir,

> Et réduisit la Muse aux règles du devoir.
> Par ce sage écrivain la langue réparée
> N'offrit plus rien de rude à l'oreille épurée;
> Les stances avec grâce apprirent à tomber,
> Et le vers sur le vers n'osa plus enjamber.

After praising Malherbe's clarity, Boileau makes a general attack on obscurity in verse, for the reason – long before the invention of the glossy magazine – that it fatigues the reader's attention:

> Si le sens de vos vers tarde à se faire entendre,
> Mon esprit aussitôt commence à se détendre,
> Et de vos vains discours prompt à se détacher,
> Ne suit point un auteur qu'il faut toujours chercher.

This develops into an attack on the 'baroque' spirit because it was not lit – we have seen why not – by the 'light of reason':

> Il est certains esprits dont les sombres pensées
> Sont d'un nuage épais toujours embarrassées:
> Le jour de la raison ne le saurait percer.
> *Avant donc que d'écrire, apprenez à penser.*
> Selon que notre idée est plus ou moins obscure,
> L'expression la suit ou moins nette, ou plus pure.
> Ce que l'on conçoit bien s'énonce clairement,
> Et les mots pour le dire arrivent aisément.

The cat is now out of the bag and we realize that Boileau – whatever he may have thought – was not writing about poetry at all. His advice, from 'Avant donc que d'écrire . . .' on, is excellent for a civil servant drawing up a report, or a philosopher expounding a reasoned argument, or a specialist setting out a difficult theory for the layman. On such principles the best journalism is still built, from a survey of a political situation to an account of a football match. But it is not the way in which imaginative literature gets written, even in prose. The poet, above all, does not first 'conceive well', and then 'state clearly'. There are not two processes, thinking and writing, or two elements, content and form, but one compound – and it is vital that they should be inseparably fused together. The medium in which the poet 'thinks' – though 'thinks' is an inadequate term – *is* words, in their mould of rhythm. Until he is actually handling them, not only the poem but the concept which he simultaneously perceives and expresses does not really exist for him. Or it exists only in embryonic form, which must be developed and may be modified. This is so universally the experience of both the writer and the reader of good poetry that one marvels that Boileau and his contemporaries should have believed themselves to be on the highway of literary orthodoxy when in fact they had strayed into a drab and narrowing back-alley which could terminate only in suicide.

If evidence is needed, one has only to follow Boileau (in his correspondence with Racine) laboriously composing his *Ode sur la prise de Namur*, from the first 'daring' draft to the final inflated platitude. More serious was the general consequence of considering poetry as a medium for 'effective communication' in a narrowly rationalistic sense. This attitude, which seems inseparable from the demand for clarity, grew by a kind of fatal logic from Malherbe's liking for clear formal arrangements, through Boileau's over-dogmatic rationalization ('clear form is based on clear thinking') to the conviction that poetic form itself is an encumbrance and had better be dispensed with. The eighteenth century, examining without enthusiasm the traditions which the seventeenth century had bequeathed it, voiced this conviction openly:

> The aim of language being simply to make oneself understood, it seems unreasonable to submit to constraints which often defeat that end and cause one to take far more time in formulating one's thought than if one merely followed the natural order of ideas.[1]

So away with poetry as a useless art, especially since it consists of well-worn clichés and 'ornaments' which actually distort meaning:

> Suppose it were discovered that these ornaments, belonging to a completely false and ridiculous system, and long familiar to every passer-by on the highways of Parnassus, are not worthy of being used, not worth the trouble they still cost when they are used? And that finally – for one must speak frankly when one attempts to prophesy – that it is somewhat puerile to constrict one's words solely to please the ear, and to constrict them to such a point that one often says less than one means, and sometimes something different.[2]

This was not what Malherbe had intended, or even Boileau. It had been less true in the seventeenth century, when the classical 'ornament' – which, it will be remembered, originally stemmed from a sober protest against the baroque 'ornament' – had expressed adequately what certain writers had to say. But by the eighteenth century the only reply would have been a complete renewal of the language of poetry from the root up. That was only to be brought about by the Romantics.

---

[1] Houdar de La Motte, *Discours sur la poésie* (1707).
[2] Fontenelle, *Traité sur la poésie en général* (1751).

Chapter 6

Irregular Seventeenth-Century Poets: Théophile de Viau, Saint-Amant, Tristan L'Hermite

AS HAS BEEN SEEN in the previous chapter, there was no clear-cut development from the 'classical' Malherbe in the first quarter of the century to Boileau, with Racine and La Fontaine, in the last third. Much of the poetry which came between and which has been claimed as baroque is in fact of such a varied nature that, if it were to be appropriately labelled, it would call for much more detailed classification. All that can be said of it in general is that it is anti-classical in several ways and that, in its entirety, it cannot be dismissed as minor, even though it has not revealed any one truly major poet.

Religious poetry continued to be written, some of it in the manner of Malherbe's paraphrases of the Psalms, but some in the tradition of the late sixteenth-century poets, which persisted with little change. La Ceppède, already mentioned on pp. 43–4, is technically a seventeenth-century poet, since the first edition of his *Théorèmes* was not published until 1613, when he was about sixty-five. Several later poets dwelt, as he had done, on the physical torments of the crucified Jesus, or, like Sponde and Chassignet, on the perishable nature of the human body, or, following d'Aubigné, drew horrifying pictures of human suffering as a consequence of war, persecution or plague. One of the most powerful of such poets was Pierre Le Moyne (1602–71), described by the modern critic Jean Rousset as 'an extraordinarily gifted poet, the Victor Hugo of his century', and by Chapelain, the official literary adviser to Louis XIII and Louis XIV, dismissed in these significant words:

> Il est guindé, diffus, enflé, et rempli de figures vicieuses ... Son style dégénère en hyperbolique ... Ce défaut ne lui vient que de trop d'imagination.[1]

[1] Quoted by J. Rousset, *Anthologie de la poésie baroque française*, II, p. 327. *Imagination* in the seventeenth century = 'fantasy, (luxuriant) fancy', seen as a bad feature.

Chapelain's comment was made in 1662. So more than forty years after Malherbe's reforms some poets were still using the hyperbolic style and the 'corrupt' imagery of the preceding century, as they were also showing a similar obsession with violence and death. If the earlier poetry is to be called baroque, the same word is fully applicable to this later poetry. Though Le Moyne may be an extreme case, he was far from unique. Some of these exponents of the religious baroque were provincial ecclesiastics out of touch with the tastes of the capital and the court – but by no means all. Several, including Le Moyne himself, formed part of the society of the salons.

Yet the strongest contrast is provided by the poetry which has come to be considered as typical of the salons and which would hardly have flourished without their influence. Almost invariably the theme is love, treated in a minor mode with ingenuity and often wit, but not passion. Not only coarseness but open sensuality are banned. Delicacy and respect are the keynotes. Hyperbolical comparisons are common, but repeated so frequently from poem to poem and from poet to poet that they become conventional and in the end unremarkable:

> Ses beaux yeux causent cent trépas:
> Ils éclairent tous les climats,
> Et portent en chaque prunelle
> Le soleil.[1]

This *précieux* idiom, most highly developed in such poets as Voiture and Sarasin, constantly recurs in other poets whose work as a whole could not be classed under *préciosité*. It is used by lovers in the plays of Corneille and Racine and for that matter, going back to a different country and period, in Shakespeare.[2] In seventeenth-century France it is the common language of *galanterie* and, like any common language, soon becomes stale and trivial, in spite of its many small-scale triumphs. Whether, in view of its dependence on metaphor (qualified by a constant refusal to use metaphor originally) it should be attached to the baroque is another question. In view of what has been said earlier of the principal baroque qualities, it would seem pointless to attempt to do so.

II

Between Malherbe and Racine, considered as the purest representative of French classicism, three poets stand out in their own right. Their

---

[1] 'Her fair eyes cause a hundred deaths: they light up every clime and in each pupil contain the sun.' (Voiture.) [2] See e.g. *Romeo and Juliet*, II, ii. Also the *Sonnets*.

verse exhibits most of the features to be found in their lesser contemporaries, but each possessed sufficient talent and originality to have formed
a poetic individuality of his own.

The oldest but shortest-lived was Théophile de Viau (1590–1626).
Little is known of his early life except that he was born of a Protestant
family, was noted for his unruliness as a student and followed a troupe
of strolling players for whom he wrote (lost) plays. At the age of
twenty-five he entered the service of the Comte de Candale – the
first of his three aristocratic patrons – and earned a reputation as an
ostentatious court gallant, over-free in his morals and his words. He
was soon in trouble for his irreverance and no doubt his Protestantism
(which he abjured in 1622). After a brief exile in 1619, his enemies the
Jesuits brought more serious charges against him which resulted in
his being thrown into prison for two years while his case was being
prepared. The eventual sentence of perpetual banishment was soon set
aside thanks to the influence of his latest patron, the Duc de Montmorency, but imprisonment in the appalling conditions then usual had so
weakened him that he died a year later.

Théophile was unfixed in his art rather than independent. He wrote
in several different manners over a comparatively short period. His
only surviving play, the tragedy of *Pyrame et Thisbé*, which enjoyed
great success, contains both ludicrously exaggerated similes and moving
natural dialogue. Naturalness has been seen as his dominant feature on
the evidence of his *Élégie à une dame*. In this long poem he rejects the
intense study and polish practiced by the ungifted followers of
Malherbe (rather than by Malherbe himself, whom he grudgingly
admires). Poetry, for him, should be more spontaneous. It should not
follow rules of composition or a premeditated plan:

> Je ne veux point unir le fil de mon sujet:
> Diversement je laisse et reprends mon objet.
> Mon âme, imaginant, n'a point la patience
> De bien polir les vers et ranger la science.
> La règle me déplaît, j'écris confusément.
> Jamais un bon esprit ne fait rien qu'aisément ...

This is a striking anticipation of Verlaine's rejection, 250 years
later, of professionally finished 'literature' in his *Art poétique*.[1] The
results are hardly comparable, but his guiding principle allowed
Théophile to describe rustic scenes in a direct way, as in his *Lettre à*

---

[1] See below, pp. 186–8.

son frère, in which, while lying in his dungeon, he longingly pictures their country home in Gascony:

> Je verrai sur nos grenadiers
> Leurs rouges pommes entr'ouvertes,
> Où le ciel, comme à ses lauriers,
> Garde toujours des feuilles vertes.
> Je verrai ce touffu jasmin
> Qui fait ombre à tout le chemin
> D'une assez spacieuse allée,
> Et la parfume d'une fleur
> Qui conserve dans la gelée
> Son odorat et sa couleur.

In his love-poetry he is capable of writing with an equally simple directness:

> Quand tu me vois baiser tes bras
> Que tu poses nus sur tes draps,
> Bien plus blancs que le linge même,
> Quand tu sens ma brûlante main
> Se promener dessus ton sein,
> Tu sens bien, Cloris, que je t'aime.

This kind of verse has a freshness lacking in *précieux* poetry. It is neither very deep nor very exciting and in some of his longer poems can become tedious, but by avoiding the trap of over-sophistication it often succeeds in rendering the perceptions of the senses with a force unusual at the time. This was Théophile's main object. He delighted in sensual pleasures of all kinds and managed in his best verse to write of them with a minimum of artifice and a complete absence of pedantry. In the circumstances it is surprising to find that, judged by the number of editions of his works,[1] he was the most popular poet of the century. La Fontaine certainly learnt something from him.

III

Antoine-Girard de Saint-Amant (1594–1661) was a friend of Théophile and had a comparable career. He also was born a Protestant and became a Catholic, quite possibly for worldly reasons. His father was a Norman sea-captain and this may account for the various voyages which the son made to America, West Africa and India, though in what capacity and at what dates is uncertain. These travels left little trace in his verse.

---

[1] There were about sixty editions between 1621 and 1677.

For the most part he depended on patrons, two of whom, the Dukes of Liancourt and Montmorency, were the patrons of Théophile. He placed his pen, his wit and his sword at their service and in short belonged to a numerous class of young men who could prosper best by attaching themselves to the aristocracy but on their own level retained a considerable measure of independence. Saint-Amant's devotion to the bottle and the brothel may have been partly a pose cultivated to amuse (in moderately bawdy verse) his contemporaries and even his patrons. But it did him no harm in the company he kept to exhibit that kind of character. He did not want to appear a mere scribe, but rather a sociable and turbulent gentleman who could toss off verse by the yard when the mood took him. In fact there is more culture and more 'art' in his work than that particular image would suggest.

His range is wider than Théophile's. It includes descriptions of natural scenes in such poems as *La Solitude*, whose theme is the pleasure of being alone in some wild spot unspoilt by man. Here the poet can wander in a mood of gentle melancholy reinforced by the discovery of some ruined house in which owls hoot, demons gibber and ghosts moan around the skeleton of a suicide. With this foretaste of eighteenth-century Gothic horror goes a prefigurement of the Romantic love of picturesque ruins and solitary communion with nature, as has often been pointed out. Though partly conventional in Saint-Amant and not always unconnected with pastoral, it does appear to contain a strong element of personal feeling and observation.[1] Certainly it includes a mythological apparatus of nymphs and dryads which no nineteenth-century Romantic could have used – though Mallarmé could – but this remains in the background. The real scene as perceived by the eyes is drawn with some faithfulness.

Elsewhere Saint-Amant can describe nature more artificially, calling birds 'les miracles volants' in the manner of Marino, whom he often imitated, or snow in the Alps as 'ce beau coton du ciel de quoi les monts s'habillent'. He can use the *précieux* technique in a poem such as *Plainte sur la mort de Silvie*, in which the poet calls on a stream to halt its current and listen to his lament on the death of his beloved; then to flow on, carrying his tears down to the salt sea. An English translation of this delicate poem was once printed in *The Stuffed Owl*, a collection

---

[1] The impulse to get away from the crowd is expressed in several poems of the time, from Racan's *Tircis, il faut penser à la retraite*, which contains the Lamartinian line: 'Vallons, fleuves, rochers, plaisante solitude,' to Marvell's *The Garden*. Théophile de Viau wrote a *Solitude* at about the same date as Saint-Amant's poem, but in his poem there is a girl and his main preoccupation is to find a spot where they can make love undisturbed. This entirely changes the emphasis.

of outstandingly bad and flat verse whose editors, rationalistic in the tradition of Boileau, entirely missed the point of this refined exercise.[1]

Such refinement is not, however, typical of Saint-Amant. He excels as a writer of burlesque poetry, a seventeenth-century mode associated particularly with Scarron but practised by numerous others. Its favourite form is the mock-heroic, in which epic characters and their actions are made to look ridiculous. A similar upturning of values gives the mock-pastoral and the mock-romantic. The commonest form of these three kinds of writing is parody containing a strong element of satire. The original masters had been Italian, then Spanish: *Don Quixote* began as a burlesque of the romances of chivalry, whatever it developed into later; Lope de Vega wrote a *Gatomaquia* or *Cat Epic* (1634), describing the loves and wars of a cat-community. Further back, of course, before the term burlesque was in use, there had been the example of Rabelais, whose work can be read as a burlesque epic in prose. Saint-Amant himself wrote a *Rome ridicule* (1643), a poem of irreverent mockery in the same spirit as the modern television series *Up Pompeii*, but in most of his work the burlesque elements are more diffused. They emerge as humour, as physical realism sometimes expressed in plainly crude terms which Malherbe would quite certainly have condemned, and as a fantastic luxuriance in the choice of metaphors which was equally 'unclassical'.

Saint-Amant's best-known poem in this vein, *Le Melon*, hymns that fruit in extravagant language which is surely the ultimate in mock-laudatory poetry:

> O manger précieux, délices de la bouche!
> O doux reptile herbu, rampant sur une couche!
> O beaucoup mieux que l'or, chef-d'œuvre d'Apollon!
> O fleur de tous les fruits! O ravissant MELON!

Describing himself lying inertly in bed. Saint-Amant's comparison is to 'a filleted hare sleeping in a pâté'. In a love-sonnet, at least half-serious, he imagines that the 'bird-god' Cupid often nests between his mistress's breasts and goes on to compare him to a sea-gull (*goilan*) laying its eggs on some rock near the sea:

> Quand je la vois, cette gorge ivoirine
> Où l'oiseau-dieu souvent se va nicher,
> Comme un goilan qui sur quelque rocher
> Fait ses petits au bord de la marine . . .

[1] *The Stuffed Owl: An Anthology of Bad Verse*, ed. D. B. Wyndham Lewis and Charles Lee (1935).

The sweet grassy reptile, the boneless hare, the gull's-nest cleavage and various other equally far-fetched similes might be classed as comic baroque and so ignored in the history of serious poetry. But they are not used exclusively for comic effect and Saint-Amant deserves consideration as a poet, unpolished but highly inventive, who effectively handled the 'corrupt' metaphor and the colloquial turn of speech until well after the middle of the century.

IV

Tristan L'Hermite (c. 1601–55) was a more courtly poet with a background similar to his two near-contemporaries. He began as a page in an aristocratic household, consorted with a company of travelling actors, fled from France to escape the consequence of some duel or brawl,[1] and returned to enter the service, first of Louis XIII, then of the King's younger brother, Gaston d'Orléans. Gaston was an unruly and intriguing prince who himself spent some time in exile with his followers when he fell foul of Richelieu. Tristan remained with him for twenty-five years, then found another patron in the Duc de Guise.

Tristan's best lyric verse is in his first two collections, *Les Plaintes d'Acante* (1633) and *Les Amours* (1638), but between these two publications he had also begun writing for the stage and it is as a dramatic author that his importance is greatest. He produced in all six tragedies, one tragi-comedy and one comedy. They appeared at a time when French 'classical' tragedy was establishing itself, but though the first, *La Mariane*, can be quoted as a pioneer experiment in regular tragedy and the others observed the main technical requirements of the genre, they have many of the qualities of baroque drama, apparent both in their construction and their style. In *La Mariane* the beheading of the heroine in front of a pitying crowd is described thus:

> Puis elle offrit sa gorge et cessa de parler.
> Et lors l'exécuteur, la voyant ainsi prête,
> D'un prompt éclair d'acier lui fit voler la tête.
> Là-dessus un grand cri tout autour s'entendit
> Qui pénétra les airs que son âme fendit.
> On vit sourdre aussitôt mille chaudes fontaines
> Des yeux de tout le peuple ainsi que de ses veines . . .[2]

---

[1] Knowledge of his early years is derived principally from his own autobiographical novel, *Le Page disgracié*. Though probably romanced in the detail, it was no doubt true as a general picture.

[2] A swift flash of steel and her head flew off. A loud cry split the skies (rose to heaven) at the same time as her soul. Hot springs welled from the people's eyes as they also did from her veins.

In his non-dramatic poetry Tristan's style is more 'prudent' and, from the point of view of the salons, in better taste. Many of his poems are completely *précieux*, ingenious variations on a limited number of accepted metaphors creating at best tiny thrills of pleasure or surprise. He was certainly influenced by Marino, the Italian poet whose glitteringly artificial *Adone* had been written at the French court not so long before under the patronage of Marie de' Medici. But Tristan goes a certain way beyond both Marinism and *préciosité*. Not far and not often enough, it might be said. He never attains the naturalness of Théophile or the bluff exuberance of Saint-Amant. But in his love-poems he achieves a certain sincerity of feeling, restrained though it is, and in his nature pieces one can discern a kind of miniature baroque in which description, transmutation and personification are combined to good effect:

> Auprès de cette grotte sombre
> Où l'on respire un air si doux,
> L'onde lutte avec les cailloux
> Et la lumière avecque l'ombre.
>
> Ces flots lassés de l'exercice
> Qu'ils ont fait dessus ce gravier
> Se reposent dans ce vivier
> Où mourut autrefois Narcisse.
>
> C'est un de ces miroirs où le faune
> Vient voir si son teint cramoisi
> Depuis que l'Amour l'a saisi
> Ne serait point devenu jaune.
>
> L'ombre[1] de cette fleur vermeille
> Et celle de ces joncs pendants
> Paraissent être là-dedans
> Les songes de l'eau qui sommeille . . .[2]

'The dreams of the sleeping water' in the last line quoted is more than a mere conceit and shows that the potentialities of this kind of poetry are not limited to prettiness or wit which, as time passes, is bound to lose much of its point.

[1] Reflection.
[2] From *Le Promenoir des deux amants.* Cf. Francis Ponge's description of pebbles (pp. 300–1 below). If Tristan's poem is stripped of its mythological references, it can be seen that both belong to the same imaginative order.

V

The three poets just considered were formerly classed as *libertins*. They were seen as free-thinking and free-living men who refused to toe the official line, whether social, ideological or literary. Up to a point this is true, though only Théophile got into serious trouble for his alleged opinions. All three led fairly boisterous lives, travelled in search of adventure or fortune, enjoyed physical pleasures and did not confine their activities to the study or the salon. This may help to characterize them biographically and even, as a first approach, to characterize their poetry.

If pushed too far, however, it revives an old idea of the French seventeenth century which has proved untenable. By singling out the 'classicism' of Malherbe, the civilizing influence of the first salons, the movement towards regularity and decorum in the drama, the role of the *Académie* (of which, incidentally, Saint-Amant was a member) in promoting uniformity of taste, a picture was built up of an ordered culture into which the 'libertine' writers did not fit. They had to be represented as rebels or eccentrics. In fact, until well into the 1650s, they were more typical of French literature than the 'regular' writers (and these, except among the critics, are hard to find). None of them achieves greatness, but for the student of poetry they are full of interest. With Saint-Amant in particular it is worth looking beyond his self-elaborated persona of 'good fat Saint-Amant' to discover a varied and gifted talent which still retains much life.

That there was life also in 'classical' poetry, written ostensibly within the conventions, is proved by the example of Racine. Some of the ways in which he achieved this feat are considered in the next chapter.

Chapter 7

Jean Racine

RACINE is considered here almost exclusively as a poet. He was, in fact, a dramatic poet and any division is necessarily artificial. But any attempt to do justice to the dramatist would lead us far beyond the bounds of our subject and we must be content with illustrating this side of his genius with a single example. To go further in that direction might obscure a truth which English readers sometimes find it difficult to accept – that, apart from the requirements of the stage, Racine was a supreme verbal artist. His verse, as verse, has been admired by poets of such radically different temperaments as Voltaire and Valéry and has influenced them profoundly.

An admirer himself of Malherbe, no rebel against the conventions of *préciosité*, an imitator of the Greeks and a respecter of contemporary good taste, his verse should have been well-mannered and slightly dull. Possibly it even appears so on a first acquaintance, but to be halted by this surface impression is to turn back on the brink of a new world – an alien world, perhaps, but one full of power, subtlety and beauty. That such qualities should have emerged from the influences current in Racine's day, and which he did not reject but fulfilled and reconciled, is one of the perennial surprises of literature. Is there, after all, a virtue in the French classical formula, as applied to poetry, which can inspire work of the highest kind, given the artist to execute it? Or can the great artist transform any formula, however unpromising, into a recipe for excellent work?

Faced with the incompatibility between 'classical' theory (words should be tailored to fit sense) and Racinian performance (words and meaning coalesce, and are impregnated in addition with a seemingly natural poetic perfume), some critics have been driven into supposing a Racine who slipped into greatness by accident and never fully realized what he was achieving. If, as a conscious artist, he followed Boileau, how could he have written as he did? The explanation is sometimes sought in the historical moment – but a moment which somehow eluded the Malherbe–Boileau hour-hand. For Jean Giraudoux,[1] writing of Racine's extraordinary psychological penetration, Racine was perhaps only a 'supreme talent'; the 'genius' was in the age which produced him and which gave him 'an inborn knowledge of great hearts and great moments'. For Marcel Raymond,[2] writing more specifically of the poet,

> he had the good fortune to appear at one of the mature stages of a culture and a language; he had mastered his technique; and an infallible intuition, a feeling of continuous beauty, enabled him to create – as though just at the emergence from sleep, in the white light of the first morning – that potent instrument, that royal language which still holds us enthralled.

This second appreciation is the more acceptable. It imputes no more to the age than can be readily conceded. One would allow the debt of almost any poet to the culture and idiom of his time. Yet even Marcel Raymond, while rightly refusing to see Racine as an unconscious operator, places him as near to the unconscious as possible – at the emergence from sleep, when the dream may still be in possession of the mind.

There should be nothing remarkable about such a process. No one is surprised when a revolutionary poet like Rimbaud produces, part consciously, part unconsciously, a highly original body of work from the books read in the classroom and in the municipal library at Charleville – and from the particular nature of his lived experience. But when Racine, who was not in appearance revolutionary, follows the same road, the need for some explanation seems to be felt. Either he was moving with some cultural current different from that of which he was aware; or perhaps he was deceiving his contemporaries into accepting at its face-value work which he knew perfectly well had another significance. Either Racine misunderstood himself, or his age misunderstood him.

Much has been written on this point and more could be. But, whatever the complexity of Racine's art and psychology, this particular difficulty need never have arisen. If Racine had been studied first as an individual case, one contradiction at least would have disappeared. But instead – as with the 'baroque' writers – a picture has been built up of 'classicism' based partly on literary theory, partly on a simplification of the historical background. Racine does not entirely fit into this picture. Hence the artificial 'paradox' of a classic who transcends classicism. Much confusion could be avoided if it were recognized that

---

[1] *Racine* (Grasset, 1930).   [2] *Génies de France* (Neuchâtel, 1942).

it is the picture, or rather the map, which is out of scale, not the individual writer. The first is always expendable and can be redrawn if necessary. The second, whether more or less well explored, is a land-mark which certainly exists. It would continue to exist if all the maps were lost.

II

Racine was the most professional of writers, capable of separating his work from what is known of his private emotions in a way not unusual in a dramatist. It is fruitless to look for any detailed reflection of his life in his writings. Nevertheless, his artistic personality as a whole was certainly moulded by his life and career.

He was born in 1639 of a family of local officials in the small town of La Ferté-Milon, in the Île de France. Both his parents died when he was a small child and he was brought up by relatives who had strong links with the Jansenist community of Port-Royal, south of Paris. His own schooling there had a powerful and somewhat sombre religious basis, though it also gave him an excellent grounding in the classical literatures. He was early attracted by the theatre and in his twenties he broke violently with his pious relatives and teachers to devote himself wholly to play-writing. His first tragedy, the immature *La Thébaïde*, was produced by Molière in 1664; this was followed by twelve years of almost consistently successful work as a tragic dramatist which set him unquestionably at the top of his profession.[1]

After the production of his greatest play, *Phèdre*, he abruptly abandoned the theatre and took up the office of Royal Historian to Louis XIV, which he shared with his friend Boileau. There were no doubt other reasons for his retirement: *Phèdre* had been attacked by a hostile clique which aimed – though finally without success – at sabotaging it in favour of a rival play; he may have begun to feel religious scruples: at any rate he sought a reconciliation with Port-Royal which had never wavered in its condemnation of the playhouses; over all, he certainly felt the need, in his thirty-eighth year, of settling down to a secure and respectable future after his comparatively dissi-pated life as a poet of the theatre.

From that moment until his death 22 years later, in 1699, he divided his time between a peaceful, solid home-life in Paris and his duties at Versailles and with the armies. These brought him increasing

[1] His plays were: *La Thébaï de* (1664), *Alexandre* (1665), *Andromaque* (1667), *Les Plaideurs* (comedy, 1668), *Britannicus* (1669), *Bérénice* (1670), *Bajazet* (1672), *Mithridate* (1673), *Iphigénie* (1674), *Phèdre* (1677), *Esther* (1689) and *Athalie* (1691).

honours and the favour of the influential, from Louis XIV downwards. In the last year of his life he fell temporarily out of favour, but the cloud soon passed and he died in possession of all his pensions and offices. Ever since *Phèdre*, he had steadily refused to write again for the professional theatre. But he was persuaded by Madame de Maintenon to write two plays on biblical subjects for performance at Saint-Cyr, the girls' school which she had founded. The second of them, *Athalie*, ranks very high among his masterpieces. Apart from *Esther* and *Athalie*, the only verse he wrote after his retirement was a handful of sacred odes, *Les Cantiques spirituels* (1694), and a few brilliantly unkind epigrams against his literary enemies. The rest of his verse, outside his plays, is almost negligible in quantity: the youthful *Paysage de Port-Royal* (*c.* 1656), three official odes (1660–3) and a verse-translation of a number of hymns from the Latin Breviary. Racine was an excellent prose-writer, pointed and lively, but all his prose was occasional. It includes the prefaces to his plays, his correspondence, shrewd and intensely human, and the *Abrégé de l'histoire de Port-Royal*, which occupied his last years.

In some respects, Racine's character is appreciably more modern than that of any other poet we have so far considered. But in others, disconcertingly though inevitably, he belonged to an age which still burnt poisoners at the stake, compromised the souls of its favourite actors by excommunication and relied on bleedings and purgations for its physical well-being. On the one hand, he was a typical man of letters of a capital city which had advanced almost unrecognizably in urbanity since Ronsard's day. Literary feuds, material ambitions, a constant competitive intercourse with the worlds of fashion and of the arts filled this side of his life and formed him into a witty, experienced and successful courtier. At the same time he possessed a delicately balanced sensibility which gave him an intuitive insight into human nature, controlled by the logic of a first-class mind. He can be defined on this score as a passionate intellectual. But a darker vein underlies his work, distinguishing his outlook from that of a writer such as Proust. Its origin may have been in the stern religious creed which he was taught in adolescence and to which he returned in his last days. But it was hardly less in his intensive study of the Greek dramatists, from whom he learnt to ponder the great spiritual crises which can befall humanity, magnified to the proportions of mythical catastrophes. Racine's scholarly interest in Greece and Rome remained with him all his life. It was not eclipsed by his more materialistic activities. It coloured his temperament no less than his religion did.

III

For all his apparent simplicity, Racine is a difficult poet. The best approach to him is to follow what was certainly his own approach and to begin by considering his dramatic verse in its functional aspect.

It is functional because it is always suited to the character who is speaking and renders every shade of his reactions to the situation in which he finds himself. At the same time, it explores for the audience, sometimes with a closely controlled irony, all the implications of that situation. It does this without becoming out of character, or rather without going beyond character to state some general truth. Racine is never the moralist that Shakespeare often is.[1] When Gloucester observes:

> As flies to wanton boys, are we to the gods;
> They kill us for their sport,

or Macbeth soliloquizes

> Tomorrow and tomorrow and tomorrow . . .

they are moving outside their immediate situation, or at least enlarging it. Racine's characters do not do this. They keep strictly to the point – to the particular circumstances which bear on their dilemma. What is lost is the more strikingly 'poetic' quality of what might possibly be called Shakespeare's baroque style – the rhetorical extension which becomes, in the right hands, a link between the particular and the universal. Racine denies himself this kind of poetry. His characters are turned inward so that all their discoveries are made in the depths of their own natures and expressed in terms of themselves. Psychologically, therefore, his plays appear self-sufficing and self-contained – which in theory is one of the attributes of French classicism. Poetically, an element is lost. This element may be called the impingement of the infinite on the finite, the association of the macrocosm with the microcosm, or simply the metaphysical imagination. In its absence, what remains but the small change of poetry – the minor and technical qualities? To this highly difficult question no wholly satisfactory answer has ever been given, yet it is a matter of experience that Racine's verse, whether read or heard in the theatre, is 'poetic'. It delights the ear, stirs the feelings, fascinates the intellect and even – both occasionally and in its total effect – excites the imagination, though along lines deliberately traced by the poet. With no justification at all could it be described as merely rhymed prose.

[1] As also were sixteenth-century French poets, including dramatists (e.g. Garnier). To a lesser extent Corneille moralizes in the same way.

This is true even when it is most 'functional'.

In the fourth act of *Britannicus*, the Dowager Empress of Rome, Agrippina, is attempting to bring to heel her son Nero. He has been made emperor by her intrigues – in plainer words, her crimes – and is now beginning to defy her. Struggling to regain her influence, the unscrupulous old woman recalls how, as a widow, she had made a second marriage with the late emperor Claudius; how she had persuaded him to set aside Britannicus, his own son by a former marriage, and to adopt her own son, Nero, as his heir; and how, when Claudius was about to die and at last realized the true position, she consummated her plan:

> Cependant Claudius penchait vers son déclin.
> Ses yeux, longtemps fermés, s'ouvrirent à la fin:
> Il connut son erreur. Occupé de sa crainte,
> Il laissa pour son fils échapper quelque plainte,
> Et voulut, mais trop tard, assembler ses amis.

The tone is factual, brisk, completely ruthless in its context. The dying Claudius, whom she had married, is envisaged purely as an instrument which must be discarded before it causes complications:

> Ses gardes, son palais, son lit m'étaient soumis.
> Je lui laissai sans fruit consumer sa tendresse;
> De ses derniers soupirs je me rendis maîtresse.

The second line – 'I let him fret out his affection fruitlessly' – must be one of the cruellest ever spoken on the stage, unless it is surpassed by the third: 'I took control of his last sighs.'

Her business now was to keep the disinherited Britannicus away from his father until the latter was dead. The death is noted in two words, the rumour that she had caused it by poison is shrugged off in seven:

> Mes soins, en apparence épargnant ses douleurs,
> De son fils, en mourant, lui cachèrent les pleurs.
> Il mourut. Mille bruits en courent à ma honte.

It will be noticed that no relevant feature of the material situation or the physical scene has been blinked. Nothing is veiled or inflated. Yet, while the reader has everything necessary to reconstruct the scene realistically in his imagination, if he so wishes, the language used is largely figurative. The figures are conventional, but instead of hanging limply they are recharged with their full literal meaning and more, so that they acquire the elastic strength of the understatement. When

Claudius was 'drawing towards his end', suddenly 'his eyes were opened'. 'He realized his mistake – but too late,' adds his widow laconically. He was completely in her power: 'Ses gardes, son palais, son lit m'étaient soumis.' 'Sans fruit' is almost a cliché. So is 'derniers soupirs', but here they are completely apt expressions. 'Mes soins' – an abstract word which might be translated here as 'ministrations' – has, of course, a double edge. This colourless word, whose associations range from the *petits soins* of the salon lover to the *soins officieux* of the poisoner Locusta who a little later in Racine's play 'zealously' provides a poison after first demonstrating its efficacy on a slave, gives an effect comparable to Lady Macbeth's:

> What cannot you and I *perform*
> On the unguarded Duncan?

But Agrippina, a more hardened criminal than Lady Macbeth and certainly no sleep-walker, has not finished her recital. She had to conceal the death of Claudius until the army had taken an oath of allegiance to Nero as his successor. Meanwhile the Roman people, on her orders, had been offering prayers to the gods for the recovery of the old emperor, until the moment came when it was safe for him to be shown to them, already dead. In these narrative lines can be detected – again if one wishes – Agrippina's sardonic pleasure in the situation. On a more open level is her insistence on her own role in the affair – 'conduit sous *mes* auspices' – '*mes* ordres trompeurs' – underlined now to stress Nero's present indebtedness to her:

> J'arrêtai de sa mort la nouvelle trop prompte;
> Et tandis que Burrhus allait secrètement
> De l'armée en vos mains exiger le serment,
> Que vous marchiez au camp, conduit sous mes auspices,
> Dans Rome les autels fumaient de sacrifices;
> Par mes ordres trompeurs tout le peuple excité
> Du prince déjà mort demandait la santé.
> Enfin des légions l'entière obéissance
> Ayant de votre empire affermi la puissance,
> On vit Claude; et le peuple, étonné de son sort,
> Apprit en même temps votre règne et sa mort.

These, concludes Agrippina (with much else previously related), were all my crimes. The tone is that of an injured lover excusing himself for having been perhaps too attentive:

> C'est le sincère aveu que je voulais vous faire:
> Voilà tous mes forfaits.

This single example must suffice to suggest the force and subtlety which lie in Racine's apparently conventional use of imagery and metre. In the same verse-form he can be ironic, vigorous, brutal, or even flat, as the situation demands:

> Est-il juste, après tout, qu'un conquérant s'abaisse
> Sous la servile loi de garder sa promesse?
>
> *(Andromaque)*

or:

> Mais je m'étonne enfin que, pour reconnaissance,
> Pour prix de tant d'amour, de tant de confiance,
> Vous ayez si longtemps, par des détours si bas,
> Feint un amour pour moi que vous ne sentiez pas.
>
> *(Bajazet)*

or simply – the depth of utility:

> Madame, tout est prêt pour la cérémonie.
>
> *(Iphigénie)*

In using and perfecting the alexandrine – his almost exclusive medium – Racine mastered it completely. It was his vehicle both for the 'Roman' tone of *Britannicus* and for the comic effects of *Les Plaideurs*:

> Voilà votre portier et votre secrétaire;
> Vous en ferez, je crois, d'excellents avocats:
> Ils sont fort ignorants.

On occasion he broke most of the technical rules laid down by his less gifted contemporaries and which the Romantics flung overboard so noisily a hundred and fifty years later. But his infringements were discreet and never wanton, dictated always by an impeccable ear. He observed Boileau's pedestrian prescription for the alexandrine.

> – Que toujours, dans vos vers, le sens, coupant les mots,
> Suspende l'hémistiche, en marque le repos –

sufficiently often for his verse to pass as 'regular' until it is carefully probed.

IV

While the functional kind of verse just examined is poetic in its compression, its economy and rightness in the choice of words, and its inconspicuous rhythms which lead the speaking voice to follow the most effective sound-patterns relative to the sense, it would hardly be enough to mark Racine as a great poet. The verse of *Britannicus* and of *Bajazet*, which were written roughly midway through his career, is perfectly dramatic and basically Racinian. But, using always the same basis, he could build higher.

In the earlier *Andromaque*, purely human passion is fanned (as in the character of Hermione) to white heat and the tone rises in places almost to a scream. It still does not break the finite barrier, but goes as close as is possible without doing so.

In *Bérénice*, the music of the Racinian line comes into play and produces some of those *tirades* which have been aptly compared to arias in which the voice can take wing on the subtly varied rhythm of the alexandrines:

> Le temps n'est plus, Phénice, où je pouvais trembler.
> Titus m'aime; il peut tout: il n'a plus qu'à parler.
> Il verra le sénat m'apporter ses hommages,
> Et le peuple de fleurs couronner ses images.
>   De cette nuit, Phénice, as-tu vu la splendeur?
> Tes yeux ne sont-ils pas tout pleins de sa grandeur?
> Ce flambeau, ce bûcher, cette nuit enflammée,
> Ces aigles, ces faisceaux, ce peuple, cette armée,
> Cette foule de rois, ces consuls, ce sénat,
> Qui tous de mon amant empruntaient leur éclat . . .

Or the still more famous:

> Je n'écoute plus rien; et pour jamais, adieu.
> Pour jamais! Ah! Seigneur, songez-vous en vous-même
> Combien ce mot cruel est affreux quand on aime?
> Dans un mois, dans un an, comment souffrirons-nous,
> Seigneur, que tant de mers me séparent de vous?
> Que le jour recommence, et que le jour finisse,
> Sans que jamais Titus puisse voir Bérénice,
> Sans que de tout le jour je puisse voir Titus?
> Mais quelle est mon erreur, et que de soins perdus!
> L'ingrat, de mon départ consolé par avance,
> Daignera-t-il compter les jours de mon absence?
> Ces jours si longs pour moi lui sembleront trop courts.

Both these passages are also 'functional', though in a less immediate way than the scene quoted from *Britannicus*. The first renders the elation of Berenice when she feels confident that her lover will marry her; the second, the pathos of her distress when she sees that they must separate. The tone, the musical quality, correspond to her feelings at those particular points in the drama. But they can be quoted apart from the drama and still retain a certain life. This becomes truer still of the last two plays which Racine wrote before his retirement: *Iphigénie* and – to a greater degree – *Phèdre*. Both were based on the Greek mythology which had persisted in Racine's mind since his schooldays and which seems to have fired his normally disciplined imagination as no other subject did. *Phèdre* in particular furnished the critic Henri Bremond, writing in the 1920s, with examples for his theory of 'pure poetry', according to which there is an autonomous language of poetry, valid in itself, as music and some painting can be argued to be valid in themselves, without reference to external associations. Just as you cannot adequately transcribe the theme of a piece of music in words, so 'pure poetry' exists independently of rational meaning and of emotions connected with the lived experience of the reader. Such a line as

La fille de Minos et de Pasiphaé

becomes a self-contained creation, having its own beauty and originating its own overtones quite apart from its significance in the mouth of a stage-character or its evocation of Greek legend. Bremond even went further and likened the language of 'pure poetry' to the language of prayer.

This theory, with its streak of mysticism, was certainly too extreme. In view of the predominantly functional qualities of Racinian verse, it would seem astonishing that it should have been applied to this particular poet at all. But he does, as we have seen, comply with one half of the requirements. By his concentration on the matter in hand he eliminates the external associations which in 'pure' poetry are worse than irrelevant: they are a distraction. It only remains to persuade oneself that he fulfils the second condition – that his verse can be detached from its dramatic context without essential loss – and he becomes the supreme example of poetic purity.

This can be done in a limited number of instances, though it may safely be said that it was never Racine's conscious intention and that the impact of his lines is always stronger when they are left in their context. Outside it, however, there is still an incantatory quality in, for example, the opening scene of *Iphigénie*, which occurs just before dawn:

A peine un faible jour vous éclaire et me guide.
Vos yeux seuls et les miens sont ouverts dans l'Aulide.

> Avez-vous dans les airs entendu quelque bruit?
> Les vents nous auraient-ils exaucés cette nuit?
> Mais tout dort, et l'armée, et les vents, et Neptune.

This is poetry at the opposite extreme to Hamlet's:

> But look, the Morn, in russet mantle clad,
> Walks o'er the dew of yon high eastward hill.

So is:

> Ariane, ma sœur, de quel amour blessée,
> Vous mourûtes aux bords où vous fûtes laissée!

Or Phèdre's querulous:

> Que ces vains ornements, que ces voiles me pèsent!
> Quelle importune main, en formant tous ces nœuds,
> A pris soin sur mon front d'assembler mes cheveux?
> Tout m'afflige et me nuit et conspire à me nuire.

Yet all these lines, perfect though they are, betray a certain conscious virtuosity on the poet's part. Just as Shakespeare, one feels, may have paused with a certain satisfaction after composing the 'russet mantle' image, so Racine must have experienced a small moment of triumph when he had written the words 'et Neptune'. No doubt he had even planned for it. The beautiful modulation of the 'Ariane' quotation, with the management of the vowels in the second line (ou-ou-u-(e)-o-o / ou-ou-u-(e)-è-é) seems hardly fortuitous. Neither does the discreet alliteration in the last passage quoted and least of all the insistent *i* sound in:

> Tout m'afflige et me nuit et conspire à me nuire.

These are nearer to what Valéry termed 'calculated lines' than to 'given lines'. It is the 'given lines', simpler and apparently spontaneous,[1] that represent Racinian poetry in its purest state.

They are so simple that they easily pass unnoticed. What is noticeable is less their presence in Racine than their absence in other poets. They seem to have been produced without effort – to occur rather

---

[1] The reader can hardly hope to distinguish spontaneity from calculation in a good poet. Nor, perhaps, can the poet himself. A 'spontaneous' line may come as the result of years of conscious or unconscious preparation. In view of the complexity of the process of poetic creation, the word is really meaningless, except to describe an appearance.

Valéry's remark was: 'Deux sortes de vers: les vers *donnés* et les vers *calculés*. Les vers calculés sont ceux qui se présentent nécessairement sous forme de problèmes à résoudre – et qui ont pour conditions initiales d'abord les vers donnés, et ensuite la rime, la syntaxe, le sens déjà engagés par ces données.' (*Littérature*, in *Tel Quel, I*.)

than to have been composed. Such are the lines which immediately
follow the passage from *Iphigénie* already quoted on pp. 76–7:

> Heureux qui, satisfait de son humble fortune,
> Libre du joug superbe où je suis attaché,
> Vit dans l'état obscur où les dieux l'ont caché.

Or, from *Athalie*:

> Promettez sur ce livre, et devant ces témoins,
> Que Dieu fera toujours le premier de vos soins;
> Que, sévère aux méchants, et des bons le refuge,
> Entre le pauvre et vous, vous prendrez Dieu pour juge;
> Vous souvenant, mon fils, que caché sous ce lin,
> Comme eux vous fûtes pauvre et comme eux orphelin.

Or, from *Phèdre*:

> Dans le fond des forêts votre image me suit.

And, perhaps the most perfect of all:

> Le jour n'est pas plus pur que le fond de mon cœur.

In these lines there is no ostentation of any kind. Imagery, rhetoric,
and the musical effects that can be drawn from alliteration and assonance
are either excluded or reduced to a minimum. Denying himself even
the barest 'ornaments', the artist has come face to face with his basic
materials, with less than which he cannot work at all: words and syntax.
To shape them, he has allowed himself only his auditory sense, a feeling for sounds and rhythm which enables him to produce the most
delicately varied effects within an apparently rigid framework. In this
sense one can say – without subscribing to the whole of Bremond's,
or even Valéry's, theory of 'pure poetry' – that Racine's verse sometimes becomes 'the language of poetry itself'.

v

Anything approaching a 'baroque' Racine is of course unthinkable.
But it must be remembered that not all his verse is so perfectly distilled
as that just described. His earliest known poems, odes describing the
country round Port-Royal, were modelled on the 'libertine' poets
Théophile de Viau and Saint-Amant, who did not conform to Malherbe's principles. They contain numerous fanciful metaphors of the
type quoted from Marino in chapter 5 (p. 50). Butterflies are 'ces
vivantes fleurs'. Birds' nests are 'ces cabinets si bien bâtis'. Oaktrees are

'ces géants de cent bras armés'. There is the pompous image of the great trees which seem to prop up the skies and 'lend their powerful backs to the thrones of the sun':

> L'on dirait même que les cieux
> Posent sur ces audacieux
> Leur pesante machine,
> Et qu'eux, d'un orgueil nonpareil,
> Prêtent leur forte échine
> A ces grands trônes du soleil.

But perhaps what Racine wrote at the age of about seventeen and never published is not evidence.[1] Or evidence only of a strain capable of development but deliberately suppressed. Yet it crops out again in a more temperate form in *Esther* and *Athalie* and the few sacred songs of his later years. The influence of the Bible, with the bold images and picturesque idioms of Hebrew poetry, is now perceptible. The English reader will feel more at home when he comes upon some violent nightmare like the dream of Athalie, or reads such lines as

> La nation entière est promise aux vautours,

or

> Et de Jérusalem l'herbe cache les murs;
> Sion, repaire affreux de reptiles impurs . . .

which are evocative in the last degree, and the opposite of 'pure' poetry. Or he will hear Racine – echoing the Psalmist and the Book of Job – speak with the authentic voice of Jehovah out of the whirlwind:

> J'ai vu l'impie adoré sur la terre;
> Pareil au cèdre, il cachait dans les cieux
> Son front audacieux;
> Il semblait à son gré gouverner le tonnerre,
> Foulait aux pieds ses ennemis vaincus:
> Je n'ai fait que passer, il n'était déjà plus.
>
> (*Esther*)

This is also Racine, writing a stanza so perfectly constructed that it floats with its own lightness. It should be compared with its own youthful embryo at the top of this page, and also with Malherbe's six-line stanzas on p. 53, which at a first glance look similar. The technical

[1] A doubt, which seems quite unjustifiable, has even been expressed as to whether *Le Paysage de Port-Royal* was by Racine. The poet's son Louis found the poems among his father's papers and accepted them as authentic. The best modern authorities are in agreement.

reasons for Malherbe's greater heaviness would require a long analysis, but it is really unnecessary. It is enough to read the two poets aloud. Some of the difference is due to the greater variety of Racine's metrical scheme. In this one stanza he uses lines of 10, 10, 6, 12, 10 and 12 syllables.

Yet Racine had learnt something from Malherbe, just as he took something from Corneille (particularly in *Britannicus*). His verse as a whole, considered over the whole of his mature period, is a compound made from these two poets, from fashionable courtly speech with the slightest touch of the *précieux*, from colloquial speech and from the Greek and Latin poets whom he read and adapted so assiduously. These various elements are so perfectly synthesized that the amalgam (unlike Ronsard's) appears as one clear, consistent material and can be held up, deservedly if paradoxically, as the model of classical purity.

The factor so far omitted from the analysis – since analysis would not show it – is Racine's personal way of approaching and handling his material. This all-important personal quality cannot of course exist in a vacuum, i.e. without the material to work on. But neither can the material exist in any coherent form without it. It is the beginning and end of art: the beginning because it provides the artist with his original bias, the end because it conditions the impression which his work will make on the reader. In both aspects it can be called his idiom. Racine's idiom, with its peculiar intonations, its mannerisms, its vocabulary, and of course its defects, is less a variety of French poetry than a poetic branch of the French language, as – though with directly contrasting qualities – Abbey-Theatre Irish is a poetic branch of English. The comparison, overlooking all other differences, can be used to explain the fascination of Racinian verse for Frenchmen. It is a delightful and irresistibly flattering idealization of his ordinary speech. So he might talk in dreams, if he were perfectly eloquent and perfectly lucid. (The Englishman, on the contrary, dreams of perfect eloquence allied to perfect intoxication, that is, freedom from inhibitions.)

In this language of the lucid dream, characters endowed with a precision of feeling which assimilates them more to passionate machines than to the untidy attempts at gods of the Shakespearian tradition speak their minds with a frankness which embraces every subtlety of perception of which they and their author are capable. Hence both the clarity which immediately strikes an audience and their interest for the modern psychologist, who has to admit the deeper accuracy of their findings. Here the dramatist joins the poet and any further division along these lines becomes unprofitable.

For Racine's immediate successors, he was the poet who had demonstrated that verse could be dignified, elegant, harmonious, supple and clear, and at the same time wholly French. He had at last realized Du Bellay's old ambition of a French literary tongue as civilized and expressive as Greek and Latin. He could therefore be quoted as a proof of national excellence and a model for imitation.

It was perhaps unfortunate. Racine is no easier to imitate than to translate. In spite of his prestige in the eighteenth century, none of his disciples surpasses the second-rate. The great Racinian scholar Paul Mesnard once listed Jean-Baptiste Rousseau and Fontanes as the sole approximate successes.[1] What a fall is here, and how dangerous it is to single out certain qualities which one finds congenial in a poet and then to believe that one holds the formula for composing similar poetry. Racine was richer than his age and, although it is unlikely that without him the poets of the next century would have followed a much different course, it is a pity that his example could be used at all to justify their mediocrity.

With time, the matter appears in better perspective. A 'classic' or not, Racine remains a great poet in his own right, to whom poets completely emancipated from the classical tradition as formulated by Boileau look back as a master. Even those Romantics who abominated it always respected him.

> Sur le Racine mort, le Campistron pullule,

wrote Hugo, conceiving the great dramatist as a dead lion infested by lice. But it is obvious today that Racine, with his lucid, wiry talent, is by no means dead. In fact, he has survived in better shape than the more massive Hugo.

[1] Except, later, Lamartine – who is a disciple with considerable reservations. Some modern critics find an affinity between Valéry and Racine. This only becomes tenable by invoking 'harmony' and the artistic conscience. But the two products are very different.

Chapter 8

Jean de La Fontaine

ANY NARROW definition of classicism equating it to the marble and the majestic would make it impossible to understand how La Fontaine flourished when he did without being at loggerheads with his age. How, if the rectangular art of Malherbe had been classic, could the same term be applied to La Fontaine's colloquial irregularity? How reconcile the notion of the linear and the grandiose as exemplified, say, in the Château de Versailles, with the whimsical manner of the *Fables* which even in form, as they stand on the printed page, cannot be fitted to any metrical norm? Such difficulties only arise if one thinks of classicism in terms of Cartesianism on the grand scale – forgetting that clarity and even logic can exist in miniature and need not entail vast constructions. Misunderstanding stems partially from an oversimplified conception of the taste of the 1660s and 1670s. The classicism of Boileau represented, at most, an official tendency in the France of Louis XIV's heyday. It was never absolute and rarely pure in the sense that it could be clearly separated from other tendencies. The nonchalant realism of much of La Fontaine's work was quite congenial to many contemporary readers who would have been incredulous if told that they were eccentric in their tastes. They belonged, in some cases, to the best culture of the time. Their appreciation of La Fontaine was a good enough guarantee, on historical grounds, of his conformity with a powerful, if – though this is contestable – not the main current. When he was attacked, it was either for personal reasons or for the bawdiness of some of his *Contes*, whose subject-matter offended the stricter moralists. It was not as an artist.

This said, we can accept at least the outline of the most cherished legend in French literature – the legend of *le bonhomme* La Fontaine who, while Molière was frantically rehearsing, Racine streamlining a new tragedy and Boileau smelling out some fresh nonentity to satirize, would be lying on his stomach watching a procession of ants across the grass. Leisure and inconsequence seem to characterize the man and his work – though for a dilettante he produced a remarkable amount of the latter.

He was born in 1621 at Château-Thierry, a town in Champagne where his father was an administrator of the Royal Forests. He belonged to the same official and professional stratum of society which produced Racine, Boileau (the son of a Clerk of the Court), La Bruyère, Corneille, and which – if one adds Molière, whose father was an upholsterer with a court appointment – was responsible for so much of the literature of the *Grand Siècle*. La Fontaine studied at first for the priesthood, then, abandoning this for reasons unknown, qualified for practice at the Paris bar. His growing connections in Paris gradually weaned him from Château-Thierry, where he inherited but eventually sold his father's post and where he left the young wife from whom he formally separated in 1658. He remained on friendly terms and continued to correspond and no doubt to see her. She was the daughter of the *Lieutenant Criminel* or Chief Constable of the neighbouring town of La Ferté-Milon and was distantly related to Racine, who was born there. For this or other reasons the two writers became acquainted and Racine, as a youth of twenty newly emancipated from Port-Royal, looked up to La Fontaine for his greater experience of the attractively naughty world.

La Fontaine had begun writing comparatively late in life, in his middle thirties. His earliest original poem was written in 1657 for his first patron, the Finance Minister Fouquet. It was an *Adonis*, just as the poem which Shakespeare described as 'the first heire of my invention' and dedicated to the Earl of Southampton was a *Venus and Adonis*. The fact is more odd than significant, except as evidence of the tastes of the English and French nobility over a span of sixty years and of the different manners in which they must be satisfied. Though Ovid was the original source of both poets, La Fontaine is immensely more urbane and there is nothing in common except the bare bones of the subject – if the expression may be applied to a post-Renaissance goddess of love.

Fouquet, after a period of opulent living during which he constructed the magnificent château and park of Vaux-le-Vicomte, aroused the jealousy of the young Louis XIV, was accused of appropriating State funds, and spent the rest of his life in prison. La Fontaine did not desert him and wrote poems begging the King to be lenient – an attitude which probably provoked Louis's lifelong coldness towards the poet. He never dipped into the generous purse which Colbert maintained for approved writers and artists, and his entry to the French Academy was delayed on the King's order until after Boileau had been elected.

He was assisted for a short time after Fouquet's fall by the powerful Bouillon family and by the Dowager Duchess of Orleans, who had her own little court; then by the wife of a wealthy financier, Madame de La Sablière, a cultured woman with a brilliant salon where he found the kind of society which was most congenial to him. At this time she was a Protestant. After her conversion to Catholicism she took the veil and went to nurse at the Hospital for Incurables, leaving La Fontaine to accept the hospitality of a distinguished lawyer, Monsieur d'Hervart. He died under his roof, having turned to religion with a kind of terror in his last days and repented also of his literary sin in writing *Les Contes*.

This roll-call of patrons need not be interpreted as a sign of a parasitic nature. No author, not even a dramatist, could hope to live then by the mere sale of his work. Patronage was his legitimate goal, though its rewards were sometimes disguised in the form of sinecure appointments or ecclesiastical livings. Pensions and other grants were dispensed by the Royal Treasury, but since La Fontaine was cut off from this source he must look for other means of support. His diversity of protectors is in fact a proof of greater independence than Racine's leaning on the single patronage of the King.

II

La Fontaine's work reflects this diversity, since much of it was intended to appeal to various paymasters or friends. It divides into three main parts: the pieces grouped in modern editions as *Poèmes et poésies diverses*, the *Contes et nouvelles*, and the *Fables*. The first of these contains, besides many occasional verses of small importance, some of La Fontaine's most interesting work – particularly to a reader surfeited by the *Fables*. It shows La Fontaine writing for Fouquet not only *Adonis*, but a long fragmentary description of the marvels of his château at Vaux (*Le Songe de Vaux*) and a group of elegies. These poems are 'classical' in their use of Greek mythology, their Cupids and their nymphs called Clymène or Philis – conventional fictions which fit marvellously into the park-like landscape of Vaux in which the poet places them. Artificial it may all be, but there is just enough imagination to give a touch of faery to the scene. La Fontaine knows, as the reader knows, that the first breath of realism would blow away the tenuous pastoral, leaving only verdigrised statues and silent fountains, but so long as the pretence lasts it lives. The verse is smooth and melodious, sometimes foreshadowing the elegiac qualities of Racine's *Bérénice*:

> Noires divinités du ténébreux empire,
> Dont le pouvoir s'étend sur tout ce qui respire,
> Rois des peuples légers, souffrez que mon amant
> De son triste départ me console un moment.
> Vous ne le perdrez point: le trésor que je pleure
> Ornera tôt ou tard votre sombre demeure.

(Adonis)

The choice of words is unremarkable. Adjectives such as *beau, doux, agréable* are sufficient to maintain without emphasis the quiet enjoyment of moods induced more by easy-flowing rhythm than by evocative imagery:

> J'ignore l'art de bien parler,
> Et n'emploirai pour tout langage
> Que ces moments qu'on voit couler
> Parmi des fleurs et de l'ombrage.
> Là luit un soleil tout nouveau;
> L'air est plus pur, le jour plus beau;
> Les nuits sont douces et tranquilles;
> Et ces agréables séjours
> Chassent le soin, hôte des villes,
> Et la crainte, hôtesse des cours.

(Le Songe de Vaux)

In their limpid simplicity, such lines as

> L'air est plus pur, le jour plus beau;
> Les nuits sont douces et tranquilles

fall into the domain of 'pure' poetry in the sense in which it is found in Racine. This kind of classicism supposes a discriminating public, to reach which the poet need never raise his voice. The baroque surprise and the Romantic scream would be equally discordant here, because unnecessary. What is required is to preserve the delicately conventional mood, to place words of proved acceptability in their rhythmic sequence with a touch so light that there is no appearance of deliberate choice. Whatever art is concealed in it, this kind of verse seems to have grown effortlessly under the poet's hand:

> Tout ce qui naît de doux en l'amoureux empire
> Quand d'une égale ardeur l'un pour l'autre on soupire,
> Et que, de la contrainte ayant banni les lois,
> On se peut assurer, au silence des bois:
> Jours devenus moments, moments filés de soie,
> Agréables soupirs, pleurs enfants de la joie,

D

Vœux, serments et regards, transports, ravissements,
Mélange dont se fait le bonheur des amants,
Tout par ce couple heureux fut lors mis en usage.

(*Adonis*)

Had Fouquet's patronage and the charm of Vaux-le-Vicomte continued to operate ... But this vein belongs chiefly to the younger La Fontaine and crops out again only in *Psyché* (1669), a graceful and sprightly retelling in prose of the love-story of Cupid and Psyche. The classical tale is intermingled with a description of the gardens of Versailles, then still being constructed, and which supply the place taken by Vaux in the earlier phase. The two things are not incongruous. Versailles and the reign of Louis XIV in their newness can be made to link up with the myth from classical antiquity, which has been interpreted as symbolizing the renewal of the seasons and so springing ultimately from the countryman's direct experience of nature. Two very different cultures meet in the atmosphere of the stylized fairy-tale peculiar to a brief moment of the seventeenth century. That moment having passed, all that one may now see is a certain faded charm, unless one can reconstruct in imagination the original climate.

A certain playful sensuality running through the early verse and prose betrays La Fontaine's strongest natural tendency. By this he belongs to the line of Marot and reaches back in some of his *ballades* and *chansons* to French poetry as it was before the Pléiade. In his own century he continues temperamentally in the 'libertine' tradition. Here and there he has a note of affectation, inherited from Voiture. La Fontaine, then, while representing in the heart of the 'classical' age the discreetly hedonistic classicism of Vaux and Versailles, also represents a freer type of more outspoken humour. It is found in some of his occasional verse, but most consistently in the *Contes*, of which he published the first in 1665.

They are rhymed stories of amorous adventures, borrowed from several sources of which the chief was Boccaccio. La Fontaine was not concerned with inventing original plots. He merely followed the four-hundred-year-old tradition of the French *fabliaux*, but took his anecdotes either from the Italian master or from later French story-tellers ranging from the author of the *Cent Nouvelles nouvelles* to Rabelais and Marguerite de Navarre. He tells his tales in a familiar, relaxed style, addressing himself directly to the reader and adding his own comments. His favourite verse-forms are built on either the eight-syllable line of the old *fabliaux*, on the ten-syllable line, or on a mixture of metres which he spins and handles at his own sweet will, as here:

Que doit faire un mari quand on aime sa femme?
  Rien.
  Voici pourquoi je lui conseille
De dormir, s'il se peut, d'un et d'autre côté.
  Si le galant est écouté,
Vos soins ne feront pas qu'on lui ferme l'oreille;
Quant à l'occasion, cent pour une. Mais si
Des discours du blondin la belle n'a souci,
Vous le lui faites naître, et la chance se tourne.
  Volontiers où Soupçon séjourne
  Cocuage séjourne aussi.

Such verse, irregular by the standards of Malherbe and Boileau, has a colloquial tone approaching that of prose. It is sometimes called *vers libres*, though the seventeenth-century term, *vers irréguliers*, is more apt. It differs from modern free verse in having rhymes (though disposed according to no set pattern) and in consisting of lines of various standard metres. In the above example, alexandrines and octosyllables are used, except for the monosyllabic *Rien*. It has a greater flexibility than anything previously written in French verse. It is wholly suited to the familiar speaking voice and has no associations with song, oratory, or stage declamation.

III

The qualities of the *Contes* – their free-and-easy tone, their narrative skill, their irregular versification – are also those of the *Fables*. La Fontaine published the first of these in 1668, was encouraged to continue them, it is thought, by Madame de La Sablière, and had produced eleven out of twelve Books – some 210 separate fables – by 1679. They were thus before the public at exactly the same time as Racine's great secular tragedies, Molière's later comedies and Boileau's *Art poétique*, which made no mention of the fable as a poetic genre. It had, however, the firmest possible roots in French literature, and here again La Fontaine had invented nothing. As with the *Contes*, he was reviving a genre much practised both in the Middle Ages and in the sixteenth century, when the verse fable had attracted numerous writers who looked back ultimately to Aesop. A second source became available to La Fontaine when a collection of Indian fables appeared in French translation in the 1640s.

Such was the well-worn material. La Fontaine's achievement was to have presented it in a form which delighted his own age and which has survived to please millions since, in spite of the familiarity induced by incessant recitation and explanation.

The greatest part of his attraction comes from a mingling of urbanity with rustic wit. The exact proportions are not, and cannot be, a matter of calculation. They were decided, one might say (as with Racine), by the age in which the poet lived, or by his own character and experience: better, by all these and an additional stroke of luck. La Fontaine is less polished than his eighteenth-century successors, less flatly simple than most of the earlier fabulists, whose tone is often that of the dogmatic monk lecturing the village school. La Fontaine marries Vaux, Versailles and Parisian sophistication with the broad strain of his native origins. Such marriages were not exceptional at the time.

If one speaks of him as a countryman, that does not make him a skilled naturalist. In spite of being a hereditary *Maître des eaux et forêts*, he may not have gone much further than the garden and the park. But at Château-Thierry he was in contact, through farmers, bailiffs and servants, with the rustic mind. A single servant hired in a nearby village would have been enough to bring in the country-shrewd proverbs, the familiarity with dogs, cats, rats, moles, birds and farm-yard animals which underlie La Fontaine's literary vein. Mice conspir-ing to bell the cat? What more natural – lending itself, that is, to natural description – in an age when night-roving fairies still left sixpence in the clean housewife's shoe, or even swept the kitchen if for some good reason she had been too tired to do it? The owl lives literally round the corner, the fox could have raided the chicken-house last night, the wolf is an actual danger to sheep. And if, even in Champagne, foxes do not eat grapes, many a country mother must have nursed her child while singing

> Petit poisson deviendra grand,
> Pourvu que Dieu lui prête vie –

so providing the opening lines of Fable III, Book V.

This interpenetration of country and town is a continuous factor in social history, but here it occurred just when the educated classes were becoming particularly conscious of their urban culture – in a way that, say, Ronsard a hundred years earlier had not been – and when a poet astride the two worlds could pick out with a sure touch the things that had most charm and savour in the country mentality. A totally rustic poet would hardly have known what to choose. A salon poet would have sneered at the whole thing, or selected only what seemed comic. La Fontaine's taste was both broader and more sure. Looking back at the result after three hundred years, one can only marvel how sure it was. The perfect balance between realism, humour and a certain stylized but easy elegance appears so simple to achieve. Perhaps it was for him. Perhaps *le bonhomme*, idling through his work, is nearer to the true La Fontaine than the conscious artist detected by Valéry. But in either case the product is unique.

It may well be asked whether, for all their qualities, the *Fables* are poetry. From the viewpoint of the Romantics they were not. They were verse, of a high order. But since the nineteenth century one has grown wary of drawing clear distinctions between verse and poetry, or even of admitting that there are two separate things to be distinguished. All that should be said is that the *Fables*, like the *Contes*, have no emotive content and awaken no immediate aesthetic response.[1] On the other hand, though the same material has been treated quite adequately by other authors in prose, the best of La Fontaine could not be recast in prose without depreciating heavily. There is therefore an element which, whether called verse or poetry, is not prose. Fundamentally, though not superficially, it is aesthetic, and depends on metre and rhyme and on an exact choice of words and expressions. It is the most economical technique possible, in ratio to its effectiveness. Perhaps the most famous fable of all, *La Cigale et la Fourmi*, is told in exactly 109 words – the length of an average gossip-paragraph in a newspaper. In that reduced space, the whole scene is drawn with picturesqueness, humour and some suggestion of character. There is no trace of compression or haste. Nothing needs adding. Intellectually and aesthetically the story and its moral are complete.

If from this one concluded, against all the other evidence, that brevity was the soul of poetry, one would eventually be reduced to the epigram. But at least it can characterize one kind of poetry, and the virtues which make for brevity while leaving an impression of leisureliness are among the highest that a writer can possess.

---

[1] Even conserving the verse-poetry distinction, few Frenchmen would agree that the *Fables* were 'mere verse'. But that is generally because of their associations with their childhood, which give them, like the nursery rhyme, an emotional value which is not inherent in them. To judge the case clearly, one would have to approach the *Fables* as though they were newly published, before the link had been forged with the nursery and the classroom.

Chapter 9

André Chénier

WHAT was likely to happen to French verse if it remained dominated by the Malherbe–Boileau tradition has been foreshadowed in an earlier chapter. In the eighteenth century the inevitable occurred – failing a poet of sufficient originality either to break the line or to conform to it with genius, as Pope may be said to have done in England. Standards of taste formulated for seventeenth-century conditions hardened into the authority of laws, and poetry, with comparatively minor exceptions, really failed to justify its existence. If one reads the verse of Voltaire, whom many contemporaries considered to be their greatest poet, one finds little that the same writer could not have expressed, and in fact did not express, better in his excellent prose. In the second half of the century, verse – of the kind conveniently called neoclassic – was set at fences which it could not jump. Arthritic in its vocabulary and generally enfeebled by decades of good taste, it was called on to describe not only the physical world as the layman perceived it, but even new scientific and philosophic discoveries. Rarely in the history of literature has the divorce between subject and diction been more apparent, chiefly because diction had become associated with fixed standards of excellence whereas the conceptions it was called on to express were in rapid evolution.

The verse produced by the eighteenth century was of three main kinds. Serious, indeed 'noble', poetry continued in the Malherbian tradition, though it lacked something of Malherbe's solidity, and resulted in grandiloquent verse cast often in the form of odes. These were the favourite vehicle for patriotic and religious themes and also for occasions when some personal sentiment struggled for expression. They then make incongruous reading and the lack of a suppler lyric idiom becomes painfully apparent. There is no reason to suppose that the poets of the eighteenth century had essentially different feelings from the Romantics. They were simply inhibited by technique.

They were more successful with light verse, which had not the same burden of dignity to carry and which, stemming from the salon tradition, was well suited to a literature closely dependent on small social groupings. Light verse comprehended the satire (usually with literary targets), the epigram, and love-poetry of the madrigal type. Here some personal emotion could certainly be shown, but the key was minor and the limits were narrowly set. The most that could be achieved was a well-groomed sensuality occasionally impinging on sentiment, or a note of restrained regret. Sometimes the tone of Ronsard is heard again faintly over a gap of two centuries, but it is now wiser, sadder and certainly more anaemic.

Finally, there was the long didactic poem, philosophical or descriptive, or both at once, which included the experiments in 'scientific' poetry. This also was written with an eye on salon society. Much of it was popularization, in an acceptably elegant form, of the kind of knowledge more solidly presented in Diderot's great *Encyclopédie*. Sometimes, however, it approached nature-poetry of the sort that Thomson and Cowper were writing in England and which can be read as a prelude to Wordsworth. In France, Saint-Lambert, the author of *Les Saisons*, Roucher, who wrote *Les Mois*, and even Delille, who described everything that came within his reach and much that did not, attain at times a feeling for country scenes very different certainly from La Fontaine's conscious acceptance of them, but which, representing the nostalgia of a now thoroughly urbanized society, deserves to be classed as an authentic emotion.

Near the end of this century André Chénier appeared. Because he was a true poet, coming after a somewhat barren period, the temptation has always been to magnify him above his real worth. Moreover, he announced certain aspects of the poetry of the next century, he died young and tragically, and his work was discovered only when the Romantic period was beginning: all these considerations have tended to mark him out as a specially significant figure. Yet he belonged entirely – even typically – to his age. Talent apart, his work contains few features that were not of the eighteenth century.

II

Chénier was born in Constantinople of well-to-do parents in 1762. His father was French Consul in that city. His mother, if not of pure Greek stock, came of a family long established in the Greek Islands. When he was five his father was transferred to Morocco, but his mother settled in Paris with her two children, André and his younger brother Marie-Joseph, who grew up to be a dramatist and poet of considerable contemporary reputation. Though educated in France, André Chénier no doubt inherited from his mother a temperamental sympathy with the Greek world which led him later to study the Greek poets with an understanding which was more than scholarship. The link of blood gave him an initial advantage over the two other great Hellenists in French poetry, Ronsard and Racine. At the same time his mother, an intelligent and accomplished woman, placed him in early contact with French culture through the writers and artists who visited her salon in Paris. Among them were the poet Lebrun (known as Lebrun-Pindare), the fable-writer Florian and the painter David.

After a short period in the army, Chénier decided against a military career and obtained a diplomatic post. He spent three years as a Secretary to the Embassy in London, with frequent visits to France. Meanwhile the Revolution had broken out, at first with the enthusiastic approval of Chénier's 'progressive' circle. He returned permanently to France but gradually grew critical of the course events were taking. He was shocked by the deposition and execution of Louis XVI and voiced his opinions in newspaper articles. Listed as a suspect during the Terror, he hid for a time in the provinces, returning to Paris only when the danger appeared to be over. He was picked up by chance while visiting a friend whose wife had been marked out for arrest. Although there was no warrant against him, he was held in prison for several months, in spite of the efforts of his father and brother to obtain his release. Two days before the fall of Robespierre and the end of the Terror, he was transferred from the prison of Saint-Lazare to the Conciergerie, summarily condemned to death and guillotined on 25 July 1794.

His tragic and – in the confusion of the times – almost accidental death at the age of thirty-two created a legend of the ill-fated young poet which need not be elaborated. One anecdote belonging to it, however, is so thoroughly in character that it seems worth preserving. Chénier and the poet Roucher were executed on the same day. The two are said to have ridden to the scaffold in the same tumbril, declaiming between them as they went the first act of Racine's *Andromaque*. Racine would have been flattered if he could have heard the story.

In his lifetime Chénier published virtually no poetry. His work was not generally known until twenty-five years later, when an imperfect edition was published by the journalist and man of letters Henri de Latouche. This was in 1819, the year before Lamartine's *Méditations*, and just at the time when the young Romantics were beginning to grow conscious of their aims. Some of them were very ready to claim Chénier as a kindred spirit.

His verse, as organized by later editors following as closely as possible the indications in his manuscripts, is classified as: *Bucoliques* and *Élégies*; *Poèmes*; *Hymnes* and *Odes*; and, finally, the *Iambes*.

III

Putting the first of these aside for the moment, the others represent Chénier's various responses to the immediate climate of his age.

The *Poèmes* were to have been 'scientific' verse and to have included an encyclopedic poem (*Hermès*) on the creation of the world – a biological rather than a religious version – and on human progress since. Another, *L'Amérique*, was to have described the geography of the world in the light of recent explorations. Of these ambitious projects to present in verse the whole knowledge of the time,[1] only some notes, an introduction entitled *L'Invention*, and a few other short fragments seem to have been written down

The *Hymnes* and *Odes* belong to another eighteenth-century convention. They comment on public or private events which impressed Chénier and are interesting chiefly for that reason. His vigorous rhetoric in defence of Charlotte Corday, the young woman who assassinated Marat, or the pathos with which he describes *La Jeune Captive* – a young woman whom he met in prison (but who was fortunate enough to escape execution) – have a certain biographical significance. But in these poems he is not essentially different from the earlier Jean-Baptiste Rousseau or from the Lebrun-Pindare whom he knew and admired. The Ode, indeed, remained in favour throughout the Revolution and was one of the most typical manifestations of the curiously inflated neoclassicism of that period.

In the *Iambes* which have, though wrongly, been considered his masterpiece, similar material is presented with an urgency rising at points to hysteria. Understandably, for these poems were composed in prison during the last months of his life while he was in daily fear of death. His themes are political satire against the enemies and betrayers of the Revolution – but satire in the form of invective or extreme sarcasm – and lamentations on his own fate. He uses a verse-form consisting of alternate alexandrines and eight-syllable lines, with cross-rhymes.

---

[1] While these and other contemporary works may remind us of the sixteenth-century Du Bartas, the conscious model, at least of Chénier, was the *De rerum natura* of the Latin philosopher-poet Lucretius.

The effect is of a short wave following a long wave and the rapid and broken tone corresponds to the emotional strain under which the poet was writing. The vocabulary, however, with its 'noble' circumlocutions, introduces a sense of remoteness and hence of unreality. How odd, one reflects, that a man in Chénier's situation should trouble to work out these elaborate abstractions. One must blame neoclassicism rather than Chénier and not forget that the most impulsive cry in a desperate situation is often a cliché. In this way Chénier records his constant terror while in prison of being called out for execution:

> Comme un dernier rayon, comme un dernier zéphire
>   Animent la fin d'un beau jour,
> Au pied de l'échafaud j'essaye encor ma lyre.
>   Peut-être est-ce bientôt mon tour.
> Peut-être avant que l'heure en cercle promenée
>   Ait posé sur l'émail brillant,
> Dans les soixante pas où sa route est bornée,
>   Son pied sonore et vigilant,
> Le sommeil du tombeau pressera ma paupière.[1]
>   Avant que de ses deux moitiés
> Ce vers que je commence ait atteint la dernière,
>   Peut-être en ces murs effrayés
> Le messager de mort, noir recruteur des ombres,
>   Escorté d'infâmes soldats,
> Ébranlant de mon nom ces longs corridors sombres,
>   Où seul dans la foule à grands pas
> J'erre, aiguisant ces dards persécuteurs du crime,[2]
>   Du juste trop faibles soutiens,
> Sur mes lèvres soudain va suspendre la rime;
>   Et chargeant mes bras de liens,
> Me traîner, amassant en foule à mon passage
>   Mes tristes compagnons reclus,
> Qui me connaissaient tous avant l'affreux message
>   Mais qui ne me connaissent plus.

If one surrenders oneself blindfold to this kind of poetry – ignorant, as was the case with Chénier's contemporaries, of other alternatives – it has a certain majestic mournfulness which is impressive in the long run. To die – with a rhetorical flourish and in impeccably laundered linen. It is not the least moving way of meeting destiny, nor necessarily the least authentic. Compare, for the exact opposite, the laconic precision of:

---

[1] i.e. within an hour perhaps I shall be dead.   [2] i.e. polishing these avenging verses.

At five in the afternoon.
It was exactly five in the afternoon.
A boy brought the white sheet
at five in the afternoon.
A frail of lime already prepared
at five in the afternoon.
The rest was death and death alone
at five in the afternoon.[1]

This type of verse was of course closed to Chénier. The line which recurs like a knell throughout the first section of the modern Spanish poem was literally impossible to write in the eighteenth century. 'At five in the afternoon' could not occur in serious French verse of the time without shocking every sense of appropriateness. It will be remembered that Malherbe's contemporaries had preferred the general to the particular, and Chénier was still spending their legacy. On the other hand, his idiom has its successes which could not be obtained in any other style.

> Le messager de mort, noir recruteur des ombres

is one. Another is the line which rhymes with it, which in a curious way is also realistic. So is the evocation, in the last four lines quoted, of his fellow prisoners flocking to see him led out by the gaoler and refusing to recognize him. One might even find considerable virtues in the long periphrasis of the minute-hand (lines 5–8) by pointing to its slow solemnity. The objection, however, must arise that Chénier in fact was thinking of the rapid passage of time, not of its measured inevitability, in which case his idiom failed his thought. What he felt was put more suitably by Baudelaire writing sixty years later:

> Trois mille six cents fois par heure, la Seconde
> Chuchote: Souviens-toi! – Rapide avec sa voix
> D'insecte, Maintenant dit: Je suis Autrefois,
> Et j'ai pompé ta vie avec ma trompe immonde!

On balance, one cannot find much more in the *Iambes* than some good verse in the eighteenth-century manner, speeded and sharpened occasionally by Chénier's own experience. The personal voice of a man is heard, pathetically, as he struggles to express his horror through layers of abstraction and coils of rhetoric. But his medium is too much for him. If the man sometimes emerges, a great artist does not.

[1] F. G. Lorca, *Lament for Ignacio Sánchez Mejías* (the bullfighter), translated by A. L. Lloyd (Heinemann, 1953).

IV

Since *Les Iambes* were Chénier's last verses, it does not appear likely that by his relatively early death a still promising poet was lost, or that the germs of romantic lyricism which have been seen in his work would have developed very far if he had lived. He is better appreciated for the sentimental 'classicism' of the *Bucoliques* and the *Élégies*, which represent his earliest manner. A number of these were written in his late teens, though he continued to work on them until near the end of his life.

They are classical in that their models, which Chénier imitates more or less closely, are the poets of antiquity – the Greeks, Theocritus, Moschus, Bion, Homer; the Latins most impregnated with the Greek tradition – Catullus, Tibullus, Ovid; also Virgil. In turning to these and reading them with appreciation in their original languages Chénier was following a movement of his time. Towards 1770 there had been a serious revival of classical studies which bore on art as well as on literature and discovered in antiquity picturesque qualities which the seventeenth century had hardly perceived.[1] Beyond this, Chénier's personal sense, through his mother, of an emotional affinity with the ancient world made it easier for him to identify his sources with his adolescent feelings. The *Bucoliques* therefore show, not so much imitation as a two-way process of assimilation and self-projection which created authentic French verse. While this verse is not totally unlike the more melodious passages of Racine and La Fontaine, it is softer and more picturesque and attains a springy, dancing rhythm within the framework of the alexandrine: as in this evocation to Bacchus, in which the god of wine is conjured by all his harmonious names:

> Viens, ô divin Bacchus, ô jeune Thyonée,
> O Dyonise, Évan, Iacchus et Lénée;
> Viens, tel que tu parus aux déserts de Naxos,
> Quand tu vins rassurer la fille de Minos.
> Le superbe éléphant, en proie à ta victoire,
> Avait de ses débris formé ton char d'ivoire.
> De pampres, de raisins mollement enchaînés,
> Le tigre aux larges flancs de taches sillonnés,
> Et le lynx étoilé, la panthère sauvage,

---

[1] Developing, it became a not unimportant strand in European Romanticism. It appears in English poetry in such well-known examples as Keats's *Ode to a Grecian Urn*; in a different form, in the admiration of Byron and Shelley for the spirit of Hellas. In France, it underlies Vigny's early poems. It raises yet another objection to an undiscriminating use of the term 'classicism' in literary criticism.

Promenaient avec toi ta cour sur ce rivage.
L'or reluisait partout aux axes de tes chars.
Les Ménades couraient en longs cheveux épars,
Et chantaient Évoé, Bacchus et Thyonée,
Et Dyonise, Évan, Iacchus et Lénée.

Invocation, with the use of series of evocative names on the Homeric
pattern, furnishes some of Chénier's happiest lines:

Dieu dont l'arc est d'argent, dieu de Claros, écoute:
O Sminthée-Apollon, je périrai sans doute
Si tu ne sers de guide à cet aveugle errant.

From the same poem, which describes the arrival of the blind Homer
on the island of Syros:

Salut, belle Syros, deux fois hospitalière!
Car sur ses bords heureux je suis déjà venu;
Amis, je la connais. Vos pères m'ont connu;
Ils croissaient comme vous, mes yeux s'ouvraient encore
Au soleil, au printemps, aux roses de l'aurore;
J'étais jeune et vaillant. Aux danses des guerriers,
A la course, aux combats, j'ai paru des premiers.
J'ai vu Corinthe, Argos et Crète et les cent villes,
Et du fleuve Égyptus les rivages fertiles.

Or there are these lovely and simple lines, which La Fontaine might
have written:[1]

Pleurez, doux alcyons! ô vous, oiseaux sacrés,
Oiseaux chers à Thétis, doux alcyons, pleurez!

The world of Chénier's *Bucoliques* is innocent, pastoral, saddened
sometimes by the untimely death of lovers, but not otherwise tragic.
Their ghosts, tender and vaporous, emanations of the summery earth
and sea, and still imprecisely sensual, wander unsatisfied among the
rose-trees, like Neaera longing to rejoin her lover Clinias:

Oh! soit que l'astre pur des deux frères d'Hélène
Calme sous ton vaisseau la vague ionienne,
Soit qu'aux bords de Paestum, sous ta soigneuse main,

---

[1] Cf.

Mes appas sont les alcyons
Par qui l'on voit cesser l'orage
Que le souffle des passions
A fait naître dans un courage.

(*Le Songe de Vaux*)

Here *courage* means *heart*, as in Chaucer:
So priketh hem nature in here corages.

Les roses deux fois l'an couronnent ton jardin,
Au coucher du soleil, si ton âme attendrie
Tombe en une muette et molle rêverie,
Alors, mon Clinias, appelle, appelle-moi.
Je viendrai, Clinias, je volerai vers toi.
Mon âme vagabonde à travers le feuillage
Frémira. Sur les vents ou sur quelque nuage
Tu la verras descendre, ou du sein de la mer,
S'élevant comme un songe, étinceler dans l'air;
Et ma voix, toujours tendre et doucement plaintive,
Caresser en fuyant ton oreille attentive.

This is not so far from Ronsard's world, though it lacks the ostentation, the frequent glitter of his more courtly poetry. It gains instead a fluidity, not always free from the shapeless and the lachrymose, and which the student of taste could certainly associate with the flowing waistless gowns worn by women at the period of the Revolution. It has not the psychological backbone present in Racine's simplest lines nor the stylistic consciousness which lends a slight but perceptible stiffening to La Fontaine. It is, in fact, the perfect expression of the *muette et molle rêverie* of the young girl and in that one respect at least is as near to nature as some of Verlaine's songs. Elegiac rather than lyric, giving the impression that the deeply passionate experiences are over – which in Chénier's case is a way of concealing that they have yet to happen – it combines Theocritus with Rousseau in a blend that would not have appeared possible, to judge only by earlier eighteenth-century verse.

For convenience, one can call this verse neoclassic. It is the last successful attempt in French poetry for some time to assimilate the Greeks and Latins to the contemporary sensibility. For this, it deserves comparison with the best poetry both of the Pléiade and of the *Grand Siècle*. Although it reaches the level of either only rarely, it has a unique if minor flavour of its own.

Chapter 10

Alphonse de Lamartine

FOR TWENTY-FIVE years after Chénier's death no poet of any importance appeared in France. Under the revolutionary governments and the Empire, already established poets and their imitators continued to write rhetorical and didactic verse in the old tradition. As late as 1809–12, Delille was still composing long, tidy poems on the Three Kingdoms of Nature and on Conversation. In a very minor mode Chênedollé and Millevoye sang of fallen leaves and the autumnal sadness of youth, but their voices were timid and insignificant except as indications. André Chénier, it will be remembered, was unknown except to the small circle who had seen his manuscripts. His brother Marie-Joseph *was* known and indeed famous for his patriotic dramas and hymns among which figured, if not the *Marseillaise*, the almost equally popular *Chant du départ*. The militant nationalism of France under both the Republic and Napoleon was not favourable to personal lyricism or to aesthetic experiment. The duty of a poet, not necessarily imposed from without, might well seem to be to support with all the enthusiasm of which he was capable the great crusade in which his country was engaged. As for the manner of doing this, coldly academic standards approved by Napoleon and formulated by such critics as La Harpe and Marie-Joseph Chénier himself ensured that the literary voice of France should have a disciplined dignity not beneath that of the parade-ground.

Nevertheless, this official enthusiasm was not shared by the more or less clandestine opponents of the régime – most of them royalist émigrés – nor, as war-weariness grew, by any of the more sensitive members of a disillusioned society. After Waterloo especially, a reaction became inevitable and was only delayed for a few years longer by the lack of any obvious foundation on which to build it. Chateaubriand, who had returned from exile in 1800 to live in uneasy hostility to Napoleon, had set an outstanding example of emotional writing in *Le Génie du christianisme*. The work of Rousseau and of the luscious Bernardin de Saint-Pierre reached from earlier days across the divide of the Revolution to move the generation of Vitoria and Leipzig. From abroad, Goethe – as the creator of the pathetic *Werther* rather than as the poet – Ossian, the ancient Scottish bard half invented by Macpherson and known in the eighteenth century but renovated by a fresh translation in 1801, and – though at the last minute – Byron,[1] came to swell the stream. But all these wrote either in prose or in a foreign language with lyric qualities for which so far there existed no corresponding vehicle in French translation. The growing thirst for a literature of the sentiments could only be satisfied by poetry, and by a native poetry which would differ radically from the current type.

In these circumstances there appeared in 1820 a short book of poems entitled *Méditations poétiques*. Simple, emotional, filled with an expansive love of nature and a sincere, if troubled, religious feeling, they came almost as the fulfilment of a national need. They were the first published work of an unknown writer of thirty, who by this one volume has been said – the claim is not much exaggerated – to have 'reinvented poetry'.

It was an unlooked-for book. But it is difficult to feel surprise that Alphonse de Lamartine should have produced it.

II

He belonged to a family of Burgundian gentry who had a town house at Mâcon (where he was born in 1790) and a couple of country estates which provided them with their income and on which they passed much of the year. Though well connected locally, they had no great influence at Court and had been scarcely important enough to emigrate. Nevertheless, they were staunch royalists. Lamartine's father had been imprisoned for a time during the Terror. Under Napoleon, the family remained by choice in a political backwater, avoiding Paris and placing somewhat exaggerated hopes on the return of the Bourbons. Lamartine's mother, a major influence in his life, endeavoured to bring up her son in the road of piety and duty, together with his five younger sisters, Cécile, Eugénie, Césarine, Suzanne and Sophie. She was a cultured and practical woman, basing her lessons on the Bible but not immune from the attractions of the sentimental novels which

---

[1] Byron's *Childe Harold* was published only in 1812. In 1816, the first French translation of one of his complete poems, *The Bride of Abydos*, was made. From then until 1820 knowledge of his work spread rapidly through discussion and critical articles. It neared idolatry when he died in 1824. (See E. Estève, *Byron et le romantisme français*, 1929.) There could be no question of Wordsworth and Coleridge, still less of Keats and Shelley. Their work was completely unknown in France at that date.

sometimes found their way into the house. Her own mother had been an assistant governess to Louis-Philippe, who was to become King of the French in 1830.

From this affectionate, high-minded and largely pastoral environment, Lamartine was sent to a boarding school at Lyons, but was so unhappy that he ran away. He then entered the college of the *Pères de la Foi* at Belley, a school run on the Jesuit model, where he was educated with understanding and formed durable friendships. School over, he continued to live an unremarkable and still unfocused life, reading widely and sketching out tragedies and an epic in the eighteenth-century manner, visiting Italy in 1811 – a journey arranged by his family to distract him from an unsuitable love-affair – and at last obtaining a coveted commission in the Household Guards on the first return of the Bourbons in 1814. He resigned it after Waterloo (in which battle, of course, no French royalist troops were engaged), believing that a military career would henceforth be a dead end, and divided between the desire to write and hopes of a diplomatic appointment.

In the autumn of 1816, he went to take the waters at Aix-les-Bains in Savoy. There he met Madame Julie Charles, a graceful invalid of thirty-two, the wife of a distinguished physicist more than twice her age. A friendship resulted which developed into a close affection during the next winter and spring, which both of them spent in Paris. In August 1817, Lamartine returned to Aix to wait for her. But Madame Charles had become too ill to travel. She died of tuberculosis in the following December without seeing him again.

His feelings for 'Elvire' were the main starting-point of the *Méditations*, some of which had been written before her death. By the time they were published, over two years later, he was preparing to marry an English girl, Marianne Eliza Birch, and immediately after the wedding he took up the appointment of attaché to the French Legation at Naples. A year there and three years as First Secretary to the Legation at Florence (1825–8) were the whole of his diplomatic experience. The intervals were filled by a country gentleman's life at the château of Saint-Point which his father had given him and which became his principal home. He continued to write poetry, but it was not until 1830 that he published his second major book, the *Harmonies poétiques*. A few weeks after this the July Revolution broke out. Under the Orleanist regime, Lamartine decided to abandon diplomacy for politics and was presently elected member for Bergues, near Dunkirk. In the interval he had made a tour of the Near East, from which he returned grief-stricken by the death of his ten-year-old daughter Julia.

Though the poet was not yet dead and the prose-writer was still to pour out several millions of words, Lamartine after forty was more conspicuous as a political than as a literary figure. In Parliament he placed himself, by nature and necessity, above the machinery of parties. Though he had some success as an orator, his influence was at first small. He was offered a minor portfolio, but refused to take anything less than the Foreign Office or the Interior. Beginning with a system of Christian liberalism, which owed much to the influence of the Catholic social visionary Lamennais, he moved gradually further to the left. Disregarded by his fellow deputies and deciding to turn to the people, he published in 1847 his *Histoire des Girondins*, an idealization of the revolutionaries of 1791 and a defence of radical republicanism within the bounds of 'order'. It had an immense popular success, as had a speech which he delivered at Mâcon in the same year, advocating the overthrow of Louis-Philippe's regime.

When the revolution of 1848 came, Lamartine played an outstanding role for a few months. He became a member of the Provisional Government and by the courage and energy of his oratory tipped the balance at a critical moment away from socialism and towards liberal democracy. Elected to the Constituent Assembly by an overwhelming vote, he joined the Executive Committee as Foreign Minister. In spite of his great prestige, he fell out almost at once with his fellow commissioners. In the struggle between democratic republicanism and socialism, he now began to incline towards the left. Soon his inconsistencies left him politically isolated. When, at the end of 1848, elections were held for the presidency of the Second Republic, Lamartine polled eighteen thousand votes. Louis Napoleon – who had now appeared on the scene – polled five and a half million.

He retired finally from politics after the *coup d'état* which confirmed the power of Louis Napoleon and led to the Second Empire. His debts at that date amounted to five million francs – the result of over twenty years of generous and extravagant living. The rest of his life was devoted to paying off this burden. He turned out an immense mass of hack work in prose, though he always refused to prostitute his poetry. He produced popular biographies, reminiscences and semi-autobiographical writings, in which his past life was often rearranged in the interests of stronger colour.[1] A new ideal presently upheld him: the cultural enlightenment of the masses. His magazine *Le Civilisateur* and

---

[1] His principal prose writings were: *Voyage en Orient* (1835), *Histoire des Girondins* (1847), *Histoire de la Révolution de 1848* (1849), *Confidences* (1849), *Nouvelles Confidences* (1851), and the autobiographical romances *Raphaël* (1849), and *Graziella* (1851).

his serial *Cours familier de littérature* were typical nineteenth-century experiments in home education. His old age was darkened by the death of his devoted wife and by the necessity of selling the family estate of Milly, though he managed to keep Saint-Point. There he was buried when he died in 1867. Two years earlier the State had come to his aid with an annual pension of 25,000 francs.

III

Through all his vicissitudes Lamartine remained an incorrigible idealist – a type ill suited to the practical business of life but indispensable at certain moments of crisis. He was remarkable in having two such moments in his life, when a long private preparation suddenly crossed the curve of history to produce a flash of greatness which appeared spontaneous. Of the two conjunctions, 1820 was more important for him than 1848 and the effects have been more lasting.

Compared to the importance of the event, the first *Méditations* may strike the modern reader as disappointingly slight. They consist of twenty-four pieces of verse on such themes as early death, sadness in solitude, man's response to nature and nature's indifference, the justice or injustice of the Creator. The key to them is easy to find in those weeks spent at Aix with Madame Julie Charles, in their drives through the autumnal landscape, their boating excursions on the lake, their metaphysical discussions, in the excitement of a probably platonic love – and then in her death a year after. But they are not directly autobiographical, nor are they explicit in their descriptions or their thought. They are the expression of a mood, sustained and cherished long after the original cause had passed and embracing perhaps other sentimental experiences as well. Indeed, the second *Méditations*, their sequel, were not published until three years after the poet's happy marriage to Marianne Birch.

The imprecision of detail in the inspiration carries over into the style – or rather, dictates it. Lamartine's first poems are murmured reveries, in which it would be discordant to find a dramatic thought or a startling image. The poet's whole skill is devoted to maintaining the reverie unbroken from the first line to the last. In such poems as *L'Isolement*, *Le Vallon* or *Le Lac*, he succeeds entirely. This incredibly smooth-flowing verse glides under its faint neoclassic haze and induces in the reader a pleasant and quite uncritical trance. Nothing would be easier than to pick out the defects of detail, the intellectual lacunae, the borrowings and the clichés in these poems, and nothing could be more

beside the point. Such verse should be judged by its total effect and by
the author's success in imposing his own mood on the reader – whether
it is a mood of melancholy, as in

> Tes jours, sombres et courts comme les jours d'automne,
> Déclinent comme l'ombre au penchant des coteaux;
> L'amitié te trahit, la pitié t'abandonne,
> Et, seule, tu descends le sentier des tombeaux,

or of regret for fleeting joys, as in *Le Lac*:

> O temps, suspends ton vol! et vous, heures propices,
>   Suspendez votre cours!
> Laissez-nous savourer les rapides délices
>   Des plus beaux de nos jours![1]

> Assez de malheureux ici-bas vous implorent:
>   Coulez, coulez pour eux;
> Prenez avec leurs jours les soins qui les dévorent;
>   Oubliez les heureux.

> Mais je demande en vain quelques moments encore,
>   Le temps m'échappe et fuit;
> Je dis à cette nuit: 'Sois plus lente', et l'aurore
>   Va dissiper la nuit.

> ... Temps jaloux, se peut-il que ces moments d'ivresse,
> Où l'amour à longs flots nous verse le bonheur,
> S'envolent loin de nous de la même vitesse
>   Que les jours de malheur?

Such verse, at its best, explains the success of the first volume of
Romantic poetry to be published in France,[2] preceding the work of
both Vigny and Hugo. Romanticism may prove on analysis to be a
scarcely more absolute term than classicism. At least it has many facets
and does not lend itself easily to a comprehensive definition. Its general
features may be allowed to emerge gradually from these chapters on
Lamartine and his contemporaries. The features which appeared in

---

[1] The improvement wrought by Lamartine's imprecision – or, one may simply say, by his
finer taste – is apparent as soon as one compares this stanza with its conscious or unconscious source:

> O temps, suspends ton vol, respecte ma jeunesse;
> Que ma mère, longtemps témoin de ma tendresse,
> Reçoive mes tributs de respect et d'amour ...
>   (Thomas, *Ode sur le temps*, 1762)

[2] Except for the *Élégies et romances* (1819) of Marceline Desbordes-Valmore, a relatively
minor poetess whose work made little impression at the time.

Lamartine's early poems and gave them their novelty were the personal emotion conveyed directly from author to reader and not through the intermediary of an imagined third character (as in Chénier's *Bucoliques*); the simplicity and music of the verse which reinforced the impression of immediate communication; the close relationship between nature and the poet's ego which made the second not only more accessible but more acceptable and more moving since it reached the reader's sensibility through emotive channels which already existed.

These points simply amount to saying that Lamartine had discarded conventions which had ceased to have a live meaning in the later eighteenth century and was speaking in a language to which his age could more intuitively respond. He had not yet, however, entirely shaken off the eighteenth century and his poetic idiom still had serious limitations. This shows whenever he passes from the imprecise to the concrete, as in a poem in *Les Nouvelles Méditations* (1823) which purports to describe the death-bed of Elvire. Here sentiment becomes bathos because of the clumsily managed realistic touches. The second *Méditations*, indeed, show a perceptible decline from the first and for the next few years Lamartine was clearly struggling to enlarge his pure but limited sources of inspiration and to surmount the handicap of his too 'poetic' vocabulary. Two long poems, *La Mort de Socrate* (1823) and *Le Dernier Chant du Pèlerinage d'Harold* (1825), were both experiments in philosophical poetry, though the philosophy was an elementary Christian one not well suited to the particular subjects. Of Socrates, Lamartine makes a precursor of Christianity. He recounts the philosopher's conversations with his friends during his last day on earth, and finally his ablutions. These are at once a Greek symbol of purification, a foreshadowing of the rite of baptism and, unfortunately but inevitably, a bath:

> 'Hâtons-nous, mes amis, voici l'heure du bain.
> Esclaves, versez l'eau dans le vase d'airain!
> Je veux offrir aux dieux une victime pure.'
> Il dit; et, se plongeant dans l'urne qui murmure,
> Comme fait à l'autel le sacrificateur,
> Il puisa dans ses mains le flot libérateur,
> Et, le versant trois fois sur son front qu'il inonde,
> Trois fois sur sa poitrine en fit ruisseler l'onde;
> Puis, d'un voile de pourpre en essuyant les flots,
> Parfuma ses cheveux et reprit en ces mots . . .

The attempt to render a familiar enough scene in non-familiar words gives an effect of false nobility which comes near to the ridiculous.

Lamartine's manipulation of *le vase d'airain* (copper basin), *l'urne qui murmure* (gurgling bath) and *le voile de pourpre* (red towel) is similar to Chénier's difficulty with the clock-hand. It is doomed to failure because these common objects, however remote their historical context, remain common objects and do not permit of a metamorphosis except in a comic sense. Boileau's advice would have been to avoid such concrete details altogether. After Lamartine, a poet such as Hugo would employ a bolder and less artificial vocabulary and carry the day by what his contemporaries considered a revolutionary redistribution of language values, though to us it seems hardly more egalitarian than poor-relief:

> Ne fermez pas la porte. Il faut ouvrir d'abord.
> Il faut qu'on laisse entrer. – Et tantôt c'est la mort,
> Tantôt l'exil qui vient, la bouche haletante,
> L'une avec un tombeau, l'autre avec une tente.
>
> (From *Les Chants du crépuscule*)

By innovating too timidly Lamartine had the worst of both worlds – the pompousness of the neoclassic without its dignity, the familiarity of the Romantic without its vigour. But it must be remembered that, while he could see behind him clearly enough, the future towards which he was groping his way was still undefined. Only six years before *La Mort de Socrate* was published, the knowledgeable publisher Didot had read some of his manuscript poems (they became the *Méditations*) and advised him to work on more traditional lines. Contemporary taste is a powerful factor, particularly when there is no obvious alternative to follow.

The flaws of idiom are less conspicuous in *Le Dernier Chant du Pèlerinage d'Harold*, which contains passages of ecstatic contemplation of nature equal to some of Byron's own. But, like other French poems inspired by the news of Byron's death at Missolonghi, this attempt to add a fifth canto to *Childe Harold's Pilgrimage* fails through incompatibility of temperament between the two poets. Lamartine depicts a Byron shedding his scepticism and being led in his last days through pantheism to repentance and a Christian end. The historical falseness of the conception hardly matters; the error was to attach it so closely to *Childe Harold*, whose form and tone Lamartine set out to imitate as faithfully as he knew how.

But out of these experiments a great work finally grew. *Les Harmonies poétiques et religieuses*, published when Lamartine was forty, at last fulfilled the promise of *Les Méditations*, and even went beyond it.

Happy in his private life and firmly reseated in a faith which the death of Elvire and other youthful uncertainties had shaken, Lamartine could give full rein to his religious optimism and seal his reputation as a poet. No clearer chant to the glory of God had been raised in French literature since *Le Génie du christianisme*, none in French verse since the choruses of *Esther* and *Athalie*. With the ardour of complete assurance Lamartine hymned in *Le Chêne*, *L'Hymne du matin*, *L'Occident*, *L'Infini dans les cieux*, the power and beneficence of the Creator and his self-manifestation in trees, stars, sunrise and evening. *L'Hymne du matin*, for example, must have been produced through a fusion of sheer physical exultancy and of faith in the Divine Being, brought together at a moment of intoxication in the natural scene. A literary historian would also add some reminiscence of Ossian's *Hymn to the Sun*, which Lamartine had probably read some twenty years earlier. In any case, there have been few more effective examples of the mating of the sensual and the emotional in literature.

In form, too, *Les Harmonies* are an advance on *Les Méditations*. While still using the alexandrine with his old fluency, he has also learnt to make it turn and twist with astonishing vigour, as in the great climax of *L'Hymne du matin*:

> Montez donc, flottez donc, roulez, volez, vents, flamme,
> Oiseaux, vagues, rayons, vapeurs, parfums et voix!

He has perfected new metres, obtaining from them the same rapid flow as in the verses of *Le Vallon* or *Le Lac*, but with less monotony. He writes of the oak-tree:

> Et pendant qu'au vent des collines
> Il berce ses toits habités,
> Des empires dans ses racines,
> Sous son écorce des cités,
> Là, près des ruches des abeilles,
> Arachné tisse ses merveilles,[1]
> Le serpent siffle, et la fourmi
> Guide à des conquêtes desables
> Ses multitudes innombrables
> Qu'écrase un lézard endormi.[2]

Finally, his vocabulary has become less conventional, his images less stereotyped and, although the liberation from neoclassicism is by no means complete, it is difficult to refuse the Lamartine of *Les*

[1] Arachne, the spider in Greek mythology.
[2] From *Le Chêne*.

Harmonies considerable credit as a verbal pioneer, though of a soberer sort than Hugo, or even Vigny.

After *Les Harmonies*, the same strong religious inspiration reappeared in two long poems which were themselves only to be parts – 'episodes' was Lamartine's word – of *Les Visions*, a vast philosophical epic of humanity which he had been meditating for a number of years. The second in order of publication, though meant as a prelude, treats the theme of an angel who falls in love with a mortal woman. His punishment is to remain on earth through numerous reincarnations, reascending by slow stages to his original perfection. Though it has its moments, this poem, *La Chute d'un ange*, is difficult to read in its entirety and its reception disappointed Lamartine when it was published in 1838. It contains the magnificent *Chœur des cèdres du Liban*, which recalls *Le Chêne* in a grander and more varied form.

The other 'episode', *Jocelyn* (1836), was a contemporary success for the reasons for which most condemn it today. This tale of a young country priest living in the Savoy Alps during the Terror unfolds in naïve and melodramatic form the conflict of human love versus priestly celibacy. Its simplifications are too insistent and its emotion too obviously stated to preserve all the freshness of the original conception. It has an incidental interest as an ancestor of the 'familiar' poetry which enjoyed a growing vogue through the nineteenth century, spreading through Hugo to François Coppée, deservedly called *le poète des humbles*. Those who are touched by lines such as

> J'ai ramené ma sœur aux bras de son époux.
> Que ce retour fut triste, et pourtant qu'il fut doux!

will find *Jocelyn* touching. Others, missing in the mass the many finer passages which the poem contains, will be stupefied by its flatness, and irresistibly reminded of the crushing parody of all such verse in Jarry's *Ubu Roi*:

> Soudain j' me sens tirer la manch' par mon épouse:
> Espèc' d'andouill' qu'ell' m'dit, v'là l'moment d'te montrer.

Nevertheless, *Jocelyn* represented in Lamartine's work a definite discarding of neoclassicism and a determination to describe ordinary things in ordinary speech which had great significance in the evolution of poetry. Like Wordsworth, he sometimes swung the pendulum too far, but the excess was salutary. More than on *Jocelyn*, he should be judged for this manner on *La Vigne et la maison*, a long poem which he wrote at the age of sixty-seven after revisiting the now deserted family home at Milly. The poem has the unashamed pathos of anecdotic art. He recalls the household as it was when his parents were still alive and he and his piano-practising sisters were still young:

> Efface ce séjour, ô Dieu! de ma paupière,
> Ou rends-le-moi semblable à celui d'autrefois,
> Quand la maison vibrait comme un grand cœur de pierre
> De tous ces cœurs joyeux qui battaient sous ses toits.
>
> A l'heure où la rosée au soleil s'évapore
> Tous ces volets fermés s'ouvraient à sa chaleur,
> Pour y laisser entrer, avec la tiède aurore,
> Les nocturnes parfums de nos vignes en fleur.
>
> . . . Et les bruits du foyer que l'aube fait renaître,
> Les pas des serviteurs sur les degrés de bois,
> Les aboiements du chien qui voit sortir son maître,
> Le mendiant plaintif qui fait pleurer sa voix,
>
> Montaient avec le jour; et, dans les intervalles,
> Sous des doigts de quinze ans répétant leur leçon,
> Les claviers résonnaient ainsi que des cigales
> Qui font tinter l'oreille au temps de la moisson.

IV

Older criticism often spoke of the 'purity' of Lamartine's poetry and the word still forces itself on the ordinary reader – though it must not be taken in the more specialized sense current in the 1920s and 1930s when, as applied particularly to Valéry, it meant that poetry was a language apart. Excluding this special sense, one can see what Gautier meant by saying that 'Lamartine est plus qu'un poète, c'est la poésie toute pure', and one can go on to inquire whether, on this ground, he has any real affinity with Racine.

First, Lamartine's poetry is pure in its inspiration. Morally pure, of course, as is obvious when it is compared to the poetry of Vigny, Baudelaire, Verlaine, Rimbaud – or indeed of any poet whose work expresses a more troubled or a richer psychology. Perhaps 'innocence' or 'simplicity' better defines this side of it. It is also inspirationally pure in that each poem expresses a single mood or feeling, with no admixture of contrary feelings or of intellectual reservations. This again is simplicity quite as much as purity. But where Lamartine is most conspicuously a 'pure poet' is in his style, and here it can be said provisionally that he seems to speak with the very voice of nature. It is apparent that his best poems first came to him as wordless harmonies, the half-conscious expression of an inner mood in tune with an outward scene. His point of departure was a rhythm; the images, the ideas, the verbal working-out were subsidiary. He himself has described the process exactly in *Le Chœur des cèdres du Liban*, which begins by saying that all living things – plants, woods, water – have a voice, even if man cannot hear it. The chant of 'le grand chœur végétal' is higher and nearer to God than the language of humanity:

> Et ces milliers de voix de tout ce qui voit Dieu,
> Le comprend, ou l'adore, ou le sent en tout lieu,
> Roulaient dans le silence en grandes harmonies,
> Sans mots articulés, sans langues définies:
> Semblables à ce vague et sourd gémissement
> Qu'une étreinte d'amour arrache au cœur aimant,
> Et qui dans un murmure enferme et signifie
> Plus d'amour qu'en cent mots l'homme n'en balbutie!

This voice of nature, which Lamartine and his contemporaries heard in the roar of forests, the whispering of foliage, or the babbling of streams, is perhaps no more 'natural' in an objective sense than the inspiration which later poets have found in the pulsing of a liner or the hum of a power-house. But the fact that they heard it at all and attached such importance to it at least shows from which angle their poetry should be approached. Music, rhythm, flow – these are its essentials and its strength. The intellectual concepts and the images are weaker because less essential.

Is it really justifiable to apply the same criteria to Racine, and so link him with Lamartine? The ears of most perceptive French critics have caught a resemblance in tone. 'Les deux seuls poètes français d'ordre lisse et coulant,' Jean Cassou once wrote,[1] referring to the smoothness of texture, the apparent lack of effort in the verse of both. But that is only one feature, discerned by considering poetry as though it were a plastic creation. Even in this respect, the Lamartinian line, for all its suavity, is more ardent, more 'lyric' than the Racinian. Enthusiasm, considered as a regrettable weakness in the pre-Romantic age, had now come into its own, and Lamartine often seems to be singing at the extreme limit of his voice, whereas Racine always appears to have something in reserve. Lamartine's enthusiasm occasionally leads him to heights which Racine could not have reached, but more often it betrays

---

[1] In *Pour la poésie* (1935).

him into exaggerations of which Racine would not have been guilty. Apart from this, Racine's deeper understanding of humanity filled his verse with a substance which Lamartine's lacks, and this difference in content is reflected in some measure in the form. It is in their religious poems that they are closest; but these, which are at the centre of Lamartine's development, occur only on the margin of Racine's poetic career.

Lamartine aspired to be a philosophical poet and, with the same character but different gifts, he might have become the French Wordsworth. But in fact, if he can be compared to any English poet, it is rather with Shelley, whose bursts of passionate and child-like lyricism he often echoes in slightly more stilted language:

> Quand la feuille des bois tombe dans la prairie,
> Le vent du soir s'élève et l'arrache aux vallons;
> Et moi, je suis semblable à la feuille flétrie:
> Emportez-moi comme elle, orageux aquilons!

Lamartine's only consistent 'philosophy' was a kind of Christian pantheism: the whole universe is an expression of the deity – the same deity, it may be added, whose image had been formed by the gentle Madame de Lamartine and the kindly fathers of the Collège de Belley, and so was beneficent. Beyond that, he is the poet of the great commonplaces – using the word in its most favourable sense. The melancholy of autumn, the exaltation of a windy day, the calm of evening inducing worship, the vigour of morning evoking praise – these universal and primarily physical experiences are rendered in verse so entirely appropriate in its music and texture that it often does seem to be the voice of the thing itself. Lamartine's strongest claims as a poet rest on this quality.

There are only a limited number of great commonplaces and, given Lamartine's simple approach to them, he soon exhausted the possibilities of his material. After reading fifty pages of him, one may well feel dissatisfied. Yet half a dozen of his poems can be repeated throughout a lifetime with no more feeling of satiety than in walking or breathing.

To have produced these – particularly in the France of that period – was a remarkable achievement.

Chapter 11

Alfred de Vigny

ALFRED DE VIGNY is a sombre figure among the French Romantics. His stoic mistrust of life contrasts with the eager response of Lamartine and the confident assertiveness of Hugo. He was one of the great doubters of literature – with some reason.

He was born at Loches in 1797 of a decaying family, the last and only surviving child of a father of sixty and a mother of forty. In place of wealth or vitality, the Vignys cherished a tradition of aristocracy which they magnified beyond its real worth. With this went a military tradition. Vigny's father was an old soldier who had served in the Seven Years War and ever after had retained that veneration of Frederick II of Prussia which was a distinguishing mark of the gentleman officers of the Old Regime. Unlike Lamartine's father, he was no enemy of Napoleon, and his son was injected in childhood with an ambition for military honours. After a schooling directed entirely to that end, he took his commission in the year before Waterloo. Very soon afterwards France, surfeited by twenty years of warfare, was to lay down her arms and embark on a long period of peace.

Vigny was ill suited to the life of a non-combatant soldier. He fretted in one garrison town after another, cut off by his aristocratic and natural reserve from the camaraderie of the mess, not interested in horses and too earnestly so in women. Once, during the French intervention in favour of the Spanish ultra-royalists in 1823, he glimpsed a hope of action, but his regiment was left in yet another garrison town on the frontier. He contrived to take longer and longer leaves and had himself invalided out at the age of thirty. The whole of his education and career until then had been wrongly orientated, as he himself recognized. Telescoped against unfavourable circumstances by the driving force of a family tradition, his character and perhaps his destiny were already misshaped. His frustrations were to continue.

In 1825 he married Lydia Jane Bunbury, the daughter of an English colonial family whom he met at Pau. (Her uncle became Governor of Jamaica.) She took no share in his intellectual life. She never learnt

French and, in the course of time, is said to have forgotten her English. Soon after their marriage she was stricken with an incurable complaint. With exemplary love and patience Vigny tended this helpless being, who became 'massive, masculine and half-blind', and who depended uniquely on him for her contacts with life. He nursed and cheered her for thirty years. Once his reserved yet ardent temperament drove him into a liaison with the actress Marie Dorval. She left him in 1837 for Alexandre Dumas.

Literature was his necessary means of expression, but here again he had more outward failures than successes. He was early in the field with his youthful poems, and for a short time was a welcome figure at the *soirées de l'Arsenal*, where the young Romantics met to exchange ideas and elaborate their doctrines. But as a poet he was soon outshone by Victor Hugo, who also turned against him for some personal reason – perhaps literary jealousy. Hugo played him as cheap a trick as a man of letters could devise. Having written an article in praise of Vigny's *Éloa*, he republished it some years later without change – except that for each mention of *Éloa* he substituted *Paradise Lost*, and for Vigny's name that of Milton.

In 1826 Vigny published *Cinq-Mars*, the first French historical novel of the lineage of Walter Scott, but here also he was soon eclipsed by Hugo and Mérimée, who did not bother to acknowledge that he had been there first. For the theatre he began translations of three Shakespearian plays, of which only one – *Othello* – was produced. The others – *Romeo and Juliet*, which he translated in collaboration with Émile Deschamps, and *The Merchant of Venice* – never reached the stage. His only big theatrical success was *Chatterton* (1835), thanks largely to the acting of Marie Dorval. When he separated from her two years later, he retired, in the phrase first coined by Sainte-Beuve to apply to him, to his 'ivory tower'. This meant in effect that he divided his time between his country-house at Le Maine-Giraud near Angoulême, where he nursed his sick wife, and Paris, where he lived in comparative isolation. He emerged from it to seek election to the French Academy. After three years of canvassing he received sufficient votes to take his seat in January 1846, but his pleasure in the occasion was dashed by a humiliating speech addressed to him by a politician who disliked him.

There were other disappointments in his life which it seems unnecessary to list. He bore them all with a superhuman charity and with no outbursts of bitterness against any living person. He spent his last years confident that his literary fame would survive, but still fettered to his

unfortunate wife Lydia. A few months after her death, he himself died
– in September 1863 – of a cancer of the stomach.

II

That Vigny's poetry would be pessimistic goes without saying. Pessimism was in his life and blood, as optimism was in Lamartine's. Both,
in the final count, were equally irrational. Yet since Vigny has been
called – by himself first and by most critics since – a philosophical
poet, we must look at this 'philosophy' briefly before passing on to
other aspects of his poems.

At best it is not a doctrine, but only a groping for one. It starts from
the fairly constant assumption that mankind are the victims of an
inescapable fatality, that unhappiness is their normal lot, and that the
nobler they are the more they will suffer. The angel Éloa is damned
for her divine pity in Vigny's first considerable poem, the Russian
princess in *Wanda* is spiritually destroyed through the same cause in
one of his last. The only answer that man can worthily return to the
malignity or indifference of the powers which oppress him – whether
their name is Fate, God or Nature – is a contemptuous silence. This
sterile and static assumption – entirely understandable in Vigny's case
– is not of course a philosophy. It barely amounts even to a philosophical approach. It has no reasoned basis, as with Schopenhauer, nor
is it fertile as in Leopardi – who in his convulsions of unhappiness
opens up perhaps accidentally new perspectives of thought as well as
of emotion.

Distinguishing him from the pessimists of his own age, Vigny's
pessimism, one might think, should carry him into the twentieth century. But he is not modern either. His disillusionments are not our
disillusionments. And when, as occasionally happens, he sheds his
pessimism and searches for relief, it is along roads which are no longer
open. He thinks he sees daylight in the hope of progress through
human intelligence (*Wanda, La Bouteille à la mer*). This was a nineteenth-century hope which has been killed by too many mechanical
shocks, from shrapnel to the atom bomb. He also had in him, profoundly ingrained, a religious faith which still insisted that the Deity
was benign in spite of all the evidence. His strongest indictment of
divine justice was the postscript which he added to *Le Mont des Oliviers*
in the year before his death:

> S'il est vrai qu'au Jardin sacré des Écritures
> Le Fils de l'Homme ait dit ce qu'on voit rapporté;

Muet, aveugle et sourd au cri des créatures,
Si le Ciel nous laissa comme un monde avorté,
Le juste opposera le dédain à l'absence,
Et ne répondra plus que par un froid silence
Au silence éternel de la Divinité.

It can hardly escape notice that this defiant manifesto begins with an 'if'.

More generally, the religious terminology which he uses and his habit of centring his chief problems upon biblical figures make it difficult to accept him today as a contemporary. The language he speaks is too noble and remote.

The most that can be said of this side of him is that he is a reflective poet – reflecting with the utmost earnestness on much the same over-riding question throughout his life. Impersonally though he words his protests, he is basically akin to those other Romantics who openly used the *moi*: he merely gives cosmic form to a personal reaction.

But this does not for a moment diminish the poet. Because his thought was stiff, his verse was too. Rather than a merit or a defect, this is a characteristic. It makes Vigny an odd poet, but only the most prudent anthologist could present him otherwise. And then he would not be Vigny.

III

Vigny's poems fall roughly into two groups, with a long interval between. The early group is represented by the first edition of the *Poèmes antiques et modernes*, and belongs to his twenties. Published in 1826, it included such poems as *Moïse*, *Le Déluge* and *Le Cor*, as well as *Éloa* (which had appeared separately in 1824) and ten poems reprinted from his first slim volume of 1822. These latter have a certain historical interest since they originally appeared only two years after Lamartine's *Méditations* and they also announce the picturesque-narrative character of Vigny's later productions. In style, and sometimes in matter, they recall Chénier, as in these lines from *La Dryade*:

Ida! j'adore Ida, la légère bacchante:
Ses cheveux noirs, mêlés de grappes et d'acanthe,
Sur le tigre, attachés par une griffe d'or,
Roulent abandonnés; sa bouche rit encor
En chantant Évoé; sa démarche chancelle;
Ses pieds nus, ses genoux que la robe décèle,

> S'élancent, et son œil, de feux étincelant,
> Brille comme Phébus sous le signe brûlant.[1]

But Vigny dated the composition of this and similar verse back to 1815–17, before he could have read Chénier, and if there is one poet whom one would trust – on grounds of moral character – not to manipulate the dating of his poems, it would be Vigny. It must therefore be accepted that the original suggestion came, as he claims, directly from Theocritus.

Such poems would not in themselves make any great mark. It was not until he moved from classical to biblical and 'modern' themes – evoking the sombre figure of Moses isolated by Jehovah's choice, or the haunting story of Roland at Roncevaux – that Vigny could be seen as an important poet.

From then until his middle forties, he published a mere half-dozen poems. Among them was *La Frégate 'La Sérieuse'* (1829), a sea-poem which, without descending to the colloquial, manages realistic description in a way that the eighteenth-century odes on sea-fights never encompassed. Vigny solved, seemingly without difficulty, the neo-classic dilemma so obtrusive in Chénier and the early Lamartine. On this ground at least his sense of language values is much surer than theirs. Here he succeeds in recapturing, through the mouth of an old sea-captain, something of the atmosphere of the days of Nelson:

> Il faisait beau. – La mer, de sable environnée,
> Brillait comme un bassin d'argent entouré d'or;
> Un vaste soleil rouge annonçait la journée
>   Du quinze Thermidor.
>
> La *Sérieuse* alors s'ébranla sur sa quille.
> Quand venait un combat, c'était toujours ainsi;
> Je le reconnus bien, et je lui dis: 'Ma fille,
>   Je te comprends, merci!'
>
> J'avais une lunette exercée aux étoiles;
> Je la pris, et la tins ferme sur l'horizon.
> – Une, deux, trois, – je vis treize et quatorze voiles:
>   Enfin, c'était Nelson.

Inevitably the poem ends in the death of the ship, sunk in the battle which follows:

> Elle plonge d'abord sa poupe, et puis sa proue;
> Mon pavillon noyé se montrait en dessous;

---

[1] Compare the passage from Chénier quoted on pp. 96–7.

Puis elle s'enfonça, tourna comme une roue,
Et la mer vint sur nous.

Another of these middle-period poems was *Les Amants de Mont-morency* (1832), which reconstructs with enchanted realism the passion of two young lovers staying at an inn who decide to shoot themselves after three days of love. Nearly everything else that he wrote at this period was in prose, with the exception of his translations from Shakespeare. His historical drama, *La Maréchale d'Ancre*, was produced in 1831. *Chatterton*, his only other original play, was a prose dramatization of part of his earlier book, *Stello*, which dealt with the lives of three ill-fated poets – Gilbert, Chénier and Chatterton. All of them died young after suffering greatly – in Vigny's version – from the world's incomprehension.[1] But the best of Vigny's 'philosophic' prose is in the three short stories of *Servitude et grandeur militaires*. This book, based on his own reactions to the army, presents the soldier as a dedicated figure, isolated from society by his calling and bound by an iron rule of duty.

In his maturity, Vigny began publishing separately in *La Revue des deux mondes* the poems of his second main group. *La Sauvage*, *La Mort du loup*, *La Flûte*, *Le Mont des Oliviers* and *La Maison du berger* appeared in 1843–4. He printed *La Bouteille à la mer* in 1854, at a date when he probably felt that he had lived his life. All these were republished in one posthumous book, *Les Destinées* (1864), together with a few other poems such as *Wanda*, *L'Esprit pur* and *La Colère de Samson*. The last-named had been written not long after his break with Marie Dorval. It was typical of Vigny not to publish it in his lifetime.

IV

In a country of sand and lions a tent has been pitched. Outside, the night wind ripples the sand lightly as though it were a lake. Through the canvas of the tent, lighted by the ostrich-egg which serves as a lamp, two long shadows can be seen. One belongs to Samson, his knees huge and monumental as those of the colossus Anubis; the other to Delilah, smooth and supple as a young leopard. Presently the poem will swell into a diatribe against the deceit of women, a discussion of the eternal battle of the sexes, its nature and causes. But it opened with a picture and will close with that other picture no less strange in which

[1] Though Vigny was not an early existentialist, this habit of reinterpreting the lives of real people in the light of a current philosophy necessarily recalls the modern existentialist treatment of such figures as de Sade, Baudelaire and Jean Genet.

Samson, loaded with his enormous chain, is brought before the god Dagon. Dagon growls softly and dips twice on his revolving base in sign of satisfaction.

> [Ils]
> Attachèrent ses mains et brûlèrent ses yeux,
> Le traînèrent sanglant et chargé d'une chaîne
> Que douze grands taureaux ne tiraient qu'avec peine,
> Le placèrent debout, silencieusement,
> Devant Dagon, leur Dieu, qui gémit sourdement
> Et deux fois, en tournant, recula sur sa base
> Et fit pâlir deux fois ses prêtres en extase,
> Allumèrent l'encens, dressèrent un festin
> Dont le bruit s'entendait du mont le plus lointain;
> Et près de la génisse aux pieds du Dieu tuée
> Placèrent Dalila, pâle prostituée,
> Couronnée, adorée et reine du repas,
> Mais tremblante et disant: IL NE ME VERRA PAS!

Such a poem, and the several others like it, is a product less of the intellect than of an imagination soaked in the atmosphere of the Bible. It is perfectly true that Vigny expressed his ideas through descriptions and symbols. It is also true that his work is rich in various textbook Romantic qualities – Orientalism, local colour (the sand and the lions) pushed sometimes as far as the grotesque (the ostrich-egg). But these features are incidental. With him, the visual image came first, coloured, solid, almost palpable. The rest was subservient to it. Summing up his own work in *L'Esprit pur*, he calls his poems *tableaux*, and in *La Maison du berger* he promises to the ideal companion whom he never found a kind of lantern-show of all the conceptions which pass through his mind:

> Tous les tableaux humains qu'un Esprit pur m'apporte
> S'animeront pour toi quand devant notre porte
> Les grands pays muets longuement s'étendront.

It would be a fascinating study, though long and very difficult, to examine in detail the imaginative processes by which this apparently conventional Frenchman of the early nineteenth century recast the barbaric material of his primitive sources. We can only say here that, while transforming it entirely, he reproduced it as concretely as it had come to him. When Blake saw the angel at Felpham, he was looking no less with his physical eyes than Vigny appears to do when he describes the Destinies weighing inflexibly on the foreheads of mankind:

Tristes divinités du monde oriental,
Femmes au voile blanc, immuables statues,
Elles nous écrasaient de leur poids colossal.

Yet Vigny was no mystic and, unlike Blake, it is very debatable
whether he was even a visionary. It is true that he wrote of his midnight labours:

The hours of the night, as they strike, are for me like the gentle voices
of loving friends calling to me and saying, one after the other: 'What
ails you?' These are the hours of the Spirits, the light Spirits who buoy
up our thoughts on their transparent wings and make them sparkle more
brightly.

But Vigny's *esprits purs*, his angels, his antique characters, seem to
have been creatures of his own mind which, to his despair, he recognized as such. He knew that nothing had reached him from outside,
but having willed these beings into some sort of existence, he worked
on to make them as real as possible. Sometimes, as in an early poem
like *Le Cor*, he worked too little and the poem as a whole was clumsy,
but the charm of faery remained in isolated passages:

Âmes des chevaliers, revenez-vous encor?
Est-ce vous qui parlez avec la voix du cor?
Roncevaux! Roncevaux! dans ta sombre vallée
L'ombre du grand Roland n'est donc pas consolée?

... Entendez-vous? dit-il. – Oui, ce sont des pasteurs
Rappelant les troupeaux épars sur les hauteurs,
Répondit l'archevêque, ou la voix étouffée
Du nain vert Obéron qui parle avec sa Fée.

More often, he worked too hard – like a sculptor, as he described
himself – hewing with chisel and hammer those ephemeral conceptions
which most writers approach with an almost fearful delicacy. And the
strangest part is that, with Vigny, they did not evaporate but remained
– by the time he had finished with them – with their leaden wings,
their bronze feet and their granite attitudes. Awkward, grotesque,
unnatural as well as unspiritual, they stand unique in French poetry
as a monument to an indomitable will.

Vigny's laborious methods of composition give to his verse, and
particularly to his images, a firmness in welcome contrast to the facile
vagueness into which Lamartine can degenerate at times. Occasionally,
without losing this firmness, Vigny manages to maintain a flow of
rhythm which combines the best features of the two extremes. This

happened notably in *La Maison du berger*, which, from whatever angle it is considered, is one of the loveliest poems ever produced by a Romantic poet. Part of its attraction springs from technical causes. It is written in seven-line stanzas, rhyming *ababccb*. This well-integrated form, with its flowing feminine rhymes and its final masculine rhyme which seems to clinch rather than close the strophe, seems to have been invented by Vigny. He used it here for the first time, and increasingly in his later poems. It suited him much better than the paired alexandrine. It could render such noble effects as the virginal voice of Nature expressing her indifference to all that concerns mankind:

> Elle me dit: 'Je suis l'impassible théâtre
> Que ne peut remuer le pied de ses acteurs;
> Mes marches d'émeraude et mes parvis d'albâtre,
> Mes colonnes de marbre ont les dieux pour sculpteurs.
> Je n'entends ni vos cris ni vos soupirs, à peine
> Je sens passer sur moi la comédie humaine
> Qui cherche en vain au ciel ses muets spectateurs.

> 'Je roule avec dédain, sans voir et sans entendre,
> A côté des fourmis les populations;
> Je ne distingue pas leur terrier de leur cendre,
> J'ignore en les portant les noms des nations.
> On me dit une mère, et je suis une tombe.
> Mon hiver prend vos morts comme son hécatombe,
> Mon printemps ne sent pas vos adorations.

> 'Avant vous, j'étais belle et toujours parfumée,
> J'abandonnais au vent mes cheveux tout entiers
> Je suivais dans les cieux ma route accoutumée
> Sur l'axe harmonieux des divins balanciers:
> Après vous, traversant l'espace où tout s'élance,
> J'irai seule et sereine, en un chaste silence
> Je fendrai l'air du front et de mes seins altiers.'

But even in this outstanding poem there is a section – often omitted in anthologies – of invective against railway-trains, then a modern invention which Vigny regarded as dangerous. Intellectually, he was perhaps right in condemning the new craze for speed. From a sentimental point of view, the section is almost worth having for the sake of one nostalgic verse in which the poet regrets the old coach journeys, with their slow and keenly tasted sensations. Yet it is very difficult to understand how a writer usually so in tune with his material could have failed to notice that his topical insertion mars the aesthetic unity of his poem as a whole.

But Vigny is a case apart. To his imagination, the Locomotive was a being not unlike Dagon, or Satan, or one of the Destinies. He demands that an angel shall watch over it with a sword in one hand and both eyes fixed on the safety-valve and piston-rods to ensure that they function safely. He might have been a still greater poet had he been either less or more eccentric.[1]

Vigny has also suffered from his exaggeratedly high conception of the poet's mission – allied, of course, to the nobility of his personal character. Had he descended to attacks on his enemies, he might have been as great an ironist as Byron in *Don Juan*. The gift was in him, as his poem *Les Oracles*, written in the last year of his life against the parliamentarians of 1848 shows:

> Les doctrines croisaient leurs glaives de chimères
> Devant les spectateurs gravement assoupis.
> Quand les lambris tombaient sur eux, ces gens austères
> Ferraillaient comme Hamlet, sous la table accroupis.
> Poursuivant, comme un rat, l'argument en détresse,
> Ces fous, qui distillaient et vendaient la sagesse,
> Tuaient Polonius à travers le tapis.

Unfortunately, he wrote little in this vein and his work as a whole stands for Dignity – but of such an endearing and original kind that it can be unreservedly accepted. The usual penalty of dignity is immobility, the pitfall which also threatens Leconte de Lisle, whose work was an extension, sometimes *ad absurdum*, of Vigny's pictorial methods and his fundamental pessimism.

From the first of these two poets to the second the nineteenth-century doubt (or 'anguish', to use the language of Vigny's contemporary Kierkegaard) can be seen hardening into despair. The characteristic of Vigny is that he was man enough to experience and state it without breaking down into the self-pity of the more feminine and certainly more superficial Musset; but, on the other hand, without the superhuman clairvoyance of Baudelaire, who could see round corners in his own and other people's natures. Vigny's vision, in comparison, is a fixed beam meeting an immovable object. He may be classed as basically Romantic because that object is himself.

[1] *Le taureau de fer, qui fume, souffle et beugle* which made such an impression on the poet was probably one of the Buddicom class of engines constructed for the French railways by a British engineering firm in 1843. A survivor of the class, still in working order, was exhibited at the Festival of Britain in 1951.

Chapter 12

Victor Hugo

VICTOR-MARIE HUGO was born in 1802 at Besançon, where his father, later a brigadier-general in Napoleon's armies, happened to be stationed at the time. The stock was robust yet somewhere strangely defective, as appeared in the poet's later life. With his two elder brothers and his mother, the daughter of a Breton sea-captain, Victor Hugo spent a year in Italy at the age of six and another year in Madrid when he was nine. Soon afterwards, the fall of Napoleon put an end to these professional journeys of Brigadier Hugo and he retired, in considerable discredit with the new regime. Much later his son drew his idealized portrait in *Les Misérables*, where he becomes *le brigand de la Loire*, but his immediate influence was eclipsed by that of Madame Hugo who, after Waterloo, was able to give full play to her royalist sympathies.

She entered enthusiastically – and her son with her – into that queer new-old society of returned *émigrés*, miraculously resurrected from before the Revolution. Courtly old gentlemen and indomitable old ladies accompanied by the perennial priests settled themselves upon a completely transformed Paris, bringing with them a bewildered younger generation whom they presented with silver fleurs-de-lys in place of a workable creed. Hugo profited greatly by the uncertainty of the restored monarchy and its search for new blood, for his early poems were rewarded by official prizes and – when he was twenty – by a yearly grant which he might not have obtained under a different regime. The grant enabled him to marry the nineteen-year-old daughter of a neighbouring family with whom he had been in love for some time. Adèle Foucher admired him for his passionate and forceful personality, though later she was to be driven into asserting her independence with a tact and courage which revealed her as no ordinary character. At the wedding-breakfast Hugo's elder brother Eugène suddenly went mad. He had been nursing a secret passion for the bride and had at last reached breaking point. He spent the remaining seventeen years of his life in an asylum.

The young couple lived in comparative harmony for some eight years, during which Hugo was establishing himself firmly as the leader of the new Romantic movement. The verse of *Les Orientales* and the great stage success of *Hernani* (February 1830) made his reputation as a poet and dramatist. His novel, *Notre-Dame de Paris*, first contemplated in 1829 and finished in January 1831 after eight months of intensive writing, carried him to a third triumph. A far more sociable and attractive personality than Lamartine or Vigny, the young writer was the centre of a literary circle which included Nodier, Musset, Gautier, the brothers Deschamps, editors of *La Muse française*, and the more conservative contributors to *Le Globe*. One of these, Sainte-Beuve, who was then a rising poet and critic, formed a personal friendship with the Hugo couple which touched off a mine. He fell ardently in love with Adèle, then confessed his feelings to the husband who at first treated him sympathetically but finally forbade him the house. The exact truth of the matter may never be clear, since each side gives its own account of it, but in the light of Hugo's character it is not unfair to suppose that what shocked him most was the fact that the two people – his wife and his disciple – who should have been uniquely interested in him, had deviated into an attraction – however innocent on Adèle's side – for each other. That he could not have forgiven. In any case his handling of the situation, difficult though it was, was certainly clumsy. It resulted in Adèle's refusal to continue living with him as his wife, though there was no outward separation. From then until the end of her life she remained with him as his faithful companion and the mother of their growing children.

This conjugal crisis, coinciding with a peak of literary activity, was one reason why, shortly after, he attached himself to the actress Juliette Drouet. As Vigny with Marie Dorval, he fell in love with her when she was acting in one of his own plays – in this case *Marion de Lorme*. But their relationship was quite different. Juliette Drouet remained with Hugo for fifty years, serving as his devoted mistress, secretary, accountant and seamstress – in all but name an exemplary second wife. Most of his finest love-poems of the 1830s were intended for her. As an inspiration she ranked equal to his little family of four children, in whom he took an almost inordinate delight.

At the age of forty he began to detach himself from literature. The failure of his play *Les Burgraves*, in 1843, disgusted him with the theatre and later in the same year he was stunned by the death of his idolized eldest daughter Léopoldine. She and the young husband whom she had recently married were drowned by the capsizing of their boat at Villequier, near the mouth of the Seine. For ten years Hugo published nothing, partly for these reasons and partly because the friendship of the Duc d'Orléans, heir to the throne, had opened up the prospect of a brilliant political career. Having long outgrown his boyish devotion to the Legitimist cause, Hugo became increasingly absorbed in politics. He was made a *Pair de France* in 1845 and spoke constantly in the Upper Chamber. But his heavy and over-general eloquence earned him the distrust of all parties. When 1848 came, he advocated a regency and not, as Lamartine did, a republic. But if at that time he had advanced less far along the democratic path, three years later his reaction to Louis Napoleon's *coup d'état* was much more energetic. He went into open opposition by joining the *Comité d'insurrection*, was in danger of his life for a few days, then escaped to Brussels and eventually to Guernsey. With his family and Juliette Drouet, he remained in the Channel Isles until the abdication of Louis Napoleon in 1870, obstinately defying the tyrant. He could have taken advantage of the amnesty of 1859 to return to France, but preferred to remain on his rock.[1] Exile and leisure renewed his literary vein, and it was during this period that the chief works of his maturity were composed: in verse *Les Châtiments* – his epic satire against Louis Napoleon – the later lyric poems in *Les Contemplations*, and most of *La Légende des siècles*; in prose the novels *Les Misérables*, *Les Travailleurs de la mer* and *L'Homme qui rit*. Uncompromised politically, he returned to Paris immediately after Sedan and was acclaimed as the idol and figurehead of the French people.

So he remained during his last years. Though his political action was unimportant (elected as Senator for the Seine, he fulfilled his duties conscientiously and inconspicuously), and though he was quite out of touch with new literary developments such as Symbolism, the Republican masses looked on him as the supreme democrat and the less advanced in literature revered him as *le père Hugo*. His personal legend survived in France for many years.

He died in 1885, having published a great deal of verse since his return from exile, and with several posthumous volumes still to come. With a final instinct for the melodramatic, he had demanded a pauper's funeral. It became one of the most impressive public ceremonies that Paris had ever seen. For six hours the coffin on its workhouse hearse moved slowly from the Arc de Triomphe, where it had lain in state,

[1] With occasional visits to the house which he took in Brussels in 1859 and where Baudelaire saw him in 1865–6 and Verlaine in 1868.

through endless crowds to the Panthéon. The impressions which the scene made on a young man of a very different generation can be read in *Les Déracinés* of Maurice Barrès.

Many Frenchmen felt – as Englishmen at the funeral of Queen Victoria – that they were burying an epoch. This man, born under the Consulate, had witnessed the fall of five regimes and the still greater revolution in the philosophy of living. He had survived Baudelaire by eighteen years, Flaubert by five. At the date he died, Leconte de Lisle, Rimbaud, Verlaine and Mallarmé had written all or most of their important work and Zola, aged forty-five, had published more than half of his great bible of naturalism.

II

Rather than a work, the writings of Hugo are a territory – so vast and so strongly characterized that few readers can pass through it and remain neutral. They are forced into adopting an attitude either of excessive admiration or of hostility.

Besides his four great and several lesser novels, a considerable body of shorter and more occasional prose-writings, and eleven dramas of which seven are in verse, Hugo published in his lifetime a dozen main collections of poetry. Before this continent of verse can be discussed, it must be charted.[1]

As a boy of sixteen Victor Hugo won the Golden Amaranth offered by the *Académie des jeux floraux de Toulouse*. It was an academic prize for a stiff and academic poem, *Les Vierges de Verdun*, and those characteristics persisted in most of the verse contained in his first published volume of 1822, *Les Odes et poésies diverses*. Two subsequent volumes completed a work which Hugo finally republished under the collective title of *Odes et ballades*. The *Odes* were declamatory historical pieces, but the *Ballades* were based on legend and folklore and were recounted with a certain warmth and fantasy, as in the English ballad. By concentrating on these qualities, Hugo went on to produce *Les Orientales*. Their appearance in December 1828 marked a second

[1] Chief novels: *Notre-Dame de Paris* (1831), *Les Misérables* (1862), *Les Travailleurs de la mer* (1866), *L'Homme qui rit* (1869).

Chief plays: *Hernani* (1830), *Marion de Lorme* (1831), *Le Roi s'amuse* (1832), *Lucrèce Borgia* (1833), *Ruy Blas* (1838), *Les Burgraves* (1843).

Chief verse collections: *Odes et ballades* (1826), *Les Orientales* (1829), *Les Feuilles d'automne* (1831), *Les Chants du crépuscule* (1835), *Les Voix intérieures* (1837), *Les Rayons et les ombres* (1840), *Les Châtiments* (1853), *Les Contemplations* (1856), *La Légende des siècles* (1859–77–83), *Les Chansons des rues et des bois* (1865), *Les Quatre Vents de l'esprit* (1881), *Toute la lyre* (1888). Also *La Fin de Satan* (1886) and *Dieu* (1891).

stage in the progress of French Romanticism hardly less significant than 1820 had been with *Les Méditations*.

Les Orientales are romantic in both the literary and the popular senses. Their setting is ostensibly that most colourful of all regions – the East. But Hugo's Orient extended little further east than Istanbul and for the most part it was North African Arabic and Spanish. His stay in Madrid as a boy, his reading of the *Romancero* – that great storehouse of medieval Spanish ballads – the poems of Byron, and the splendour of summer sunsets over Paris – these were the chief sources of his 'local colour'. From such materials he built up an exotic-seeming world which warmed the imagination without over-taxing it. Lamartine's evocations of nature had been based on landscapes which, however mistily, he had observed. Hugo was bound by no such limitations. Rather than the Lake of Annecy, he could describe the Alhambra by moonlight, or the Nile whipped by a desert wind:

> On entendait mugir le simoun meurtrier,
> Et sur les cailloux blancs les écailles crier
> Sous le ventre des crocodiles.
> Les obélisques gris s'élançaient d'un seul jet.
> Comme une peau de tigre, au couchant s'allongeait
> Le Nil jaune, tacheté d'îles.

By means of this synthetic Orientalism, Hugo treated the kind of subjects that Delacroix treated in painting – the sack of eastern towns, foaming steeds and mustachioed janissaries, languishing harem-queens, minarets and palm-trees. None of it was entirely new, for even Racine, in *Bajazet*, had written on an 'eastern' subject. The novel of the first half of the seventeenth century (de Gomberville and Madeleine de Scudéry) had hinted at similarly exotic settings, while in the eighteenth century Orientalism had permeated both novel and drama. But not poetry. And, besides this, Hugo's handling of such themes was more full-blooded and was carried out with a conscious intention of revolt. His avoidance of Greek and Latin subjects was deliberate. It enabled him to contrast his own work with that of the drier writers of the two previous centuries and so exaggerate the distinction between the coldness of the classics and the warmth of the Romantics. Having applied his new principles to the theory of the drama in the preface to his un-acted play *Cromwell* in 1827, he went on to state his conception of poetry in the shorter preface to the *Orientales*:

> The author is not unaware that many critics will think him rash and absurd to desire for France a literature comparable to a medieval town.

It is one of the maddest ideas that one could have. It means openly desiring disorder, abundance, eccentricity, bad taste. How much better is a fine, regular nudity, high walls entirely *plain*, as they say, with a few sober ornaments *in good taste* – scrolls and ovals, a bronze garland for the cornices, a marble ceiling with cherubs' heads for the vaulting! The Palace of Versailles, the Place Louis XV [Place de la Concorde], the Rue de Rivoli – there you have it. That gives you a nice literature ruled on the line.

Other nations say Homer, Dante, Shakespeare. We say Boileau.

If Hugo had added Corneille, Molière, Racine, La Bruyère, Lesage, his argument would have been considerably weakened, but he and his contemporaries were irked more by the hand of a debased classicism which had grown academic than by the original masters. Though overstated, their protest was genuine.

By this time Hugo was a sufficiently accomplished poet to lead his own revolt. The verse of *Les Orientales* shows great virtuosity in the handling of rhythm and metre. Technically, he is both varied and sure. He can write plain rollicking poems of the ballad type:

> Don Rodrigue est à la chasse.
> Sans épée et sans cuirasse
> Un jour d'été, vers midi,
> Sous la feuillée et sur l'herbe
> Il s'assied, l'homme superbe,
> Don Rodrigue le hardi.

He can also accomplish a metrical *tour de force* like *Les Djinns*, which swells through seven changes of metre to its climax, then diminishes through the same changes in reverse until it dies away in the two-syllable lines with which it began:

> On doute
> La nuit ...
> J'écoute:
> Tout fuit,
> Tout passe;
> L'espace
> Efface
> Le bruit.

It was artificial, but it was a change – as Hugo intended – from Boileau, and even from Chénier and Lamartine. At some periods poetry should be sublime, at others exploratory and sensitive, but this was a time when a poet's most urgent duty was to be read. If we look on the

early Hugo as a great resuscitator, shocking French poetry back to
life by methods which his contemporaries were too fastidious or too
slow to apply, we shall be doing him justice.

His metrical revolution was completed by an attack on the 'regular'
alexandrine. He began to break it up, to displace the caesura from the
exact middle of the line and to carry on his sentences over the rhyme
from one line to the next (*enjambement*). Other poets around and before
him had done the same, but an 'irregularity' which in Racine, La Fontaine or even Chénier is something of an event, in Hugo is a characteristic. His most conspicuous challenge to the belated classicists was made
in his drama *Hernani*, of which the opening lines:

> Serait-ce déjà lui? C'est bien à l'escalier
> Dérobé ...

caused, according to Théophile Gautier, almost a riot in the audience.

After this, Hugo was ready to exploit the positions he had conquered. In his four great books of lyric verse – on which the least
contestable part of his reputation is based – he writes with the same
metrical freedom and originality, but with less desire to startle. He has
grown accustomed to his own virtuosity, and in its place two different
monsters are beginning to take shape: one is the personality of Hugo,
and the other his windy, thundering rhetoric. But in the 1830s their
outline was not yet perfectly clear, and to discuss them now would be
to anticipate.

The four books reflect a certain growth in maturity from the first
to the last, but in essentials they form a single body of poetry, beginning with *Les Feuilles d'automne* in 1831, through *Les Chants du
crépuscule* (1835) and *Les Voix intérieures* (1837), to *Les Rayons et les
ombres* of 1840. These poems are nearly all personal, in a perfectly
open way. Whether Hugo speaks in the first person, or renames himself 'the poet' or Olympio – or, more familiarly, Ol – there is no real
concealment that he is expressing the spontaneous reactions of Hugo.
Spontaneity in love, in his response to nature, in his views on political
questions, in his impressions of past ages (*Le Passé, La Statue*), expressed with that amazing fluency which caused Barrès to dub him 'Le
maître des mots français'. Unsubtle and uninhibited, he gives himself
away with the lavishness of a born showman. There is something for
everyone, even the most fastidious if they happen to come his way, for
who can really resist the lure of so opulent a sensuality? His emotional
gusto is not forced. He believes in it completely, and why not, since
these are the feelings which carry most conviction with the common

man? His sensual approach is a universal approach, whether he is writing to Juliette such a lyric as:

> Puisque j'ai mis ma lèvre à ta coupe encor pleine,
> Puisque j'ai dans tes mains posé mon front pâli,
> Puisque j'ai respiré parfois la douce haleine
> De ton âme, parfum dans l'ombre enseveli . . .

with its mounting accumulation of *puisque*'s which is a hallmark of his rhetoric; or whether, more delicately, he is describing a luminous mid-summer night as in the short *Nuits de juin*, or regretting past happiness, as in *Tristesse d'Olympio*, or apostrophizing the ghosts of drowned sailors, as in *Oceano Nox*:

> On s'entretient de vous parfois dans les veillées.
> Maint joyeux cercle, assis sur des ancres rouillées,
> Mêle encor quelque temps vos noms d'ombre couverts
> Aux rires, aux refrains, aux récits d'aventures,
> Aux baisers qu'on dérobe à vos belles futures,
> Tandis que vous dormez dans les goëmons verts.
>
> On demande: – Où sont-ils? sont-ils rois dans quelque île?
> Nous ont-ils délaissés pour un bord plus fertile? –
> Puis votre souvenir même est enseveli.
> Le corps se perd dans l'eau, le nom dans la mémoire.
> Le temps, qui sur toute ombre en jette une plus noire,
> Sur le sombre océan jette le sombre oubli.

What has been most admired in these poems, and what remains, are the great commonplaces of feeling, expressed with more richness and a stronger *souffle* than in Lamartine. Hugo insists too much, it is agreed, but without him some of the most moving and lovely sentiments of ordinary humanity would have been left without adequate expression. This was no doubt his greatest achievement, and one which is easy to overlook unless it is replaced in its historical context. We have grown so used to supposing that normal 'poetic' diction is like this (ordinary speech emotionally heightened by rhyme and rhythm and by an occasional admixture of oratory) that we forget that for a hundred and fifty years before Hugo (in French poetry at least) it was not so. Poetry used a language composed of special ingredients which were out of reach of the average education. The opposition aroused in the twentieth century by various poetic techniques sometimes indiscriminately classed as 'modern' is due largely to a return to pre-Romantic practice. The film-star who was everyone's darling suddenly turns highbrow, or develops complicated sensibilities which cannot be expressed in the language to which we have grown accustomed. In the 1830s this was a new language of which Hugo can justly be considered to have been the father. But today . . . today it belongs to the world. To tear something from the world before it has finished chewing it is to invite those bellows of indignation still heard even now, though more faintly as time passes. In other terms, Hugo was too successful for the well-being of the Muse. He democratized her, as he claimed, leaving it painfully difficult for her to alter her status in the future.

III

If after this Victor Hugo had died, or had ceased writing for good, he would have taken his place with the three other great Romantics on about equal terms – a less tortured poet than Vigny, less limpid than Lamartine, heavier yet less passionate than Musset – but a necessary member of the quartet to complete its combined range. We have to consider whether, by beginning to publish and write again after a ten years' break, he increased his poetic stature.

There can be little doubt about *Les Contemplations*. At first sight these poems – nearly all composed between 1840 and 1852 (they were published in 1856) – continue the personal, lyric manner of the earlier volumes. They are divided into two parts by a page left blank except for the words: 'Quatre Septembre 1843', and the tragedy of Léopoldine's death becomes the leitmotiv of the poems grouped after it. Hugo's new attitude of despair is summed up in the poem *Veni, vidi, vixi*:

> Puisque l'espoir serein dans mon âme est vaincu,
> Puisqu'en cette saison des parfums et des roses,
> O ma fille! j'aspire à l'ombre où tu reposes,
> Puisque mon cœur est mort, j'ai bien assez vécu.

Yet it is doubtful if the blow of his daughter's death alone accounts for the underlying difference between these poems and, say, *Les Rayons et les ombres*. Something besides a tragic accident had occurred since 1840, and that was the natural cessation of the young Romantic's inner source of poetry. He had exhausted the novelty of sensual experience and was prepared to 'contemplate' it rather than to express it directly. The poems of the first part of *Les Contemplations* are invectives such as *Réponse à un acte d'accusation* or *A propos d'Horace*, quiet records of daily life or of communings with nature, searchings after the destiny

of man, eclogues where the inspiration is still erotic, songs where it is
more generally sentimental. An act or an impression is now the material
for a poem; it no longer is a poem of itself, spontaneously.

The second part of *Les Contemplations* confirms the evidence of the
first. Here are verses of subdued pathos, laments, nightmare specula-
tions on death and eternity.

Hugo's chief poems on the death of Léopoldine (*A Villequier*,
Demain dès l'aube, *Paroles sur la dune*) stand as great 'commonplace'
pieces beside his own *Tristesse d'Olympio*, Lamartine's *Le Vallon*, or
Tennyson's *In Memoriam*:

> J'entends le vent dans l'air, la mer sur le récif,
> L'homme liant la gerbe mûre;
> J'écoute, et je confronte en mon esprit pensif
> Ce qui parle à ce qui murmure;
>
> Et je reste parfois couché sans me lever
> Sur l'herbe rare de la dune,
> Jusqu'à l'heure où l'on voit apparaître et rêver
> Les yeux sinistres de la lune.
>
> . . . Comme le souvenir est voisin du remord!
> Comme à pleurer tout nous ramène!
> Et que je te sens froide en te touchant, ô mort,
> Noir verrou de la porte humaine!
>
> Et je pense, écoutant gémir le vent amer,
> Et l'onde aux plis infranchissables;
> L'été rit, et l'on voit sur le bord de la mer
> Fleurir le chardon bleu des sables.

Such poems form an essential part of a nation's stock of distinguished
verse on universal themes. The word 'classic', in one of its most important senses, must certainly be applied to them. But they are elegiac
rather than lyric. They are bets on immortality at such short odds that,
though successful, they do not thrill very much. It is when an outside
chance like *Bateau ivre* comes off that the heart is astonished and uplifted. But for the obvious futility of the living advising the dead and
the critic the poet, one would say that Hugo ought to have devoted
the whole of his second literary existence to this quieter and safer vein.
We should then have had two very good poets instead of one vast but
uneven writer. At the cost of a narrowing of range we should have
been rid of a great mass of repetitive verbiage and should have been

able to see some rare blooms of impersonal art. We should have had sharper satire in *Les Châtiments* to give point to its great Meissonier pictures of battles and defeats, and we might have had an unquestionable masterpiece in *La Légende des siècles*.

This was Hugo's epic of humanity, as *Les Visions* was to have been Lamartine's and *L'Histoire de France* was Michelet's. A fruit of his first years in the Channel Islands, the first volume was published in 1859. By that date the whole work had been conceived, though the second and third volumes followed only in 1877 and 1883. Its very loose theme is the progress of the human spirit from the earliest days of the Creation, as described in the Bible, though the ancient civilizations of Assyria and Egypt to the European Middle Ages, finally reaching forward into a cloudy future with the poems *Dieu* and *La Fin de Satan*, which were published posthumously. The grand design was a noble one typical of the aspirations of the mid-nineteenth century, though it took no account of the evolutionist theories which were already well established by the time the second volume of *La Légende* appeared. Apart from this, Hugo's knowledge of history and pre-history was too incomplete for his work to be more than a series of dips into a huge bran-tub of legend, mythology and literature out of which almost anything might come.

The resulting poems are best appreciated as separate *tableaux* – far more fluent than Vigny's evocations of the past, yet, in their totality, far less memorable. The most impressive have been skimmed by anthologists and the traditional choices are sound – *La Conscience, Booz endormi, Le Satyre, La Rose de l'Infante* foremost among them. Of the many others, few are entirely first-rate, some are ridiculous, but most repay reading for the occasional strange or startling passages which they contain. As random examples from the second volume there is the story of Zim-Zizimi, a kind of Sardanapalus who conquers the world only to be snuffed out by a supernatural force:

> Il a dompté Bagdad, Trébizonde et Mossul
> Que conquit le premier Duilius, ce consul
> Qui marchait précédé de flûtes tibicines;
> Il a soumis Gophna, les forêts abyssines,
> L'Arabie, où l'aurore a d'immenses rougeurs
> . . . Et le Sahara fauve, où l'oiseau vert asfir
> Vient becqueter la mouche aux pieds des dromadaires.

A few pages further on is the legend of Sultan Mourad, a bloodthirsty tyrant who in his lifetime has slain thousands of human beings.

In his last hours he relieves the sufferings of a pig, and when he appears before the Judgement Seat this single good deed saves him:

> Soudain, du plus profond des nuits, sur la nuée,
> Une bête difforme, affreuse, exténuée,
> Un être abject et sombre, un pourceau, s'éleva,
> Ouvrant un œil sanglant qui cherchait Jéhovah.
> . . . Le pourceau misérable et Dieu se regardèrent.

During and after the composition of *La Légende des siècles,* the torrent of other poems continued. They were collected in *Les Chansons des rues et des bois* (1865), which were chiefly light pieces, *L'Art d'être grand-père* (1877), familiar poems reflecting his delight in his grandchildren Georges and Jeanne, several volumes of philosophic and religious poems (some perhaps deserve to be called mystical) running from *La Pitié suprême* (1879) to *Les Quatre Vents de l'esprit* (1881) and prolonged in the posthumous *Fin de Satan* and *Dieu,* and in certain pieces of *Toute la lyre* (1888–93). There are also the patriotic verse of *L'Année terrible* (1872) and the Republican, anti-clerical tirades of *Les Années funestes* (1898). Many of these pieces deserve to be read more than they are. While some are senile vapourings, others are illuminations of the human mind, and the poet – unselective by temperament – often mingles the two in the same poem.

IV

There are three levels of approach to Hugo. If one cannot penetrate to the third, it is perhaps best to stay on the first. One then remains free to appreciate, without hindrance or annoyance, some three or four dozen poems including all those which we have mentioned by their title.

But by penetrating beyond this, the reader becomes inescapably conscious of the poison which flows through all Hugo's work – the personality of Victor Hugo. It is this Hugo who writes with affectionate pride of himself in the first poem of *Les Feuilles d'automne,* who at the age of twenty-eight weeps over his love-letters written ten years before – not because they recall the woman he wrote them to, but because they recall his own younger self – who addresses to Juliette that cruelly patronizing poem, *Oh, n'insultez jamais une femme qui tombe!* and the greater cruelty of

> Quand tu me parles de gloire,
> Je souris amèrement.

Cette voix que tu veux croire,
Moi, je sais qu'elle ment.

Hugo, who had tasted the delights of fame, could now preach disdain of such vanities to the woman whose stage ambitions he had stifled. This was the Hugo who kept human beings as pets, so long as they would perform for him, and posed as a martyr in the exile to which he condemned not only himself, but his entire family – with the result that his younger daughter was finally driven into madness. (There is plenty of grief in his verse for the dead Léopoldine, *cet autre moi-meme*, but not a word of sympathy for the unfortunate Adèle, who dared to defy him.) Finally there is the megalomaniac's self-identification with God, easily discoverable in his later poems and well illustrated by his remark to a tongue-tied workman who approached him in his old age: 'N'ayez pas peur. Je ne suis qu'un homme.'

This ridiculously inflated egoism cannot be ignored, because Hugo makes it the basis of his theory and practice. Once realized by the reader, it can be seen to be everywhere, and then every line he writes is suspect. 'Hélas!' he writes in the preface to *Les Contemplations*, 'quand je vous parle de moi, je vous parle de vous.' But this is precisely what he never succeeds in doing. Never was a writer more lacking in his perception of the feelings of others, yet few writers have based so much of their work on their personal relationships. Those he loved go in alive and come out as wax models, labelled *the fiancée, the mistress, the dead daughter, the grandchild*, with hardly a name or a human face among them. The only living presence in that booming echo-room is Hugo's.

But is it? What was Victor Hugo? If there is no satisfactory answer, does not that explain everything? Cocteau summed up the matter when he remarked: 'Hugo était un fou qui se croyait Hugo'. Suppose that the whole of Hugo's life, and his work which was so closely bound to it, was a series of impersonations of some ideal figure: the Lover, the Poet, the Seer, the Exile, the Democrat, the Grand Old Man, the God-inspired. That would explain our exasperation with his egotism, which is not of itself an unusual or repulsive quality in literature and is not displeasing in a Villon, a Rousseau or a Verlaine. But if the ego is placed at the centre of the work, and there is nothing at the centre of the ego, disappointment is inevitable.

We now reach the third level, which transcends the usual limits of literary appreciation. Certain critics have suggested that at the centre of the Hugolian ego was God, or a god. This would make of Hugo one of the great mystics and of his cloud-capped, thundering rhetoric a sublime attempt to express the inexpressible.

While only a celestial judge would be really competent to decide whether this is true or false, we can at least see how it may affect our opinion of Hugo as a poet. What appear most important in this light are not the plainly sensual earlier poems, not the picture-poems, but some of the later *Contemplations* and the pantheistic (or deistic?) broodings expressed intermittently from then until his death in such poems as *Religio, Ce que dit la bouche d'ombre, La Vision des montagnes,* or *Dieu,* of which the final lines are:

> Veux-tu planer plus haut que la sombre nature?
> Veux-tu dans la lumière inconcevable et pure
> Ouvrir tes yeux, par l'ombre affreuse appesentis?
> Le veux-tu? Réponds.
>   – Oui, criai-je.
>   Et je sentis
> Que la création tremblait comme une toile.
> Alors levant un bras et d'un pan de son voile
> Couvrant tous les objets terrestres disparus,
> Il [*the angel*] me toucha le front du doigt.
>   Et je mourus.

One would read with closer attention Hugo's description of the Day of Judgement, comparing it perhaps to d'Aubigné's description:[1]

> On comprenait que tant que ce clairon suprême
> Se tairait, le sépulcre, obscur, raidi, béant,
> Garderait l'attitude horrible du néant,
> ... Mais qu'à l'heure où soudain, dans l'espace sans rives,
> Cette trompette vaste et sombre sonnerait,
> On verrait, comme un tas d'oiseaux d'une forêt,
> Toutes les âmes, cygne, aigle, éperviers, colombes,
> Frémissantes, sortir du tremblement des tombes.
> Et tous les spectres faire un bruit de grandes eaux,
> Et se dresser, et prendre à la hâte leurs os,
> Tandis qu'au fond, au fond du gouffre, au fond du rêve,
> Blanchissant l'absolu, comme un jour qui se lève,
> Le front mystérieux du Juge apparaîtrait!

And, reading on in the same long poem,[2] one would wonder whether, and in what sense, Hugo had *seen* the immense trumpet of the final

---

[1] See pp. 41–2.
[2] *La Trompette du jugement,* in *La Légende des siècles,* I (1859).

angel, with its symbolic dimensions – or whether it was just another instrument forged by his excessive mastery of words:

> Pensif, je regardais l'incorruptible airain . . .
> Sa dimension vague, ineffable, spectrale,
> Sortant de l'éternel, entrait dans l'absolu.
> Pour pouvoir mesurer ce tube, il eût fallu
> Prendre la toise au fond du rêve, et la coudée
> Dans la profondeur trouble et sombre de l'idée;
> Un de ses bouts touchait le bien, l'autre le mal;
> Et sa longueur allait de l'homme à l'animal,
> Quoiqu'on ne vît point là d'animal et point d'homme;
> Couché sur terre, il eût joint Éden à Sodome.
>
> Son embouchure, gouffre où plongeait mon regard,
> Cercle de l'Inconnu ténébreux et hagard,
> Pleine de cette horreur que le mystère exhale,
> M'apparaissait ainsi qu'une offre colossale
> D'entrer dans l'ombre où Dieu même est évanoui.
> Cette gueule, avec l'air d'un redoutable ennui
> Morne, s'élargissait sur l'homme et la nature;
> Et cette épouvantable et muette ouverture
> Semblait le bâillement noir de l'éternité.

Reported or invented? The answer matters a great deal. In its absence one can certainly surrender oneself to a shudder – of some magnitude, but which never goes as near the nerve as the *frisson nouveau* which Hugo himself acutely detected in Baudelaire and such as is contained in Baudelaire's *Le Gouffre* or *L'Irrémédiable*.

In a less cosmic vein, Hugo also has his surprises for those who would confine him to the sensual platitude. There is this Blake-like verse to the *Horse*, from *Les Chansons des rues et des bois*:

> Monstre, à présent reprends ton vol.
> Approche que je te déboucle.
> Je te lâche, ôte ton licol,
> Rallume en tes yeux l'escarboucle.

And this from the first stanza of *Crépuscule*, in *Les Contemplations*:

> L'étang mystérieux, suaire aux blanches moires,
> Frissonne: au fond du bois la clairière apparaît;
> Les arbres sont profonds et les branches sont noires;
> Avez-vous vu Vénus à travers la forêt?

And this, which foreshadows Baudelaire:

> Et la vase – fond morne, affreux, sombre et dormant,
> Où des reptiles noirs fourmillent vaguement.
>
> (*Les Rayons et les ombres*)

In justice to Hugo such poems should be even better known, and a considerable volume could be made from them. Taken in isolation and subjected to examination by an expert alienist, they might enable us to decide whether Hugo, who was near the verge of madness in 1855, became or remained technically mad – and not merely in Cocteau's half-joking sense – like his brother Eugène and his daughter Adèle. The usual view is that he recovered most of his sanity after a period of intense spiritual concentration and solitude, with which went adventures into spiritualism (the table-turning seances held in Guernsey) and some initiation into the Oriental religions. In that case, his remarkable self-identification with the forces of nature grew out of a perhaps superficial study of Buddhism, and once again he is the *écho sonore* and not the creative spirit.

Certainly the voice of the earlier Hugo persists, now amplified, in his later poems, and the mere hint of those swelling tones causes the too experienced reader to wince away. Perhaps it will be less apparent to some future generation which, knowing nothing of his biography, having lost three-quarters of his work, and reading what they have in the wrong chronological order, will be inclined to set him without reserve on the level of Virgil and Dante. Hugo badly needs a new 'legend', based quite unscientifically on his work and as little as possible on the known facts of his biography.

V

Hugo never asked or doubted where he stood, but his compatriots have constantly asked the question, not without a certain embarrassment. Gide's 'Le plus grand poète français, hélas,' best sums up their perplexities. Putting aside for the moment the seer, the satyr and the democrat, each of whom deserve their separate admirations, we have a poet who, in spite of his compelling eloquence, suffers from the very serious fault that his verse is static. Except in a small number of his best poems, there is no development from stanza to stanza, or from image to image, but only a constant variation of words and images all expressing the same concept. In Hugo's mind, ideas did not beget ideas: words begat words. He saw his outline too clearly before he began to write and his poems, instead of being a chain or a spiral of discoveries shared by the reader, are one long circling round in search of a better formula. And his megalomania compels him to efface nothing, because his first formulation, as much as his last, was part of Hugo. Ironically enough, he almost obeys Boileau's precept of

> Avant donc que d'écrire, apprenez à penser.

But their kinship is concealed by the immense verbal richness with which Hugo floods and covers the single concept with which he starts and ends. Instead of the organic movement which good poetry ought to have, there is only a series of resounding[1] hammer-blows on the same spot. The stationariness of the concepts contrasted with the mechanically rapid flow of the rhythms and the rhetoric points to a disunity between Hugo's thought and his medium, and is the chief reason why he cannot be considered a supremely great artist.

But is he still, for all his faults, the greatest French poet? He has in him the elements of half a dozen poets, none of whom he surpasses on their own relatively narrow ground. We have pointed to certain foreshadowings or reminiscences of Baudelaire (pp. 136–7), but such passages would be eclipsed or ignored in the work of Baudelaire as a whole. We have quoted examples of Hugo's shorter strophes (pp. 126, 129). If they are compared, purely as technical achievements, with the strophe from Racine on p. 79, it is obvious that Racine was a superior artist. Many of Hugo's verses, particularly in *La Légende des siècles*, have a strong Parnassian tinge, but placed beside the exact and powerful work of Leconte de Lisle their weakness becomes apparent.[2]

As a writer of light poetry Hugo is often charming. Many of his songs have grace and wit, as in:

> Moi, seize ans, et l'air morose,
> Elle, vingt; ses yeux brillaient.
> Les rossignols chantaient Rose,
> Et les merles me sifflaient.

Or, more sentimental:

> Et j'entendais, parmi le thym et le muguet,
> Les vagues violons de la mère Saguet.

But next to Musset, the master of this genre, how heavy and fumbling is Hugo. How pompously he writes to his mistress:

---

[1] They are resounding, wherein he differs from Malherbe (see pp. 54–5.)
[2] Compare the sketch of the eagle in *Masferrer* (*Légende des siècles*, II) with L. de Lisle's *Sommeil du condor*.

Tu peux, comme il te plaît, me faire jeune ou vieux.
Comme le soleil fait serein ou pluvieux
L'azur dont il est l'âme et que sa clarté dore,
Tu peux m'emplir de brume ou m'inonder d'aurore,

while Musset carelessly, almost mockingly, observes:

Oui, femmes, quoi qu'on puisse dire,
Vous avez le fatal pouvoir
De nous jeter par un sourire
Dans l'ivresse ou le désespoir.

Hugo consistently ignores the golden rule of love-poetry, whether light or serious, which is to write of the beloved and not of the lover, and in one more instant we must confront him with a poet who was a master of that art. Hugo writes *A une femme*:

Enfant! si j'étais roi, je donnerais l'empire,
Et mon char, et mon sceptre, et mon peuple à genoux,
Et ma couronne d'or, et mes bains de porphyre,
Et mes flottes, à qui la mer ne peut suffire,
    Pour un regard de vous!

Si j'étais Dieu, la terre et l'air avec les ondes,
Les anges, les démons courbés devant ma loi,
Et le profond chaos aux entrailles fécondes,
L'éternité, l'espace, et les cieux, et les mondes,
    Pour un baiser de toi!

(*Les Feuilles d'automne*)

Ronsard, promising little less, writes in an entirely different spirit and his final sestet saves everything:

Si j'étais Jupiter, maîtresse, vous seriez
Mon épouse Junon; si j'étais roi des ondes,
Vous seriez ma Téthys, reine des eaux profondes,
Et pour votre palais le monde vous auriez.

Si le monde était mien, avec moi vous tiendriez
L'empire de la Terre aux mamelles fécondes,
Et dessus un beau coche, en longues tresses blondes,
Par le peuple en honneur Déesse vous iriez.

Mais je ne suis pas Dieu, et si[1] ne le puis être;
Le ciel pour vous servir seulement m'a fait naître,
De vous seule je prends mon sort aventureux.

[1] *Si = ainsi.* 'Thus (or this) I can never be.'

> Vous êtes tout mon bien, mon mal, et ma fortune:
> S'il vous plaît de m'aimer, je deviendrai Neptune,
> Tout Jupiter, tout roi, tout riche et tout heureux.

Yet to conclude that Hugo was jack-of-all-trades and master of none would be an absurd underestimate. He attempted more things than he achieved successfully, yet in his totality he was unlike any other poet and in his own speciality – the voice of Jupiter-Prometheus – he could be magnificent. Perhaps as the nineteenth century recedes still further from us and takes on more of the attributes of a teeming, boisterous second Renaissance, Hugo will be prized as its most perfect representative.

Chapter 13

Alfred de Musset

THE PERSONALITY and work of Musset offer a strong contrast to those of Hugo, yet he is less read than he deserves by those who find Hugo over-heavy. Verlaine, Laforgue, even Apollinaire have all reaped some benefit from the reaction, while Musset remains half-neglected, his poems slipped – as in his own time and so unsuitably – 'under the ribbons in the sewing-basket'.

He was born in 1810 of an old family which originated in the Vendômois. Among his ancestors his biographers have been able to place Ronsard's Cassandre Salviati, while his great-grandmother was a Du Bellay. These distant connections with literature become more precise in his father, a cultivated official in the War Ministry. He was an authority on J.-J. Rousseau, on whom he published a book.

The young Musset glanced very briefly at the law, medicine and a business career before deciding that literature was his true vocation. At eighteen he was admitted, an elegant and brilliant youth, to the *Cénacle* which revolved round Hugo. He had just published his first poems in reviews and at the same age he made a free translation of De Quincey's *Opium Eater*. In 1830 came *Les Contes d'Espagne et d'Italie*, which were his *Orientales*, but also contained pieces of independent or more playful tendencies, such as *Les Marrons du feu* and *Mardoche*. It was already obvious that he was not going to follow tamely in the steps of Hugo, but what would he be?

The question was not entirely resolved in the next three years, during which he wrote *Namouna*, *Les Secrètes Pensées de Rafaël*, and *Rolla* – on which poems the strongest single influence was Byron – and *Le Spectacle dans un fauteuil*, which contained two short plays intended only for reading. At this time he was leading a life of precocious debauch, provoked by, but also increasing his nervous instability. He realized that he must somehow break the vicious circle before it sterilized his talent. 'Je sens qu'il me manque encore je ne sais quoi,' he confessed to his elder brother Paul. 'Est-ce un grand amour? Est-ce un malheur? Peut-être tous deux.'

The double requirement was met by his liaison with the novelist George Sand which began in the summer of 1833 and was finally broken off in the spring of 1835. During that stormy period the couple travelled to Italy where Musset fell ill and found on recovering that his mistress had fallen in love with his doctor, the Venetian Pagello. Back in Paris, the relationship was resumed, but became more than ever a clash of two tempestuous and supremely egoistic temperaments. Much has been written about the insatiable sensuality of George Sand and it is obvious that Musset, who was six years younger than her, was no match for her. But when they first met he was by no means an inexperienced adolescent and his hysterical nature was such that almost any woman would have had difficulty in living with him in harmony. The 'wounds' which he suffered in the affair were largely self-inflicted.

The only certain profit was for Musset's art. The experience directly inspired his group of serious poems *Les Nuits* (1835–7), on which his chief claim to greatness rests, and also his autobiographical novel, *La Confession d'un enfant du siècle*. In an outburst of creative activity he wrote in the one year 1834 his three most important plays, *Lorenzaccio*, *Fantasio* and *On ne badine pas avec l'amour*.

By the age of thirty Musset was practically burnt out. Though strictly he cannot be included in the long list of Romantic poets who died young – since he lived until 1857 – in effect he gave almost all he had in some ten years. After this he was pathetically conscious of a growing lethargy caused by his enfeebled health, his alcoholism and his disgust with the bitter taste of life, which his palate never matured sufficiently to appreciate. His *Poésies nouvelles*, published in 1852, contained few poems of interest later than *Une Soirée perdue* and *Simone*, both written in 1840.

Some pleasure came to him, however, from his delayed success as a playwright. After the failure of his one-act comedy, *La Nuit vénitienne*, on the stage of the Odéon in 1830, he had decided to write plays for publication only. Most of them appeared in *La Revue des deux mondes* between 1833 and 1837 without exciting any great interest. But in 1846 a French actress on tour at St Petersburg performed one of them – *Un Caprice* – before the Imperial Court as an experiment. It was so successful that on her return to Paris she asked for the others and the next few years saw most of Musset's shorter plays produced at the Comédie-Française. They are now as integral a part of the répertoire as Marivaux and Molière.

This recognition of his work encouraged Musset to write a few more of his *Comédies et proverbes*, including *On ne saurait penser à tout*.

He is also the author of a dozen short stories and *nouvelles*, among them *Fréderic et Bernerette*, *L'Histoire d'un merle blanc* and *Mimi Pinson*, the most typical of his outlook and period. Its pathos is novelettish but its fancy can be found amusing. The finest example of his teasing humour is in the *Lettres de Dupuis et Cotonet* (1836–7). In these four letters to the editor of the *Revue des deux mondes*, ostensibly written by two provincial seekers after truth and culture, Musset brilliantly derides the literary and social catchphrases of his day, and indirectly shows himself an acute critic. As a gently satirical review of the ideas current during the most active years of the French Romantic movement, by a man who lived through them, the *Lettres* are as enlightening as they are entertaining.

II

The mixed nature of Musset's talent appears most clearly in his sequence of big serious poems, *Les Nuits*, which can be roughly described as the product of an eighteenth-century intelligence crossed with a nineteenth-century sensibility. The sequence begins with *La Nuit de mai*, written in May 1835, and continues with *La Nuit de décembre* (1835), *d'août* (1836), and *d'octobre* (1837). To the same group, and completing the story of the same emotional crisis, belong *La Lettre à Lamartine* (February 1836), *L'Espoir en Dieu* (February 1838), and *Souvenir* (September 1840).

Two months after the final break with George Sand, Musset walked under the chestnut trees in the Tuileries, treading on perhaps exactly the same ground that Racine had paced as he walked there over a hundred and fifty years before declaiming the still molten verse of *Mithridate*. Then he went home, called for all the available candles in the house to be lit and taken to his room, and worked among them until morning on the composition of his poem. If we did not know that *La Nuit de mai* was composed in this way, we could almost deduce it. Such a poem would be launched in an illumination and finished in a fever. Once begun, it sings itself on inevitably, and there is little that the author can afterwards do to correct or change it. In form it is a dialogue between the Muse and the Poet – as are all the *Nuits*, except *La Nuit de décembre*. It contains the master-theme of them all – that a good poet must have had experience of suffering:

> Quel que soit le souci que ta jeunesse endure,
> Laisse-la s'élargir, cette sainte blessure

> Que les noirs sérafins t'ont faite au fond du cœur;
> Rien ne nous rend si grands qu'une grande douleur.

The enthusiasm of the spring-drunk Muse, eager to express her rapture, is opposed to the muteness of the Poet, too broken to respond. These artificial-looking figures stand for something much deeper than a literary convention. The Muse can be taken as the Ideal Woman, the *âme sœur* of nearly all the Romantics, but more properly this is a debate between Musset's natural vitality, beginning to reassert itself after his emotional buffeting by George Sand, and his despair which he is beginning to realize and define. Unless one objects to the dialogue form as such in poetry, it is difficult to object to Musset's useful device.

In *La Nuit de décembre*, it is winter. The theme of despair has moved up into full focus. The Muse is absent, and in her place is a mysterious black-clad double who has appeared to the poet at all the critical moments of his life, particularly the saddest ones:

> Partout où j'ai voulu dormir,
> Partout où j'ai voulu mourir,
> Partout où j'ai touché la terre,
> Sur ma route est venu s'asseoir
> Un malheureux vêtu de noir,
> Qui me ressemblait comme un frère.

This *Doppelgänger* (an early example of a figure soon to be familiar in literature – as in E. A. Poe's *William Wilson*) seems to have been an actual hallucination which Musset experienced at least once. It seems to have been less consciously conjured up than the White Lady who appeared to Victor Hugo in Guernsey, or the visions which just eluded Vigny. But it also admits of the most ordinary symbolical explanations, and could be taken simply as a mental projection of the grief-absorbed poet weeping *from outside* over his own sufferings.

As though feeling that an inner dialogue is not enough, Musset addresses his next poem in the sequence to Lamartine. As Lamartine had once turned to Byron (in *L'Homme*, in *Les Méditations*), Musset now looks to Lamartine, his elder in poetry and in suffering, and pours out to him the story of his tormented heart. The poem opens with a superb flourish and, though it seems longer than the theme justifies, it is irreducible. Like *La Nuit de mai*, *La Lettre à Lamartine* moves forward in a single, sustained flow, too organic to be cut without crippling it. In the five final quatrains it raises itself to one of the most moving climaxes in French poetry:

Créature d'un jour qui t'agites une heure,
De quoi viens-tu te plaindre et qui te fait gémir?
Ton âme t'inquiète, et tu crois qu'elle pleure:
Ton âme est immortelle, et tes pleurs vont tarir.

Tu te sens le cœur pris d'un caprice de femme,
Et tu dis qu'il se brise à force de souffrir.
Tu demandes à Dieu de soulager ton âme:
Ton âme est immortelle et ton cœur va guérir.

Le regret d'un instant te trouble et te dévore;
Tu dis que le passé te voile l'avenir.
Ne te plains pas d'hier, laisse venir l'aurore:
Ton âme est immortelle, et le temps va s'enfuir.

Ton corps est abattu du mal de ta pensée;
Tu sens ton front peser et tes genoux fléchir.
Tombe, agenouille-toi, créature insensée;
Ton âme est immortelle et la mort va venir.

Tes os dans le cercueil vont tomber en poussière,
Ta mémoire, ton nom, ta gloire vont périr,
Mais non pas ton amour, si ton amour t'est chère;
Ton âme est immortelle, et va s'en souvenir.

After this, Musset returns to *Les Nuits*, though his mood is now less closely linked to the calendar. *La Nuit d'août* is really a spring or early-summer poem, and is best appreciated when read as the counterpart of *La Nuit de mai*. This time it is the poet who, having partly recovered from his original despair, announces that he intends to love elsewhere and, if necessary, to suffer again. The Muse tries to dissuade him, telling him that he will wear out his heart and his poetic talent in these exhausting experiences. Here, of course, was the hub of Musset's dilemma, the tragic either – or against which he beat out his vitality. Without emotional and sensual excitement he had no sensation of living and no stimulus to write. With it, he knew that his energy and his interest in life must dwindle year by year like a *peau de chagrin*. This inescapable dilemma – and not a spoilt-child screaming for one particular woman – forms the tragic heart of the *Nuits* poems. It explains their intensity, their impatience, their exaggerations of emotion, for – as Musset too lucidly saw – time and youth were running out, and his was not a nature capable of recollecting emotion in tranquillity.

As though to prove it, he writes *La Nuit d'octobre*, in which he begins by saying that he has at last recovered from the sickness which almost destroyed him, and can now recall its details dispassionately. The Muse hesitates, doubting whether his wounds are really healed, and her doubts are justified when the poet works himself into a new frenzy of grief and abhorrence for the woman who betrayed him. He ends, however, in a calmer mood, resolved to forgive and forget and to be reborn, with nature and the sun, to new joys. Biographically, this was a pathetic illusion.

L'Espoir en Dieu, which follows the four *Nuits*, is a hurried search for a philosophical or religious faith to replace Musset's lost emotional enthusiasms, but the real epilogue is provided by *Souvenir*, written after a visit to the Forest of Fontainebleau where the poet had once walked with George Sand. The appeasement of which he had spoken prematurely in *La Nuit d'octobre* has now really come to him. He can bury his bitterness but still keep as a secure possession the memory of his one great passion. But with this calmness there has come an evident decline in poetic force. *Souvenir* is inferior to *Les Nuits* as well as less original, for it carries many echoes of Lamartine's *Le Lac*, which it partly resembles in form. No doubt Musset had meant to add to the older poet without precisely imitating him, but the comparison brings out a new flabbiness and lack of spontaneity in Musset's verse which would have been unthinkable three or four years earlier.

These poems, then, are the record of the effects of a violent emotional experience upon a highly sensitive and unstable temperament. They combine an intensity of personal feeling and an undisguised exposure of the poet's *moi* with a certain artificiality in the form and idiom. In them, Musset writes as the Romantics would have liked to picture Chénier writing had he lived on into the nineteenth century to compose verse contemporary with Chateaubriand's prose and hereditary to Rousseau's. In short, he was the poet who was missing in the Napoleonic era. But writing when he did, in a decade of bourgeois sentimentality from which Hugo had already swept the neo-classic ornamentation, his verse was too readily accepted as the outpourings of a simple heart own brother to the midinette's. The artifice, the style, the distinctive stamp were lost sight of, and only the tear-provoking sentiments were seen. If Musset is considered, because of *Les Nuits*, as the poet-patron of self-pity, it was largely his own fault, yet many of his imitators and admirers overlooked the stiffening framework, the stylization of sorrow which distinguishes these poems from, say, a Dickensian death-bed scene. There is an essential dis-

tinction – though Musset does not invariably observe it – between an
artist's pride in his suffering because it brings him good artistic material
and an unorganized clamour of grief.

III

The rest of Musset's work contains little that resembles *Les Nuits* at
all closely; its distinguishing marks are lightness, grace and wit. These
qualities were the product of several influences, from Byron's in the
early poems to La Fontaine's, Chénier's and then the spirit of the
eighteenth century more generally in his later verse. But however
numerous his – freely acknowledged – masters, Musset used them only
as a basis for work which is quite distinctive and full of small but delightful surprises.

Much of it is written in the form of sonnets, *rondeaux* and short song-
poems such as *La Chanson de Fortunio, J'ai dit à mon cœur, à mon
faible cœur...*, *Fut-il jamais douceur de cœur pareille...*, *Tristesse,
Mimi Pinson, A M. Victor Hugo, A Sainte-Beuve.* These poems are
intentionally insubstantial and their point must be taken at once or
not at all. Only pedantry would stop to analyse it. But in such longer
poems as *Mardoche, Namouna, Une Bonne Fortune,* the wit is more
sustained. The first two were offshoots of Byron's *Don Juan,* whose
tone only Musset really succeeded in echoing in France:

> J'ai connu, l'an dernier, un jeune homme nommé
> Mardoche, qui vivait jour et nuit enfermé.
> O prodige! il n'avait jamais lu de sa vie
> Le *Journal de Paris,* ni n'en avait envie.
> Il n'avait vu ni Kean, ni Bonaparte, ni
> Monsieur de Metternich; quand il avait fini
> De souper, se couchait, précisément à l'heure
> Où (quand par le brouillard la chatte rôde et pleure)
> Monsieur Hugo va voir mourir Phébus le blond.
> Vous dire ses parents, cela serait trop long.

Hassan, the young hero of *Namouna,* sits in his emptying bath while
the 'green-eyed naiad' of the water slips out down the waste:

> Un silence parfait règne dans cette histoire,
> Sur les bras du jeune homme et sur ses pieds d'ivoire.
> La naïade aux yeux verts pleurait en le quittant.
> On entendait à peine au fond de la baignoire
> Glisser l'eau fugitive, et d'instant en instant
> Les robinets d'airain chanter en s'égouttant.

This poem is worth reading rapidly, or rather reads itself, through the whole length of its 147 stanzas.

Une Bonne Fortune contains such lines as:

> Il faut en convenir, l'antique Modestie
> Faisait bâiller son monde, et nous n'y tenions plus.
> Grâce à Dieu, pour New-York elle est enfin partie . . .

and in many less expected places Musset's impish wit breaks through. It has none of the violence of paradox or the obviousness of the Wildean epigram, but ripples quietly over the surface of verse which reads more like familiar conversation than like fully dressed poetry. It is compounded of many small qualities, of which perhaps the most striking is Musset's beautifully appropriate handling of proper names. This appears in the poem *Dupont et Durand*, which recounts the story of a pair more drab but no less idiotic than Dupuis and Cotonet. It is also found in such serious poems as *Le Saule*:

> Il se fit tout à coup le plus profond silence
> Quand Georgina Smollen se leva pour chanter . . .

and in the Muse's suggestions for escape from reality in *La Nuit de mai*:

> Inventons quelque part des lieux où l'on oublie;
> Partons, nous sommes seuls, l'univers est à nous.
> Voici la verte Écosse et la brune Italie,
> Et la Grèce, ma mère, où le miel est si doux,
> Argos, et Ptéléon, ville des hécatombes,
> Et Messa la divine, agréable aux colombes;
> Et le front chevelu du Pélion changeant;
> Et le bleu Titarèse, et le golfe d'argent
> Qui montre dans ses eaux, où le cygne se mire,
> La blanche Oloossone à la blanche Camyre.

There is more than an echo here of Chénier's verse, whether of:

> . . . N'invoquent, au milieu de la tourmente amère,
> La blanche Galatée et la blanche Néère,
>
> (*Bucoliques*)

or of his third *Élégie*, where the Muses perform exactly the same function for the poet, but in a less urgently feverish spirit than in Musset:

> O mes Muses, c'est vous; vous mon premier amour,
> Vous qui m'avez aimé dès que j'ai vu le jour.
> . . . Elles viennent! leur voix, leur aspect me rassure:
> Leur chant mélodieux assoupit ma blessure;

Je me fuis, je m'oublie, et mes esprits distraits
Se plaisent à les suivre et retrouvent la paix.
Par vous, Muses, par vous, franchissant les collines,
Soit que j'aime l'aspect des campagnes Sabines,
Soit Catile ou Falerne et leurs riches coteaux,
Ou l'air de Blandusie et l'azur de ses eaux:
Par vous de l'Anio j'admire le rivage,
Par vous de Tivoli le poétique ombrage,
. . . Par vous, mon âme, au gré de ses illusions,
Vole et franchit les temps, les mers, les nations.

But there is no parallel in Chénier to Musset's humour. Much of it
is 'period', reflecting the assumed detachment of the dandy of the
1830s, whose motto might have been *Surtout, pas de sérieux*, but who
was only half cured of *René* and the *mal du siècle* and was ironically
aware of the old dichotomy of body and spirit experienced also by
Villon and by the 'baroque' Sponde:

L'âme et le corps, hélas, ils iront deux à deux,
Tant que le monde ira – pas à pas, côte à côte,
Comme s'en vont les vers classiques et les bœufs,
L'un disant: 'Tu fais mal!' et l'autre: 'C'est ta faute!'
Ah! misérable hôtesse et plus misérable hôte!
Ce n'est vraiment pas vrai que tout soit pour le mieux.

If Musset has dated in places, in others he remains very fresh, and
in any case the reader is carried on by the rapid movement of his verse.
This feature distinguishes him markedly from Hugo, and often from
Vigny. It can be studied as a technical quality and related to the great
variety of metres which Musset handled and his ingenuity in linking
'natural' speech with complicated rhyme-patterns, as few French
poets except La Fontaine had done before him. Thus, the six-line
stanzas of *Namouna* are rhymed in some ten different ways. *Les
Nuits* show a mobility of metre and a variety of rhyme-changes which
make them comparable to *Lycidas* in their forward-moving effect. But
this is not only a matter of technique – indeed Musset disclaimed all
pretension to studied effects, insisting that he wrote purely as an
amateur when the mood came to him. It rests on some mysterious
quality inherent in the poet's mind, or his ear, or even his respiratory
system. As Milton wrote most naturally not in couplets, or in quatrains,
but in long soaring verse-paragraphs, Musset also, in his less sublime
way, spins out his verse in integrated paragraphs. For example, the
first seven lines of *La Lettre à Lamartine* are one sentence, conceived

F

and expressed in a single piece, with no forcing of the rhymes or meddling with the normal word-order:

> Lorsque le grand Byron allait quitter Ravenne
> Et chercher sur les mers quelque plage lointaine
> Où finir en héros son immortel ennui,
> Comme ie était assis aux pieds de sa maîtresse,
> Pâle et déjà tourné du côté de la Grèce,
> Celle qu'il appelait alors sa Guiccioli
> Ouvrit un soir un livre où l'on parlait de lui.

The confident march of Musset's style is too easily obscured by the pathos of his subject. Here is a man who seems to be humiliating himself in language more suitable for defiance. But when it is remembered that he was proud to exhibit his suffering, the contradiction disappears.

In one other respect he equals, or sometimes excels, the three other great Romantics. His use of imagery is as bold as in any of them, but more varied and often more apposite. In his early work he writes of monks at a funeral as

> Les moines, s'agitant comme de noirs cyprès,

of the moon seen above a steeple as

> La lune,
> Comme un point sur un i,

or, to return to *La Nuit de mai*, writes of all tormented poets:

> Leurs déclamations sont comme des épées:
> Elles tracent dans l'air un cercle éblouissant,
> Mais il y pend toujours quelque goutte de sang.

But, unlike more luscious-sounding poets, he was not carried away by his imagery. His use of it was discreet, varied and controlled. He has nothing comparable to that eternal contrasting of the cradle and the tomb, the dawn and the sunset, which obsessed Hugo. Yet on the other hand, when he used metaphors he developed them to the full, drawing in all their implications, and so he cannot be thought of as a forerunner of the Symbolists. In his treatment of imagery he falls between Hugo and Verlaine and, unless it is recognized that there is a third place for him, he disappears.

That would be more than a pity. It would leave French Romantic poetry without humour. It would mean that for lightness and grace in the expression of personal passion we should have to go back to the sixteenth century, or else forward some forty years. Musset was a necessary poet in his generation. Still better, he was an unexpected one.

Chapter 14

Charles Baudelaire

BAUDELAIRE once observed that one should read Musset only in adolescence, obviously having done so. A more than casual resemblance between the two men is easily overlooked by reason of the vast influence which Baudelaire was to exercise on future poets eager to cultivate every seed he had sown, whereas Musset remained more or less blocked in his period. Yet some of the temperamental and circumstantial resemblances are sufficiently striking to suggest that one approach to Baudelaire is to regard him as a Musset who became adult very early, who recognized and faced his destiny and, rather than toy with illusory hope, constructed a scheme of things for his own use. This scheme embraced not only an 'artificial paradise' but also an artificial hell – both necessary elaborations in his attempt to control by form, of which he was a master, the nauseating spiritual anarchy which otherwise would have overwhelmed him. In this sense art, which for Musset was an overloading of pressure, for Baudelaire was a girding-up for salvation. This is at the root of their different attitudes towards poetry and of the divergent results they achieved.

Both poets died miserably in their middle forties after lives of excess which rapidly ruined their already vitiated constitutions. Both craved inordinately for sensual and cerebral excitement, had recourse to drugs or alcohol as both stimulants and opiates, and incidentally both admired and translated De Quincey. Both, as a result of the nervous tensions under which they lived, were perverse – that is, they went out of their way to flout received opinion, in small things as in big, rather than ignore it. Both contrived to show some detachment through humour, though Musset's humour is irresponsible, Baudelaire's sardonic. Both were attracted by 'dandyism', which might be broadly defined as a convention-sanctioned fastidiousness fortified by impeccable tailoring: e.g. a conformist Byron or an aesthetically minded Guards officer. For Musset this desire to belong to some sort of élite was principally a social attitude, adopted in the 1830s when it was really fashionable. For Baudelaire, ten years later, it was a personal discipline adopted to combat his natural instincts and the horror which he felt lay beneath them.

'The dandy', he writes in *Mon Cœur mis à nu*, 'should aspire to be sublime without respite. He should live and sleep before a mirror.' And nearby: 'Woman is the opposite of the dandy. . . . Woman is *natural*, i.e. abominable.' This, which may appear as a desperately contrived narcissism, is part of a larger system of introspection which, for Baudelaire as for Musset, focuses the whole universe in a single well of personality. Everything is in it – self, God, Satan, humanity – a loathsome mixture. Finally, Musset's insistence on suffering is echoed by Baudelaire in a somewhat wider sense. He seems to see it not only as a condition of poetry but as a condition of all humanity – from which, however, he would exclude Monsieur Prudhomme and similar wearers of the *Légion d'honneur*. It is true that between Musset's

> Rien ne nous rend *si grands* qu'une grande douleur

and Baudelaire's

> Soyez béni, mon Dieu, qui donnez la souffrance
> Comme *un divin remède à nos impuretés* –

there appears to lie the world of difference between the humanist's horizon and the religious man's. Yet, properly considered, the difference narrows when Baudelaire continues:

> Et comme la meilleure et la plus pure essence
> *Qui prépare les forts aux saintes voluptés,*

since one of the *saintes voluptés* might well be a merited consciousness of superiority. In short, the parallel can be maintained for a considerable distance without breaking down, and if it were of interest no doubt it could be demonstrated that the poet Baudelaire contained, or was capable of containing, the poet Musset. The point, however, is not there, but in the proposition that Baudelaire contained Romanticism and nothing else that was not already explicit or implied in other Romantic writers. If by some fearful accident French culture and poetry had been cut short soon after Baudelaire's death – say by the Franco-Prussian War and its aftermath – there would be no difficulty whatever in seeing his work as the crown and epitome of the Romantic movement, and Baudelaire himself as the last and greatest of the French Romantics.

As it is, continuous lines can be traced from him to the Parnassians (regard for formal excellence – though this is only one aspect of his much wider art), to the Symbolists (poetry as music, as evocation, and the 'correspondences' between the senses and the material and ideal worlds), to the Surrealists ('correspondences' again, the importance of dreams, the sometimes arbitrary introduction of the macabre). Since the 1880s until today, Baudelaire has been claimed as the chief master of 'modern' poetry. It is at least not difficult to consider him as the greatest of the French nineteenth-century poets and the most comprehensive, in spite of his restricted output; and, ranging over the whole rich field of post-medieval poetry, to place him beside Ronsard, Racine and Rimbaud as one of the supreme representatives of the poetic art in France.

II

His biography provides a pasture-ground for the psychologist, who can find in it almost everything that makes life not worth living. He was born in Paris in 1821. When he was six he lost his father, a sexagenarian civil servant who had been a friend of the *Idéologues* – the last representatives of eighteenth-century rationalism. His young mother, whom he adored, soon remarried a brilliant officer and diplomat, Major Aupick, who later became a general and was French Ambassador in Constantinople and Madrid. Aupick did nothing to soften the feeling of intrusion which the small boy inevitably experienced and his social and military qualities increased the antagonism between the two as Baudelaire grew older. After unhappy schooldays at Lyons (where Aupick was stationed) and at the Lycée Louis-le-Grand in Paris, from which he was expelled, Baudelaire was offered a diplomatic career but refused, insisting on literature. He was left for a time to his own devices, led a Bohemian existence in the Latin Quarter, and at that time probably contracted the venereal disease which contributed to embitter his life. When he was twenty, his stepfather packed him off in the captain's care on a voyage to India, but Baudelaire left the ship at Réunion and returned home. Though he evidently detested the voyage at the time, it gave him an experience of the sea and of exotic scenes which was to re-emerge effectively in his poetry.

On his return he was of age. He demanded his whole share in his father's inheritance, took and furnished an elegant flat on the Île Saint-Louis (part of the ancient centre of Paris) and began to lead the life of artificial refinement which he connected with the 'dandy'.[1] He took as a

---

[1] The same impulse, which, heavily loaded with literary invention, forty years later inspired Huysman's *A rebours* (1884) and hence Wilde's *Picture of Dorian Gray*.

mistress Jeanne Duval, a half-caste woman of low origins and mentality, the 'Black Venus' of his poems. He kept her with him for most of
his life, linked to her by a sense of duty long after the perhaps perverse
attraction she had exercised was dead.

Two years of luxurious living almost exhausted his capital. The
debris was taken over by trustees, who doled him out a small monthly
income of 200 francs (about £10) for the remainder of his life. Henceforth he was engaged in a continual struggle against poverty and debt
which he was never within sight of winning by his literary work. At
the age of twenty-four he contemplated, and perhaps seriously attempted, suicide. At about the same date he began to use drugs
(laudanum and opium). He published in reviews the first of his remarkable essays in art criticism – the *Salons* of 1845 and 1846 – and began
writing some of the poems which were to appear later in *Les Fleurs du
mal*. Soon after he discovered the work of Edgar Allan Poe, which led
to one of the most remarkable cases of transferred identity in literature.
That Scève should partially take over Petrarch or Boileau should
appropriate Horace can be explained as examples of imitation wedded
to some conscious exploitation of already established prestige. But for
Baudelaire, Poe seemed both the man and the artist which he himself
was groping to be – or, rather, to define. His desperate search for a
personality could concentrate, in his middle twenties, round this distant figure, with whose tragic and 'Satanic' destiny (as he conceived
it) he could intimately sympathize, in whose *Tales of Mystery and
Imagination* he found 'an insatiable love of the Beautiful which had
assumed the potency of a morbid passion', and whom he revered, as
Mallarmé was to do later, as a perfectionist in art, 'whom a single false
note tortured'. Most commentators have realized that this was a characterization of Baudelaire far more than of Poe and have still not been
able to conceal their wonder that the well-nigh impeccable artist of the
Fleurs de mal (and the declared disciple of Théophile Gautier) should
have esteemed the doggerel of *For Annie* or of *The Raven*:

> Much I marvelled this ungainly fowl to hear discourse so plainly,
> Though its answer little meaning – little relevancy bore;
> For we cannot help agreeing that no living human being
> Ever yet was blest with seeing bird above his chamber door –
> Bird or beast upon the sculptured bust above his chamber door,
> With such name as 'Nevermore'.

But it came to him in a foreign language, and he was no doubt able
to believe that Poe's verse was a successful application of Poe's aesthetic

doctrine as set out in his critical writings: that poetry is not utilitarian, is independent of moral values, and is the product of conscious and careful workmanship rather than of 'inspiration'. Baudelaire at once set out to translate Poe's prose *Tales* – whose quality is so much higher than that of his verse – and published three volumes of them (*Histoires extraordinaires*, etc.) in 1856, 1857 and 1865. But on his poems, when they appeared, the direct influence of Poe's work was extremely slight, and it is hard to believe that the *Fleurs du mal* would have been much different if he had never read the American.

Some of these poems date from before 1844. Other appeared in reviews between 1850 and 1855. For some time Baudelaire, encouraged by Madame Sabatier, a charming and cultured *demi-mondaine* (his 'White Venus') to whom he became attached, had been planning to publish them in book form. In 1857 he found a publisher in his friend, Poulet-Malassis. Two months later author and publisher appeared before a Paris court, following a newspaper protest against the *Fleurs du mal*, and six of the poems were condemned as harmful to public morality. They were ordered to be deleted from the book and Baudelaire was fined 300 francs and costs. This ridiculously petty prosecution can be ascribed to an excess of civic virtue displayed by the press – watchful, as always, against corruptive influences – by the courts and by the general public in a self-consciously respectable period. Earlier in the same year Flaubert's *Madame Bovary* had been the object of a similar, but unsuccessful, prosecution.

That his work should be condemned for the wrong reasons by those whose judgement in both art and morality he most despised, was a cutting blow to Baudelaire. His attitude towards his judges, and more generally towards the whole uniformed public, is expressed with characteristic outspokenness in his journal:

All these imbeciles of the bourgeoisie who constantly repeat the words 'immoral, immorality, immorality in art' and comparable idiocies remind me of Louise Villedieu, a five-franc tart I once took to the Louvre, where she had never been before. She began to blush, to cover her eyes and, pulling continually at my sleeve, asked me before the immortal pictures and statues how it was possible to display such indecencies in public.

Four years later Baudelaire published an entirely new edition of the *Fleurs du mal*, excluding the condemned poems and correcting the others and rearranging their order. This edition has provided the main basis for modern editors, who tend to see a general design in the whole book and quote in support Baudelaire's own remark that 'this is not simply an album'. While this is true, the fact that it has some architecture is not of the first importance. It cannot be read as a spiritual sequence like the work of Petrarch or of Scève and the reader's gain in attempting to do so is not very great. Baudelaire did not live to see a further collected edition through the press, but published separately *Les Épaves* (1866), containing particularly the condemned poems, and *Les Nouvelles Fleurs du mal* (1866), which included ten new pieces, among them *Examen de minuit* and the famous sonnets *Recueillement* and *Le Gouffre*. Adding his juvenilia and a few occasional and bawdy pieces, his whole verse production consists of some two hundred poems in all. None is very long and many are of sonnet length.

He contributed to an innovation in his *Petits poèmes en prose*, on which he worked during the last ten years of his life and which were published in complete form posthumously (1869). But, although he conceived the prose poem and wrote a few good examples of it, a number of these short pieces are imaginative or symbolic anecdotes written in straightforward prose. He does not attain the dreamlike quality of Nerval's novel *Aurélia* or the lyrical concentration of Rimbaud's *Illuminations*, which last remains the most perfect nineteenth-century example of the genre.

His other prose works include *Les Paradis artificiels* (1860), in which he introduced and enlarged on De Quincey; his critical writings on painting, literature and music (*Curiosités esthétiques* and *L'Art romantique*) and his journals (*Fusées* and *Mon Cœur mis à nu*) which give the best possible key to his mind and character.

To return to the external events of 1857. In that year General Aupick died and Baudelaire drew closer, as far as lay in his nature, to his mother. She responded as well as she could and deprived herself to meet his constant calls for money. From that year also Baudelaire was a sick man; at times he felt the wind of madness blowing over him, but he never quite fell into that – for him – most terrible abyss of all. In 1863 he undertook a disastrous tour in Belgium. With failing powers, he remained in that country for three years, then he had a stroke which left him half-paralysed and speechless. He was brought back to Paris where he died a year later, on 31 August 1867. Towards the end he could neither articulate his words nor write them, yet seems to have retained his mental lucidity.[1] His mother, whom he had adored, then

---

[1] For a medical summing-up:
'Baudelaire was not insane in the strict sense of the word. His intelligence, even when impaired, remained superior to that of the average Frenchman; until death, he retained his power of self-criticism. No signs of delirium have been noted in him, except for the nocturnal episode related by Catulle Mendès [when Baudelaire had identified himself with

hated, then forgave, and had cruelly but not deliberately tormented, saw him buried in the Cimetière Montparnasse. She survived him for four years, having helped to arrange for an edition of his complete works which would preserve his memory. But it is doubtful whether she ever realized his genius as a writer or understood that his art alone had saved him from complete collapse as a human being.

III

Until quite recently responsible historians of literature could present Baudelaire as a kind of early Toulouse-Lautrec, moving in a Parisian dream-underworld in which the criminal and the courtesan rub shoulders with the grave-digger. The back of the music-hall opens on to the cemetery, like the tavern in Villon. But before you get there you must pass through eye-splitting perspectives of pink and black, rooms of incredible dilapidation tenanted by moustached harpies, fungous alleys haunted by cats, boudoirs rancid with rotting flowers, the whole evening tour of tawdry vice. These, it is true, are the hallmarks of much of Baudelaire's poetry, and not only of the section which he grouped as *Tableaux parisiens*. Enlarging the quest a little, we find the vampire bat, Lucifer, and a majestically defiant Satan – all the trappings, it would appear, of Black Romanticism. This gamey atmosphere of evil is Baudelaire's most immediately striking feature, particularly to the adolescent reader. (Adolescence is the time to begin reading him, provided he is not dropped afterwards, for recollection alone in later life will leave an entirely false impression.)

Even at that, it is a considerable triumph, which might be summarized as: Out of this dunghill we pluck this orchid, Beauty. The corruption of what he understood as 'modern life' gave him his local colour, deliberately preferred by him to evocations of remoter settings – the medieval, the oriental or the biblical. It is so well rendered, by subtly mingled description and suggestion, that it gives his work the localization it needs, without sacrificing the 'strangeness' which, following Poe, he considered indispensable to poetry. Moreover Paris, the inexhaustible modern city, was for him what nature was for such Romantics as Lamartine. Incapable, as he admitted, of 'shedding tears over vegetation', he could find in the sounds and sights of Paris the

Gérard de Nerval and had screamed that he was not mad and had not killed himself] which belongs rather to the nightmare; no states of mental disturbance, no marked perturbations of the mechanism of thought. We will conclude that he bordered on insanity.' Dr R. Trial, *La Maladie de Baudelaire: Étude médico-psychologique* (Paris, 1926).

same exhilaration that other poets derived from the mountain or the desert. And even here nature of a sort filtered through in sunsets, moonlight, fogs and rain.

This décor, then, powerfully realized and fully integrated into his verse, is the entrance to Baudelaire – but only that. Further in is the Inhabitant, at first sight matching the entrance, a voluptuary – surely? – looking for every kind of sensual pleasure but always driven to mix into it some morbid imagining. An intellectual sadism, a thought of death in its most repugnant forms, a reminder that beauty and happiness are not for a moment secure – are these the seasonings invented by a perverse refinement to heighten pleasure, or are they a poison which runs in the poet's veins, and so irremediable?

Surely the second. It is quite inadequate to consider Baudelaire as a distorted libertine, however shudderingly picturesque, or as a superficial Romantic turned sour. He has been seen, on the contrary, as a deeply religious man, deprived perhaps of grace, and in the theological terms he himself would have approved, he certainly felt in his own flesh the pricking of original sin, the bitterness of the Fall repeated in each new individual and the unholy allurements of Satan which precede it. He aspires, falls back and regrets with a heavy remorse which envelops his own life and that of the other human beings implicated in it:

> Je suis un cimetière abhorré de la lune,
> Où comme des remords se traînent de longs vers
> Qui s'acharnent toujours sur mes morts les plus chers.

This fundamental part of his nature is expressed in the well-known entry in his journal: 'There are in every man at every moment two simultaneous aspirations, one towards God, the other towards Satan. The urge towards God, or *spirituality*, is a desire to rise; the urge towards Satan, or *animality*, is a joy in descent.' *A joy*. That was the rub, and it also explains why Baudelaire always remained within the limits of humanity. There could never be a Saint Baudelaire. But another passage in the journal, written certainly when he was no longer young, reveals better the efforts of a sick and struggling man to rise above his difficulties. It shows a childlike simplicity which cannot be reconciled with the idea of an immoral sensationalist. Representing his spiritual and practical preoccupations when he was about forty, it is headed *Hygiene, Conduct, Method*, and runs:

I swear to myself to adopt henceforth the following rules as the eternal rules of my life:
    Every morning to say my prayers to God, the fountain of all strength

and all justice, to my father, to Mariette [the servant who had looked after him as a child] and to Poe, as intercessors; to pray to them to give me the necessary strength to perform all my duties and to grant my mother a long enough life to enjoy my transformation; to work all day, or at least as long as my strength allows me; to trust in God, that is, in perfect Justice, for the success of my plans; every evening to say another prayer to ask God for life and strength for my mother and myself; to divide all that I earn into four parts – one for ordinary living, one for my creditors, one for my friends and one for my mother; to obey the rules of the strictest sobriety, the first of which is to cut out all stimulants, of every sort and kind.

Such resolutions do not explain the artist. They do, however, indicate that the poet Baudelaire was not simply the man Baudelaire fancily dressed for some decadent *danse macabre*; that *les soubresauts de la conscience* were not due to the manipulations of a puppet-master, but were real uncontrollable jerkings. Also, from this and other overwhelming evidence, we can be sure that at no period of his life did Baudelaire ever separate his art from his personal anguish or his religious faith. Even towards the end there was no renunciation of *Les Fleurs du mal*, either as a corruptive influence on others or as a now discarded reflection of his own fallible self. For better or worse, his poetry always remained part of him.

IV

Because of his experiences in life, Baudelaire was inclined to feel that some ironic force was working against him. Other men, in their complacency, were confident and happy; he, in his tormented lucidity, could not be. While Musset, in his much simpler way, also felt singled out for unhappiness, he had expressed his reaction in personal terms. Vigny, highly conscious of a joyless isolation, generalized the experience into a principle anticipatory of Nietzsche's conception of the superman. Baudelaire did neither. He does not generalize explicitly, and seldom moralizes. Yet at the same time, unlike Musset, he assumes that his is part of the universal human experience and treats it with the depth and seriousness which that deserves. Feeling that his own destiny is exceptional but not unique, he considers it as representative of at least a minority of other human destinies. Much more than Hugo he was entitled to say: 'Quand je vous parle de moi, je vous parle de vous.' In fact, he did say so, though in less flattering terms:

Hypocrite lecteur, – mon semblable, – mon frère!

Within this general obsession with the representative irony of his own destiny, two themes – or better, perhaps, two sensations – appear and reappear in his work. One is the sense of hurrying time, of the minutes which tick past inexorably, and which the poet, according to a very probable anecdote, symbolized by a notice stuck over the face of his clock, reading, in English: 'It's later than you think.' The most complete expression of this feeling is found in *L'Horloge*, of which a verse has already been quoted[1] and which reaches the desolate and sardonic conclusion:

> Tantôt sonnera l'heure où le divin Hasard,
> Où l'auguste Vertu, ton épouse encor vierge,
> Où le Repentir même (oh! la dernière auberge!),
> Où tout te dira: Meurs, vieux lâche! il est trop tard!

Allied to this is the condition called by Baudelaire *ennui*, or in its more virulent states *spleen*, then *dégoût*. This is the 'fastidious monster' of the searing apostrophe *To the Reader* which opens the *Fleurs du mal*. It is the motif of the four successive poems entitled *Spleen*, with their wonderfully rendered atmosphere of rain descending endlessly from wintry skies, while indoors the domestic cat restlessly seeks a more comfortable position and the greasy and abandoned playing-cards gossip darkly together of happier times:

> Pluviôse, irrité contre la ville entière,
> Dans son urne à grands flots verse un froid ténébreux
> Aux pâles habitants du voisin cimetière
> Et la mortalité sur les faubourgs brumeux.
>
> Mon chat sur le carreau cherchant une litière
> Agite sans repos son corps maigre et galeux:
> L'âme d'un vieux poète erre dans la gouttière
> Avec la triste voix d'un fantôme frileux.
>
> Le bourdon se lamente, et la bûche enfumée
> Accompagne en fausset la pendule enrhumée,
> Cependant qu'en un jeu plein de sales parfums,
>
> Héritage fatal d'une vieille hydropique,
> Le beau valet de cœur et la dame de pique
> Causent sinistrement de leurs amours défunts.

This is in minor vein and might seem to express little more than the Spirit of Influenza, were there not graver and longer poems in the same

---

[1] See p. 95.

mood. From these it is clear that Baudelaire's *ennui* was one of the Dark Forces, paralysing virtue, activity, and life itself, opposed – once again, ironically – to the unforgiving Clock.

The sensation of being stuck, when it is essential to advance, can be related simply to the writer's attitude to his work when this refuses to 'run' for him; in Baudelaire's particular case, to his physical constitution, which would suddenly fail him when an effort was required and which constantly reminded him that his days were numbered (he died, in fact, at forty-six). But more than this, he saw and expressed it as a condition of existence to which we are all subject, men and angels alike:

> Une Idée, une Forme, un Être
> Parti de l'azur et tombé
> Dans un Styx bourbeux et plombé
> Où nul œil du Ciel ne pénètre;
>
> Un Ange, imprudent voyageur
> Qu'a tenté l'amour du difforme,
> Au fond d'un cauchemar énorme
> Se débattant comme un nageur,
>
> Et luttant, angoisses funèbres!
> Contre un gigantesque remous
> Qui va chantant comme les fous
> Et pirouettant dans les ténèbres;
>
> . . . Un damné descendant sans lampe,
> Au bord d'un gouffre dont l'odeur
> Trahit l'humide profondeur
> D'éternels escaliers sans rampe,
>
> Où veillent des monstres visqueux
> Dont les larges yeux de phosphore
> Font une nuit plus noire encore
> Et ne rendent visibles qu'eux.

We are all trapped, in a nightmare whirlpool, on an endlessly descending staircase, in the ice of the Pole, in a snake-pit, and – most helplessly of all – in our own natures, which allow of no illusions once we have learnt to see into them. For this terrible and possibly true poem, *L'Irrémédiable*, concludes:

> Tête-à-tête sombre et limpide
> Qu'un cœur devenu son miroir!

Puits de Vérité, clair et noir,
Où tremble une étoile livide,

Un phare ironique, infernal,
Flambeau des glaces sataniques,
Soulagement et gloire uniques,
– *La conscience dans le Mal!*

'Irony', 'remorse', 'irremediable', 'lucidity' are the key-words in approaching Baudelaire, and may seem to characterize the whole poet. One might compare, at first purely as an expression of the same idea in two different idioms, these lines of Marvell's:

But at my back I always hear
Time's wingèd chariot hurrying near:
And yonder, all before us lie
Deserts of vast eternity.
Thy beauty shall no more be found;
Nor, in thy marble vault, shall sound
My echoing song. Then worms shall try
That long preserved virginity;
And your quaint honour turn to dust,
And into ashes all my lust.
The grave's a fine and private place,
But none, I think, do there embrace.[1]

with this sonnet of Baudelaire's:

Lorsque tu dormiras, ma belle ténébreuse,
Au fond d'un monument construit en marbre noir,
Et lorsque tu n'auras pour alcôve et manoir
Qu'un caveau pluvieux et qu'une fosse creuse;

Quand la pierre, opprimant ta poitrine peureuse
Et tes flancs qu'assouplit un charmant nonchaloir,
Empêchera ton cœur de battre et de vouloir,
Et tes pieds de courir leur course aventureuse,

Le tombeau, confident de mon rêve infini
(Car le tombeau toujours comprendra le poète)
Durant ces grandes nuits d'où le somme est banni,

Te dira: 'Que vous sert, courtisane imparfaite,
De n'avoir pas connu ce que pleurent les morts?'
– Et le ver rongera ta peau comme un remords.

[1] *To his Coy Mistress.*

That is the whole of Baudelaire's poem. The situation is contemplated as finished and irremediable. But Marvell's lines, of course, are extracted from a longer poem, and he goes on to look to a possible future and to draw Ronsard's moral of *Cueillez dès aujourd'hui les roses de la vie*, though with a humour and a ferocious gaiety that were not in Ronsard's nature:

> . . . Let us roll all our strength, and all
> Our sweetness, up into one ball;
> And tear our pleasures, with rough strife,
> Through the iron gates of life.
>   Thus, though we cannot make our sun
> Stand still, yet we will make him run!

V

Yet Baudelaire was not, as the quaint phrase has it, 'anti-life'. If he were, he would be the poet of an at first thrilling but ultimately self-defeating and sterile despair and his appeal would be limited to small groups of exceptional temperaments dotted here and there in history. He demands a more general response and has found it. There are excellent reasons for this.

First, on moral grounds, a man who faces up honestly to the whole of the human situation as he can see it, however sombrely, is worthy of respect and attention. He has something true to declare, even if it is contested that it is the whole truth.

Secondly, the artist is intimately present in what might be described as his most depressing poems. Lines already quoted will have illustrated this. Others, almost at random are:

> Et de longs corbillards, sans tambours ni musique
> Défilent lentement dans mon âme . . .

or:

> Ma jeunesse ne fut qu'un ténébreux orage,
> Traversé çà et là par de brillants soleils,

or:

> Je jalouse le sort des plus vils animaux
> Qui peuvent se plonger dans un sommeil stupide,
> Tant l'écheveau du temps lentement se dévide!

or, of old women in Paris, observed with an eye more pitiless than Villon's:

Où serez-vous demain, Èves octogénaires,
Sur qui pèse la griffe effroyable de Dieu?

In all such poems the skill and love of the poet in his handling of words show through, and this creative touch, to whatever purposes it is applied, cannot be called a refusal of life. It is, on the contrary, the triumph of a vital talent, which we may as well call genius, over its material. Much more could be written on this point, but it is sufficient to read Baudelaire without preconceptions to confirm it.

Thirdly, there is in many of the *Fleurs du mal* a deep response to the beauty and even to the wonder of the external world, tinged usually with melancholy, but often quite free of bitterness. Baudelaire does not always snarl. He is perfectly capable of accepting what life has to offer, though naturally with a lurking fear that it will be snatched away from him. But this only makes it more desirable. It is then that he writes his most musical and airy verse, which can enchant by its sheer rhythmic qualities:

Mère des souvenirs, maîtresse des maîtresses,
O toi, tous mes plaisirs! ô toi, tous mes devoirs!
Tu te rappelleras la beauté des caresses,
La douceur du foyer et le charme des soirs,
Mère des souvenirs, maîtresse des maîtresses!

But Baudelaire's greatest quality as a writer of verse lies in his use of a poetic idiom which, while always retaining a certain *allure* or presence (he is never loose or trivial), can nevertheless encompass the plain adjective or the familiar phrase without falseness of tone. Here he was as much the creator of a new language as Hugo, although his language, being more difficult, has become less vulgarized since by common use. For the youthful Rimbaud, Baudelaire was 'the king of poets, a real God, but he lived in too artistic a *milieu*, and his much-praised form is a poor thing.' Coming from Rimbaud, the reservation is understandable, but less than just. It was the 'artistic' backbone, the immense discrimination which underlies Baudelaire's choice of words and images, that gave his verse its original force and has now raised him, with no suspicion of paradox, to the status of a 'classic'.

Chapter 15

Leconte de Lisle and Heredia

IT IS customary to place after the Romantic heyday a reaction in favour of impersonality known as Parnassianism and roughly contemporaneous with the Second Empire. Revolting against the excessively self-revelatory manner of Musset and his lesser disciples, the Parnassians took up Théophile Gautier's somewhat frigid doctrine of 'art for art's sake', married it to the cult of form prescribed by Théodore de Banville, and produced a type of poetry distinguished by pictorial rather than by emotional or musical qualities. Carefully wrought in detail and definite in outline, this poetry belonged to the same artistic order as Flaubert's prose – particularly in *Salammbô* and the *Trois Contes* – and to the same intellectual climate as the materialistic philosophies of Renan and Taine. In the 1880s it began to be superseded in its turn by Symbolism, with its fluid and twilight intimations of the unconscious. After Romantic subjectivity, Parnassian objectivity, and after that an integration of the two in such poets as Verlaine and Mallarmé and a number of lesser writers.

So long as this is regarded as a simplified outline, it helps us considerably in following the main currents of French poetry after 1850, as it helped poets of the time to define what they were for and against. Moreover, *parnassien* is a useful critical term which serves to define a recognizable type of verse by no means limited to the contributors to *Le Parnasse contemporain*. But the theory must not be applied too narrowly. For one thing, the greatest poet writing under the Second Empire, Baudelaire, sometimes joins hands with the Parnassians yet can never be confined within their aesthetic. Verlaine and Mallarmé wrote first as Parnassians, and Mallarmé in his own way developed their insistence on formal perfection into the austerest canon of pure Symbolism. No poet of any stature at all remained a pure Parnassian except Heredia, whose poems were not published as a collection until 1893 – though it is true that most of them had appeared considerably earlier in reviews. Finally, Parnassianism is better regarded as an extension, or late phase, of Romanticism, rather than as a negation of it.

With these reservations we can approach the work of the man who has gone down to literary history as the leader of the Parnassians, Charles-Marie René Leconte de Lisle.

He was born in 1818 in Réunion of a family of sugar-planters and spent most of his youth on the hot, colourful island. Looking back to it in middle age, Leconte de Lisle no doubt exaggerated the charm that it had had for him, for as a young man he felt stifled by the narrow mental outlook of the colony. But the natural features of the place – its glaring sunshine, its tropical vegetation, its population of Indians, negroes and mulattoes – left a permanent impression on him. At eighteen he was sent to France by his family to study law. He spent six years with relatives in Brittany and at the University of Rennes, then returned to Réunion without a degree but with a taste for literature so strongly developed that he could settle to nothing else. Eventually he was offered through a school-friend a small post on a Parisian left-wing review, *La Phalange*. His family consented to help him with a small allowance and he departed for Paris at the age of twenty-seven with the intention of making his way as a writer.

For the rest of his life he never left France and hardly stirred from the capital. He married and lived for many years as a poverty-haunted man of letters, his physical existence bounded by the library, the publisher's office, the café and his fifth-floor flat on the Boulevard des Invalides. All his journeys were in the imagination, which is perhaps only a redeployment of memory. But for a short time at the beginning he had a glimpse of a more active existence.

La Phalange, to which he contributed, was a mouthpiece of the idealistic socialism which had been preached by Fourier. Leconte de Lisle adhered to the movement and in 1848 it seemed to him for a moment that the *Fouriériste* dream might come true. Among other political activities, he headed a deputation calling upon the Provisional Government to abolish slavery in the colonies. Slavery was abolished, but the measure meant ruin for the sugar-planters, and Leconte de Lisle's family stopped his allowance. In later years, indeed, he was obliged to support his mother and sisters on his own meagre earnings.

Soon afterwards Louis Napoleon seized power and a disillusioned Leconte de Lisle dropped politics for good. He turned instead to the ancient cultures and religions which other thinkers besides himself were beginning to re-examine in the light of the new theories of evolution. This can easily be called 'escapism', but he was in fact groping down to the philosophic centre of his age by his reading of Lamarck, Darwin and of the Buddhist and Hindu sacred books. Out of it he developed his own philosophy of scientific atheism. Meanwhile he was making a precarious living by occasional journalism, lessons and a series of excellent translations of the classics, but winning very little recognition as a poet. The reception given to his first books of poems made it appear possible that he would be almost as unrecognized in his lifetime as Baudelaire. But in 1862 his *Poèmes barbares* – though still not widely read – attracted round him younger men who were in revolt against the over-emotional work of the poets whom they dubbed *passionistes*. At first they called themselves *stylistes* and *formistes*, but their name was finally fixed by the publication of *Le Parnasse contemporain*, an anthology of contemporary poetry whose first volume appeared in 1866. Other numbers followed in 1871 and 1876.

The contributors to *Le Parnasse contemporain* were much too numerous and varied to form a school. They included almost every poet of any quality who was then writing, from Baudelaire, Mallarmé and Verlaine to Sully Prudhomme and François Coppée. But while other contributors disappeared or deviated, Leconte de Lisle continued to write in the same manner and by the date of the second number he was generally recognized as the high priest of *Le Parnasse*.

After 1870, his prestige was sufficient to guarantee him a reasonably secure existence. He was appointed assistant librarian to the Senate and the Republic confirmed the small pension of 300 francs a month which he had accepted reluctantly from Louis Napoleon. His literary position was that of successor-designate – on a smaller scale – to Victor Hugo, to whose chair in the Academy he was elected in 1886. He died eight years later in his house at Louveciennes. His studious existence with its final academic honours inadequately suggests the splendour and ferocity of his work.

II

Leconte de Lisle's poetry was published in the three main divisions of the *Poèmes antiques* (1852, augmented 1872), the *Poèmes barbares* (1862, augmented 1874 and 1878) and the *Poèmes tragiques* (1884), to which the posthumous *Derniers Poèmes* (1895) must be added for completeness. But the dates have no great significance as stages of the poet's development. His work can be treated as one body without insistence on its chronological order.

The first impression which this verse would make on a reader coming straight from Musset or Verlaine would be of entering a heavily furnished room of the period. The hangings are of the best velvet, the furniture of ebony and mahogany, the ornaments of massive gilded bronze. An indefinable atmosphere of apprehension broods over this opulent solidity. Absurdly, one hesitates to lift the silver cover of the bacon-dish lest underneath should be the head of the Count with its staring eyes. The tiger-headed rug lies ready to tear at the suddenly writhing legs of the dining-table. Passive, of course, are displayed various exotic trophies: a stuffed eagle, a shark's fin, a four-armed Vishnu. These objects have not been assembled haphazard. As we grow accustomed to the scene we are aware of a powerful harmony uniting its components. Leconte de Lisle is as much in control of his material as Matthew Arnold was of his. Neither was a collector of purposeless bric-à-brac. In the French poet's décor there is unity, there is movement, and there is even something that might be called life if we could find some more familiar form of life to which to relate it. In one of his finest poems, *Qaïn*, the seer Thogorma sees in a vision the gigantic children of Cain walking back into their citadel at the end of the day. Clearly this cannot be classed simply as a frieze:

> Thogorma dans ses yeux vit monter des murailles
> De fer d'où s'enroulaient des spirales de tours
> Et de palais cerclés d'airain sur des blocs lourds;
> Ruche énorme, géhenne aux lugubres entrailles
> Où s'engouffraient les Forts, princes des anciens jours.
>
> Ils s'en venaient de la montagne et de la plaine,
> Du fond des sombres bois et du désert sans fin,
> Plus massifs que le cèdre et plus hauts que le pin,
> Suants, échevelés, soufflant leur rude haleine
> Avec leur bouche épaisse et rouge, et pleins de faim.
>
> C'est ainsi qu'ils rentraient, l'ours velu des cavernes
> A l'épaule, ou le cerf ou le lion sanglant.
> Et les femmes marchaient, géantes, d'un pas lent,
> Sous des vases d'airain qu'emplit l'eau des citernes,
> Graves, et les bras nus, et les mains sur le flanc.
>
> Elles allaient, dardant leurs prunelles superbes,
> Les seins droits, le col haut, dans la sérénité
> Terrible de la force et de la liberté,
> Et posant tour à tour dans les ronces et les herbes
> Leurs pieds fermes et blancs avec tranquillité.
>
> Le vent respectueux, parmi leurs tresses sombres,
> Sur leur nuque de marbre errait en frémissant,

> Tandis que les parois des rocs couleur de sang,
> Comme de grands miroirs supendus dans les ombres,
> De la pourpre du soir baignaient leur dos puissant.

Though 'sculptural', such verse is not static. It has a slow, pro-cessional movement in keeping with the whole poem from which it is taken – a long one. Poetry conceived on this scale can afford to be majestic and unhurried – there can be no quarrel with it on that ground. As for the weakness of some Parnassian poets and sometimes of Balzac, Flaubert and Zola in prose – their piling-up of secondary details – Leconte de Lisle avoids this too. His details and his adjectives are carefully selected with a view to the total effect and his description is not so exclusively concrete that it fails to convey an atmosphere. *Le vent respectueux*, in the last strophe quoted, is a comment, bordering on humour, on the monumental dignity of the biblical women. It both sums up and lightens the pictorial aspects of the passage.

Later in the same poem, Leconte de Lisle describes the bursting of the cataclysmic storm which began the Flood:

> Tout se tut. Le Silence élargi déploya
> Ses deux ailes de plomb sur les choses tremblantes.
> Puis, brusquement, le ciel convulsif flamboya.

> Et le sceau fut rompu des hautes cataractes.
> Le poids supérieur fendit et crevassa
> Le couvercle du monde. Un long frisson passa
> Dans toute chair vivante; et par nappes compactes
> Et par torrents la Pluie horrible commença.

There are weaknesses in this: *Tout se tut* is unpleasant to the ear; *la Pluie horrible* seems inadequate – but there is daring and brilliance in *le silence élargi, le ciel convulsif, crevassa* and *par nappes compactes.* Leconte de Lisle's main concern as a poet – it appears all through his work – was to find the words which most adequately conveyed his unusual concepts, without much regard for their musical or other aesthetic qualities. Sometimes this led him to an exact visual adjective, sometimes to a technical or semi-technical term, and often to an archaic or pedantic spelling of proper names – *Qaïn for Caïn, Héva* for *Ève.* But it goes further than a preoccupation with the externally picturesque. It reveals a constant effort to preserve the original flavour of the material he was transposing. It is the opposite of the classic search for the *mot juste*, which meant – or was debased to mean – the word which most satisfied the expectation of conventionally educated people.

Leconte de Lisle did not engage in this harmless pastime. His interest was in characterizing the peculiar, in rendering, for example, the essence and appearance of the god Bhagavat:

> C'était le Dieu. Sa noire et lisse chevelure,
> Ceinte de fleurs des bois et vierge de souillure,
> Tombait divinement sur son dos radieux.
> Le sourire animait le lotus de ses yeux.
> Et dans ses vêtements, jaunes comme la flamme,
> Avec son large sein où s'anéantit l'âme,
> Et ses bracelets d'or de joyaux enrichis,
> Et ses ongles pourprés qu'adorent les Richis,
> Son nombril merveilleux, centre unique des choses,
> Ses lèvres de corail où fleurissent les roses,
> Ses éventails de cygne et son parasol blanc,
> Il siégeait . . .

Only a poet-scholar with a complete disregard for salon standards and devoid also of Baudelaire's flair for themes relevant to 'modern life' could have composed towards 1880 'The Death-song of a Gaelic Warrior of the Sixth Century' in which the severed head of the dead chieftain is carried on a spear in the van of the charging Celts:

> Je ne l'entendrai plus, cette tête héroïque,
> Sous la torque d'or roux commander et crier;
> Mais je la planterai sur le fer de ma pique:
> Elle ira devant moi dans l'ouragan guerrier.
>
> Oc'h! Oc'h! c'est le Saxon qui l'entendra crier!
>
> Elle me mènera, Kenwarc'h! jusques au lâche
> Qui t'a troué le dos sur le cap de Penn'hor.
> Je lui romprai le cou du marteau de ma hache
> Et je lui mangerai le cœur tout vif encor!
>
> Kenwarc'h! Loup de Kambrie! Oh! le Cap de Penn'hor!

Here, and in many other poems, Leconte de Lisle seems to have followed up the hint thrown out by Hugo in *Les Orientales* and to have carried the Romantic taste for local colour to its furthest limits. But with him it was more than colour; it was form and texture as well. His imagination was so impregnated with the atmosphere of the exotic – apart from the fact that his research into it was much more thorough than Hugo's – that he gives it back as though it were a lived experience. Impersonal as his verse appears (and as he strove to make it), it is thus not anti-Romantic. The generation of 1830, fascinated by the strangeness of the exotic, had tried to express it in French without sufficiently assimilating its spirit. Almost inevitably, they failed. Hugo's early work, Gautier's verses on Spain, remain a painted décor. Leconte de Lisle comes nearer to achieving the impossible. His poems on India are about as Indian, on primitive Scandinavia about as Scandinavian, as *The Three-corned Hat,* danced at Covent Garden, is Spanish, or Fitzgerald's *Rubáiyát* is Persian. That, for anyone who is neither a native nor a specialist, is good enough – provided that one looks to poetry for aesthetic pleasure and not for exact instruction or for new light on experience.

III

The correspondence between Leconte de Lisle's work and Hugo's *Légende des siècles* has often been noticed, but it is hardly close enough for a charge of imitation to be brought against either poet. Hugo conceived a huge epic with the progress of the human spirit as its motif. Leconte de Lisle interpreted history as a descent rather than as an ascent, and his treatment was considerably more fragmentary, if more scientific. On the dates, either one could have influenced the other, and since *Les Poèmes antiques* appeared seven years before the first volume of *La Légende des siècles,* it is probable that Hugo borrowed something from Leconte de Lisle's descriptive methods. On the other hand, *Qaïn* was first published ten years after Hugo's *La Conscience,* which also deals with Cain in his old age and may have suggested the subject to the younger poet, who treated it, however, on a grander scale and in a very different spirit. In general, it would appear that the two poets glanced occasionally at each other's work before writing from their own strongly held, and different, points of view.

Another ghost walks through Leconte de Lisle's work – the ghost of Vigny. It is difficult to seize, but impossible to lay. Leconte de Lisle could have read nearly all Vigny's work before publishing a line of his own, and it is certain that he did so. Similar themes, verse-forms and even isolated lines occur here and there in his pages. But more striking than any resemblances of detail was the deep compatibility of temperament between the two. The iron world of Vigny was Leconte de Lisle's world – more profusely decorated no doubt, but at least as hard and hostile at the centre. In fact, it was more so, for while Vigny still belonged to the Christian tradition and still thought, in however disillusioned a way, in terms of a moral universe, Leconte de

Lisle had taken a further step and believed only in a mechanistic uni-verse. The groundwork of his poetry was his study of the various gods and religions which, according to the evolutionist explanation, man had devised for himself in various historical and geographical circum-stances. Brahma, Vishnu and Siva, the Hellenic Pantheon, the Nordic Valhalla, the Egyptian gods had all been valid in their time and place before giving way to Christianity. Christianity in its turn would be-come outworn and disappear,

> Laissant l'homme futur, indifférent et vieux,
> Se coucher et dormir en blasphémant les Dieux.

Leconte de Lisle's pessimism, as it is found in such poems as *Dies Irae*, *Midi*, *Le Vent froid de la nuit*, *L'Illusion suprême*, is complete. Recoiling in horror from the idea of immortality – 'Le long rugisse-ment de la vie éternelle' – he concludes that the only desirable end is the annihilation of the individual personality:

> Et toi, divine Mort, où tout rentre et s'efface,
> Accueille tes enfants dans ton sein étoilé;
> Affranchis-nous du Temps, du Nombre et de l'Espace,
> Et rends-nous le repos que la vie a troublé.

His conception of the 'divine nothingness' into which all life returns derived from Buddhism or Vedaism, which he found the most attractive among the different religions he studied. From the same sources, with a certain admixture of Darwinism, came his conviction that all life, whether human or animal, is fundamentally the same, and that the one common factor in the universe is suffering. This philosophy, with its scientific basis, would no doubt have been accept-able to Vigny had he belonged to the same generation and it would have given him a stronger intellectual justification for his personal pessimism. But as it was, Vigny remained a desolate and lonely seeker while Leconte de Lisle was linked to the advanced thought of his age.

But he too was a poet before he was a philosopher and it seems that his philosophy developed out of his subjects rather than the opposite. He was not led by systematic research alone to the Icelandic runes or the war-songs of the Gaelic bards. Temperament drew him to some of the most ferocious episodes in folklore and early literature and par-ticularly to those descriptions of beasts and birds of prey in which he excels. He was more fascinated by the example than by the rule. His Mongolian eagle swoops from the sky to peck out the eyes of the wild stallion; his jaguar, sleeping on a rock in the jungle, dreams that she is tearing at the flanks of plunging buffaloes; his shark and his python slide through their native elements in search of their quarry. The thesis behind this is that nature is amoral – the law is to kill or to be killed and no guilt attaches to the act. Man is as much subject to it as the animals. But in reading these bloodthirsty poems, it is impossible not to remark that the poet's first pleasure was to re-create these beasts by an imaginative attempt to enter into their spirit.

In such a poem as *L'Incantation du loup*, he takes up a subject which Vigny had used in *La Mort du loup*, but instead of narrating the wolf-hunt and ending his poem with a moralizing passage to explain its intention, he simply describes the he-wolf sitting on the snow after the tragedy has occurred. The she-wolf and the cubs have been killed by the hunters and the survivor gazes up at the moon and chews over his hatred of Man. The poem ends with this quaint and powerful passage:

> Lui, le chef du haut Hartz, tous l'ont trahi, le Nain
> Et le Géant, le Bouc, l'Orfraie et la Sorcière,
> Accroupis près du feu de tourbe et de bruyère
> Où l'eau sinistre bout dans le chaudron d'airain.
>
> Sa langue fume et pend de la gueule profonde.
> Sans lécher le sang noir qui s'égoutte du flanc,
> Il érige sa tête aiguë en grommelant,
> Et la haine, dans ses entrailles, brûle et gronde.
>
> L'Homme, le massacreur antique des aïeux,
> De ses enfants et de la royale femelle
> Qui leur versait le lait ardent de sa mamelle,
> Hante immuablement son rêve furieux.
>
> Une braise rougit sa prunelle énergique,
> Et, redressant ses poils raides comme des clous,
> Il évoque, en hurlant, l'âme des anciens loups
> Qui dorment dans la lune éclatante et magique.

Such poetry may not be the highest art, but at least it is original, and represents as energetic an attempt as that made by the early Romantics to break out of the urban, polished world inhabited by the neoclassics. This casting-back to barbarism and magic is Leconte de Lisle's most durable feature. Sometimes it raises a smile; occasionally it is overdone and smells artificial, but on the whole his world can be accepted. One walks respectfully through it, noting with awe those huge, abandoned constructions of the human mind. One admires his jackal-headed carvings and his monstrous stone flowers and, although all this was created only a century ago, the modern imagination is stirred in much the same way as the poet was stirred by the thought of ancient Egypt or the halls of the Nibelungen. As long as his work communicates this impression, it must be counted as successful. The reservation, which the Symbolists were quick to exploit, and which was presently to be weighted with all the authority of Freud, is that contemporary man cannot be excluded for long from poetry. With his pettiness and his inconsistencies, he forces his way into the foreground and everything that does not converge directly on him is thought of as stage furniture. But is it not possible that a section of the audience should be more fascinated by the décor than by the actors?

IV

Although Leconte de Lisle's work contains all the Parnassian features, he was too definite a personality to be a Parnassian and nothing more. For the perfect example we must look to his friend and disciple, José-Maria de Heredia, who was born in 1842 (more than twenty years later than his master) at Santiago de Cuba of a Spanish father and a French mother. Like Leconte de Lisle, he spent most of his life in Paris, where he studied at the École des Chartes and became expert in the handling of ancient manuscripts. And in much the same way his early foreign background lent an imaginative warmth to his scholarship.

But it is less warm than in Leconte de Lisle, and uncomplicated or unburdened by any attempt at a cosmic philosophy. His work loses in vigour while it gains in delicacy. It was composed slowly, with a meticulous regard for exactness of atmosphere. His whole published work consisted of the 118 sonnets of *Les Trophées* and of the two longer poems *Romancero* and *Les Conquérants d'or*, neither of which is first-rate. Heredia's real talent was for the sonnet, in which he could work, it has been said, like an engraver of antique medallions who evokes a whole civilization in a few characteristic lines. He took his subjects from Greek mythology – his sequence on the Centaurs and his three sonnets on Perseus and Andromeda are particularly good – and from Roman history: here *La Trebbia* and the triptych on Anthony and Cleopatra stand out. He moved to the Middle Ages and the Renaissance with his sonnets on the Venice of the Doges and on the Spanish *Conquistadores.* He painted his own direct impressions of nature –

taken chiefly from the coast of Brittany – less well than the half-imagined, half-remembered tropical sea-bottom of *Le Récif de corail*. He adventured in a few sonnets as far as Egypt and Japan.

His usual method, so precise that it can easily be analysed, is to set the scene with carefully chosen 'colour' or 'atmosphere' words in the first quatrain, then to bring forward the particular figure or characteristic which he wishes to stress during the next lines of the poem. With the last tercet the image moves into full focus and the final line adds some significant feature which fixes it. A good example of this technique is his description, in *Le Samouraï*, of the Japanese warrior in his lacquered armour moving across the sands towards the window of the waiting girl:

> D'un doigt distrait frôlant la sonore bîva,
> A travers les bambous tressés en fine latte
> Elle a vu, par la plage éblouissante et plate,
> S'avancer le vainqueur que son amour rêva.
>
> C'est lui. Sabres au flanc, l'éventail haut, il va.
> La cordelière rouge et le gland écarlate
> Coupent l'armure sombre, et sur l'épaule éclate
> Le blason de Hizen ou de Tokungawa.
>
> Ce beau guerrier vêtu de lames et de plaques,
> Sous le bronze, la soie et les brillantes laques,
> Semble un crustacé noir, gigantesque et vermeil.
>
> Il l'a vue. Il sourit dans la barbe du masque,
> Et son pas plus hâtif fait reluire au soleil
> Les deux antennes d'or qui tremblent à son casque.

Such verse requires great precision in the choice of words and a power of condensation which no poet in a hurry or a passion could contrive. The reader, too, must have a patient appreciation of exact craftsmanship and must be prepared to 'taste' each sonnet slowly.

Les Trophées were not published in book form until 1893. But even then, though they were out of their period, they had many admirers. Perceptibly donnish in their inspiration and in their references to ancient history and mythology, they were poetry for the connoisseur who had enjoyed a classical education. Equally, they were models of economy, clarity and the evocative force of a few well-assembled words and, by implication, a condemnation of the opposite tendencies towards vagueness and verbosity. Historically they can be seen as the ultimate development of Gautier's theory of *l'art pour l'art*. While there is more in them than mere naturalistic description, they also crown a long and rich tradition of descriptive poetry which is much older than Gautier. Their interest and attraction today lie principally in that quality.

Chapter 16

Paul Verlaine

THE deplorable Verlaine – for so, from the moral point of view, he must be considered – traversed in his life various psychological crises which, if lived experience alone were decisive, should have yielded poetry comparable to Baudelaire's. Yet, for all his self-inclusion among the *poètes maudits* or 'doomed poets' of the eighties, Verlaine is not a Satanic, or even a tragic, figure. It is not possible to take him so seriously, nor does he often demand it. When he does, one is inclined to smile rather than to participate. It is always 'pauvre Lélian' in trouble again, never a clairvoyant fellow man playing on one's own fears and vices. Certainly he can sometimes be touching, with oblique, unexpected strokes which awaken a momentary sentiment, a probably literary nostalgia, but do not last. Their effect can be quite pleasing.

He is not to be criticized for the fact that he is relatively superficial. It was part of a valid conception of poetry which he evolved to harmonize with his own temperament. He aimed at other effects than the effect in depth. His work marks the beginning of Symbolism, and if he is now more usually classed as an Impressionist, in this instance the one led to the other. In any case, in spite of his openly personal and 'intimate' style, he marks very clearly the end of Romanticism as poets from Lamartine to Hugo had conceived it. The *moi* in Verlaine no longer performs the same function as in them. It is more like the 'I' in Marot, or even in La Fontaine. It is, though on several levels higher, the 'I' of the pop-singer and not of the guide or prophet who leads us by the hand into our own natures.

He was born at Metz in 1844, the only surviving child of conventional but indulgent parents. His father was a captain of Engineers who had risen from the ranks and whose family came from the Ardennes. His mother was a daughter of beet-farmers established near Arras. Notwithstanding this north-eastern ancestry, Verlaine was brought up as a Parisian, for his father resigned his commission in 1851 and went to live in the capital. Verlaine took his *baccalauréat* at the Lycée Bonaparte (now the Lycée Condorcet) and found employment at the age of twenty as a clerk in the Hôtel de Ville. He was beginning to publish poems in reviews and to mingle in the advanced literary circles to which he was introduced in salons and cafés. Among his young acquaintances were such coming writers as Villiers de l'Isle-Adam, François Coppée, Anatole France, Léon Dierx, Catulle Mendès and Heredia. His chief admirations were for Baudelaire (who died when he was twenty-three and never met him) and Hugo, whom he visited in Brussels in 1868. But the active 'leaders' whom he followed were Leconte de Lisle and Théodore de Banville. He was printed in one of the first numbers of the *Parnasse contemporain*, with Mallarmé and others, and in the same year (1866), the publisher of *Le Parnasse*, Lemerre, brought out his first book of verse, the *Poèmes saturniens*. It was followed by the *Fêtes galantes* (1869) and by *La Bonne Chanson* (1870), inspired by his feelings for Mathilde Mauté.

His marriage to this seventeen-year-old girl, the half-sister of a musician friend of his, Charles de Sivry, called at least a halt on the slope of alcoholism down which Verlaine had been slipping since his father's death five years before. That steadying influence gone, Verlaine had been left by an adoring mother to his own devices, of which not the least harmful was the consumption of absinth. But the marriage was not a sufficient antidote and there had already been signs of trouble before the appearance of Rimbaud in the Verlaine household in September 1871. The sixteen-year-old Rimbaud had sent Verlaine some of his poems and had received in return a cordial invitation to come to Paris. In the upshot, Verlaine abandoned his wife and his infant son and wandered off with Rimbaud. Their association, in Paris, Belgium and London, lasted some eighteen months and was cut short when Verlaine, who had bought a revolver with some idea of suicide, fired at Rimbaud in a Brussels hotel and wounded him slightly in the wrist. He was sentenced, by a Belgian court strongly influenced by the immoral appearances of the two men, to the maximum penalty of two years' imprisonment.[1]

During his wandering with Rimbaud he had written *Romances sans paroles* (1874), his finest book of short lyrics. His experiences in Mons gaol led directly to *Sagesse*, though this was not published until 1881. The book reflects his conversion to Catholic piety, to which he turned with the help of the prison chaplain after receiving the news that his wife had obtained a separation from him. Oddly yet typically, Verlaine had always hoped, as he put it, that Mathilde would return to him ('It is *I* who have been deserted,' he protested in a letter to Victor

[1] Shortened by good conduct to seventeenth months (August 1873 to January 1875).

Hugo), and for some years after he still sought for the reconciliation which he himself had made hopeless, and then fought to see the son whom Mathilde's family carefully kept away from him.

After his release from prison there was a final meeting with the now embittered Rimbaud. It turned into a pub-crawl at the end of which Rimbaud, drunk and indignant at Verlaine's pious efforts to convert him, knocked his companion senseless and left him to lie in the gutter. Verlaine's attempt to reform himself was, however, genuine. During the next few years he took a number of teaching posts, both at private schools in England – at Stickney in Lincolnshire, at Bournemouth and at Lymington in Hampshire – and in France; one of these was in a college run by priests in the French Ardennes. He even inquired about recovering his post of municipal clerk, which he had abandoned rather than lost more than ten years previously in the confusion of the Commune. A new protégé, in the shape of Lucien Létinois, a peasant's son, was the cause of his buying, with his mother's help, a farm to be managed by the young man's parents, where he himself lent a hand with a hayrake. The venture failed with disastrous rapidity. In January 1883 Lucien died suddenly of typhoid fever, aged twenty-three. It seems most probable that his significance for Verlaine was that of a foster-son, filling the place of his own son Georges. Three years later Verlaine's devoted mother died and in the same winter Verlaine heard of the remarriage of Mathilde, now in her thirties. Nothing remained to halt his demoralization.

Most of his old literary friends had long since turned their backs on him. In 1875 the compilers of the third volume of *Le Parnasse contemporain* had refused the work of the ex-gaolbird. He had great difficulty in finding publishers – even at his own expense – and certainly his verse did not sell. But after *Sagesse* a new publisher, Vanier, became interested in him and printed his next three books: *Jadis et naguère* (1884), *Amour* (1888) and *Parallèlement* (1889). The last, containing much licentious verse, was to run 'parallel' to the more edifying *Sagesse* and *Amour*. From that date Verlaine's poetry declined greatly. The rest is full of an often maudlin sensuality, relieved sometimes by bursts of savage humour.[1]

But as his talent declined his literary reputation grew. Young poets admired his work and sought him out. He offered himself as a candi-

[1] His other volumes were: *Femmes* (1890), *Dédicaces* (1890), *Bonheur* (1891), *Chansons pour elle* (1891), *Liturgies intimes* (1892), *Odes en son honneur* (1893), *Élégies* (1893), *Dans les limbes* (1894), *Épigrammes* (1894); also *Chair* (1896), *Invectives* (1896) and other posthumous collections.

date for the *Académie française* – repeating the gesture which Baudelaire had made in the same defiant spirit, and with as little hope as he
of a place among the Immortals. He was, however, given the title of
Prince of Poets by a group of younger writers. He was invited to
lecture in England by Arthur Symons and others interested in the new
doctrine of Symbolism. Meanwhile, he was living in increasing in-
firmity and squalor, looked after, when not in hospital, by two elderly
prostitutes and somewhat relieved financially by a subscription
arranged by a committee of literary men. He died in January 1896, aged
fifty-one.

Much more than Banville, who said it of himself, Verlaine was
'a lyric poet'. His mismanaged and not very creditable life was reflected
– often all too clearly, if never very deeply – in his verse. One is dissuaded from separating the two by Verlaine's retort to a now forgotten
journalist named Bertol-Graivil:

> Ce monsieur crut plaisant de me couper en deux:
> Le poète, très chic – l'homme, une sale bête.
> Voyez-vous ce monsieur qui me coupait en deux?
>
> Rentre, imbécile, ton 'estime' pour mes livres.
> Mais ton mépris pour moi m'indiffère, étant vil.
> Garde, imbécile, ton 'estime' pour mes livres.
> Dernier des reporters, et premier des Graivil.

Not the least of Verlaine's achievements was the part he played in
preserving Rimbaud's name. In 1883, eight years after he had last seen
him, he devoted one of his articles on the *Poètes maudits*[1] to an enthusiastic account of his old companion, quoting some of his poems evidently from memory. Rimbaud, who was then trading in Abyssinia,
had been completely forgotten and was even thought to be dead.
The interest aroused by Verlaine's article and quotations started a hunt
for more poems by the young genius. In 1886 Vanier published *Les
Illuminations* with a preface by Verlaine which dated their composition
to 1873–5. Without Verlaine, it seems certain that the Rimbaud cult
could not have been born at that highly opportune moment, if at all,
and even possible that his work would never have been brought to
light.

---

[1] In the review *Lutèce*. Vanier republished the articles in book form in 1884. This series
discussed Corbière, Rimbaud and Mallarmé. A second series (1888) was on Marceline
Desbordes-Valmore, Villiers de l'Isle-Adam and Verlaine himself.

II

But Verlaine, whose reputation today stands considerably lower than that of his friend, was an excellent poet in his own right. His work follows a curve which is clear enough in outline. There is a first phase of imitation and experiment, containing some poems stamped with the contemporary impersonality and even 'impassibility', though stamped with a feather if one compares them with the massive castings of Leconte de Lisle. Then follows the truly feathery phase of *La Bonne Chanson* and *Romances sans paroles* – which is the characteristic Verlaine at his best. After this he embarks on his long adventure into piety, which must be described as a one-sided flirtation with a God whom he knew only through such edifying works as the eight-volume *Catechism of Perseverance* which the prison chaplain gave him to read. Verlaine, of all people, could never take fire through a duenna and the result in his poetry is too often the cultivation of the hackneyed symbol or else that tearful diffuseness which was always the defect of his virtues. His faith, in any case, brought no stiffening into either his concepts or his vocabulary – and how much that was needed is evident in nearly all the poems he published in the last eight years of his life. Not that these are unreadable. The mordant shaft, the humour, the direct sensuality, the touching piety, the growingly conscious but sometimes amateurish echoes of Villon, still give life to the occasional poem if not to the mass. But really by this time Verlaine had disintegrated, and what flies about us as we progress through his increasingly fluffed-out verse is no longer feathers but kapok. To the student of the literary scene of the nineties, such collections as *Dédicaces*, *Invectives* and *Épigrammes* have an immense interest. They are highly ingenious as verse and sometimes very funny. But that is incidental to whatever pleasure one may take in poetry.

When he was first published, Verlaine was described by a hostile critic, Barbey d'Aurevilly, as: 'A puritan Baudelaire – an unfortunate and comic combination, without the brilliant talents of M. Baudelaire, and with reflections here and there of M. Hugo and Alfred de Musset.' Verlaine, in the dedication of the *Poèmes saturniens*, conceived himself in the Baudelairean role of one of those ill-starred poets, born under the sign of Saturn, who

> Ont entre tous, d'après les grimoires anciens,
> Bonne part de malheur et bonne part de bile.
> L'imagination, inquiète et débile,
> Vient rendre nul en eux l'effort de la Raison.

The desire to continue Baudelaire (as well as Gautier and Leconte de Lisle at their most stiffly picturesque) is evident in this first collection and breaks down in ways already prophetic of the mature Verlaine. Thus, his youthful sonnet to a statuesque, impassive courtesan, in which she is finally compared to a dahlia, opens:

> Courtisane au sein dur, à l'œil opaque et brun
> S'ouvrant avec lenteur comme celui d'un bœuf,
> Ton grand torse reluit ainsi qu'un marbre neuf.

Whatever Baudelaire's verbal maltreatment of women, he never suggested the comparison to an ox.[1] There are no such glimpses of the incongruous – and so openings for the Verlainean type of humour – in his verse. Verlaine was, of course, entitled not to take his subjects quite seriously since he did not take himself quite seriously. In the poem *Sérénade*, also clearly modelled on Baudelaire, he begins:

> Comme la voix d'un mort qui chanterait
> Du fond de sa fosse,
> Maîtresse, entends monter vers ton retrait
> Ma voix aigre et fausse.

From such small signs it could have been deduced (as it was by the acute Barbey d'Aurevilly, when he wrote: 'An unfortunate and comic combination') that Verlaine had the makings of a clown unless he could shift his whole work on to a lighter register. Fortunately he was beginning to do this even in the *Poèmes saturniens*. They contain, for example, two well-known sonnets which just succeed in conveying a straightforward pathos without heaviness or anticlimax. One is *Après trois ans*, which treats in fourteen lines the theme of Hugo's *Tristesse d'Olympio* (the revisiting of a scene of past happiness) and opens in a perfect minor key:

> Ayant poussé la porte étroite qui chancelle,
> Je me suis promené dans le petit jardin
> Qu'éclairait doucement le soleil du matin,
> Pailletant chaque fleur d'une humide étincelle.

Another is *Mon Rêve familier* – the old Romantic dream of the woman who 'understands', and who in Verlaine's life might well have been represented by his cousin and adoptive sister Élisa Moncomble, who paid for the printing of the *Poèmes saturniens* and died soon after their publication. But when this poem was written she was still alive.

---

[1] Verlaine probably had in mind such Baudelairean lines as:

> Statue aux yeux de jais, grand ange au front d'airain!

The only person near to him who had died at that date was his father. The poem is either prophetic or it expresses a generalized nostalgia. It is distinguished not so much by the too *recherché* eleventh line (the third quoted below) as by the simple and unemphatic last line:

> Est-elle brune, blonde ou rousse? – Je l'ignore.
> Son nom? Je me souviens qu'il est doux et sonore
> Comme ceux des aimés que la Vie exila.
>
> Son regard est pareil à celui des statues,
> Et, pour sa voix, lointaine et calme et grave, elle a
> L'inflexion des voix chères qui se sont tues.

When it is recalled that this earliest volume contains the universally quoted *Chanson d'automne*, as well as the mischievous *Chanson des ingénues:*

> – Nous sommes les Ingénues
> Aux bandeaux plats, à l'œil bleu,
> Qui vivons, presque inconnues,
> Dans les romans qu'on lit peu. –

it is obvious that, among an interesting selection of echoes and imitations, the true Verlaine had already been born.

In the score of pieces which make up the short *Fêtes galantes*, the same playful and regretful[1] Verlaine continues, submitting now to a light discipline which consists in a stylization and unification of mood rather than of form. The points of departure were Victor Hugo's *Fête chez Thérèse* (in *Les Contemplations*), which Verlaine knew by heart, and the writings of the Goncourt brothers on eighteenth-century painting, which led Verlaine to the painters themselves as he could see them at the Louvre. From the artificial charm of Watteau, Lancret and others, he evolved his delicate verbal pastels. It was one of those 'transpositions of art' (painting into poetry) which Gautier had recommended and attempted, but carried out now in a different spirit. Several of these groupings of puppet-like characters from the *commedia dell'arte* or from French eighteenth-century comedy (as Marivaux) in park-like settings are interior landscapes as well. There is a vaguely felt sentiment in them of the kind which thirty years later would become one of the occupational diseases of minor Symbolists:

> – Votre âme est un paysage choisi,

---

[1] 'Melancholy', an adjective often applied to him, is altogether too strong, unless qualified.

or

> Leur élégance, leur joie,
> ... Tourbillonnent dans l'extase
> D'une lune rose et grise –

but which is appropriate here to Verlaine's particular mood and setting.

III

The *Fêtes galantes* represented a transition from the Parnassianism and the Baudelairean *ennui* of some of the *Poèmes saturniens* to the freer music of the next two books. *La Bonne Chanson* is full of Verlaine's delight in his approaching marriage with Mathilde. *Romances sans paroles*, though it contains sadder poems written for Mathilde, is as spontaneous as the other book in the impressions he shared with Rimbaud – of Belgian landscapes or London scenes. Through those two people, by and between whom Verlaine maintained with some truth that his life had been torn, he recaptured a youthful freshness of feeling nonexistent in his Parisian literary world. His dealings with both of them were in the first place a pilgrimage in search of innocence, to which the immorality and irresponsibility which also resulted were incidental. In Rimbaud's company he could yearn as imprecisely as any young girl of the time over her piano:

> Il pleure dans mon cœur
> Comme il pleut sur la ville.
> Quelle est cette langueur
> Qui pénètre mon cœur?
>
> O bruit doux de la pluie
> Par terre et sur les toits!
> Pour un cœur qui s'ennuie,
> O le chant de la pluie!

He could write for Mathilde from London a short lyric like *Green*, which opens:

> Voici des fruits, des feuilles et des branches,
> Et puis voici mon cœur, qui ne bat que pour vous.
> Ne le déchirez pas avec vos deux mains blanches,
> Et qu'à vos yeux si beaux l'humble présent soit doux.

He follows it with *Spleen*, a title borrowed from Baudelaire, but

how different was the canker in Baudelaire's 'spleen' poems[1] from the
sobered butterfly in Verlaine's:

> Les roses étaient toutes rouges,
> Et les lierres étaient tout noirs.
>
> Chère, pour peu que tu te bouges,
> Renaissent tous mes désespoirs.
>
> Le ciel était trop bleu, trop tendre,
> La mer trop verte et l'air trop doux.
>
> Je crains toujours – ce qu'est d'attendre! –
> Quelque fuite atroce de vous.
>
> Du houx à la feuille vernie
> Et du luisant buis je suis las.
>
> Et de la campagne infinie,
> Et de tout, fors de vous, hélas!

In the imponderable qualities of the verse of this period consists
Verlaine's chief gift to French poetry (Rimbaud's song-poems were
similar and were written at the same date, but they were not known
until later). They avoid all definition of feeling and, still more, all
summing-up of feeling or comment upon it. Their landscapes are
imprecisely sketched and related to the inner mood. Their language
is unemphatic and colloquial. Their versification is correspondingly
fluid, running over on occasion from line to line, ignoring conventional
rules of scansion and rhyming, sometimes employing assonance. His
work now embodies the exact opposite of the Parnassian ideal, in both
themes and technique. While it may properly be called impressionistic,
it also contains the main qualities of Symbolism as it was before an
exact artist like Mallarmé had gone to work on it.

During his first winter in prison, Verlaine's chief interest was to
prepare *Romances sans paroles* for the press. The book appeared, after
much difficulty in finding a printer, in March 1874. In April he wrote
his poem *Art poétique*, containing his reflections on poetry at that date.
(The poem was not printed until 1882 and was later included in *Jadis et
naguère*.)

He begins by saying that poetry should be *musical* and gives a practical hint on how to make it so:

[1] One is quoted on p. 161.

> De la musique avant toute chose,
> Et pour cela préfère l'Impair.

That is, the line with an uneven number of syllables – seven, nine or eleven – instead of the more usual metres of eight, ten or twelve syllables. *Art poétique* itself is written in nine-syllable lines.

He recommends a misty technique, in which words are *not* always chosen with precision:

> Il faut aussi que tu n'ailles point
> Choisir tes mots sans quelque méprise:
> Rien de plus cher que la chanson grise
> Où l'Indécis au Précis se joint.

Only in this way can 'shading' be introduced into poetry.

This was a direct attack both on the definite outlines cultivated by the Parnassians and on the whole classic doctrine of exactness in the use of language.[1] He goes on to attack other qualities associated with that doctrine: the 'murderous conceit' – *la pointe assassine* – wit, rhetoric:

> Prends l'éloquence et tords-lui son cou!

And finally Rhyme, the sacred rhyme with which Malherbe had once squared off his lines and stanzas, which Leconte de Lisle and Heredia led up to in their verse, with which Banville had juggled until it became an obsession, as Rostand was to do later in such lines as these:

> Impossible, Monsieur; mon sang se coagule
> En pensant qu'on peut y changer une virgule.

Poetry, Verlaine concludes poetically, should be as perfumed and unpremeditated as the morning breeze. Not an art – above all, not 'literature':

> Que ton vers soit la bonne aventure
> Éparse au vent crispé du matin
> Qui va fleurant la menthe et le thym . . .
> Et tout le reste est littérature.

This was one of those periodic and necessary protests against professionalism which, in its general drift if not in its particulars, is as pertinent today as yesterday. It is the protest of any 'natural' writer against the academic on one hand and the smart commercial on the other. Later, Verlaine withdrew the more extreme implications of *Art poétique* which, after all, was only a song written in prison. He recoiled

---

[1] For Boileau's *Art poétique*, see pp. 55–6.

before the extreme formlessness which younger poets, invoking his
recommendations, allowed themselves.[1] In logic, his advice led to
unrhymed free verse. He had not meant that, he said. But he might just
as well have admitted it, while himself keeping nearly always within
the limits of rhyme and of a nonchalant but approximately regular
scansion, which resulted in what he called the *vers libéré*.

IV

The religious poems in *Sagesse* have moved many Catholics and in
a few of his best sonnets Verlaine is not greatly inferior to the French
religious poets of the late Renaissance. Yet his dialogue with the
Creator lacks animation: one misses both the battle of doubt and the
ecstatic resignation of the true mystic. Biographically, of course, it
soon became apparent that neither of these was for Verlaine. As he goes
downhill his characteristics become over-stressed. The aery vagueness
of his youth becomes a middle-aged flabbiness; his bright-eyed sensuality becomes grossness; his glancing allusions, just chatter. The volume
Amour contains a moving sequence of poems on Lucien Létinois, here
regarded as an adopted son. His reflections after Lucien's death might
be compared to Hugo's meditations after the death of his daughter
Léopoldine. At first the contrast, the complete lack of 'eloquence' and
emphasis, is refreshing. Here grief speaks naturally. He is remembering
Lucien as he saw him during his military service:

> Je te vois encore à cheval
> Tandis que chantaient les trompettes
> Et ton petit air martial
> Chantait aussi quand les trompettes:

[1] His main repudiations of such developments were given first in an interview, published
by J. Huret, *Enquête sur l'évolution littéraire* (1891), in the course of which he said: 'J'ai
élargi la discipline du vers et cela est bon; mais je ne l'ai pas supprimé. Pour qu'il y ait vers,
il faut qu'il y ait rythme. A présent, on fait des vers à mille pattes. Ça n'est plus des vers,
c'est de la prose . . . et surtout, ça n'est pas français, non, ça n'est pas français, nom de
Dieu!'

His second pronouncement was a more cautious head-shaking over the young *vers-
libristes* – 'gay colts who go gambolling over the grass' – in which he defended rhymes:

> . . . la rime, un abus que je sais
> Combien il pèse et combien il encombre,
> Mais indispensable à notre art français,
> Autrement muet dans la poésie,
> Puisque le langage est sourd à l'accent.
>
> (*Épigrammes*, II, 2, 1894.)

Je te vois toujours en treillis[1]
Comme un long Pierrot de corvée,
Très élégant sous le treillis,
D'une allure toute trouvée;

... Et je te rêvais une mort
Militaire, sûre et splendide,
Mais Dieu vint qui te fit la mort
Confuse de la typhoïde ...

Seigneur, j'adore vos desseins,
Mais comme ils sont impénétrables!
Je les adore, vos desseins,
Mais comme ils sont impénétrables!

But it becomes obvious that 'naturalness' is not enough. Who is this speaking – a poet who can either ennoble or illuminate the occasion, or an old woman, loquacious, sentimental and querulously pious? Only pathos is communicated and other poets have accustomed us to expect more from poetry.

Nevertheless, Verlaine's work as a whole still interests for its power of sentimental and visual suggestion, its flickering use of imagery, its easy-going rhythms and language. If Hugo had once 'put a red cap on the old dictionary', Verlaine went much further, writing argot and slang as freely as he evidently spoke them. This enlivens but also dates him. The current slang of the 1880s – except for a few words which are always with us – has faded while not yet acquiring the historical interest of, say, Villon's slang. His poetic stock, for a long time quoted over-highly, has now fallen much lower than Mallarmé's or Rimbaud's. Yet his influence on twentieth-century poetry has been as great as either of theirs. It is felt from Apollinaire to Aragon, while his vein if not precisely his influence can be discovered in many of the poets who have rejected the appearance of conscious art to give the first place to *fantaisie*.

[1] *Treillis*: fatigue-dress, 'denims'.

Chapter 17

Arthur Rimbaud

FRENCH poetry has never been quite the same since Rimbaud. Some of it in particular, following the *Illuminations*, which are easier to admire than to imitate, has been written in prose. But there are varying degrees of imaginative power and it is arguable that more averagely endowed talents have been led astray by Rimbaud's example of freedom than were ever stunted in their reasonable growth by the example of Racine's polished 'regularity'. Both great originals have overstrained their imitators, but while Racine did so unwittingly, Rimbaud might be held more responsible because – though at the age of sixteen and in private correspondence – he formulated a theory of poetry.

Everything has conspired to make Rimbaud, as person and poet, an almost incredible figure. One can still say, when adulation and legend have been cleared away,[1] that he was remarkable.

He was born on 20 October 1854 in the small industrial town of Charleville, near the Belgian frontier. Charleville has open spaces with trees and is bordered by the river Meuse on which the schoolboy Rimbaud, violently rocking a moored punt, may have had his first prefigurement of the *bateau ivre*. His father, like Verlaine's, was a professional soldier who had begun as a ranker. He came ultimately of Provençal stock and had an expansive and adventurous nature which made home life in a small town intolerable to him. After service in Algeria and the Crimea, he separated from his wife when Rimbaud was six, leaving the young boy with his brother and two sisters to be brought up by their mother. The severity of the poet's upbringing, in which piety and economy were the guiding principles, sufficiently explain his rebellion against the world of narrow respectability which his mother personified. She demanded, and for a time obtained, an outward conformism. He eluded her in clandestine escapades and through literature. His precocious feeling for poetry made him an outstanding pupil at the local school, where his Latin verses won him the first prize

---

[1] Though there is no pressing reason why they should be. A writer's legend, if properly focused, is at least as revealing as any 'document'.

in the *Concours général* of 1869, open to all the schools of France, and where he was encouraged by a young master, Georges Izambard, who recognized his brilliant possibilities.

He left school in his sixteenth year a few days before the Franco-Prussian War broke out. Against that unsettled background, he ran away to Paris, then Brussels, then Paris again, with intervals of lounging and reading at Charleville. Sometimes he travelled without a ticket or on foot. He learnt the technique of vagabondage: how to sleep under a rick, to dodge patrols of suspicious Prussians, to beg at farms for a hunk of bread or a few sous to spend at the nearest inn. But he was also meditating on poetry and writing it. Having read and admired Verlaine's verse, he sent some of his own to the older poet (encouraged by a mutual friend, who added a postscript) and received the invitation to visit him in Paris.

Early in September 1871 he arrived at the Verlaines' home[1] with *Bateau ivre*, written shortly before, in his pocket. He was not yet seventeen. At first he had no doubt hoped that he could begin a literary, or at least a journalistic career in Paris, and Verlaine duly introduced him to the poets and painters whom he knew. The effect was disastrous. Though the young writers of the seventies were not conventional, their unconventionality was that of the city-dweller, and in the last resort superficial. The anti-salon is still a salon. Rimbaud's originality was of a more primitive, personal kind. He was dirty and surly and would spend whole evenings enveloped in a silent cloud of tobacco-smoke. He poured acid into a companion's beer and, at a 'Bohemian' dinner, jeered at every pause in the recitation of an *avant-garde* poem and ended up by attempting to stab one of the guests. His aggressive awkwardness was no doubt partly assumed in self-defence against the manners of the capital. But it was also dictated by a real contempt for an art still dominated by Parnassian standards.

Only Verlaine was both aware of Rimbaud's talent and fascinated by his personality. They eventually left Paris together, with the results described in the previous chapter. Nearly half of the next year was spent in London (1872–3), with shorter stays in Brussels and two visits by Rimbaud to his home at Charleville. As soon as he had reluctantly given evidence in the shooting affair which led to Verlaine's imprisonment, Rimbaud hurried home, and, at the small farm which his mother owned at Roche, finished writing *Une Saison en enfer*. Whether he had already written *Les Illuminations* is a disputed point which is discussed

---

[1] At the time they were occupying the second floor of the house of Verlaine's parents-in-law, the Mautés.

below. Most probably he turned his back finally on literature when he was just nineteen. The most that is claimed by another school of thought is that he continued writing until he was twenty-one. Within those limits of time he made a complete change of direction.

One can either say flatly that he stopped dreaming, or that exactly the same urge to know and to dominate runs through the second phase of his life as through the first, but exteriorized now and with less fruitful results.

While Verlaine was in prison, Rimbaud returned to London with the young poet Germain Nouveau. He apparently worked in a box factory, gave private lessons, and taught in a school at Reading. The next year he was at Stuttgart, where the final meeting with Verlaine took place – though Verlaine continued to post him his religious poems, which exasperated and disgusted him. He journeyed on foot to Italy, worked on the docks at Marseille, and studied languages to equip himself for the battle of life. At the age of twenty-one the poet of the *Illuminations* seriously thought of working for his *baccalauréat*, the matriculation examination which he had not bothered to take at school.

His travels continued. He enlisted in a contingent of the Dutch army bound for Java, deserted on arrival and worked his passage home on an English ship. He sold bootlaces in Vienna, roved through Scandinavia with a circus, was an overseer in the quarries of Cyprus. Seven years after his break with Verlaine he was seeking employment in the ports of the Red Sea. He found it with a French trading firm at Aden, which put him in charge of their newly opened branch at Harrar in Abyssinia.

The Abyssinian Rimbaud showed a toughness of purpose and a forceful curiosity which still linked him to the adolescent poet. He equipped a caravan and led it through desert and hostile country to Antotto, the future Addis Ababa. He traded in arms, and probably in slaves. He also dreamed of being an explorer and sent his mother a list of books and scientific instruments which she grudgingly sent him, deploring what she considered as the useless expense. He reconnoitred the country round Harrar, reached the Wabi River and discovered the Ogaden, a country of nomad tribes and big game which no European had so far visited. There is no sign that he relented in his rejection of literature, but journalism was another matter. He sent articles on Abyssinia to *Le Figaro* and *Le Temps* and even, it seems, to the local Charleville paper, which he had once derided as the supreme example of provincial inanity. None of them printed him.

He wrote again to offer his services to *Le Temps* as a correspondent in the Italo-Abyssinian war of 1887. An old schoolfriend on the staff was charged to convey the editor's refusal, which he softened by adding:

No doubt you do not know, living so far away from us, that you have become in Paris, in a very small circle, a sort of legendary character – one of those characters whose death has been announced, but in whose existence a few faithful persist in believing, and for whose return they obstinately wait. Your work, verse and prose, has appeared in Latin Quarter reviews and has even been published in book form.[1] A few young men (whom I think over-simple) have tried to found a literary theory on your sonnet on the colour of the letters. This little group has recognized you as its master, not knowing what has become of you, but hoping that you will reappear one day to rescue it from its own obscurity.

Not wishing to arouse false hopes, his friend continued:

I must hasten to add in all conscience that all this has no practical bearing of any kind. But in spite – to write frankly – of many incoherences and exaggerations, I have been struck by the astonishing skill of those early productions of yours.

By that date it is probable that Rimbaud thought even less than his correspondent of his youthful writings and of the disciples who were gathering round his name. Had he survived long enough he would probably have been bored by his literary apotheosis. The only counter-indication, slight indeed, has been pointed out by Dr Enid Starkie. When Rimbaud returned to France to die, he carried among his necessary business papers an invitation which the editor of an *avant-garde* review had written him. But with what object he had kept it, it is impossible to say.

A painful tumour on his right knee forced him back to France. Amputation of the leg did not save him and, after a few months at Charleville, he returned to the Hospital of the Conception at Marseille. Here he died on 10 November 1891. His mother and his sister Isabelle buried him hurriedly at Charleville. A few days before his death he had professed the Catholic faith. Perhaps it was a true conversion. Perhaps, out of lassitude, he had yielded to Isabelle, who had nursed him so devotedly. In any case, the black sheep had come home, and without making a fortune. His sister did her best to represent him as the conscientious employee of a colonial business house. She glossed over every reference to his early escapades, distorted every fact that did not square with her conception of an honest but

---

[1] A reference to Verlaine's articles on the *Poètes maudits* and to Vanier's edition of the *Illuminations*.

unremarkable citizen. Like her mother, she belonged to the race which regards every departure from the norm as shocking, especially genius. Yet Rimbaud was produced, and only could have been produced, by the inner pressures generated in that same race.

Perhaps the oddest postscript is provided by the marriage of Isabelle to the earliest and least critical of her brother's biographers, Paterne Berrichon. Already worshipping the poet he had never known, Berrichon approached the family for information and ended by becoming, posthumously, Arthur Rimbaud's brother-in-law. In that way he could share the slightest recollections of the sister and draw nearer in spirit to his idol.

II

Rimbaud's work consists of his verse poems, all written, with one exception,[1] between 1870 and 1872, and the prose or prose poetry of *Les Illuminations* and *Une Saison en enfer*. His earliest verse corresponded to a not uncommon adolescent urge and was produced in his sixteenth year during his last summer at school, or soon after he had left school and was enjoying his new-found freedom. To begin with there are echoes of Hugo and Baudelaire, but these disappear astonishingly quickly and almost at once a new poet appears, writing boldly and inventively (as to language) of his childhood, of Charleville, of the mixed sexual and religious obsessions of puberty and of the impressions made by his first wanderings. There is an early lightness akin to some of Verlaine's *Poèmes saturniens*, yet already different and original:

> On n'est pas sérieux quand on a dix-sept ans.
> Un beau soir – foin des bocks et de la limonade,
> Des cafés tapageurs aux lustres éclatants! –
> On va sous les tilleuls verts de la promenade.

> Les tilleuls sentent bon dans les bons soirs de juin.
> L'air est parfois si doux qu'on ferme la paupière.
> Le vent chargé de bruits – la ville n'est pas loin –
> A des parfums de vigne et des parfums de bière.

> ... Le cœur fou robinsonne[2] à travers les romans
> Lorsque, dans la clarté pâle d'un réverbère,

[1] *Les Étrennes des orphelins*, written late in 1869 and published in *La Revue pour tous* (January 1870). It was one of the very few poems published by Rimbaud himself, apart from the privately printed *Saison en enfer*.
[2] 'Goes Robinson Crusoe-ing' – a word of Rimbaud's invention.

> Passe une demoiselle aux petits airs charmants,
> Sous l'ombre du faux-col effrayant de son père.
>
> Et comme elle vous trouve immensément naïf,
> Tout en faisant trotter ses petites bottines,
> Elle se tourne alerte et d'un mouvement vif,
> Sur vos lèvres, alors, meurent les cavatines.[1]

Then, rapidly enough, experience matures, sensation grows more complex, and the language becomes correspondingly richer and denser:

> Le jeune homme dont l'œil est brillant, la peau brune,
> Le beau corps de vingt ans qui devrait aller nu
> Et qu'eût, le front cerclé de cuivre, sous la lune,
> Adoré, dans la Perse, un génie inconnu,
>
> Impétueux avec des douceurs virginales
> Et noires, fier de ses premiers entêtements,
> Pareil aux jeunes mers, pleurs des nuits estivales
> Qui se retournent sur des lits de diamants;
>
> Le jeune homme, devant les laideurs de ce monde,
> Tressaillant dans son cœur, largement irrité
> Et plein d'une blessure éternelle et profonde,
> Se prend à désirer sa sœur de charité.[2]

At about this time Rimbaud became conscious of the nature of his poetic vocation. The poet, he now believed, should be a *voyant*, a 'see-er', penetrating by his own insight and experience into the true nature of things and self. In May 1871 he wrote two letters to friends – the first to his old schoolmaster, Izambard, the second to a young contemporary, Paul Demeny – in which he set down his ideas. In the second letter he gave his comments on other French poets. Some were remarkable anticipations of later criticism. Others, though youthfully exaggerated, help to situate Rimbaud's own position, both as he saw it himself and as time has confirmed it:

> Lamartine is sometimes a see-er, but strangled by old forms. Hugo, too
> pig-headed [i.e. insistent], has a lot of *seen* in his later books – *Les*

---

[1] Cavatinas, simple arias – a rare word. From *Roman*, written in September 1870, when Rimbaud was not, as the first line implies, seventeen but just under sixteen. Later, he wished to suppress this poem as too juvenile.

[2] From *Les Sœurs de charité*, written in 1871, when Rimbaud was seventeen: again he suggests that he is older.

Misérables is a true poem[1] . . . Musset is fourteen times detestable to us –
suffering generations beset with visions – whom his angel laziness has
insulted. Oh, the sickly stories and proverbs! Oh, *Les Nuits*, oh, *Rolla*,
oh, *Namouna*, oh, *La Coupe* [*aux lèvres*]! All French – that is, hateful to the
last degree; French, not Parisian! Another product of that odious genius
which inspired Rabelais, Voltaire, Jean La Fontaine, commented by
M. Taine! Sprightly, the spirit of Musset! Charming, his love! There you
have painting on enamel, solid poetry! There is a grand future for French
poetry, but in France . . .

The second Romantics are good see-ers: Théophile Gautier, Leconte de
Lisle, Théodore de Banville. But since to inspect the invisible and to hear
the unheard is something else than to take up the spirit of dead things,
Baudelaire is the first see-er, the king of poets, a *real God*. But even he
lived in too artistic a milieu and his much-praised form is a poor thing.
Inventions of unknownness demand new forms.

What is this 'unknownness' and how is it to be approached?

The first study of a man who wishes to be a poet is knowledge of himself
– entire knowledge. He searches for his soul, inspects it, tries it out,
learns it.

So far, this is orthodox: a statement of principle to which almost any
serious poet would subscribe. But Rimbaud takes it further:

As soon as he knows it, he must cultivate it. That appears simple. A
natural development goes on in every brain. So many *egoists* set up as
authors. And many others attribute their intellectual progress to it!

After this hit at the cultivation of egoism, which he associated with
such Romantics as Musset, the absolute Rimbaud goes on to draw the
extreme consequences of his theory:

But it is necessary to make the soul into a monster – like the *comprachicos*,[2]
say! Imagine a man implanting and cultivating warts on his own face. I say
that one must be a *voyant*, make oneself clairvoyant. The poet makes himself a *voyant* by a long, immense and deliberate disordering of all the senses.
Every form of love, suffering, madness. He searches for himself, he ex-
hausts every poison upon himself, to retain only their quintessences. An
unspeakable torture in which he has need of superhuman faith and
strength, in which he becomes above all others the arch-sufferer, the arch-
criminal, the arch-damned soul [*maudit*] – and the supreme sage. For he

---

[1] It is significant that he quotes a novel in prose as his example. The social-revolutionary
side of *Les Misérables* would have attracted him. Though not 'active' politically, the
young Rimbaud was a natural anarchist, with ideas of a humanitarian Utopia.
[2] Buyers of children to be 'made' into circus freaks.

has reached the *unknown*! Because he has cultivated his soul, rich already, more than anyone else! He reaches the unknown and even if, demented, he ends by losing the understanding of his visions, he has seen them! Let him burst himself in his leap through unheard-of and unnameable things; other horrible workers will come; they will begin from the horizons where the other has disappeared.

So the poet must distort himself into a specialized instrument of perception. He will do this by a deliberate disordering (*dérèglement*) of the senses, which eventually makes of him a *grand malade* (one thinks of Rousseau and Proust), a great criminal (Villon, de Sade, Jean Genet, at least in their legends), a *grand maudit* (the word used by Rimbaud well before Verlaine relaunched it in his *Poètes maudits*, and applicable to the doomed outcast of the Byronic tradition, the self-characterized Baudelaire of *Les Fleurs du mal*, and even the noble pariahs of Vigny's poems).

There are two main components in this theory of Rimbaud's. First, a fairly direct development from the Satanism of Baudelaire, which led him to believe that physical debauch of various kinds, including the use of drugs (particularly cannabis), would broaden experience of evil as of good and would lead to spiritual lucidity. Secondly, Rimbaud the adolescent – his adolescence is always important – feels himself on the brink of life and has no patience with the prospect of maturing slowly. He must snatch at everything – experience, knowledge, understanding – and get it at once in its integrity. The only way to do this is by the short cut which is also the direct route: through sensation, which is instantaneous and within his immediate grasp. Afterwards, it will not matter if he has destroyed himself. At least he will have *been there* and others can go on (he believes) from the point which he has reached.

The conception of the poet as *voyant* has caused Rimbaud to be interpreted as an actual student of occultism, a disciple of various writers on the methods and practice of magic who undoubtedly exercised a considerable influence on nineteenth-century literature – though that influence cannot easily be isolated. But such an approach, though sustainable,[1] is not necessary to explain Rimbaud's work, in the way that it helps in deciphering certain sonnets of Gérard de Nerval. One need not go beyond 'nature' and the example of Baudelaire to explain such phrases as *l'alchimie poétique*. Claudel's description of Rimbaud as *un mystique à l'état sauvage* seems nearer the truth. A

[1] The most plausible case for it is put forward by Enid Starkie in her *Arthur Rimbaud* (rev. ed. 1961). She also proposed the alchemical explanation of the *Sonnet des voyelles* discussed below on p. 201.

mystic or not, he flourished 'in a wild state' and is not made more intelligible by references to any formal hermetic system.

There is much greater significance in the stress which he lays in the *lettre du voyant* on pre-rational or anti-rational methods of apprehending reality. The notion of the unconscious is certainly there, though he did not find the word. Still, he was writing thirty years before Freud, though more than fifty after Coleridge. He also points – certainly in his results and partly in his theory – to Surrealism, but with an important distinction. He prescribes a deliberately willed sacrifice at the outset of the experiment and by his reference to 'suffering', 'torture', and to 'losing the understanding (*intelligence*) of his visions' seems to have in mind a consciously lucid victim on the Racinian model. The disintegration of the understanding is the end for him, as also for Baudelaire.[1] Beyond that point, 'other horrible workers' must take up the search. But that was precisely the point at which the Surrealists began to become interested. A state of no-reason – but drifted into automatically, and without deliberate effort or suffering – was for them the state in which 'real reality' was attained. Although Rimbaud can be claimed as a forerunner of the Surrealists, his kinship with them is thus incomplete. He belongs collaterally to the family of the despised Musset, who conceived the poet as performing a voluntary sacrifice in which his rational identity remains intact to the last.

III

In Rimbaud's development the *lettre du voyant* implied both a plan for living and a plan for poetry. Soon after, he wrote his magnificent *Bateau ivre*, which can be described from one point of view as the first great Symbolist poem.[2] The 'drunken boat' is a ship which has gone adrift down some American river when its haulers were captured and massacred by 'shrieking redskins'. Free and crewless it is carried about the seas, traversing storms, amid seascapes and landfalls of incredible strangeness and beauty. The underwater world and the sky display their terrors and marvels while it drifts for months as almost a part of them:

[1] 'J'ai *cultivé mon hystérie* avec jouissance et terreur. Aujourd'hui 23 janvier 1862 j'ai subi *un singulier avertissement*; j'ai senti passer sur moi le vent de l'imbécillité' (Baudelaire, *Fusées*).
[2] Another claimant to the title, Mallarmé's *Après-midi d'un faune*, was written in a first version six years earlier (1865), but published in its third and definitive version only in 1876.

Presqu'île ballottant sur mes bords les querelles
Et les fientes d'oiseaux clabaudeurs aux yeux blonds;
Et je voguais, lorsque à travers mes liens frêles
Des noyés descendaient dormir, à reculons . . .

But it is still the boat, even if 'drunk' with sensation, still a conscious identity.

Finally, it grows weary of its incessant wanderings and desires to break up or else to creep into some European water – say a puddle on which a child is sadly launching a toy boat:

Si je désire une eau d'Europe, c'est la flache
Noire et froide, où vers le crépuscule embaumé
Un enfant accroupi plein de tristesses, lâche
Un bateau frêle comme un papillon de mai.

The young poet seems to have identified himself with the boat – prophetically so if one thinks of his two existences: the first escape from home and Charleville with the intoxicating adventures of the senses which lay ahead, then the return, sobered and disillusioned, after Verlaine's condemnation; next, the geographically distant adventures of the traveller, ending in his death at Marseille from disease and exhaustion. It is not necessary to believe that Rimbaud foresaw these things with clarity in order to agree that he may have guessed at the general pattern of his destiny. Such is the more obvious symbolism of the poem.

Its great strength lies, however, in its evocations of the violence and colours of the sea and of their concordances with human experience. As all his biographers point out, he had not yet seen the sea, yet far more truly and successfully than Hugo he is a cosmic poet. He suggests the unity of all forms of life at an intuitive level by his mastery of the image which, whether implicit or fully worked-out, is greater than that of any French poet before him. Since, he has been equalled only by Mallarmé and Valéry, who worked, however, on a more intellectual level and a different scale.

Je sais les cieux crevant en éclairs, et les trombes
Et les ressacs et les courants; je sais le soir,
L'aube exaltée ainsi qu'un peuple de colombes,
Et j'ai vu quelquefois ce que l'homme a cru voir.

J'ai vu le soleil bas taché d'horreurs mystiques
Illuminant de longs figements violets,
Pareils à des acteurs de drames très antiques,
Les flots roulant au loin leurs frissons de volets.

J'ai rêvé la nuit verte aux neiges éblouies,
Baisers montant aux yeux des mers avec lenteur,
La circulation des sèves inouies
Et l'éveil jaune et bleu des phosphores chanteurs.

... J'ai heurté, savez-vous? d'incroyables Florides
Mêlant aux fleurs des yeux de panthères aux peaux
D'hommes, des arcs-en-ciel tendus comme des brides,
Sous l'horizon des mers, à de glauques troupeaux.

J'ai vu fermenter les marais, énormes nasses
Où pourrit dans les joncs tout un Léviathan,
Des écroulements d'eaux au milieu des bonaces
Et les lointains vers les gouffres cataractant![1]

Glaciers, soleils d'argent, flots nacreux, cieux de braises,
Échouages hideux au fond des golfes bruns
Où les serpents géants dévorés des punaises
Choient des arbres tordus avec de noirs parfums!

... J'ai vu des archipels sidéraux! et des îles
Dont les cieux délirants sont ouverts au vogueur!
Est-ce en ces nuits sans fond que tu dors et t'exiles,
Million d'oiseaux d'or, ô future Vigueur?[2]

---

[1] Cf. Leconte de Lisle's description of the Flood (p. 170).
[2] A nearly literal translation will suggest the particular quality of this verse better than further commentary:

I know the skies splitting in lightning, the waterspouts, the undertows and the currents; I know the evening, the dawn uplifted like a tribe of doves, and sometimes I have seen what man has believed he saw.

I've seen the sinking sun spotted with mystic horrors, lighting up with long stiff violet streaks, like actors in very ancient dramas, the waves rolling afar their corrugated shudders.

I've dreamt in the green nights of the dazzled snows, kisses rising slowly to the eyes of the seas, the circulation of the unheard-of saps [tides], the yellow and blue awakening of the singing phosphorescences.

... I've jostled, do you know? incredible Floridas, where the eyes of man-skinned panthers mingle with the flowers, [I've bumped against] rainbows taut like reins on fishy flocks beneath the horizon of the seas.

I've seen the marshes fermenting, enormous nets where a whole Leviathan rots in the rushes, [sudden] collapses of water in the midst of calms, and the distances Niagaraing towards the depths.

Ice-floes, silver suns, nacreous waters, burning skies, hideous groundings in the depths of brown gulfs where the giant bug-riddled serpents fall with black perfumes from the twisted trees.

... I've seen starry archipelagos and islands whose delirious skies are open to the wanderer. Is it in those bottomless nights that you sleep and are exiled, you million golden birds, O future Strength?

In Rimbaud's verse, *Bateau ivre* is the peak of this kind of writing, not equalled in any of his other poems. But similar mergings of sensations and concepts – the comparison of the dawn to a flock of doves rising into the sky, of rising sap to rising tide, metaphors like 'black perfumes' – and some of the same verbal richness, run through several of his poems. His sonnets on the colour of the vowels is an example of an apparent attempt to find equivalences between two different senses, seeing and hearing. But though poetic theories have been constructed around his visual scale of

> A noir, E blanc, I rouge, U vert, O bleu,

they do not yield any coherent system and it must be concluded that Rimbaud was writing quite subjectively. One key to his 'colour-scheme' has been found in an illustrated alphabet which he might have used as a child. It could have begun *A pour Abeille*, with a drawing of a black bee. Another explanation relies on the sequence of the colours through which the base metals of the medieval alchemist is said to have passed in his attempt to make gold. Such ingenious suggestions leave the reader still free to interpret this poem – and others – with whatever imagination he cares or is able to bring to it. It is useless to apply too much logic to a poet who deliberately rejected it. What does emerge, however, is that Rimbaud's perceptions were not primarily aural. His poetry in general is not 'musical' or noticeably sensitive to combinations of sound. On the contrary, the visual impression predominates. A true 'musician' would have felt no need to transpose sounds into colours; it would contaminate them for him. One recalls Verlaine's *Art poétique*:

> Car nous voulons la Nuance encor,
> *Pas la couleur*, rien que la nuance!
> Oh! la nuance seule fiance
> Le rêve au rêve et la flûte au cor!

What is this but a refutation by a poet who certainly was a 'musician' of Rimbaud's over-crude or over-rich preoccupation with 'colour'?

IV

The lighter manner of Verlaine probably influenced the last verse-poems of Rimbaud. At about the time when the older poet was writing *Romances sans paroles*, Rimbaud was rhyming such mysteriously simple lines as:

> O saisons, ô châteaux,
> Quelle âme est sans défauts?

or:

> Oisive jeunesse
> A tout asservie,
> Par délicatesse
> J'ai perdu ma vie.

These lighter poems – some can be described as song-poems – were probably all written in 1872. There are about a score of them in all. Some were attached to the *Illuminations* in prose, in the edition arranged by Verlaine. Others – in some instances the same poems in slightly different versions – were quoted by Rimbaud himself in *Une Saison en enfer* – a work which brings us to a consideration of his prose writings.

It is not known when *Une Saison en enfer* was begun. It may have been as early as his stay in London with Verlaine. But it was certainly completed and prepared for publication after the shooting affair in Brussels, when Rimbaud was recuperating at his mother's farm at Roche (August 1873). It tells, symbolically but clearly enough for the attentive reader, the story of his spiritual adventure and its failure. From the opening: 'In other days, if I remember rightly, my life was a feast at which all hearts were open, all wines flowed,' it leads up to his reaction against not only the companionship of Verlaine, but the whole of his superhuman effort to live by the senses. Overstrained physically, in revulsion against alcohol and drugs, he is inclined, as Baudelaire once had been, to seek a healthy rule of life. But at the same time he is spiritually disintoxicated. The vision glimpsed two years earlier in the *lettre du voyant* is now admitted to have been false – or unattainable. He renounces it expressly, calling it 'delirium', 'folly'. And, though not without a last regretful glance backward, he braces himself to go forward into the 'real' world of practical achievement, of science, hard work and hard hearts:

> 'I created all festivals, all triumphs, all dramas. I tried to invent new flowers, new stars, new flesh, new tongues. I thought I had acquired supernatural powers. Well, I must bury my imagination and my memories. A fine reputation for art and story-telling has collapsed!
> 'I! I who called myself Magus or angel, excused from all morality, I am brought back to earth, with a duty to discover and rugged reality to embrace. Peasant!
> 'Was I mistaken? Could charity be the sister of death for me?
> 'Anyhow, I will ask pardon for having fed myself on lies. And let's get going.'

This farewell to literature – or, more exactly, this renunciation of the stimulated imagination as a means of possessing life – was printed privately in Brussels on Rimbaud's order. Since he failed to pay for the work, the edition lay undisturbed in the publisher's stockroom for nearly thirty years. Rimbaud received a few author's copies of which some were sent to friends, while it is supposed that the others were burnt by him together with all his manuscripts and letters in November 1873. Thus his renunciation was complete, since even the literary expression of it was annihilated.

This version of events, psychologically consistent as it is, was disturbed recently by the debate on the *Illuminations*. This was the other of Rimbaud's main prose-writings and in many ways the more interesting. It recounts, in prose-poems of great imaginative richness, his dreams, his hallucinations, his voyages beyond reality or his transpositions of it. It is the book of a great visionary. But for some justified doubts about Rimbaud's religious vocation, one would be tempted to call it the chief work of pure mysticism in French. It should be read through with sympathetic attention, with or without notes, but it cannot be properly illustrated by detached quotations. Even more than his poetry in verse, it is the realization of Rimbaud's conception of the poet as *voyant*. It corresponds to his view that 'inventions of unknownness demand new forms', and supposedly was the work he was writing in 1872–3 during his period of a general 'disordering of the senses'. It and it alone of his surviving writings belongs naturally to the phase which came to an end with *Une Saison en enfer* and it fits his description in the latter work of the 'lying visions' which he has renounced.

This sequence was accepted unquestioningly until 1949, when a new study contested the priority of the *Illuminations* and maintained that it was composed between 1873 and 1875.[1] These were the dates given by Verlaine in his preface to the first (1886) edition of *Les Illuminations*, but no one had supposed Verlaine to be a very reliable witness. On consideration, however, it seems strange that Verlaine should have thought that these particular prose poems were written *after* his association with Rimbaud if, in fact, they were written during it. He would surely have known what his friend was producing at that particularly memorable time.

But M. de Lacoste's principal argument rested on Rimbaud's handwriting, which appears more mature in the *Illuminations* than in his other work. His contention would mean that Rimbaud went back on the decision so firmly stated in *Une Saison en enfer*, and if he did so only to the extent of revising and copying work already composed in draft, even that would be a compromise foreign to everything that is

[1] *Rimbaud et le problème des Illuminations*, by H. de Bouillane de Lacoste (Paris, 1949).

known of his absolute and stubborn character. Another difficulty which arises is to know what work Rimbaud was writing during the year when he was away with Verlaine (January 1872 to February 1873) presumably before he began *Une Saison en enfer*. If it was not *Les Illuminations*, what was it? The few lightly phrased poems mentioned at the beginning of this section hardly fill the gap. A manuscript referred to by Verlaine as *La Chasse spirituelle* might do so, but this has been lost, and with it all hope of discovering whether it was the same as the *Illuminations* or a different work.

This question, which still divides authorities on Rimbaud, may never be solved with absolute certainty.[1] But, however, it may affect our interpretation of his psychological development, in the wider sense it makes no difference to an appreciation of his work. Whenever it was composed, completed or redrafted, *Les Illuminations* is what survives of the great visionary work he had contemplated before he met Verlaine. It should not depend for its effect on biographical references, or indeed on any detailed knowledge of its author. Like all great poems – and this is one – it can be read in a spirit of discovery rather than with the idea of recognition. What will always be worth finding in it will be new, with a novelty varying from reader to reader.

[1] That is still the position at this date. See review by C. A. Hackett of Albert Py's edition of the *Illuminations* (Droz, 1967) in *French Studies*, January 1971: '. . . he is content to place the *Illuminations* (rightly, in our view) as a "suite d'écrits" within the period 1872 to 1874 or, at latest, 1875.' The general inference is that, after Rimbaud had renounced the 'lying visions' of his *voyant* period in *Une Saison en enfer*, he nevertheless continued to add to the *Illuminations* and to fair-copy them for a year or two longer.

Chapter 18

Stéphane Mallarmé

WITH Mallarmé we leave the domain of Bohemianism, passion, guilt and ethics, to enter the office of a kind of mad statistician who manipulates words instead of figures. Greatest of white-collar poets, high priest of Symbolism, don's delight and reincarnation of Baudelaire's cat,[1] such are the attributes of this outwardly drab personality. Of him it could be said more truly than of most people that he led a life in which nothing happened. We are left with the adventures of the spirit, on whose extent and interest the greatness of his poetry must finally depend. But the man himself is not at first sight promising.

He was born in 1842 of Parisian middle-class parents and, since his mother died when he was six, he was brought up dutifully by his grandmother. At the age of twenty he crossed the Channel to London – having already begun to study English in order, he said later, to read Edgar Allan Poe in the original; the desire had been kindled in him by Baudelaire's writings. He took with him a German girl, to whom he was married in Kensington, and returned to France after a nine-months' stay equipped with enough English to teach it in French schools. The next thirty years of his life were spent in various *lycées*, at first in the south and east (Tournon, Besançon and Avignon), but after 1871 in Paris, where he found a post at the Lycée Condorcet which Verlaine had attended as a pupil some ten years earlier. Two further moves were made to other Parisian *lycées* before he thankfully took his retirement and his pension at the age of fifty-one. He was an unimpressive if conscientious teacher who seems to have bored his pupils as much as they must have bored him. He enjoyed his release from this drudgery for only five years. He died of an attack of laryngitis in September 1898.

His private life was almost as colourless as his professional career.

[1] Les amoureux fervents et les savants austères
Aiment également, dans leur mûre saison,
Les chats puissants et doux, orgueil de la maison,
Qui comme eux sont frileux et comme eux sédentaires.
Fleurs de mal, LXVI.

With his wife Marie, he soon settled down to a humdrum existence on small means. A daughter, Geneviève, was born, and later a son who died in childhood. One can make either much or little of his friendship with Méry Laurent, an ex-dancer and *demi-mondaine* who was the Mallarmés' neighbour in Paris. He found in her a sympathetic comrade and the kind of model of human beauty which the Pre-Raphaelites had looked for in their friends, but it seems unlikely that she was his mistress. In any case, their association was not passionate. He lived without love or hate and even without travel, being content to spend his summers at Valvins, near Fontainebleau, where he sailed his small boat on the Seine. Yet this apparently negative character had a talent for friendship which drew some of the most remarkable men of two generations to his side and gradually made his modest home one of the main centres of French intellectual life.

It began in his schooldays when he attracted the sympathy of a young teacher, Emmanuel des Essarts (a poet himself), who encouraged him in literature. While teaching at Avignon he was on cordial terms with some of the *Félibrige* poets – particularly Aubanel and Mistral – who were working to revive Provençal literature. When he moved to Paris his name was already known through his contributions to reviews and he quickly established personal contact with such contemporary poets as Verlaine, Heredia and Catulle Mendès. He kept all these friends and added new ones through his interests in music and painting. Manet became his particular friend, while later Whistler, Gauguin and Rodin knew him and paid him homage. After 1880 his small flat in the Rue de Rome, behind Saint-Lazare station, became a rendezvous for writers who grew more and more to look on Mallarmé as their master. His reputation was increased by Verlaine's article on him in *Les Poètes maudits* and by the references to his verse in *A rebours*, the novel by Joris-Karl Huysmans, another personal friend. Both of these were published in 1884, at which date numerous young poets were groping for a new literary doctrine, soon to be called Symbolism. They grouped themselves round Mallarmé and the famous Tuesdays in the Rue de Rome were attended by such poets as Gustave Kahn, Stuart Merrill, Jean Moréas, Henri de Régnier, Vielé-Griffin and the Belgians Rodenbach, Fontainas and Mockel. It was a more talented salon than any that could have been brought together at that date by social influence, though its proceedings usually took the form of a three-hour monologue by Mallarmé, to which the visitors listened in respectful silence. In course of time, still younger writers were introduced and profited by Mallarmé's teaching, Gide and Valéry among them.

It may be objected that Mallarmé's contacts with so many friends and admirers were through the arts and so on a remoter plane than the ordinary human relationship. But in some cases – notably with Huysmans and Verlaine – this relationship existed also, while in general some personal attraction was necessary to bind together so many devoted disciples. Doctrine alone would never have been enough. The personality which had proved too rare and elusive for the class-room blossomed with tremendous authority in a more adult circle.

Mallarmé's influence was the more remarkable because he published little, and that comparatively late. Two of his longest poems, *Hérodiade* and *L'Après-midi d'un faune*, had been begun when he was teaching at Tournon in 1863–6. Both were originally conceived as dramatic pieces. The first was never finished. The second was pub-lished, after two rewritings, in 1876. Although he appeared in reviews, it was not until 1887 that he published a collective edition of his shorter poems, limited to forty-seven copies. With a few later additions, this accounts for almost his entire poetic production – some sixty pieces of verse in all, many of them sonnets. He wrote much less than Bau-delaire and is in extreme contrast to the prolific Hugo and even to Verlaine.

A final, highly enigmatic, poem appeared in a review in 1897. This was *Un Coup de dés jamais n'abolira le hasard*, of which the main feature was the elaborate typographical arrangement. Special significance was given to spacing and the use of capital letters. A single word might occupy a whole page. This attempt to bring the page itself into physical collaboration with the poet's mind was a highly interesting experiment, but too difficult to succeed as a means of communication. Besides this, Mallarmé made a prose translation of Poe's poems – 'a legacy from Baudelaire', he called it – and expounded his views on literature and art in the intricate prose essays of *Divagations* (1897). An earlier prose work, *Igitur*, was discovered and published posthumously. Written between 1867 and 1870, it is the veiled symbolic record of a psycho-logical crisis through which Mallarmé passed at Besançon and Avignon and it belongs to the same family as Rimbaud's *Une Saison en enfer*.

II

The difficulty of Mallarmé's verse attracts some readers as strongly as it repels others, but both classes of readers should remember that it is not so much a willed quality (though the will entered into the actual process of composition) as a logical consequence of the poet's nature.

He wrote with great difficulty, haunted always by the fear of sterility. In the plainest terms, he was afraid not so much of writing common-place verse – the conscious avoidance of which might lead to affecta-tion – as of being incapable of writing at all. Since the fluent com-mand of language which the majority of great poets have enjoyed was not for him, he made the most – sometimes, perhaps, more than the most – of the words of which he did dispose. He cherished them individually, turning and displaying them so as to lose no facet of possible meaning. He arranged them in special orders and settings in an attempt to bring out their most subtle qualities, straining normal French syntax to do so. He dispensed largely with punctuation, or played it down, leaving the word and phrase as unfettered as possible; not, it may be hazarded, with a deliberate intention of ambiguity, but in the more humble belief that by running free his phrases might set up resonances of which he himself had not originally been aware.

When he wrote, though in a slightly different context, that: '*To name* an object is to destroy three quarters of the enjoyment of a poem, which is made up of the pleasure of guessing little by little; *to suggest it* – that is the ideal', he was thinking not only of the reader. The poet also, given a sufficient respect for the possibilities of his medium, may always expect to have written more than he knew and to have the same pleasure afterwards of discovering new extensions of meaning. In this Mallarmé differs from the opposite type of laborious poet represented by Malherbe, who is clear and limited because of his determination to control the full implication of every word he puts down. To do this is to regard language primarily as a vehicle for com-munication. But Mallarmé considered it as potentially live material, which in certain combinations could bring into existence what had not existed before.

Besides meaning, words have another property: sound. One too easily writes 'music' in this connection, prompted by Mallarmé's deep interest in music proper, particularly Wagner's music, and by his conviction that poetry ought to be suggestive and moving in the same way. But Mallarmé is not 'musical' as Baudelaire sometimes is, or like Verlaine, some of whose verses can even be sung without doing too much violence to them. He shows only rarely the melodious quali-ties which Valéry was to develop with deliberate virtuosity through whole passages of verse. His concern is rather with the sound of the separate word or small group of words, as in:

Que vêt parmi *l'exil inutile* le Cygne,

or:

<blockquote>Aboli bibelot d'inanité sonore.</blockquote>

In reading his carefully chosen but short sound-combinations one is less aware of the musician than of the magician or oracle who seeks by a few sibylline phrases to intrigue the mind through the ear, but is not trying to compose a verbal 'movement'. Aesthetic in the detail, he is less so in his general design. In his sonnets and other short poems especially, the controlling factor which gives the piece its unity is generally an intellectual factor. This is noticeable even when the point of departure is a pictorial conception.

Mallarmé's attitude towards words – his material and his instrument of discovery – changed somewhat during his life, though basically he remained the same poet. At the age of twenty he underwent, like other poets, the fascination of Baudelaire and his early verse bears the master's imprint. It appears in such sonnets as *Angoisse*, *Le Sonneur* and *Tristesse d'été*, the last of which speaks of the oblivion he hopes to find in his mistress's hair and in the make-up (presumably mascara) 'wept by her eyelids';

<blockquote>Mais ta chevelure est une rivière tiède,
Où noyer sans frissons l'âme qui nous obsède
Et trouver ce Néant que tu ne connais pas.</blockquote>

<blockquote>Je goûterai le fard pleuré par tes paupières,
Pour voir s'il sait donner au cœur que tu frappas
L'insensibilité de l'azur et des pierres.</blockquote>

While this is well below the best Baudelaire, it is interesting for the last line, in which the fastidious Mallarmé is already selecting words on his own initiative. *L'azur*, his favourite word for 'the sky', is unexpectedly coupled with another insensible substance, stones. The idea of the whole tercet is out of life or out of realism (one might lick mascara for a number of reasons, but hardly to see if it would bring insensibility), is not particularly Satanic, and is at least halfway to aestheticism: the urge to experiment with artistic material (here, words) rather than with actual physical sensations.

If we take a leap from such early poems, relatively clear in their sense and straightforward in their syntax and word-values, to Mallarmé's late work, we find an extreme contrast. Twenty years of practice in compression and distortion had led to such verse as:

<blockquote>A la nue accablante tu
Basse de basalte et de laves</blockquote>

> A même les échos esclaves
> Par une trompe sans vertu
>
> Quel sépulcral naufrage (tu
> Le sais, écume, mais y baves)
> Suprême une entre les épaves
> Abolit le mât dévêtu

This might be first approached as a conundrum, made more difficult by the lack of punctuation and some forcing of the word-order. Restoring these and making other slight changes, we have in prose:

Tu à la nue accablante (basse de basalte et de laves), et même aux échos esclaves, par une trompe sans vertu, quel sépulcral naufrage (tu le sais, écume, mais y baves) abolit – suprême et unique épave – le mât dévêtu?

The English would then be:

Silenced to the overwhelming cloud, which is low with basalt and lava [black and solid-looking], and even to the slavish echoes, by an ineffectual trumpet, what sepulchral shipwreck (you know it, foam, but slobber over it) abolishes – supreme [highest or final] piece among the wreckage – the stripped mast?

There are several possible alternative meanings. *A même les échos* could also mean *alongside the echoes*, while *une trompe sans vertu* might imply either that the trumpet was not sounded or that it was too feeble to be heard above the echoes of the storm. (Evidently it was a signal of distress.) *Abolit* can be either past or present tense. Such verse is full of puzzles whose working-out can provide endless pleasure of a fairly low order. If one does not wish to work them out, one can merely say that this particular sonnet as a whole[1] refers to a shipwreck, symbolical no doubt of some psychological disaster. Something is sinking or has sunk without warning or trace in a storm whose causes are uncertain. Some commentators see in this an allegory of life, or of the poet's destiny, but if that were the main point of the poem it is obvious that almost anyone could do as well. Mallarmé's peculiar talent appears in such touches as the assonance in the first line ('A la

---

[1] The remaining lines are:

> Ou cela que furibonde faute
> De quelque perdition haute
> Tout l'abîme vain éployé
>
> Dans le si blanc cheveu qui traîne
> Avarement aura noyé
> Le flanc enfant d'une sirène.

nue accablante tu') and the consonance in the second ('*Basse* de *basalte*')
and the puzzling and intrusive placing of the word *tu*. The meaning of
this, as the past participle of *taire*, only becomes clear when one reaches
line 5, which contains the subject of the phrase and the first noun with
which *tu* could agree: *sépulcral naufrage*. Nearly each one of these lines,
taken separately, is a small organization of sound with a concealed or
withheld meaning, and has some kind of virtue in itself even before
it is fitted into the complete picture. If it had not, one could only say
that Mallarmé was absurdly incompetent to write his poems in this way.

Such a sonnet is an extreme example of ingenuity rather than a great
poem, but before he reached this point Mallarmé had written verse
which is better than ingenious. There is the relatively long *Après-midi
d'un faune*, subtitled 'an eclogue', which is fairly clear in outline as
the erotic and aesthetic musings of a classical faun on a warm southern
afternoon. It should be read first in a state of intellectual trance, with
the mind closed, and then with the help of one or more of the detailed
commentaries upon it. Parallel to this outstandingly sensuous poem
is *Hérodiade*, a hymn to chastity or sterility. It was this in a second sense
because Mallarmé was never able to finish it. Unlike *L'Après-midi
d'un faune*, the total intention of *Hérodiade* is still debatable, but the
detail is clear; as in the lovely lines in which the virgin princess meditates on her own nature:

> Oui, c'est pour moi, pour moi, que je fleuris, déserte!
> Vous le savez, jardins d'améthyste, enfouis
> Sans fin dans de savants abîmes éblouis,
> Ors ignorés, gardant votre antique lumière
> Sous le sombre sommeil d'une terre première,
> Vous pierres où mes yeux comme de purs bijoux
> Empruntent leur clarté mélodieuse, et vous
> Métaux qui donnez à ma jeune chevelure
> Une splendeur fatale et sa massive allure!
>
> ... J'aime l'horreur d'être vierge et je veux
> Vivre parmi l'effroi que me font mes cheveux
> Pour, le soir, retirée en ma couche, reptile
> Inviolé sentir en la chair inutile
> Le froid scintillement de ta pâle clarté
> Toi qui te meurs, toi qui brûles de chasteté,
> Nuit blanche de glaçons et de neige cruelle!

Similar preoccupations underlie one of the best known of all Mallarmé's poems, the sonnet beginning *Le vierge, le vivace et le bel
aujourd'hui*. It contains the pictorial image of the swan trapped in the

ice of a frozen lake and by its insistence on whiteness, sterility and cold
has affinities with the last few lines of the passage from *Hérodiade* just
quoted. The barren coldness of the physical scene is suggested by the
recurrent *i*-sound which runs through all the end-rhymes, dominates
several of the lines internally, and is of course the vowel of the master-
word *cygne*. It is not merely a subjective reaction to hear the French *i*
as a desolate sound in itself,[1] made more desolate by the sense-associations of such words as *cri, agonie, bise, siffle, givre, hiver, stérile,*
exil, ennui. Mallarmé introduces most of these words into his poem,
in which we have emphasized the words or lines containing the most
telling assonances:

> Le vierge, le *vivace* et le bel *aujourd'hui*
> Va-t-il nous *déchirer* avec un coup d'aile *ivre*
> Ce lac dur *oublié* que hante sous le *givre*
> Le transparent glacier des vols qui n'ont pas *fui*!
>
> Un *cygne* d'autrefois se souvient que c'est *lui*
> *Magnifique* mais qui sans espoir se *délivre*
> Pour n'avoir pas chanté la région où *vivre*
> Quand *du stérile hiver* a resplendi *l'ennui.*
>
> Tout son col secouera cette blanche *agonie*
> Par l'espace *infligée* à l'oiseau qui le *nie,*
> Mais non l'horreur du sol où le plumage est *pris.*
>
> Fantôme qu'à ce lieu son pur éclat *assigne,*
> Il s'*immobilise* au songe froid de *mépris*
> Que vêt *parmi l'exil inutile le Cygne.*

The swan's plight is of course an allegory, open to diverse interpretations, but applied most plausibly to the poet or artist who is
trapped in his own love of perfection (the pure waters of the lake)
which then freezes over and becomes his prison. Winter has surprised
him there when he ought to have been migrating towards the warmth
of life and after a short struggle he is immobilized by the 'gleaming
purity' which is his element.

III

Another view of the poet, this time in his relation to society, is in
Le Tombeau d'Edgar Poe, which Mallarmé wrote as though it were to

---

[1] Cf. Racine's line:

> Tout m'afflige et me nuit et conspire à me nuire.

For Rimbaud, however, the vowel *i* was red, associated with crimson, blood, lips, and
so suggestive of the opposite conception of warmth.

be recited at the unveiling of a monument to Poe at Baltimore in 1875. In fact the poem was not written until the following year, but in reading the last few lines it is useful to remember that Mallarmé had an actual monument in mind. The general theme is this: Now that the poet has been changed by death into his eternally true self, his contemporaries are horror-struck not to have realized his true significance (as a messenger of death) while he was still alive. The many-headed public (hydra), when they originally heard his angelic voice giving a purer sense to the tribal catchwords (language debased by current usage), derided him as a drunken soothsayer. If from this conflict between earth and sky, 'real' and ideal, our mind does not construct an ornament for Poe's tomb (a metaphorical ornament, such as the sonnet itself), then let at least the granite block of the tomb stand to protect him once and for all against future slander:

> Tel qu'en Lui-même enfin l'éternité le change,
> Le Poëte suscite avec un glaive nu
> Son siècle épouvanté de n'avoir pas connu
> Que la mort triomphait dans cette voix étrange!
>
> Eux, comme un vil sursaut d'hydre oyant jadis l'ange
> Donner un sens plus pur aux mots de la tribu
> Proclamèrent très haut le sortilège bu
> Dans le flot sans honneur de quelque noir mélange
>
> Du sol et de la nue hostiles, ô grief!
> Si notre idée avec ne sculpte un bas-relief
> Dont la tombe de Poe éblouissante s'orne
>
> Calme bloc ici-bas chu d'un désastre obscur
> Que ce granit du moins montre à jamais sa borne
> Aux noirs vols du Blasphème épars dans le futur.

Mallarmé's first version of the sonnet differed somewhat from the definitive version printed here.[1] He himself made the following English translation[2] of the earlier version:

> Such as into himself at last Eternity changes him,
> The poet arouses with a naked hymn[a]

---

[1] The chief differences are: l. 2, *hymne* for *glaive*. l. 4, *s'exaltait* for *triomphait*. l. 5, *Mais comme un vil tressaut d'hydre* . . . l. 7, *Tous pensèrent entre eux le sortilège bu*. l. 9, *Du sol et de l'éther*. . . l. 10, *Mon* for *notre*. l. 12, *Sombre bloc à jamais chu*. . . l. 14, *Aux vieux vols de blasphème*. . .

[2] First published by Charles Chassé in *Revue de littérature comparée* (1949).

His century overawed not to have known
That death extolled itself in this[b] strange voice:

But, in a vile writhing of an hydra, (they) once hearing
    the Angel[c]
To give[d] too pure a meaning to the words of the tribe,
They (between themselves) thought (by him) the spell drunk
In the honourless flood of some dark mixture[e]

Of the soil and the ether (which are) enemies, o struggle!
If with it my idea does not carve a bas-relief
Of which Poe's dazzling[f] tomb be adorned,

(A) stern block here fallen from a mysterious disaster,
Let this granite at least show forever their bound
To the old flights of Blasphemy (still) spread in the future.[g]

To this, Mallarmé added his own explanatory notes, also in English:
    [a] Naked hymn means when the words take in death their absolute
value.
    [b] This means his own.
    [c] The Angel means the above said poet.
    [d] To give means giving.
    [e] In plain prose: charged him with always being drunk.
    [f] Dazzling means with the idea of such a bas-relief.
    [g] Blasphemy means against poets, such as the charge of Poe's
always being drunk.

It will be noticed that, apart from one or two minor faults in English
idiom, Mallarmé appears to mistranslate *grief* in line 9. Normally it
means, not 'struggle' but 'grievance' or 'complaint'. Except where they
are obvious, his elucidatory notes if anything obscure his translation
and point to the conclusion that a difficult writer does not really know
where his work is difficult.

After the sense has been pieced together, the most striking feature
of the sonnet is the pomp of such lines as:

Dont la tombe de Poe éblouissante s'orne

and of:

Aux noirs vols du Blasphème épars dans le futur.

The flourish of these is paralleled by lines 8 and 14 of the Swan
Sonnet quoted earlier. But the most typical strength of the sonnet for

Poe is in its compression, a quality which has made the opening line one of the most famous in European poetry. For a comparison one naturally turns to *Adonais*, Shelley's lament for a brother poet, Keats, who was also calumniated in his life and – Shelley believed – killed by his calumniators. One reads through the fifty-five flowing stanzas with mounting impatience against the wholly innocent Shelley. He seems so near to hitting the target of 'Eternity at last changes him into himself', but again and again swerves away at the critical point. In the opening stanza:

> ... his fate and fame shall be
> An echo and a light unto eternity.

In the fourth:

> ... he went, unterrified,
> Into the gulf of death: but his clear Sprite
> Yet reigns o'er earth.

Surely the idea must occur in the lovely sequence which begins:

> Nor let us weep that our delight is fled
> Far from these carrion kites that scream below;[1]
> He wakes or sleeps with the enduring dead:
> Thou canst not soar where he is sitting now.
> Dust to the dust! but the pure spirit shall flow
> Back to the burning fountain whence it came,
> A portion of the Eternal, which must glow.
> Through time and change, unquenchably the same.
> Whilst thy cold embers[2] choke the sordid hearth of shame.

But in the end we realize that it will not and cannot occur. Partly because Shelley's conception of the dead poet becoming one with the universal spirit is irreconcilable with Mallarmé's conception of the poet becoming (through his work rather than in any other manifestation of his spirit) unalterably himself. Partly because Shelley's rhetoric, like all Romantic rhetoric, is based on cumulation, not concentration, on a building-up of phrases and images to a staggering grand total.[3] Mallarmé's is compressed to contain the maximum force in the minimum space and this difference in idiom must to some extent affect the concepts.

One further comparison is interesting. In 1889 Verlaine, who of

---

[1] Cf. Mallarmé's more abstract *noirs vols du Blasphème*.
[2] The ashes of the slanderer.
[3] Cf. the passage from Musset's *Lettre à Lamartine* quoted on p. 145.

course knew Mallarmé's sonnet – he had printed it himself in the *Poètes maudits* – published a sonnet on Rimbaud, whom he believed to be dead. The hints taken from Mallarmé – detraction of the poet, drunkenness, sculpture – are apparent, while the style is rather more compressed than is usual in Verlaine. But he cannot go far in Mallarmé's direction and the only original things he has to say about Rimbaud are that Rimbaud loved him and was attractive to women because of his rustic good looks and his lazy cheekiness! It is not one of his best poems, but it points the contrast between three very different poets: Shelley, all fire and spirit; Verlaine, engaged on characterizing the physical, Mallarmé, preoccupied with the intellectual essence of subject and situation. This is Verlaine's sonnet:

> Mortel, ange ET démon, autant dire Rimbaud,
> Tu mérites la prime place en ce mien livre,
> Bien que tel sot grimaud t'ait traité de ribaud
>   Imberbe et de monstre en herbe et de potache ivre.
>
> Les spirales d'encens et les accords de luth
> Signalent ton entrée au temple de mémoire
> Et ton nom radieux chantera dans la gloire,
> Parce que tu m'aimas ainsi qu'il le fallut.
>
> Les femmes te verront grand jeune homme très fort,
> Très beau d'une beauté paysanne et rusée,
> Très désirable d'une indolence qu'osée!
>
> L'histoire t'a sculpté triomphant de la mort
> Et jusqu'aux purs excès triomphant de la vie,
> Tes pieds blancs posés sur la tête de l'Envie![1]

IV

The urge to work out Mallarmé's meaning for oneself and then to 'explicate' it to others is an addiction which the nature of his poetry encourages. Sometimes it is raised to the status of exegesis, a term more properly reserved for the exposition of the Scriptures and which supposes at least an expert knowledge based on some body of accepted doctrine. Any such assumption is misleading where Mallarmé is concerned, since no one authoritative interpretation of his work exists, but only more or less percipient commentaries. To expect more than this is to regard the poet as the exponent of some coherent if hermetic system which he either created or represented – but in any case a

[1] *Dédicaces*, LVI.

system. What then becomes of the explorer, using words to make his discoveries and suggesting further discoveries to his various readers?

It is much better to concede that poetry for Mallarmé was a game, even though he considered it as the greatest of all games. On the level of serious play he is fascinating and a wonderful companion for nights of insomnia. (One would not recommend Baudelaire for the same occasions.) Anyone faced with his professional explicators should realize from the start that they are experienced fellow players in the same game, worthy of respect for that reason, but open to suspicion when they grow dogmatic. Of most of Mallarmé's more knotty poems there is no one unchallengeable explanation on an intellectual level, but several possible or alternative explanations. This seems to have been Mallarmé's intention and it would be fatuous to know better than the author. Moreover, a purely intellectual explanation does not exhaust appreciation of the poet and should be used simply as a convenient handrail.

Mallarmé can be approached most satisfactorily as a strayed, or an evolved, Parnassian. He started from a position very near to Gautier's theory of 'art for art's sake' and was at first interested in the pictorial qualities of verse. In an early poem such as *Soupir*, he compares his soul aspiring to his mistress to a fountain rising in a park in autumn, but the image carries him away and the last half of the poem is predominantly pictorial:

> Mon âme vers ton front où rêve, ô calme sœur,
> Un automne jonché de taches de rousseur
> Et vers le ciel errant de ton œil angélique
> Monte, comme dans un jardin mélancolique,
> Fidèle, un blanc jet d'eau soupire vers l'Azur!
> – Vers l'Azur attendri d'Octobre pâle et pur
> Qui mire aux grands bassins sa langueur infinie
> Et laisse, sur l'eau morte où la fauve agonie
> Des feuilles erre au vent et creuse un long sillon,
> Se traîner le soleil jaune d'un long rayon.

But he came to realize the inadequacy of the outer landscape and perhaps his own incapacity to paint it without being imitative and decided to treat 'not the object, but the effect which it produces'. With most poets this would necessitate a switch from the objective to the subjective, supposing that poetry must oscillate between those two poles. But the Parnassian element in Mallarmé led him to attempt the portrayal of the essences of objects which for him were more real than the objects themselves. No doubt it was an illusion and he fell into subjectivity. Yet one can but admit that the effort and intention shown in Mallarmé's sonnets runs parallel to that shown in Heredia's work. There is the same exacting craftsmanship, the same – or rather, a much greater – care in the selection and disposition of words.[1] To what end? To paint the phantom or ideal picture which should always accompany the visible picture of the universe as the human mind apprehends it.

What prevents Mallarmé from being an incontestably great poet is his failure to achieve this. He does not seem to have known the physical universe well enough before undertaking to express its spirit. And he could draw on no great religious or metaphysical tradition which might have supplied him with that knowledge or have taken its place. The teaching of Edgar Allan Poe was an inadequate substitute. If we look at Mallarmé's physical world as it is revealed in his more original poems, we find that it contains the common objects in a poor writer's home – a lamp, curtains, flowers – a few usual ornaments such as fans and jewels, and some marble slabs suggesting either mantelpieces or tombs. There are no animals, except the Swan; no people, except the cipher Hérodiade and some virtually anonymous women evoked from a conventionally erotic viewpoint.[2] Beyond this, his great symbols involve the sea, ships, rocks, and the sky by day and by night.

These are generalized to a point at which hardly any true direct

---

[1] That the art of Mallarmé seemed to contemporaries to contain at least one important Parnassian feature is borne out by the first letter which Paul Valéry wrote to him. The young poet, subscribing himself as a fervent admirer of *Hérodiade* and of the 'doctrines savantes du grand Edgar Allan Poe', declares that he prefers 'les poèmes courts, *concentrés pour un éclat final, où les rhythmes sont comme les marches marmoréennes de l'autel que couronne le dernier vers*'. (Letter of 14 July 1890.) While such a technique, as handled by Mallarmé, can lend itself to Symbolist poetry, it has a clear affinity with the *vers définitif* of the Parnassians and is the opposite to Verlaine's preference for the drifting final line. See p. 187 above.

[2] His poem most peopled with sensory images is *L'Après-midi d'un faune*, but to a large degree they are literary. It must also be remembered that erotic imagery is the commonest and easiest kind of all. There are other common objects in the small poems significantly entitled *Chansons bas*, which Mallarmé intended humorously.

Comparisons between painting and poetry are full of pitfalls, but it is tempting to contrast the aridity of Mallarmé's renderings with the warmth and richness which such late Impressionists as Vuillard and Bonnard discovered in the same simple domestic material. The gulf between them suggests that a truer analogy for Mallarmé's verse might be with 'abstract' painting. But to pursue this would entail lifting Mallarmé right out of his period and detaching him from the Symbolist movement, with its insistence on 'music' and its vaguely apprehended transcendental values. He would cease to be at the heart of Symbolism. Moreover, it would suppose a development in the work of a single poet from the representational art of the Parnassians to the abstractionism of a Braque or of a Picasso. Such a development is not theoretically impossible, and our view of Mallarmé as well as of the whole course of modern aesthetics might well be renewed by a successful demonstration that it did in fact occur. But this would require more than a footnote, or a chapter.

observation need be implied. On such evidence one may well ask what was Mallarmé's authority to describe the essence of a universe which he does not appear to have known. The usual answer is to call him the poet of absence or of the void. This appears not unacceptable. The sense of absence and emptiness is a deep human reaction to a common situation and if Mallarmé expresses it he can be placed beside Pascal, Baudelaire and Du Bellay. But it ought to be accompanied by a desire for presence and fullness and there is little sign in Mallarmé's mature work that he either regretted or aspired to anything other than he had. We are left with immensely skilful poetry about a negative state in which the poet seems to have acquiesced[1] and which he indeed elaborated as the only state in which he could imagine himself existing – or, if one prefers it, nonexisting.

The lack of correspondences between Mallarmé's poetry and the external universe is his weakest point. The attempt to create something perfect in itself has led to self-containment and then to isolation from both material and spiritual values. This isolation can be attributed to too high a conception of the poet's function rather than the reverse. For it would seem that the poet should not endeavour to *create*, in the strict sense of the word. His function is to *re-create*, by combining in new ways elements which are already familiar. Sometimes Mallarmé does this, but more often everything he uses appears to be his own invention. In its way, it is a vast achievement. But it is unproductive and sets up no resonances outside itself. His work demands to be admired for the beauty of its own complex patterns rather than to be related to any kind of lived experience. It illustrates both the triumph of 'pure poetry' and its limitations.

[1] There is, however, an indication of the contrary in a letter from Claudel to Gide (27 January 1913). Claudel speaks of: '. . . ce mot que Mallarmé a dit à l'un de nous: "Je suis un désespéré." ' He adds: 'Car au fond Mallarmé était un mystique, il est resté prisonnier de cette vitre froide et nue qu'il n'a jamais pu rompre.' But Claudel's interpretation of Mallarmé, like his interpretation of Rimbaud, may well have been coloured by his own religious convictions.

Chapter 19

Other Nineteenth-Century Poets

THE nineteenth century can be seen today as the greatest age of French poetry, surpassing even the Renaissance in wealth of themes and variety of treatment, and certainly not yet equalled by the twentieth century, which in some essentials derives from it. It was an age in which poetry was perhaps the most popular of all mediums of expression, attracting a high proportion of first-class writers and a veritable army of the less great. Among all these were poets of strong talent who deserve to be remembered either because of the general level of their achievement or because of some particularly original contribution to literature. At least twenty such poets might be listed, some of them approaching in interest the major poets described in the nine previous chapters.

But twenty is too many, except as an illustration of the vigour of the nineteenth-century Muse. The majority must be left to the anthologies and the more exhaustive manuals of literature, where they will usually be found classed, conveniently if roughly, in three main generations as Romantics, Parnassians and Symbolists. In such places the reader may sometimes experience the pleasure of discovering for himself a minor poet whose work he finds particularly congenial, or even one whose value seems to have been unjustly overlooked. The most promising ground for such discoveries is among the later Symbolists, while, if the Parnassian aesthetic ever returned to favour, there would be obvious scope for rehabilitation among some of Leconte de Lisle's neglected contemporaries. Meanwhile, it is only proposed in this chapter to consider four poets of especial interest: Nerval, Gautier, Corbière and Laforgue.

II

Gérard de Nerval (the pseudonym adopted by Gérard Labrunie) was born in 1808 and belonged, like his contemporaries Musset and Gautier, to the Romantic generation of 1830. His early work would hardly have distinguished him from other young and secondary writers

of the time and it was not until the last years of his life that he wrote
the stories and the handful of sonnets which have earned him a unique
place in French literature. He was by then living in a state of great
emotional tension and was afflicted by intermittent spells of madness
which ultimately drove him to suicide in 1855. Shortly before his
death he produced in rapid succession an autobiographical prose-work,
Aurélia, a volume of short stories, *Les Filles du feu*, and his sonnets,
Les Chimères. Through all these runs the common Romantic motif
of regret for what might have been, crystallized round a feminine
figure who, biographically speaking, was a reminiscence of three
women: his mother, who died when he was a child; a girl met once at
a dance in his youth (the 'Adrienne' of one of his stories); and, most
important of the three, an actress called Jenny Colon with whom he
fell in love towards the age of thirty. She refused Nerval to marry
another man and died not long after. This lived experience was trans-
muted by long brooding into a kind of mysticism whose character was
determined by two main factors: the influence of the German Romantics, more metaphysical than their French counterparts, and particularly of Goethe's *Faust*, which Nerval translated;[1] and then the
influence of various religious myths, sometimes described as 'oriental',
but more precisely Greek, Egyptian and even Christian. Nerval studied
these for their occult or hidden meanings, and believed that he found
in them truths of world import as well as others bearing on his own
immediate situation.

From these varied elements, to which he added other reminiscences
of his life and reading, Nerval compounded the six sonnets which
make up the *Chimères*. Two of these, *El Desdichado* and *Artémis*, are
among the most famous in the French language.

Their power lies in their use of mysterious symbols and allusions
which affect the reader in much the same way as a magic incantation.
He recognizes some of the allusions, guesses at others, and takes the
rest on trust because it is stated so confidently and beautifully. He
willingly allows himself to be led into a kingdom of hidden significance just beyond the frontiers of his known world and surrenders
to a charm of the same nature as that contained in Coleridge's *Kubla
Khan*, except that Nerval is less clear. This is especially true of *El
Desdichado*:

> Je suis le ténébreux, – le veuf, – l'inconsolé,
> Le prince d'Aquitaine à la tour abolie;

---

[1] Women (Margaret and Helen) play an important part among the redemptive influences
at work on Faust. Margaret becomes one of the spirits who greet Faust in his apotheosis.

Ma seule *étoile* est morte, – et mon luth constellé
Porte le *soleil noir* de la *Mélancolie.*

Dans la nuit du tombeau toi qui m'as consolé,
Rends-moi le Pausilippe et la mer d'Italie,
La *fleur* qui plaisait tant à mon cœur désolé,
Et la treille où le pampre à la rose s'allie.

Suis-je Amour ou Phébus, Lusignan ou Biron?
Mon front est rouge encor du baiser de la reine;
J'ai rêvé dans la grotte où nage la sirène . . .

Et j'ai deux fois vainqueur traversé l'Achéron,
Modulant tour à tour sur la lyre d'Orphée
Les soupirs de la sainte et les cris de la fée.

To the reader of such a sonnet two courses are open. Either he can leave it in its general context of the complaint of the *desdichado* – the ill-starred man – and interpret its obscurer lines in whatever way his own imagination or his experience suggests. This, which might seem to be the refuge of the idle or the ignorant, is a perfectly legitimate approach to poetry of this kind, and one which Nerval himself encouraged when he wrote that *Les Chimères* 'would lose their charm by being explained, supposing that were possible'. Most poets would willingly sacrifice complete comprehension for the much greater triumph of entering into the live imagination of their readers. That is perhaps the main function of the poetic medium and is certainly its highest achievement.

If, on the other hand, one wishes to know exactly what was in Nerval's mind as he wrote each line of his sonnet, the answer can be given with a fair degree of certainty.[1] By referring to his autobiographical prose writings and to the books he is known to have read, almost every allusion can be made clear. Thus, the clue to the title and to the opening quatrain is furnished by Walter Scott's *Ivanhoe,* in which a mysterious knight bears on his shield the words *El Desdichado.* Taking this from Scott, though not from Spanish, to mean 'disinherited', Nerval goes on to see himself as 'the Aquitanian prince of the abolished tower' – a reference to an ancient southern family from which Nerval

[1] The fullest annotations of his verse are in Jeanine Moulin, *Gérard de Nerval: Les Chimères* (Lille and Geneva, 1949). *El Desdichado* and *Artémis* are also annotated in A. M. Boase, *The Poetry of France,* Vol. III (Methuen, 1967); *El Desdichado* only in Castex and Surer, *Manuel des études littéraires françaises, XIXᵉ siècle* (Hachette, 1950). For Nerval and the occult more generally, see J. Richer, *G. de Nerval et les doctrines ésotériques* (Paris, 1947).

claimed to descend, whose titles of nobility were abolished in the Revolution, and whose arms were Three Towers Argent. In the third line, his 'star' is probably his love, the women whom he has lost and whom he considers as different facets of the same female principle. Imposed upon this there might, however, be a further allusion to heraldry, and there is almost certainly an allusion to one of the cards of the Tarot pack, used by fortune-tellers.[1] This card is called 'The Star', while others, relevant to the same quatrain, are 'The Prince of Darkness' and 'The Blasted Tower'. In the same line the Dark Knight becomes also a troubadour, carrying a lute painted with stars and among them the device of the 'black (eclipsed) sun' which was suggested to Nerval by a picture of Dürer's entitled *Melancolia*.[2]

The second quatrain evokes a personal experience of the poet's, as recounted in one of his short stories. On Mount Posilippo, overlooking the Bay of Naples, he had been contemplating suicide (hence: *dans la nuit du tombeau*) but had been dissuaded by the prospect of a meeting with a young Englishwoman, a chance travel-acquaintance, to whom he sat and talked in an arbour overgrown with vines and roses. The *fleur* (the italics in the sonnet are all Nerval's) could be any flower associated in his memory with the occasion, but even this has been precisely identified as a columbine thanks to a note made by the poet in the still extant manuscript.

In the ninth line, Nerval, attempting to define his own identity, invokes Cupid and Apollo from classical mythology, Lusignan and Biron from French folklore. The latter turns his thoughts to his childhood in the Valois country and to a scene at a dance when 'the Queen' (Adrienne) kissed him. The 'siren's cave' no doubt refers to one of the local legends which he himself re-told in prose.

In the last tercet, the central concept is of Orpheus descending to the Underworld to recover Eurydice – for Nerval the woman whom

[1] Cf. T. S. Eliot, *The Waste Land*, I, lines 46–55:

> Here, said she,
> Is your card, the drowned Phoenician sailor, etc.

See particularly Eliot's note on this passage, with his remarks on the other symbols which he associates somewhat arbitrarily with the Tarot cards. As in Nerval, there is an admixture of symbols.

[2] In his poem entitled *Melancolia* (1834), Théophile Gautier gave a long description of this picture. It contains the lines:

> Dans le fond du tableau, sur l'horizon sans borne,
> Le vieux père Océan lève sa face morne,
> Et dans le bleu cristal de son profond miroir
> Réfléchit les rayons d'un grand soleil tout noir.

he saw in the two guises of 'the saint' (Adrienne, who became a nun and died in the convent) and 'the fairy' (Jenny Colon, the actress). He did not in fact recover either of these lost loves in any ordinary sense, yet, taking his two descents into hell to mean two of his spells of insanity, he may be said to have emerged from them 'victorious' in the sense that he brought back the assurance that the two women still existed for him in another world.

Such is the explanation of the more external symbolism of the sonnet. It could be developed in greater detail to show the complicated interlinking of the symbols and their wealth of overtones. The first interest of any such analysis is to show the general working of a particular poet's mind. The second is that, in a poet of Nerval's type, the mythological and cultural elements are identified almost inseparably with his own experience. This is true also of Baudelaire, but much less of Musset, and hardly at all of Gautier. Thirdly, it will now be apparent that much of the wealth, as well as the obscurity, of Nerval's verse is due to his simultaneous use of several different mythologies and planes of reference. There enter into this one sonnet the Romantic mystique of medieval chivalry and the troubadours, the occult symbolism of the Tarot cards, Greek mythology and French folklore. Compared to poetry based on a single cultural reference (classical as in Ronsard and Chénier, or biblical as in d'Aubigné and Vigny, various certainly in Leconte de Lisle – but never mixed within the same poem), here is confusion so rich as to appear indigestible. But in his slender body of work Nerval does digest it and manages to assimilate still other mythologies. Within a very small compass, therefore, he foreshadows a poetic process developed later by T. S. Eliot and, even more, by Ezra Pound. The latter has been attacked on grounds of scholarship, on which he is clearly vulnerable. But if one wished to attack him as a poet, it would seem much more relevant to examine his assimilation of his material. With Nerval, the assimilation is total, while the scholarship is so uninsistent and elusive that it hardly provokes a challenge.

Nerval uses 'symbols' – the Disinherited Knight, the Black Sun, several kinds of flower, the Thirteenth (hour) – to represent certain phases and factors in his lived experience; the reader who traces those symbols to their source can reconstruct the experience fairly clearly. This use of symbolism has to be distinguished from the methods of the Symbolist school as exemplified in Mallarmé. Unfortunately, the limited terminology of literary criticism may lead to a confusion between the two things, distinguished only by the use or avoidance of a capital letter. The poetry of the Symbolist school does not usually

refer back directly to phases of lived experience. It aims rather at
reaching an entirely new plane of experience (as in Rimbaud) or at
constructing a new technique of perception (Mallarmé). Nerval, who
is fundamentally a Romantic in his nostalgia for the past, the submerged and the unattained, and in his perplexed distaste for the actual,
never, for example, resembles Mallarmé in the latter's revolutionary
use of language. In his vocabulary and syntax he is perfectly straightforward, conventional even. That is perhaps the most radical difference
between the two.

Beyond that, the symbols used by Mallarmé and by some other
Symbolist poets are exclusively their own. Even where there seems to
be a link with some generally known myth or legend (evoked, for
example, by the Faun or the Swan), the original has been so overlaid
or transformed by the poet's own application of it that the myth hardly
provides a 'key'. At best, it may on occasion suggest a starting-point
for a reconstruction of the poet's imaginative processes, but it will
show no easy way through the labyrinth which the poet is creating
with each line that he writes. It is then best to forget the myth and to
follow the poet as patiently and imaginatively as possible.

The difference might be summed up by saying that a poet like
Nerval records experience already suffered and accepted, however
cryptically he does so; whereas Mallarmé is attempting to realize – and
so, in effect, to create – experience by the act of writing. The first
obeys one of the great Romantic formulas: the 'recollection of emotion' (not necessarily in tranquillity). Mallarmé, and with him, at least
in intention, the whole of the French Symbolist school proper, is
engaged far less in recollection than on reconnaissance. This is not
to deny that Nerval has certain apparent affinities with the Symbolists,
due as much to the metaphysical features in his prose writings as to
his verse. An apparent affinity can become an attraction and even an
influence, so that it is not altogether wrong to say that Nerval points
forward to the Symbolists. But when analysed, with the help of the
exceptionally abundant clues which he has left behind, it becomes clear
that there was a fundamental divergence between his conception of
poetry and theirs.

III

The saying which has stuck to Théophile Gautier (1811–72) and
which serves to point an immediate contrast with the introspective
Nerval, is: 'I am a man for whom the external world exists.' Because

of his talent for objective description, added to the importance which he attached to poetic form, he became the chief forerunner of the Parnassians, the master to whom they could look for the basis of their aesthetic.

In his early days Gautier belonged to the most frenzied wing of the young Romantic movement. With Gérard de Nerval he joined the group known as the *petit cénacle*, whose members' names or pseudonyms, matching their flowing hair, their horrific beards, and their clothes of a medieval picturesqueness, rang like a defiant roll-call in the ears of the despised *bourgeoisie*: Petrus Borel, Philothée O'Neddy, Jehan du Seigneur, Augustus MacKeat, Napoléon Tom. Some of the group were painters or sculptors and Gautier himself studied for a time in an artist's studio before shortness of sight obliged him to give up painting. He always regretted this and continued to look at objects with a painter's eye.

His early works were in keeping with the atmosphere of the *petit cénacle*. At twenty-one he published *Albertus, ou l'âme et le péché*, a medieval story in verse of a man who sells his soul to the devil for love of a witch. Other poems showed a preoccupation with the macabre in which the externally picturesque is mingled with at least traces of a personal obsession. In 1836 he published his first novel, *Mademoiselle de Maupin*, a wildly emotional fantasy of sex, in the preface of which he first sketched out a theory of *l'art pour l'art*.[1] In the same year he became a regular journalist and for the rest of his life was overloaded with routine work for various periodicals, producing, however, stories also and much interesting dramatic and art criticism. This somewhat monotonous existence was relieved by travel. His first journey abroad was made in 1840, when he visited Spain, the Mecca of the good Romantic, and was enchanted by the experience. It gave him a travel book, *Voyage en Espagne* (1841) and a volume of poems, *España* (1845), consisting of careful and sometimes powerful exercises in description and 'colour'. His last and principal book of verse, *Émaux et camées*, appeared in 1852.

At that period the reaction was just setting in against the poetry of Lamartine and Musset, considered to be over-facile and the product of a now unfashionable emotionalism. Gautier was to benefit from this reaction. It corresponded to his own line of development and was in harmony with his own theory and practice.

His theory, as expressed in the preface to *Mademoiselle de Maupin*

[1] Much later, Hugo claimed to have launched this phrase in a verbal discussion in 1829. See P. Van Tieghem, *Petite histoire des grandes doctrines littéraires* (Paris, 1946), p. 236.

and, later, in the Introduction which he wrote for an edition of Baude-laire's *Fleurs du mal*, was that the artist is not concerned with moral, social, or political considerations. His duty is to his art, which he should cultivate to the highest point of excellence that he is capable of reach-ing, taking beauty and not utility as his criterion. As a good craftsman, he must submit himself to his material and sink his own personality in his search for perfect execution and form. His work will therefore tend to be impersonal, at least when he is compared to the more subjective of the Romantics.

It is noteworthy that the two men whose theories were at the origins of the allied doctrines of 'art for art's sake', 'pure poetry' and the cult of ideal beauty (leading to aestheticism) – Gautier in France and Edgar Allan Poe in America – were both reacting against a contem-porary demand that art should fulfil a social function. They identified this demand with the bourgeois tendency to exploit every activity for practical ends. In both cases, they staged a further revolt by specializing in the strange and the macabre. They thus consistently opposed on every point the bourgeois scheme of things, which was based on (1) thrift and profit, (2) conventional behaviour, (3) cosy living and dying.[1] In a comparable manner, Leconte de Lisle contracted out of the movement of social optimism to concentrate on the past and the pic-turesque.

The private circumstances of all these three writers furnish a reason why they tended to regard art – or poetry – as something remote from topical considerations. All were over-burdened by journalism or other kinds of hack-work (as was Mallarmé later by teaching). They resented this work as unworthy of their talents. It merely enabled them to pay their bills. When they could turn from it, it was with feelings which caused them to magnify the higher, more 'eternal' aspects of non-remunerative art. In their experience there was an absolute divorce between the materialistic daily grind and the disinterested labour of the artist. It was essential not to allow the second to be contaminated by the first. From such a point of view, any kind of 'engagement' is simply a surrender to the values of the trader and the politician. It would seem that theories of artistic purity, and particularly the distinction between the language of 'communication' and true poetry, owe less historically to the leisured aesthete than to harassed men who were forced into

[1] By a wholly intelligible turn of the wheel, Communism now requires of the artist pre-cisely what the bourgeoisie demanded in the nineteenth century; while, as a corollary, it stigmatizes anything remotely savouring of 'art for art's sake' as 'bourgeois'. Today, Poe and Gautier would be in revolt against 'socialist realism' and would be considered as 'bourgeois escapists'.

them as a means of preserving at least some measure of spiritual independence. To speak of escapism in such a context is grossly to simplify,
if not to falsify, the question.

In practice, Gautier's poetry (the poetry of *Émaux et camées*) is
certainly asocial; but it is by no means as impersonal as his aesthetic
idealism might seem to demand. The author is continually present
in his touches of humour, irony, sarcasm and sometimes of ferocity.
Occasionally he recounts his own experiences. Yet on the whole the
tone is restrained. The voice belongs to a commentator more than to
an advocate or a victim. As to the form, *Émaux et camées* are written
almost throughout on one simple pattern: a cross-rhymed stanza of
four octosyllabic lines, as in this description of Paris in winter:

> Dans le bassin des Tuileries
> Le cygne s'est pris en nageant,
> Et les arbres, comme aux féeries,
> Sont en filigrane d'argent.
>
> Les vases ont des fleurs de givre
> Sous la charmille aux blancs réseaux;
> Et sur la neige on voit se suivre
> Les pas étoilés des oiseaux.[1]

On the score of technical inventiveness Gautier's virtuosity is
cramped and he is nowhere comparable to that brilliant if shallow
versifier, Théodore de Banville, who was also a Parnassian in his worship of poetic form. Gautier's skill shows in the regularity and richness
of his rhymes and in his strict observance of the chosen metre; also in
the care with which he selects his words, usually in view of an exact
descriptive effect. These are somewhat negative qualities and although
today it is still possible to admire some of his best poems in the same
way that one admires a medieval *ballade* by Chartier or Charles
d'Orléans, it is difficult to feel much warmth for his work as a whole.
His sound craftsmanship neither communicates a compelling emotion,
nor has it the qualities of the master-artist innovating, like Mallarmé,
a new mode of expression. Yet it is possible to see why Mallarmé
revered Gautier on an equal plane with Poe, chiefly as an advocate of
non-utilitarian art. And it is even more understandable that Baudelaire
should have acclaimed him, in the dedication of the *Fleurs du mal*, as
'the impeccable poet, the perfect magician of French letters, my most
beloved master and friend'.

[1] From *Fantaisies d'hiver.*

Gautier often prefigures Baudelaire: in his grim humour, his sense of the macabre, his treatment of the Parisian scene. One can amuse oneself by reading through Gautier in search of particular passages which Baudelaire echoed or imitated. There are a number of them, such as:

> Devers Paris, un soir, dans la campagne,
> J'allais suivant l'ornière d'un chemin,
> Seul avec moi, n'ayant d'autre compagne
> Que ma douleur qui me donnait la main.

This preceded the

> Ma Douleur, donne-moi la main . . .

of Baudelaire's sonnet *Recueillement*.

In Gautier's sonnet *La Chimère* (1837) occur the lines:

> Par delà le soleil et par delà l'espace,
> Où Dieu n'arriverait qu'après l'éternité.

For many readers, this will have a very familiar ring. They will have heard it, in all probability, in Baudelaire's poem *Élévation*:

> Par delà le soleil, par delà les éthers,
> Par delà les confins des sphères étoilées.

The traffic may not have been all in one direction. Baudelaire's terrible poem, *Une Charogne*, in which he imagines his mistress rotting in the grave, was not published before 1857, but it probably existed in manuscript as early as 1844. In that case, Gautier's *Bûchers et tombeaux*, in *Émaux et camées*, may well contain not only Gautier's renunciation of his own earlier obsession with death, but a deliberate reply to Baudelaire. In the happy days of classical art, says Gautier, men did not probe beneath the flesh but accepted the outward form as the image of ideal beauty:

> Le squelette était invisible
> Au temps heureux de l'Art païen;
> L'homme, sous la forme sensible,
> Content du beau, ne cherchait rien.

The dead were burnt on funeral pyres, so eliminating the whole medieval obsession with the *danse macabre* and the charnel-house. In the final stanza of his poem (and the last quoted below) he would seem to be giving his answer to Baudelaire:

> Reviens, reviens, bel art antique,
> De ton paros[1] étincelant

---

[1] Marble, from the island of Paros.

Couvrir ce squelette gothique;
Dévore-le, bûcher brûlant!

Si nous sommes une statue
Sculptée à l'image de Dieu,
Quand cette image est abattue,
Jetons-en les débris au feu.

Toi, forme immortelle, remonte
Dans la flamme aux sources du beau,
Sans que ton argile ait la honte
Et les misères du tombeau.[1]

But whatever parallels may be drawn, Gautier rarely touches Baudelaire's level. His effects are superficial and mechanical in comparison. His material never became part of his life-stream. As he presents it, it may interest but never absorbs us. As an artist, Baudelaire was greatly superior. His verse shows a technical mastery, a cadence and a music which were beyond Gautier's command, for all his respect for aesthetic qualities. Yet it is greatly to Gautier's credit that he helped to show Baudelaire his way.

In an earlier chapter on Baudelaire, a parallel with Musset was indicated which some critics would certainly reject out of hand, considering those two poets to be absolutely incompatible. Gautier touches Musset at several points, particularly in his playfully conversational passages and in some of his song-poems and love-poems. If carefully read, he will be seen to provide a bridge between Musset and Baudelaire, an intermediate kind of verse which might well soften the shock of passing too rapidly from the one to the other and suggest that it is more appropriate to speak of gradations than of opposites.

IV

Between the Gautier of *l'art pour l'art* and Tristan Corbière it would be useless to attempt a transition. Corbière was a poet of a different species, though he had certain slender affinities with Musset and Hugo, which appear chiefly in the perverse form of parody of those – for him – too literary writers. With Baudelaire he had a deeper affinity of temperament, which runs constantly beneath his rougher and more

---

[1] Cf. Baudelaire's conclusion:

Alors, ô ma beauté! dites à la vermine
Qui vous mangera de baisers
Que j'ai gardé la forme et l'essence divine
De mes amours décomposés!

immediately rebellious verse. But he belonged to a later generation, the generation of Verlaine. In 1873 he produced one remarkable book of poems, *Les Amours jaunes*, and died soon after at the age of twenty-nine.

He was born in Brittany in 1845 and spent most of his short life in that province – first as a schoolboy at Saint-Brieuc and Nantes and later, for reasons of health, in the small port of Roscoff, on the north coast of Finistère. From boyhood he suffered from arthritis and this prevented him from following the sailor's career which he would no doubt have chosen. The sea was in his blood. His father had been a naval officer before becoming director of a company of coastal steamers and a writer of excellent sea-stories. The son could imitate him only to the extent of sailing his small cutter as an amateur in the sufficiently dangerous waters of the Channel. On shore, he led a free and somewhat wild life. One Sunday he alarmed the inhabitants of Roscoff by setting up at his window a battery of sporting guns which fired a simultaneous volley just as they were coming out of church. On another occasion he led out his dog on a cord of immense length which rapidly entangled a whole streetful of pedestrians. His reputation for unconventional behaviour was supported by his lean, cadaverous appearance, of which he was acutely conscious and which undoubtedly complicated his sexual life. At the age of twenty-six he fell desperately in love with the Italian mistress of a French count when the pair came to Roscoff as summer visitors. He followed them back to Paris and spent the next three years in Bohemian squalor in Montmartre. He fell critically ill and returned to Brittany only to die in 1875.

While he was in Paris, he had his poems published at his own expense. Their appearance went unnoticed. Corbière himself seems to have taken no further interest in them. Ten years later, through the intermediary of a cousin, they were shown to Verlaine, who was so impressed that he devoted the first of his articles on the *Poètes maudits* to Corbière. A certain posthumous fame now came to him, resulting in the publication of a new edition of his poems in 1891. But, although he was henceforth known as a curious and vigorous poet, it was not until the 1940s that interest in him became intense and that he was recognized as one of the outstanding poets of his age.

It might be possible to describe all Corbière's work in terms of frustration; frustration in love, resulting in the humorous bawdiness of those poems which account for his title of *Amours jaunes* – bilious, off-colour loves, neither grimly black nor cosily pink;[1] the frustration

---

[1] Cf. *rire jaune*, to give a wry, sickly smile.

of not being a 'real' sailor which caused him to emphasize the virile fatalism of the seaman in his immensely racy salt-water ballads; frustration in travel (a short journey in Italy, then the three years in Paris) and in his reading of literature, both of which filled him with mockery instead of admiration; finally, the insidious general frustration of the Celtic race to which he belonged, and whose spirit he caught in a few great regional poems.

But 'frustration' suggests discouragement, while Corbière's mood is more often one of impatience. He has the brusque energy of the out-of-doors man, brilliant gifts of sarcastic observation, a rueful self-knowledge nicely posed between self-mockery and self-pity, and a reckless command of language and metre.

The difficulty of much of his verse for the English reader is mainly one of vocabulary. Local terms, sea terms and colloquialisms of various kinds play an important part in it. In these typical lines, the crew of a pirate ship are hoisting the sails and making ready to leave port:

> Cent vingt *corsairiens*, gens de corde et de sac,
> A bord de la *Mary-Gratis* ont mis leur sac.
> – Il est temps, les enfants! on a roulé sa bosse . . .
> Hisse! – C'est le grand foc qui va payer la noce.
> Étarque! Leur argent les fasse tous cocus! . . .
> La drisse du grand foc leur rendra leurs écus . . .
> – Hisse hoé! . . . *C'est pas tant le gendarm' qué jé r'grette!*
> – Hisse hoà . . . *C'est pas ça! Naviguons, ma brunette!*

Just as in Masefield's *Salt-Water Ballads* one needs to know, or to guess, something of nautical language, here it is helpful to know such things as that *rouler sa bosse* means 'to knock about the world' or 'to paint the town red' in sailor parlance; *étarque* means 'made fast', and *la drisse du grand foc* is the main foresail halyard. The second parts of the last two lines are snatches adapted from a sea-shanty. Elsewhere, the difficulty, and the strength, of Corbière consists in the rapidity of his allusions, often complicated by his love of paradox and punning. A few lines from his magnificent *Litanie du sommeil* provide an example:

> SOMMEIL – Loup-garou gris! Sommeil! Noir de fumée!
> SOMMEIL! Loup de velours, de dentelle embaumée!
> Baiser de l'Inconnue, et Baiser de l'Aimée!
> – SOMMEIL! Voleur de nuit! Folle-brise pâmée!
> Parfum qui monte au ciel des tombes parfumées!
> *Carrosse à Cendrillon* ramassant *les Traînées*!
> Obscène Confesseur des dévotes mort-nées!

... Trop-plein de l'existence et Torchon neuf qu'on passe,
Au café de la vie, à chaque assiette grasse!
Grain d'ennui qui nous pleut de l'ennui des espaces!
Chose qui court encor, sans sillage et sans traces!
Pont-levis des fossés! Passage des impasses!

... Voix mortelle qui vibre aux immortelles ondes!
Réveil des échos morts et des choses profondes,
– Journal du soir: temps, siècle et revue des
    deux mondes!

In quite another vein is the best-known of his Breton poems, *La
Rapsode foraine et le Pardon de Sainte-Anne*, which mixes simplicity
with compassion. It is too long to quote here, but part of it at least is
in every anthology. His *Épitaphe*, beginning:

Il se tua d'ardeur, ou mourut de paresse.
S'il vit, c'est par oubli; voici ce qu'il se laisse:[1]

is another widely quoted poem, but somewhat over-mannered in its
display of paradox. One would prefer any of the six poems grouped
as *Rondels pour après*, marvellous in their grace and lightness. Almost
song-poems, they are a surprising extension of Corbière's range. In
this *Rondel*, the poet, a child again, imagines himself in his grave,
visited by the women he has loved:

Il fait noir, enfant, voleur d'étincelles!
Il n'est plus de nuits, il n'est plus de jours;
Dors ... en attendant venir toutes celles
Qui disaient: Jamais! Qui disaient: Toujours!

Entends-tu leurs pas? ... Ils ne sont pas lourds:
Oh! les pieds légers! – l'Amour a des ailes ...
Il fait noir, enfant, voleur d'étincelles!

Entends-tu leurs voix? ... Les caveaux sont sourds.
Dors: il pèse peu, ton faix d'immortelles;
Ils ne viendront pas, tes amis les ours,
Jeter leur pavé sur tes demoiselles ...
Il fait noir, enfant, voleur d'étincelles.

Even today, Corbière may still await discovery by many readers.
He is well worth it. In terms of 'greatness' he still needs to be adequately assessed; in the long run, his eccentricities may tell against him.

---

[1] Or, in a second version:

Mélange adultère de tout
De la fortune, et pas le sou.

For his tone and his execution he can be placed somewhere between Baudelaire and Rimbaud. He knew the first, but not the second. He is by no means dwarfed in their company.

V

Jules Laforgue was fifteen years younger than Corbière; his work belongs to the 1880s. Unlike Corbière, he has long been widely known and appreciated. His approach to life, expressed with many shy and ironical nuances but basically uncomplicated, has been thoroughly understood and assimilated by later writers. He has exercised an influence second only to Verlaine's, dependent partly on manner, partly on technique. He has been classed as a Decadent-Impressionist, which is reasonable as classifications go. His reputation, one would say, has for some time stood in just proportion to his talent.

He was born in 1860 of French parents at Montevideo, where his father ran an unprofitable school. At the age of six he was sent back to France with part of the family and was educated in his father's native town of Tarbes, in Gascony, and later in Paris. His first post was that of secretary to an art critic, but at twenty-one he obtained an appointment as French reader to the Empress Augusta of Germany. He spent five impressionable and unhappy years at the German court, leading a life of formalized leisure which increased his fundamental loneliness. He gave up this post when he became engaged to an English girl whom he had met in Berlin. They were married in London, then went to settle in Paris. Here, after a few months of poverty and ill health, Laforgue died of tuberculosis at the age of twenty-seven.

Most of his verse was written in Berlin. His chief collections were *Les Complaintes* (1885) and *L'Imitation de Notre-Dame la Lune* (1886), both containing experimental forms of verse, and the posthumous *Derniers vers* (1890), which are frankly in free verse. His copious production also included a poem in dialogue, *Le Concile féerique* (1886), a number of critical essays, and the *Moralités légendaires* (1887), which were prose versions, with a modern malicious slant, of famous stories such as *Lohengrin* and *Hamlet*. His earliest poems, written in conventional forms, were published posthumously in 1903 with the title of *Le Sanglot de la terre*.

Laforgue would seem to be cut on the exact Romantic pattern of the ill-fated and unfulfilled poet who dies young. Born fifty years earlier, he would possibly have lamented his destiny in verse like Musset's or even like Hégésippe Moreau's. But by his time the century had grown older and more sceptical. It had at last learned caution in its approach to the *moi*, which was beginning to be recognized as a more complex thing than it had appeared in the confident 1830s. Then, the liberation of the *moi* from its conventional environment had seemed a sufficient objective. Now, its very nature was uncertain. It had to be shaped by an act of will (Rimbaud). Or it was not truly separable from its environment (Verlaine), and had to be surprised in various revealing but fugitive attitudes. The charging boar of the Romantics had come straight at the camera, trumpeting 'Ego Hugo' or some other instantly identifiable cry. But Symbolism required the reader to go out stalking exceedingly elusive deer – so elusive that they might sometimes seem to be phantoms, when they were not (as with the more imitative and minor Symbolists) Bambi-like creatures of a calculated coyness complete with studio-designed dapplings:

> Mon cœur, tremblant des lendemains,
> Est comme un oiseau dans tes mains,
> Qui s'effarouche et qui frissonne.
>
> Il est si timide qu'il faut
> Ne lui parler que pas trop haut,
> Pour que sans crainte il s'abandonne.
>
> *(Albert Samain)*

Or, of later date but similar colour:

> Mon âme est une rue en province, le soir.
> *(A. Foulon de Vaulx)*

Laforgue is not like this. His elusive appearance is a genuine image of his adolescent indecision, a product of emotional difficulties, ill-health, and a precociously keen intelligence. He combines a feminine sensitiveness with a certain bitter edge which is also feminine. He responds temperamentally to the sadness of autumn and winter, with their thinly orchestrated breezes, their wet streets and watery sunsets:

> O Soleil! l'autre été, magnifique en ta gloire,
> Tu sombrais, radieux comme un grand Saint-Ciboire,
> Incendiant l'azur! A présent, nous voyons
> Un disque safrané, malade, sans rayons,
> Qui meurt à l'horizon balayé de cinabre,
> Tout seul, dans un décor poitrinaire et macabre.[1]

---

[1] *Couchant d'h ver*, in *Le Sanglot de la terre*.

He experiences something of the Baudelaire *ennui:*

> Un couchant des cosmogonies!
> Ah! que la vie est quotidienne . . .
> Et du plus vrai qu'on s'en souvienne,
> Comme on fut piètre et sans génie . . .

He exteriorizes his own lassitude and attaches it to the outside world of nature and humanity, which in some poems he pictures as moving towards an *impasse*. This attitude would justify terming him a 'decadent' in one important sense of the word. It is not a sense that can be extended to Verlaine, Rimbaud or Mallarmé and is peculiar to Laforgue among the poets of his generation. It is reminiscent of the pessimism of Leconte de Lisle, from whom Laforgue might conceivably have learnt his own, though his treatment was entirely different.[1] Whereas Leconte de Lisle advances towards annihilation with a thunder of alexandrines and a drumming of epithets,[2] Laforgue, no member of the old guard, fades out yet cannot fade out; his mood is minor, realistic and modernistic:

> If faut trouver d'autres thèmes
> Plus mortels et plus suprêmes.
> Oh! bien, avec le monde tel quel,
> Je vais me faire un monde plus mortel!

> . . . Enquêtes, enquêtes
> Seront l'unique fête!
> Qui m'en défie?
> J'entasse sur mon lit les journaux, linge sale,
> Dessins de mode, photographies quelconques,
> Toute la capitale,
> Matrice sociale.

> . . . Alléluia, Terre paria.
> Ce sera sans espoir,
> De l'aurore au soir,
> Quand il n'y en aura plus il y en aura encore,

---

[1] A search for influences would be more profitably directed to the Germans whom he had read, Heine and Schopenhauer.

[2] As in:

> Et vous, joyeux soleils des naïves années,
> Vous, éclatantes nuits de l'infini béant,
> Qui versiez votre gloire aux mers illuminées,
> L'esprit qui vous songea vous entraîne au néant.
>
> (*L'Illusion suprême*, in *Poèmes tragiques*, 1884)

Du soir à l'aurore.
Alléluia, Terre paria!
Les hommes de l'art
Ont dit: 'Vrai, c'est trop tard.'
Pas de raison
Pour ne pas activer sa crevaison.
Aux armes, citoyens! Il n'y a plus de RAISON.

So things finish, not with a bang but a whimper. The quotation is inevitable, since some of the spirit of Laforgue still persisted forty years later in *The Waste Land* of T. S. Eliot. It was no accident, and the English poet has acknowledged Laforgue's influence on his early work. By another route – the *fantaisistes* and Apollinaire – Laforgue reaches the French 1920s and is echoed in some of the poetry of that period. In foreshadowing the spiritual emptiness which characterized the years following the First World War, he was thus much ahead of his time, but the mood would have been nothing without the manner of expression. What made Laforgue seem particularly modern in the twenties and after were his colloquial, casual style (*J'entasse sur mon lit les journaux* . . .), his anticlimatic use of the everyday, even trivial allusion (*Le sobre et vespéral mystère hebdomadaire / Des statistiques sanitaires / Dans les journaux*), his wry humour and self-deprecation. Some of this was cast, almost inevitably, in free verse, of which Laforgue was one of the pioneers in France.

His verse was evolving towards freedom rather than entirely 'free'. Much of his production is as regular as Verlaine's, with a singing tone belonging to some of the basic metres of French poetry, frequently varied or alternated but still respected. Even in the *Derniers vers*, from which the quotation above is taken, rhyme is used almost throughout; only a few of the end-words (as *quelconques, paria*) have no rhyme. But there is no regular metre – only, at most, a rhythm – and it is because of this feature that his work is most original from the technical point of view. It indicates that he was moving – until his early death silenced him for good and stamped him as a potentially great but still immature poet – towards a type of poetry fundamentally opposed to the 'music' of Verlaine and the polished art of Mallarmé. It was a type which the twentieth century was to develop until it became for many poets an entirely natural and necessary medium of expression.

Chapter 20

Claudel and Apollinaire

THE most striking development in French poetry in the twentieth century has been the breakdown of regular versification. As has been seen, experiments in free verse had already been made in the late nineteenth century by Laforgue, who died too young to follow up his own innovations. At much the same time, however, other poets – notably Gustave Kahn – went to work on similar lines and by 1900 the cultivation of free verse had become an important by-product of the Symbolist movement. The ground was now prepared for one of the greatest of literary revolutions – far more radical than its relatively tardy counterpart in England. The French, hitherto wedded, as it appeared, to a rigid system of prosody based on the recurrence of uniform numbers of syllables, became completely at home in a generation or two with poetry which cannot be scanned by any rules. It is, of course, true that some of the theorists of prosody have represented traditional French verse as more systematized than it actually was in the practice of most poets. Ambitious theories have been aired which attempted to show that the alexandrine corresponded to the natural rhythm of breathing, or that its twelve syllables could be felt as a necessity by the ear, which instinctively rejected a 'false' alexandrine of eleven or thirteen syllables. But such theories had their basis in long-ingrained habit rather than in nature. The reasons why the alexandrine and a few other metres dominated French poetry for so long are to be sought in aural education, not in physiology. Similarly, all the ingenuity expended in proving that rhyme was indispensable to French poetry can now be seen to have been misplaced. As soon as new rhythms emerged with which rhyme was not traditionally associated, its absence was not felt.[1]

Nevertheless, it is still a matter for wonder that aural habits which had stood for four centuries could be so easily discarded in a few decades. For anything comparable, we must look to modern develop-

---

[1] And even – though this is more surprising – traditional metres, including the alexandrine, have come to be used quite commonly without rhymes.

ments in music: combinations of sound which the twentieth century accepts as normal could hardly have been tolerated by the nineteenth-century ear. In poetry, the revolution has been at least as extreme. After being the instrument of a small minority, free verse of various kinds has become the more usual medium, while the regular forms tend to be the exception. Either they are the property of consciously traditionalist poets whose gaze is fixed somewhat defiantly on the past, or they are regarded by other poets simply as alternatives to the less stylized forms. Valéry was the last great poet to use them exclusively[1] and in this respect his example has not been followed.

Yet, in spite of the immense changes which have occurred, it might be misleading to speak of a total transformation in poetic technique. Apart from the evident fact that the traditional forms and metres, as handled by poets of the past, still remain acceptable to the modern ear, they often survive as a basis for free verse. In certain varieties of this it is easy to perceive, more or less overlaid according to the particular case, the irreducible skeleton of the alexandrine and other 'conventional' metres. In other types no metrical pattern whatever may be discernible, yet there will be a certain rhythm, possibly emphasized by assonance. Rhyme is not outlawed. In different poems by the same poet, it may occur regularly, rarely, or not at all. What is broadly called free verse therefore ranges from a fairly direct development of Verlaine's conception of the *vers libéré* to kinds of writing in which the poet seems to reject all metrical precedent and assumes entire responsibility for his own rhythmic patterns.

Is any classification of the 'free' forms possible? The answer is surely that, if thoroughly carried out, it would be far too complex to be at all enlightening. It has to be recognized that form, as commonly understood, has ceased to be of the first importance in judging a poet. A complicating factor is introduced by poetic prose and the prose poem. The ancestry of these – without necessarily going back to Chateaubriand, or further still to Rousseau – may be traced to such sources as Baudelaire's *Petits poèmes en prose*, Lautréamont's *Chants de Maldoror* and – by far the most influential – Rimbaud's *Illuminations* and *Saison en enfer*. In such works there is nothing that can be related to the traditional metres of French verse. What rhythms there are belong rather to oratory or to impassioned private speech. But far more than in rhythm their 'poetic' quality consists in their imaginative originality and in the strength of the images. In certain modern writers the prose-

---

[1] And even Valéry experimented with prose poems, as the posthumous publication of his entire work now reveals.

poem is indistinguishable (except typographically) from free verse, and conversely. It would be unprofitable to attempt to establish distinctions of kind along those lines. But distinctions of more limited application can often be drawn between those poets whose work (however it is printed) stems conspicuously from regular verse and those whose work cannot be so characterized. They will not point to any rigorous division into categories, but they will frequently provide a valid starting-point for the analysis of individual poets and may also reveal where the true talents and affinities of these lie.

The two very different poets described in this chapter represented the new tendencies in French literature at a relatively early stage and exercised a considerable influence on the changing course of poetry. They may also stand for the two types of writer just indicated. Apollinaire derives principally from the verse-poets. Claudel claimed, for that part of his work which is most interesting from the point of view of form, to derive from the prose-writers. He was, in fact, the great exponent of the *verset*, or verse as found in the Bible. Whether this should strictly be regarded as an offshoot of prose – since much of the Bible is unequivocally poetry in the original – is open to question. It is at least certain, however, that Claudel's most characteristic work owes nothing to the traditions of French prosody.

II

Paul Claudel was born in 1868 in the village of Villeneuve-sur-Fère in the Aisne *département* of north-east France. His grandfather was the village doctor and one of his great-uncles the parish priest. He took a justifiable pride in coming from simple, healthy stock in which were incarnated the solid qualities of traditional France. When he was thirteen, his parents took him to Paris to be educated at the Lycée Louis-le-Grand. At twenty-two, ignoring the attractions of a full-time literary career (for he had already begun to write), he gained the first place in the examination for the Foreign Service and embarked on his long and successful career as a consul and diplomat, from which he retired only at the age of sixty-six. It enabled him to marry and to bring up a large family in comfort. Near the outset, his duties took him to China, where he spent fourteen years (1895–1909). Later, he was French Ambassador successively in Tokyo, Washington and Brussels. Other posts in South America and various European capitals contributed to broaden and colour his outlook, but in spite of this he was always the widely travelled Frenchman rather than the cosmopolitan.

Postings and leaves in Paris kept him in touch with the cultural life of the capital. In fact, he took some part in it, primarily through his early friendship with André Gide and his other connections with the group of the *Nouvelle Revue Française*. His independence as a writer was not due to exile, which simply served his temperament, giving him new positions and settings in which to deepen his essential Frenchness, though without nostalgia. His true independence sprang from earlier causes rooted in his character.

Among the young Symbolists of the eighties and nineties, among whom Claudel moved, vague metaphysical aspirations were common enough. In Claudel almost alone they were not vague. At the age of eighteen he adopted irrevocably the fervent Catholic faith which was to dominate his whole life's work. He attributed the first step in his conversion – strangely, for some minds – to his discovery of Rimbaud, whose prose poems he read when they were published in 1886. In Rimbaud he believed that he found 'a mystic in a wild state'. The voice which Rimbaud had heard was God's voice, though he did not recognize it as such at the time. But from where else could have come that note of pure sincerity in so crassly materialistic an age?

Arthur Rimbaud [wrote Claudel][1] appeared in 1870, one of the saddest dates in our history – a time of utter defeat, of civil war, of material and moral confusion, of positivist stupor. He rose up suddenly – '*like Joan of Arc!*' was his desolate cry later. One must read in Paterne Berrichon's book [the first, sanctimonious, biography of Rimbaud] the tragic account of this vocation. But it was not *a word* that he heard, or even a voice. It was a mere inflexion, but enough to make repose and 'the comradeship of women' henceforth impossible for him. So is it so rash to think that he was raised up by a higher will, in whose hand we all are, but which was silent and chose to be silent?

This explanation of the 'miracle' of the sixteen-year-old Rimbaud entirely suited Claudel's conception of poetry and of life. Rimbaud's idea of the poet as *voyant* and his attempt to embrace the entire universe in a single sensibility were Claudel's also, but Claudel held a key which Rimbaud lacked. For him, the universal sensibility was of course the divine sensibility, in which the poet shares through his religion:

Salut donc, ô monde nouveau à mes yeux, ô monde maintenant total!
O credo entier des choses visibles et invisibles, je vous accepte avec un
  cœur catholique!
Où que je tourne la tête

[1] In his preface to the *Mercure de France* edition of Rimbaud's works (1912).

J'envisage l'immense octave de la Création!
Le monde s'ouvre et, si large qu'en soit l'empan, mon regard le traverse
d'un bout à l'autre.[1]

The huge accession of confidence and energy which religion
brought to Claudel's writing is exteriorized in exuberance but never in
the kind of megalomania so obtrusive in Hugo. Hugo seems to swell
himself up to converse with God, while Claudel accepts with a natural
exhilaration the premise that the Creator must be in all his creatures. If
one recognizes God everywhere, there should be no conflict between the
human ego and the divine, or between the inner and outer worlds. The
business of poetry is to establish their essential sameness, not to per-
petuate distinctions based on false notions of the nature of the universe.
And the poet himself does not stand apart. He belongs inescapably to
the order of things which he is describing.

Such an attitude is really far removed from Rimbaud's conception
of the poet as an explorer on dangerous seas, risking his sanity to find
the 'unknown'. The poet, for Claudel too, is a searcher, and the search
may be long and painful. But at its end, if it is successful, he finds the
ecstatic happiness of fulfilling his own nature: everything will be
friendly and familiar. There can be no question at all of the monstrous
distortions which Rimbaud believed necessary to the attainment of
the lucid vision.[2]

Nor is there a place for Mallarmé's obsession with language as an
autonomous process. However language is manipulated it cannot of
itself spell out TRUTH for Claudel. It is only valid as a representation of things already in existence. When it is a true representation,
it fulfils its highest function. But when words fail to hit the mark,
nothing of importance has been lost. They can be left to lie there and
others can be used. Valéry's distinction between the language of pure
poetry and that of 'communication' also disappears, since everything
that exists is potentially in communication because of its divine source
and art is merely one means among others of showing this or, at most,
of facilitating it.

This attitude towards literature undoubtedly helped Claudel to
write prolifically, with constant recastings, as new ways of presenting
his subjects occurred to him. The greater and best part of his work was
written in dramatic form. Such plays as *Partage de midi* (1906), *L'Annonce faite à Marie* (1912) and *Le Soulier de satin* (1929) established him
as one of the most original dramatists of his age, though they ignored

---

[1] From *L'Esprit et l'eau* in *Cinq grandes odes*.   [2] See pp. 196–7 above.

most of the requirements of the ordinary theatre. He wrote prose-poems (*Connaissance de l'Est*, 1900) and poems which approximate to regular verse in such volumes as *Poèmes de guerre* (1922) and *Feuilles de saints* (1925). But these last are comparatively unimportant beside his earlier and more revolutionary work, the *Cinq grandes odes*, composed while he was in China and published in 1910. It was here that he used most successfully a type of poetic prose which may be considered his own invention. It is found also, in conjunction with more regular verse, in *La Cantate à trois voix* (1913), and it is the medium of his plays, in which it performs admirably the function which no other playwright's language has wholly fulfilled since Racine's day of permitting a transition from ordinary conversation to high lyric feeling without the alternate use of prose and verse.

III

As used in the *Cinq grandes odes*, this language is biblical in its general contours and occasionally also suggestive of Walt Whitman.[1] Without rhyme or regular rhythms, it moves forward under the pressure of the poet's 'inspiration', sweeping with it whatever associations and images occur to him at the moment. It is an extraordinary turgid stream, this outpouring of Claudel's faith, and liable to take in anything, from the most simple play on words to the breathtaking metaphor. He is 'baroque' beyond the nightmares of the seventeenth-century classicists and it is useless to sift out the sublime from the trivial. His force is in the two combined. One might begin reading his dialogue between the Poet and Muse[2] as though it were a burlesque of all such dialogues when treated conventionally – as, for example, in Musset's *Nuit de mai*. The parable by which Claudel's Muse urges the Poet to surrender to the divine intoxication appears at first comic in its naturalism:

> Celui qui a bu seulement plein son écuelle de vin nouveau, il ne connaît plus le créancier et le propriétaire;

[1] The rhythms and articulations of Claudel's free verse are so different as to rule out the close influence which Gide was inclined to detect. Claudel, however, knew Whitman's work almost certainly before he began *Cinq grandes odes*. Later, in February 1913, he wrote to Gide, who was planning a collective translation of Whitman.

'J'ai bien les *Leaves of Grass*, mais à Paris ou à la campagne et ce sera toute une histoire de les retrouver. Si je traduisais quelque chose de Whitman, ce serait les pieces sur le Sud: "Oh South, my South" (je ne me rappelle plus le titre), ou cette autre pièce également assez courte où il parle des voix des chanteurs, ténor, contralto.' (*Correspondance Claudel et Gide*, Gallimard, 1949.)

[2] In *La Muse qui est la Grâce*.

Il n'est plus l'époux d'une terre maigre et le colon d'une femme querelleuse
avec quatre filles à la maison;
Mais le voici qui bondit tout nu comme un dieu sur le théâtre, la tête
coiffée de pampres, tout violet et poisseux du pis sucré de la grappe,
Comme un dieu au côté de la thymélé, brandissant la peau d'un petit
cochon plein de vin qui est la tête du roi Panthée,
Cependant qu'attendant son tour le chœur des garçons et petites filles aux
voix fraîches le regarde en croquant des olives salées!

But what is comic here is appropriate and this is not burlesque.
Claudel's Muse, unlike Mallarmé's Hérodiade or Valéry's Jeune
Parque, is not self-conscious. She cannot be ridiculous because she is
present only in her argument, whose force and exactness are her whole
concern. And as she develops it, the argument is quite consistent and
capable of leading to the most lofty conclusions:

Telle est la vertu de cette boisson terrestre: l'ivrogne peu à peu, plein de
gaieté, voit double,
Les choses à la fois comme elles sont et comme elles ne sont pas et les gens
commencent à ne pas comprendre ce qu'il dit.
La vérité serait-elle moins forte que le mensonge?
Ferme les yeux seulement et respire la vie froide! Fi de vous, ô chiches
jours terrestres! O noces! ô prémices de l'esprit! Bois de ce vin non
fermenté seulement!
Avance-toi et vois l'éternel matin, la terre et la mer sous le soleil du matin,
comme quelqu'un qui paraît devant le trône de Dieu!

From such passages it becomes evident that Claudel's chief strength
lies in his concrete similes and images. These make his didacticism
acceptable by linking it to the experiences of ordinary life and, more
particularly, to its sensations. The method may seem to be that of the
rustic preacher condemned by Malherbe's generation,[1] but what
counts is less the method than the talent which uses it. Its occasional
weaknesses are cancelled out by unquestionable successes, such as
'Ferme les yeux seulement et respire la vie froide!' in the lines just
quoted. Claudel's work is full of similar achievements, which would
necessarily be beyond the reach of a more prudent technique.
In:

La terre bien chauffante, tendre-feuillante et nourrie du lait de la pluie,

or in:

O mon âme, il ne faut concerter aucun plan! ô mon âme sauvage, il nous
faut tenir libres et prêts,

[1] See p. 52.

Comme les immenses bandes fragiles d'hirondelles quand sans voix
retentit l'appel automnal!

or in this evocation of the sparkle and elasticity of sea-water:

Comme du fond de l'eau on voit à la fois une douzaine de déesses aux
beaux membres
Verdâtres monter dans une éruption de bulles d'air,
Elles se jouent au lever du jour divin dans la grande dentelle blanche, dans
le feu jaune et froid, dans la mer gazeuse et pétillante!

the metaphor is triumphantly at work in a region where distinctions
between verse and prose are no longer important. Metre and rhyme
would add nothing to what is already complete. Considerations of
prosodic form become irrelevant, or rather, the metaphor creates its
own form for the duration of its existence.

In the intervals, it might be expected that there would be descents
into flatness, since it is scarcely possible to maintain the metaphor-
making faculty at a continuous height throughout a long poem – and
in any case Claudel does not attempt it. His solution is in 'eloquence',
the quality condemned by Verlaine and shunned by Mallarmé, and
which can sustain the bad orator indefinitely even when he has nothing
to say. But Claudel's eloquence is sufficiently dynamic, or original, or
downright odd to escape serious censure. It is a product of the Dionysian conception of poetry, according to which the poet writes in a kind
of delirium, blindly obedient to the voice of the god which has taken
possession of him:

Ah, je suis ivre! ah, je suis livré au dieu! j'entends une voix en moi et la
mesure qui s'accélère, le mouvement de la joie,
L'ébranlement de la cohorte Olympique, la marche divinement tempérée!
. . . O le cri de la trompette bouchée! O le coup sourd sur la tonne
orgiaque!

In this enfevered state, what language will the poet use to express his
ecstasy? The language of everyday speech, Claudel appears to say,
stripped of conventional 'music' and of other kinds of poetic artifice,
yet deformed or elevated to a point at which it is not immediately
recognized for what it is:

Les mots que j'emploie,
Ce sont les mots de tous les jours, et ce ne sont point les mêmes!
Vous ne trouverez point de rimes dans mes vers ni aucun sortilège. Ce

I

sont vos phrases mêmes. Pas aucune de vos phrases que je ne sache reprendre![1]
  Ces fleurs sont vos fleurs et vous dites que vous ne les reconnaissez pas.[2]

While it would be forcing such a passage to deduce from it a definite
statement of poetic doctrine, it can be said that Claudel intends his
poetry to be accessible to any reader who will take trouble over it.
What he demands is spiritual insight – the approach through intuition
and experience – rather than the approach through literature in its
technical and 'hermetic' aspects. He therefore takes the kind of language
which comes first to hand and requires the least premeditation and
blows into it with the full force of his eloquence to create now gor-
geous, now monstrous, serpentine shapes. Occasionally the language
collapses before him and the result is limp and ludicrous, but that risk
has to be taken. In the last resort he does not care about language,
or rather, he regards it as infinitely expendable. He views it with the
same piratical eye as a character in one of his plays, the adventurer
Amalric, viewed the prospect of the commercial plunder of the
East:

Je reconnais mon brave Levant, hourra! *'I'm wild and woolly and full of
fleas!'*
. . . Évidemment au lieu de ce commerce ignoble,
Il vaudrait mieux entrer le sabre au poing épouvantablement
Dans les vieilles villes toutes fondantes de chair humaine,
Résolu de revenir avec quatre tonneaux pour sa part tout remplis de
bijoux avec par-ci par-là quelques oreilles d'infidèles et doigts coupés de
dames et demoiselles,
Ou de périr avec honneur au milieu de ses compagnons!
Cela vaudrait mieux que de transpirer en pyjama devant son *ledger*![3]

Other poets might sit and sweat over their ledgers, but Claudel
quickly realized that this could not be his method. The 'accountancy'
of verse, with all the labour of concentration and selection which it involves, was not for him. To save time and to keep pace with the rhythm
of his own thought, he was quite ready to write in prose. Soon after
the publication of *Cinq grandes odes*, he described his poetic writing,
'not as a disintegration of the traditional verse-line, but as the supreme
and final development of prose. . . . Its descent is not from the French

---

[1] Like *to take up*, *reprendre* has the two senses of *to re-use* and *to correct*.
[2] *La Muse qui est la Grâce.* This ode as a whole contains a debate on the Dionysian
(inspired) and the Apollonian (artistically conscious) conceptions of poetry.
[3] *Partage de midi*, Act I.

poets, but from the continuous line of great prose-writers which runs from the origins of our language to Arthur Rimbaud.'[1]

There the matter might be left, except that it is not possible to regard the Rimbaud of the *Illuminations* or Claudel himself simply as prose-writers. Whatever their intentions, both have contributed to the 'disintegration of the traditional verse-line' by offering alternatives to that line. Their example has led other poets to experiment with freer rhythms which can be seen today to belong to poetry because of the richness of their imagery and because of a stylization which is after all greater than the ear could tolerate in prose.

Considered as an innovator who refused to compromise with the accepted literary approach to the French language, Claudel was as bold and as great in his way as Mallarmé. But he launched his attack from the directly opposite quarter and there is, of course, an absolute incompatibility between the two.

Mallarmé never entered the *Académie*. Claudel was elected to it, after an earlier failure, at the age of seventy-nine. He died in 1955.

IV

Claudel's work appears relatively timeless beside that of Apollinaire, who was a typical and brilliant product of the first decade of the present century. The period is difficult to pin down, since it was at the same time (as in Edwardian England) vulgarly brassy, aimlessly playful, and fertile in true novelties. Some of these novelties were to dominate life in the 1920s, which were a direct development of certain aspects of the 'Edwardian' era, too rapidly forced into maturity by the pressure of the First World War. It was the period – to give a random list not irrelevant to Apollinaire's eclectic talents – of the early motor-car, the first aeroplane, the first great generation of the School of Paris, including the Fauves and the Cubists, the Diaghilev ballet, the rise of Montparnasse, the whimsy of the French *fantaisiste* poets. Surrealism was germinating and could claim Apollinaire as one of its precursors, though it did not emerge as a movement until after his death.

Guillaume Apollinaire represented primarily the irresponsible side of his period and was blind to some of its most important features. Yet he had an intuition of its complexity and was aware of living in an age of far-reaching changes. If their nature sometimes escaped him, as was inevitable, he fought for them in his fashion, which may now seem

[1] Letter quoted in H. Clouard, *Histoire de la littérature française du symbolisme à nos jours* (1947), Vol. I, p. 467.

somewhat old-fashioned. To be in turns jumpy, pathetic, humorous, imitative and original was his temperamental limitation; but it also qualifies him to represent a particular point in time better than any other poet.

His whole life was unsettled but full of zest. Its ups-and-downs go some way to explain the erratic spirit behind his work. He was born in Rome in 1880, the illegitimate son of a Swiss-Italian nobleman and a Polish girl of good family, Angélique Kostrowitzky. He changed this name to Apollinaire in his early twenties when he began to write. His father disappeared from his life when he was a child, but with the assistance of his father's family he was given a wholly French education at a Catholic college at Monaco and other schools in the neighbourhood. His adolescent years were complicated by his mother's sentimental and financial difficulties, which necessitated frequent changes of address. With his younger brother, he was parked one summer at a small hotel at Stavelot, in the Belgian Ardennes, from which the two youths decamped at dawn without paying the bill. They had received instructions from their mother to join them in Paris, with sufficient money for the train-fare, but none for the landlord.

In Paris, the young man found various odd jobs, tried freelance journalism, placed a few poems in literary reviews and undertook a commission to write a pornographic work. He evidently found this task congenial, since several works of the same kind followed in the course of his career. An important interlude was the year he spent in Germany at the age of twenty-one as tutor to the daughter of a wealthy widow. His experience of Germany, together with his earlier impressions of the Ardennes and his parental background, formed the basis of his cosmopolitanism.[1] He also fell in love, seriously but vainly, with the governess of his young pupil, an English girl called Annie Playden. Her continued refusals of him dictated the pattern of *Apollinaire le mal-aimé*, which was to figure as an important motif in his poetry and, to a considerable extent, in his life.

Back in Paris, he gradually made his way in *avant-garde* circles, edited a short-lived review and wrote his early stories, *L'Hérésiarque* and *L'Enchanteur pourrissant*, in the fantasy of which might be found a foretaste of Surrealism. At least as important were the friendships which he struck up with several young painters: Derain and Vlaminck

---

[1] Apollinaire, who loved to surround himself with mystery, often presented himself as a widely travelled man. In fact, the above was the whole extent of his wanderings, apart from two or three short trips to London. During his year as tutor, he obtained leave of absence from his employer to visit various German towns, and also went as far as Prague and Vienna.

and, a little later, Picasso and Braque. He lived for some six years with the painter Marie Laurencin, who finally left him in 1913. In articles and prefaces he made himself the mouthpiece of the new movement in art, published his study, *Les Peintres cubistes*, in 1913, and in the same year produced his first volume of collected poems, *Alcools*.

In the 1914 war, Apollinaire, though not yet a French national, joined up as an artilleryman and later became an infantry officer. Army life seemed to give him some of the stability and security for which he had been subconsciously seeking throughout his years of experimentation. Those experiments – literary, critical and emotional, enlivened often by a disconcerting puckishness – drew towards their end in 1916, when he was wounded in the head by a shell-splinter. He lived on for two and a half years, but dulled and more sober, comforted in his last months by his marriage to Jacqueline Kolb. His second collection of poems, *Calligrammes* (1918), and his 'surrealist' play, *Les Mamelles de Tirésias* (1917), made him appear to be still in the van of the *avant-garde*; but the play had been first written in 1904, while *Calligrammes* contains, besides experimental work, that poem *La Jolie Rousse*, a pathetic confession of possible error, the tired man's first dubious glance backward:

> Vous dont la bouche est faite à l'image de
>   celle de Dieu
> Bouche qui est l'ordre même
> Soyez indulgents quand vous nous comparez
> A ceux qui furent la perfection de l'ordre
> Nous qui quêtons partout l'aventure
>
> Nous ne sommes pas vos ennemis . . .

What Apollinaire might have become had he lived beyond November 1918 is no doubt an idle question. The reputation which he has left is that of an innovator and to a large extent it is justified. Discarding extravagant claims made on his behalf to be considered as the father of modern poetry, one can at least regard him as one of its most amusing and versatile uncles.

v

Apollinaire's earliest poems, like those of Laforgue, whom he nevertheless expressly disclaimed having imitated,[1] were in regular verse.

---

[1] Letter to Max Jacob, 14 March 1916, quoted in Marcel Adéma, *Apollinaire* (Heinemann, 1954).

He continued to use the regular metres, sometimes without rhyme, practically to the end of his life. They occur in his early Rhenish poems, inspired by his stay in Germany:

> Mon verre est plein d'un vin trembleur comme une
> flamme
> Écoutez la chanson lente d'un batelier
> Qui raconte avoir vu sous la lune sept femmes
> Tordre leurs cheveux verts et longs jusqu'à leurs pieds.

They appear in the short song-poems, which for many readers are the most precious and moving part of Apollinaire's work. Some, such as *Le Pont Mirabeau,* are most carefully composed from the metrical and 'musical' point of view:

> Sous le pont Mirabeau coule la Seine
> Et nos amours
> Faut-il qu'il m'en souvienne
> Le jour venait toujours après la peine
>
> Vienne la nuit sonne l'heure
> Les jours s'en vont je demeure.

A rhythm which evidently rang in Apollinaire's head was the jog-trot octosyllable, used with rhyme or near-rhyme in one of his finest 'regular' poems, *La Chanson du mal-aimé*:[1]

> Un soir de demi-brume à Londres
> Un voyou qui ressemblait à
> Mon amour vint à ma rencontre
> Et le regard qu'il me jeta
> Me fit baisser les yeux de honte.

It appears without rhyme in later poems such as *Les Collines*:

> Profondeurs de la conscience
> On vous explorera demain
> Et qui sait quels êtres vivants
> Seront tirés de ces abîmes
> Avec des univers entiers.

But even more than the octosyllabic line, it was the alexandrine which dominated Apollinaire's ear. He uses it with the same sinewy pomp as Rimbaud in *Bateau ivre*:

[1] Inspired by his fruitless pursuit of Annie Playden, whom he followed to London after her departure from Germany.

> Gonfle-toi vers la nuit O mer Les yeux des squales
> Jusqu'à l'aube ont guetté de loin avidement
> Des cadavres de jours rongés par les étoiles
> Parmi le bruit des flots et les derniers serments.[1]

He writes it, slightly disguised by the typographical arrangement in a poem such as *Les Colchiques*:

> Le pré est vénéneux mais joli en automne
> Les vaches y paissant
> Lentement s'empoisonnent
> Le colchique couleur de cerne et de lilas
> Y fleurit tes yeux sont comme cette fleur-là
> Violâtres comme leur cerne et comme cette automne
> Et ma vie pour tes yeux lentement s'empoisonne.

Here lines 2 and 3 are the two halves of a regular alexandrine. Line 6 may appear to have thirteen syllables, but is again an alexandrine when scanned as the voice will inevitably read it:

> 1 2 3   4   5   6   7   8   9 10 11 12
> Violâtres comm' leur cern' / et comme cett' automne

As for the rhymes, *automne* with *s'empoisonnent* and *lilas* with *là* may be incorrect according to 'classical' rules, but they are impeccable to the ear. In short, the licences taken are no greater than those practised by Verlaine, whose methods and spirit persist through a great deal of Apollinaire's work.

Apollinaire was rightly regarded in his early days as a young poet who was continuing Symbolism. It was the first stage in his search for a poetic identity which he never completely found. His break-out from the traditional verse-form, which seems to constitute his strongest claim to originality, was a continuation of that search and its fruits were willed; they were not the product of any deep emotional, or aesthetic impulsion.

Nevertheless, they were striking and even startling. For example, the suppression of all punctuation was a measure deliberately decided by Apollinaire while reading the proofs of *Alcools*. The poems had been normally punctuated when first sent to the printer. This was a stunt-decision, though Apollinaire could justify it afterwards by remarking that 'the rhythm and division of the lines are the real punctuation and nothing else is needed'. It was, in fact, simply an extreme development of the practice of Mallarmé, who punctuated very sparsely.

---

[1] *L'Émigrant de Landor Road*, in *Alcools*.

Another of Apollinaire's typographical experiments may also have derived from Mallarmé, who in *Un Coup de dés* had given his work a special visual presentation in print. Apollinaire's 1918 volume contained twenty *calligrammes* (which gave their name to the volume as a whole). These were short pieces disposed on the page in some such form as a flower or a heart, or in more abstract shapes intended to lead the eye to the words in certain significant orders and to establish various spatial relationships between them. Apollinaire did not take these experiments very seriously. They were amusing to contrive and effectively unconventional and they increased, at least temporarily, his reputation for modernity.

This, however, requires a more solid basis if it is not to be just modishness. One might be found in the startling mixtures of rhythms and of imagery to which Apollinaire hardly came until after the publication of *Alcools* in 1913, though the most recent piece in that collection, the long poem *Zone*, pointed clearly in a new direction. This loosely rhymed poem opens with a regular alexandrine:

> A la fin tu es las de ce monde ancien

and a metrical analysis will reveal a number of comparable alexandrines throughout the poem, together with other lines which start with the first hemistich of an alexandrine, then develop into something longer and less obviously metrical:

> Des troupeaux d'autobus / mugissants près de toi roulent

or again:

> Tu es dans le jardin / d'une auberge aux environs de Prague

Zone can be seen as a free-verse poem constructed on the skeleton of the alexandrine, but thereafter distended and distorted to obtain new – and sophisticated – metrical effects. The imagery and the diction are equally heterogeneous. In them a conscious if somewhat relaxed virtuosity is clearly at work:

> C'est le Christ qui monte au ciel mieux que les aviateurs
> Il détient le record du monde pour la hauteur
> Pupille Christ de l'œil
> Vingtième pupille des siècles il sait y faire
> Et changé en oiseau ce siècle comme Jésus monte dans l'air
> Les diables dans les abîmes lèvent la tête pour le regarder
> Ils disent qu'il imite Simon Mage en Judée
> Ils crient s'il sait voler qu'on l'appelle voleur

Les anges voltigent autour du joli voltigeur
Icare Énoch Élie Apollonius de Thyane
Flottent autour du premier aéroplane

Had something like this been written towards 1650, it would be a nice point to decide how far it falls into the category of the baroque. The poem as a whole is a straggling meditation in which Apollinaire includes whatever comes uppermost at the moment in his mind or his memory. Because of its intellectual formlessness, it differs strongly from anything written by Claudel, Mallarmé or Valéry. Because of the same quality, it looks forward to post-1918 poetry even more than it looks back to the sometimes whimsical and inconsequential Verlaine.

From about the date of *Zone*, Apollinaire, while yet to amuse himself with the 'representational' *calligramme* and still capable of writing verses filled with a simple personal sentimentality, seems to have set out deliberately to develop a new manner. In the *poème-promenade* and the *poème-conversation* he noted down the random impressions which came to him as he walked about Paris or sat in a café hearing disconnected snatches of talk:

Cher Monsieur
Vous être un mec à la mie de pain[1]
Cette dame a le nez comme un ver solitaire
Louise a oublié sa fourrure
Moi je n'ai pas de fourrure et je n'ai pas froid
Le Danois fume sa cigarette en regardant l'horaire
Le chat noir traverse la brasserie.[2]

Though such a piece is quite different in the result from *Zone*, the intention is similar: to present a kaleidoscopic series of observations linked only by the poet's fantasy, or by his momentary point of view. The observations are entirely arbitrary. The reader may, or may not, be given the key to them. If he has it, everything is probably clear to him. If not, the poem is likely to be completely obscure. In any case, remove the poet – fail to know the exact circumstances in which he was writing – and nine times out of ten this kind of poem collapses when written by Apollinaire. The elements for an imaginative interpretation (Nerval) or for an interpretation through the logic of language (Mallarmé) are simply not there. Instead, subjectivism is rampant.

Mistakenly, it must be concluded, Apollinaire gave a more ambitious name to this phase of his work. Anxious to associate himself with a movement in painting which he admired and defended, he spoke of

_____
[1] A gormless individual.   [2] From *Lundi Rue Christine* (*Calligrammes*).

Cubist poetry, as others have done since. What is meant is a schematic art, constructed on planes disposed at different angles and displaying various intersecting facets, as it were geometrically, to the reader. Poetry as well as painting can certainly be described in such terms, though it is doubtful whether the description will lead the poet, as composer, or the reader, as appreciator, very far. At least it helps little with Apollinaire, who lacks both the abstract sense of order and the capacity for geometrical reconstruction displayed by the masters of Cubist painting. If his work is to be characterized in this sort of idiom, it would be put for preference in the category of 'fragmented impressionism'. The desire to paint from life is there, with no abstraction, no attempt at construction or reconstruction, and no overall design. In, for example, his *poèmes-conversation*, Apollinaire removes the rational links which hold together more conventional poetry, but does not supply links of other kinds – whether musical or aesthetic in other ways, emotional, or (again as in Mallarmé) near-mathematical. In a small number of his less simply conceived poems he does, however, appear to foreshadow the 'free associations' of Surrealism, naming whatever comes out of the hat – no longer of his observation of the external scene, but of his own unconscious – in the unpremeditated order in which it comes. This technique is used notably in parts of the long poem *Les Collines*, from which a verse has already been quoted.[1]

To true Surrealist poetry the word *technique* would be inapplicable, but in Apollinaire's case there are strong grounds for using it. His earlier method of composition, the evidence of some of his manuscript poems, his cultivated habit of surprise, and the relatively narrow circumference of his imagination as it appears in his work as a whole, all suggests that Apollinaire was picking at random deliberately and even, where necessary, fabricating, rather than allowing his irrational images to float up naturally to the surface of consciousness. While therefore he appears to be a Surrealist in certain writings, and while one can but admire his remarkable sensitivity to a trend which art was about to take, his real method is that of the *collage*, in which a number of apparently unrelated objects are stuck together with a view to a total effect. When a *collage* is not a composition, it is studiedly a non-composition, and there is as much premeditation in the second case as in the first.

To sum up Apollinaire briefly is impossible because of his diversity. In some writers this is an outstanding virtue because it stems from a passionate exploration of the various means by which truth as they

[1] On p. 250.

conceive it can be attained. But it is hard to detect any passion of this kind in Apollinaire's shifts of ground or any development in his art which can be related to an inner compulsion. Nor is it easy to know what ends he was seeking, except notoriety and stability. On the level on which Apollinaire pursued them, neither of these absolutely necessitates poetry. He came perhaps nearest to the second during his year's service at the front. He remains as a copious if shallow source of ideas and rhythms – particularly to free-verse poets – as the author of a number of hauntingly simple verses in an older manner, and as a foil to such monolithic figures as Claudel, Péguy and Romain Rolland. He represents an important side of a period which in their work is hardly even indicated. He has become still more closely identified with it because of his early death. Had he survived, he might have developed his *disponibilité* fruitfully as did his contemporary Gide. But the signs are that middle age was about to bring him caution and perhaps atrophy rather than increased daring and depth.

Meanwhile, through the second half of the twentieth century, Apollinaire's reputation and his appeal for many readers have continued to grow. I cannot feel that this invalidates the analysis of his work given in the last few pages. His liking for the inconsequential, and the fact that he apparently 'suffers' but refuses to labour his suffering, have kept him attuned to a trend in modern French poetry whose importance is undeniable. His technical experiments have also proved surprisingly fruitful and, this being so, the spirit in which he undertook them matters far less than the results.

Chapter 21

Paul Valéry

PAUL VALÉRY was born in 1871 and so was of about the same age as Claudel, but nine years older than Apollinaire. He published nothing of note until he was forty-six, by which date Claudel had written nearly all his best work and Apollinaire had only a year to live. Compared to theirs, his poetry might seem to be retrograde. He can be seen as the last and greatest representative of the Symbolism of the 1890s, but – the qualification is important – he was able to accommodate it to the taste of the twentieth century. His poetry derives from Mallarmé, but takes on a greater movement and warmth imputable to the twenty years during which he virtually abstained from publishing, allowing himself simply to meditate and mature. He then became famous within a few years. The chronology of his literary production (one cannot write 'cycle' or 'rhythm') is extremely curious. His personality had some affinities with Mallarmé's, but the differences were important enough to foreshadow a different poet.

He was born at the sea-port of Sète, on the Mediterranean, where his father – a Corsican – was employed in the Customs and Excise. His mother was the daughter of the Italian Consul at Sète, Giulio Grassi. With this Mediterranean ancestry went an early familiarity with the sea, ships and sailors which filled Valéry's world during the formative years of childhood. The less conscious background of his poetry owes much to the hours spent wandering and playing by the waterside – hours, he wrote later, 'of apparent idleness, but dedicated really to the unconscious worship of three or four uncontestable deities, the Sea, the Sky, the Sun'. When he was thirteen, his parents moved a few miles inland to Montpellier, but he spent his summer holidays with his mother's family at Genoa, and so in another port.

Valéry at first wanted to be a sailor, but was discouraged by his weakness in mathematics while at school. Nevertheless, mathematics remained one of his passions throughout life, surpassing in time his other early enthusiasms for architecture, anthropology and painting. Literature was only one of his youthful interests, though for a few years it was dominant. He began to write poetry at about the age of eighteen and discovered for himself Edgar Allan Poe, 'perhaps the subtlest artist of this century', as well as more contemporary gods such as Mallarmé, Heredia and Huysmans. In 1890 he met by chance the young writer Pierre Louÿs, to whom he was to owe not only the friendship of André Gide but a personal introduction to Mallarmé when he went to Paris in the following year. By 1892 he had composed some two dozen known poems in the Symbolist-aesthetic manner of the nineties and was looked on as a promising and personally agreeable recruit to Mallarmé's circle. In the same year he passed through a psychological upheaval which culminated in a night of crisis when he was at Genoa. This, called over-importantly by some biographers 'The Night of Genoa', had evidently a bearing on his decision to give up poetry and a faint parallel might be drawn with Rimbaud's renunciation. However, the poems he had so far written showed no great spiritual pressure. Their importance, even in his own life, had not been paramount. And the renunciation was not absolute, since he continued to write verse occasionally. The crisis is important only in the light of later developments.

It is partially explained by two long essays which he published soon afterwards in reviews: *Introduction à la méthode de Léonard de Vinci* (1895) and *Une Soirée avec Monsieur Teste* (1896). These closely argued essays are both concerned in different ways with the problems of intellectual and artistic creation. They show Valéry inclining to a perfectionism which forbids creation, since the product must always be inferior to the idea of it which exists in the artists' mind. They also show the intense interest which he already took in the actual process of creation as it goes on in the artist's mind – an interest which for Valéry took precedence over any that he could feel in the finished work, for the second brings the first to an end. As early as this, means and not ends were the study which attracted him, and this preference remained with him throughout life.

His search for a career led him to London, where he was employed for a time in Cecil Rhodes's Chartered Company, then back to France to a civil servant's post in the War Ministry. He resigned after three years to marry Jeannie Gobillard, the niece of the painter Berthe Morisot, and to become the private secretary of Édouard Lebey, the blind and crippled director of the Havas Agency. His duties were light and left him free to enjoy a quietly civilized life with his friends and his wife's family. He spent many hours reading and meditating at his own desk and rose at dawn – when his mind was always most active – to do so. But there were no concrete results and the writer might never have revived if his friends on the newly launched *Nouvelle Revue Française*, including Gide, had not urged him to look over his early poems with a view to publication in a volume. So stimulated, he began a new work, *La Jeune Parque*, which occupied him, through many rewritings, from 1913 until its publication in 1917. It was an immediate success with the discriminating public and was followed by various separate shorter poems such as *Le Cimetière marin*, *La Pythie*, *Palme* (all 1920) and *L'Ébauche d'un serpent* (1921). These were all included in the collection *Charmes* (1922). Meanwhile, the old poems of the nineties which had originally caused this rekindling had appeared in 1920 as *Album de vers anciens*.

Thus in the five years from 1917 to 1922, and around Valéry's fiftieth year, was published all the verse which established him as unquestionably the greatest poet of his time. Henceforth he wrote little more verse, and none that added to his essential reputation, but contented himself with the three short librettos of the *Cantate du Narcisse*, *Amphion* and *Sémiramis*. The first of these was a simplified popularization of an earlier poem, while the last two were written for performance at the Paris Opéra with Honegger's music. Parts of his unfinished play, *Mon Faust* (published 1946), were also in verse.

From the springboard of his great poems Valéry began a second career as a prose-writer. His employer Lebey having died in 1922, the year of *Charmes*, he set out to live as a freelance intellectual and poured out essays, comments and prefaces. The work most nearly related to his poetry is found in such carefully composed dialogues and meditations as *L'Âme et la danse* (1912), *Eupalinos ou l'architecte* (1923), *Dialogue de l'arbre* (1923), *Degas, danse, dessein*, (1938). His chief collections of essays were *Variété*, *I-V* (1924–44), *Regards sur le monde actuel* (1931 and 1945) and *Tel quel*, *I–II* (1941–3). His inexhaustably interesting *Cahiers*, filling twenty-nine volumes, were published in 1957–61. It says much for the French character that this acute but unspecialized artist and thinker, comparable as a figure to a less retiring and more prolific E. M. Forster, should have been adopted between the wars as the unofficial mouthpiece of French culture. Neither Gide nor the younger men who more truly represented that tumultuous period had the same authority, though they may have had greater influence. The many honours awarded to Valéry included election to the *Académie française* (1925), honorary doctorates at Oxford and Coïmbra, and the Grand Cross of the Legion of Honour. He served on several cultural bodies and was elected President of the League of

Nations Committee for Intellectual Co-operation. In 1937 a new Chair of Poetry was created for him at the Collège de France, where he gave public lectures twice a week. In spite of these distinctions, Valéry always remained an informal, modest and occasionally impish figure, displaying the intellectual fruits of his twenty years of independent study with no descent into the academic. During the German occupation he adopted a courageously non-cooperative attitude and continued to lecture at the Collège de France. He died in July 1945 and was buried in the *cimetière marin* of his birthplace, Sète.

II

There is Valéry's poetry and there is his poetic theory, formulated for the most part after the poetry had been written. While it would be too exacting to require an absolute concordance between the two, the second still provides the best way of approach to the first. It is, moreover, an important contribution to the understanding of poetry in general.[1]

Valéry drew a clear distinction between the language of prose (including ordinary speech) and the language of poetry. The first is a practical instrument of communication: 'It solves immediate problems on the spot. Its field and limit is comprehension.'[2] But language in poetry 'assumes a value of its own, which must be preserved intact, *in spite of* the working of the intellect on the given material. The language of poetry must preserve itself, through itself, and remain identical, unchangeable by the intelligence which finds or gives it a sense.'

This corresponds closely to what we have already seen of Mallarmé's poetry and it is clear that Valéry's theory owed much to Mallarmé. It was evidently with Mallarmé in mind that he wrote:

> Every literature which has passed a certain age shows a tendency to create a poetic language separated from the ordinary language, with a vocabulary, a syntax, licences and inhibitions differing more or less from those in common use.

The point made is no more than that 'poetry is a separate language', but Valéry suggested further (and other critics were to develop or

---

[1] The best recent exposition of Valéry's poetic theory and practice is in Francis Scarfe's *The Art of Paul Valéry* (Heinemann, 1954), pp. 38–106. I am indebted to Mr Scarfe for much that is written here.

[2] *La compréhension est son terme.* Even in prose, Valéry employs language capable of extensions and gradations of meaning. *Terme* has two basic senses, both appropriate here: *field of reference* and *end*.

exaggerate what he said) that it is (a) higher or more absolute than the ordinary language of communication, and (b) purer.[1]

If we examine these two related conceptions, we find the first leading to an idea of poetry as 'the Paradise of language' – a term used by Valéry in writing of the mystic poet St John of the Cross. In this Paradise, the different virtues of language meet for a time (i.e. during a few lines of verse) in complete and perfect union. Developed very slightly, this will mean that a poem, ideally, is a place in which the true essences of words meet in their true relationships. It would justify seeing poetry as potentially the highest expression of reality – once it is conceded that reality can be attained at all through the medium of words. This transcendental doctrine can lend itself to a mystical and religious conception of poetry, though it does not necessarily contain it.

Incidentally, it will be noticed that the conception of a Paradise of language was suggested to Valéry by his subject, St John of the Cross. It is therefore an example of 'impure' thinking – of contamination of the essence of the thought by an example taken from a different order. To remain, in his own sense, pure above suspicion, Valéry should not have connected his theory with a religious mystic. In other words, the notion of 'divine poetry' ought not to be confused with the theological divine.

The conception of a 'pure' language can, however, hardly be kept entirely separate from other ideals of purity. At the supreme height of abstraction the various ideals are bound to meet anyway, in such a conception as 'pure essences'. But there is a different application of the term 'pure poetry'. It is often used to justify aestheticism. Poetry which is didactic, narrative or descriptive is impure in the sense of *mixed* because it employs functions of 'the language of communication' and uses words in their common or 'tribal' sense.[1] A poet who makes this distinction will strive to avoid the current and the familiar because they are contaminated by external associations, but he will be considered, by those who do use words in that way, as an affected writer.

Certain analogies can now be drawn, as they were in fact drawn by Valéry. He saw the possibility of a poetic language 'as different from practical language as artificial language is from algebra or that of chemistry'. This reference to mathematical and chemical symbolism is at first sight very suggestive. It helps us to understand the methods of 'hermetic' poetry, of Scève and Nerval as well as Mallarmé. A passage in one of these is often constructed on similar principles to the equation

[1] Cf. the qualities of Racine's poetry, discussed on pp. 75–8.
[2] See Mallarmé's sonnet on Poe, pp. 213–14.

or the formula. Thus,

> Tel qu'en Lui-même enfin l'éternité le change

might well be expressed as

$$a^n = x$$

or, to put it on a more metaphysical level,

$a^n = x = a$, where a = Edgar Allan Poe.

The only concept not rendered by such a formula is the concept contained in *enfin*. This cannot be transcribed, since algebra is too absolute a science to take account of time-lapses.

A formula without an equation is suggested by Nerval's:

> Je suis le ténébreux, – le veuf, – l'inconsolé,
> Le prince d'Aquitaine à la tour abolie,

or by Baudelaire's:

> . . . vieux flacon désolé,
> Décrépit, poudreux, sale, abject, visqueux, fêlé.

These express compounds of qualities in a form of the same order as $CHCl_3$. The poetic formula is less condensed than the chemical formula, and also less precise; but it allows of greater shading.

But such analogies cannot be pressed too far. The formulas of particular sciences or specializations represent agreed values with fixed meanings for the initiated; but there is no one 'poetic language' which can be learnt rationally and which enjoys general recognition. Within certain groups or traditions of poets – as some of the medieval *ballade*-writers or the nineteenth-century Symbolists – there is a tendency to create fixed symbols and language-values, but these are only partial and local. They do not give a 'language of poetry' comparable as a whole to the 'language' of mathematical symbols.

Another analogy, between poetry and music, was also suggested by Valéry. This is more satisfactory because it allows room for aesthetic considerations.[1] It would also permit poetry to be discussed on an emotional and even spiritual plane, related to the notion of a 'higher language' mentioned above. One need only quote such expressions as 'heavenly strains', 'divine harmony', which stem from Renaissance Neoplatonic thought, or: 'The music yearning like a god in pain', a product of Romantic aestheticism. Valéry, however, would have discouraged such associations and would have been content merely to

[1] One also speaks of the 'beauty' of an abstract formula, or of the working-out of a problem, whether in mathematics or chess. But the pagan in most of us does not concede true aesthetic qualities to such things until they are translated into physical terms, as the mathematical formula into a work of architecture.

claim that the language of poetry is nearer to the language of music than to that of prose.

Here some confusion is possible, which Valéry's practice as a poet tends to encourage. On the one hand is the perfectly tenable comparison between poetry and music on a general level: both may make a direct appeal to the emotions without the intermediary of a rational process; both admit of values which cannot be – or more truly, perhaps, have not been – exactly formulated and which we therefore tend to relate to the unconscious; both lay much insistence on aesthetic qualities. On the other hand, the comparison of the 'music of poetry' to music proper is usually misleading. Certainly it is fruitful as a source of metaphors – *melodious, harmonious, jarring, contrapuntal* – and as a reminder of the importance of sound-patterns in verse. But if taken further than this it runs against the insuperable objection that poetry does not command the same technical resources as music, so that the application of musical terms to poetry can only be an approximation. We are left with the sound but limited conclusion that the language of poetry is often 'like' the language of music in its processes and effects.

From what has been written so far it will emerge that to regard poetry as a language separate from the language of ordinary speech is not to confine it to the irrational or the aesthetic to the exclusion of the intellectual. On the contrary, the analogies with mathematics and chemistry show that the intellect can play a vital part in poetry. This was so with Valéry. On the other hand, the analogy with music, the insistence on sound-patterns, the use of 'incantation' and 'invocation', show that the intellectual element will be manifest, not in abstractions, but in sensory embodiments. Any absolute distinction between the mind (the intellectual) and the body (the sensory) is a false distinction, as modern medical science and psychiatry amply prove. To show the basis-in-nature of Valéry's poetry, it is enough to say that he already realized this and suggested it in his verse. His poetry, in agreement with his theories, relies on sensations for its primary contact with the reader – the aural sensation of the sound of the verse, the evocation of physical sensations through imagery – while revealing on examination the existence of an intellectual process running through, or behind, the physical texture. This is precisely the manner and order in which a live human being presents himself to us: the physical presence first, and afterwards the intellectual or spiritual *persona*. It distinguishes Valéry from his master, Mallarmé, who strikes us as an intelligence without an adequate, or with a contrived physical presence.

Another consequence which emerges is that 'pure' poetry is a myth, though like most myths it may shed new light on reality. But it can never be realized integrally, since the medium of poetry is words, and it is inconceivable that poetry should be written in which *all* the significant words were stripped of their current 'tribal' associations. (Valéry admitted that this could be done only during a few lines, but even that is doubtful.) A truly 'hermetic' school of poets would have, in fact, more chance of success if they set out to invent an entirely new language.[1] But taking poetry as it is – and not only those types which lend themselves to the 'pure' theory – it seems best to regard it, for each culture, as a second and more secret tribal language. Like the various *argots* and technical jargons, it is a language within a language, but not *by nature* either higher or lower than the language of current usage. The foreigner may never learn it, or even come across it, but if he does he will be initiated more deeply into the psychology of the people whose poets produced it than in any other way.

III

Nearly all the foregoing considerations could arise spontaneously from a study of *La Jeune Parque*, which has been described as one of the most obscure poems in the French language. From its midnight opening:

> Qui pleure là, sinon le vent simple, à cette heure
> Seule avec diamants extrêmes? . . . Mais qui pleure,
> Si proche de moi-même au moment de pleurer?

to its sunrise ending:

> Alors, malgré moi-même, il le faut, ô Soleil,
> Que j'adore mon cœur où tu te viens connaître,
> Doux et puissant retour du délice de naître,
> Feu vers qui se soulève une vierge de sang
> Sous les espèces d'or d'un sein reconnaissant!

[1] This is broadly what the *lettriste* poets, taking a hint from Dadaism, did in the forties and fifties. Their 'poems' were made up of combinations of onomatopoeic syllables. Similar inventions have been tried out by such poets as Henri Michaux:

> Et go to go and go
> Et sucre!
> Sarcospèle sur Saricot
> Bourbourane à talico
> Ou te bourdourra le bodogo, etc.

But the range of expression of such compositions is limited while the 'language', which is really anti-language, varies unpredictably from poet to poet and poem to poem. Also, as the above lines show, words are used which, though free of sense-associations in French, have a plainly rational meaning in other languages.

it is, in some five hundred alexandrine lines, the monologue of a mysterious being in whom it is possible to see a young girl turning towards womanhood and life, though the title suggests that the 'Young Fate' symbolizes more than this. The physical setting is a night under the open sky (the *diamants extrêmes* of the second line are the stars.) Nearby is the sea, which in the final passage adds its thundering invitation to life and action to that of the rising sun. There is an obvious contrast between the vaguely sensuous *vierge de sang* of this great poem and Mallarmé's coldly withdrawn *Hérodiade*. Valéry's poem also carries some reminiscences of *L'Après-midi d'un faune*, particularly in its mingling of physical feeling and dream. But while both Mallarmé's major poems remain largely within the limits of aestheticism, *La Jeune Parque* has intimate if secret connections with the life of common experience. Its many possible meanings have been amply discussed and commented, but it starts from the conception of the virgin awakening to life with both regret for the 'Mystérieuse Moi' which she is leaving behind and desire for the fulfilment which lies before her. This theme alone, explored with sufficient subtlety and perception, can become in itself an allegory of humanity. It need not be confined to feminine experience. It can be extended to embrace the acceptance by the individual of 'reality' or the external world, the acceptance of responsibilities, whether human or divine, the struggle between 'the desire for solitude and the vital instinct . . . or more generally between the self and the non-self', the passage from an unconscious to a conscious mode of perception, the desire for the knowledge of experience (especially if the 'Cher Serpent' of the poem is taken as the Serpent of Genesis).

Valéry himself, who had ample opportunities to clear up these points, contented himself with a few enigmatic comments and smiled with equal benevolence on his various interpreters. His interest had been less in an exact theme than in its execution and in the complex web of psychological suggestions which this brought into existence. In a letter written in 1922, he observed:

> Figurez-vous que l'on s'éveille au milieu de la nuit, et que toute la vie se revive et se parle à soi-même . . . Sensualité, souvenirs, émotions, sentiment de son corps, profondeur de la mémoire et lumières ou cieux antérieurs revus, etc. Cette trame qui n'a ni commencement ni fin, mais des nœuds, – j'en ai fait un monologue auquel j'avais imposé, avant de l'entreprendre, des conditions de forme aussi sévères que je laissais au *fond* de liberté.[1]

[1] See Francis Scarfe, op. cit., p. 182.

When, nearly twenty years after the composition of the poem, the philosopher Alain published a commentary on it, Valéry wrote an amused but modest reply entitled *Le Philosophe et la 'Jeune Parque'*. Borrowing the tone of La Fontaine, the Young Fate explains:

> CERTES, d'un grand désir je fus l'œuvre anxieuse . . .
> Mais je ne suis en moi pas plus mystérieuse
> Que le plus simple d'entre vous . . .
> Mortels, vous êtes chair, souvenance, présage;
> Vous fûtes; vous serez; vous portez tel visage:
> Vous êtes tout, vous n'êtes rien,
> Supports du monde et roseaux que l'air brise,
> Vous VIVEZ . . . Quelle surprise! . . .
> Un mystère est tout votre bien,
> Et cet arcane en vous s'étonnerait du mien?

And after praising mystery which is the salt of life and distinguishes men from the beasts, she concludes:

> Et si j'inspire quelque effroi,
> Poème que je suis, à qui ne peut me suivre,
> Quoi de plus prompt que de fermer un livre?

> C'est ainsi qu'on se délivre
> De ces écrits si clairs qu'on n'y trouve que soi.

A hostile reader might think Valéry wantonly enigmatic, safeguarding by riddles the prestige of his work and thought. But his whole attitude to poetic composition, as well as the poetry itself, excludes such a view. He is, he could have maintained, as clear as his subject warrants, since the subject is 'sensuality, memories, emotions, awareness of the body, depths of the memory, and former lights or skies seen again' – all this passing through a half-awakened mind in the middle of the night. Since such states are part of general human experience – almost classically general – the poet has a duty to attempt to render them. Valéry's poem is a conscious and polished attempt to transcribe some such experience as faithfully as possible. It is polished in form, because he did not believe, with the Surrealists, that the unconscious can be dredged up in a presentable condition. The artist must go to work on it before it has any value. He is, of course, working to communicate something, and in that respect appears to contradict his own theory of the language of poetry. But *La Jeune Parque* is certainly not written in the language of direct and functional communication. It operates at a greater depth. His refusal to define the

Young Fate while readily discussing the composition of the poem allows for all the interpretations mentioned earlier – rightly, because they may be said to be all contained in the poem. His execution is a masterpiece, not of evasion, but of eclecticism. It allows many possible interpretations of the basic theme without opting too strongly for any one of them. The imagery is deliberately blurred or ambiguous. The complicated sound-patterns – depending mainly on alliteration – have as one of their functions to lull the intellectual side of the reader's attention and to produce a musical and incantatory effect:

> Harmonieuse MOI, différente d'un songe,
> Femme flexible et ferme aux silences suivis
> D'actes purs! . . . Front limpide, et par ondes ravis,
> Si loin que le vent vague et velu les achève,
> Longs brins légers qu'au large un vol mêle et soulève,
> Dites! . . . J'étais l'égale et l'épouse du jour,
> Seul support souriant que je formais d'amour
> A la toute-puissante altitude adorée. . . .

Or here, where the play of the vowels more particularly reinforces the impression of the sea-noises below the precipice over which she fears to slip:

> Non loin, parmi ces pas, rêve mon précipice . . .
> L'insensible rocher, glissant d'algues, propice
> A fuir (comme en soi-même ineffablement seul),
> Commence . . . Et le vent semble au travers d'un linceul
> Ourdir de bruits marins une confuse trame,
> Mélange de la lame en ruine, et de rame . . .
> Tant de hoquets longtemps, et de râles heurtés,
> Brisés, repris au large . . . et tous les sorts jetés
> Éperdument divers roulant l'oubli vorace. . . .

It is, however, unsatisfactory to detach passages for examination only on stylistic grounds. Form and theme are so closely interknitted that each part of the poem demands to be related to its context.

IV

The same might be said, not only of this poem, but of almost the whole of Valéry's verse. One poem completes or illuminates another, so that for a full understanding his work should really be considered *en bloc*. This is truer of Valéry than of most poets because he spoke for preference through various mouthpieces which might be said – though this is an over-simplification – to reflect different facets of his consciousness. The Young Fate needs to be completed by Narcissus, the hero-martyr of the contemplation of the Ideal in oneself,[1] by the Delphic Oracle of *La Pythie*, by the Snake in *Ébauche d'un serpent*, and even by the trees of *Au platane* and *Palme*. Such creations, mythical, animistic or inanimate, belong to that tradition of Symbolist poetry which projected the self, or elements of the self, into another form. Rimbaud's Drunken Boat, Mallarmé's Faun and his frigid Hérodiade are the most illustrious examples. But in Valéry these are more than projections in the ordinary sense: they are half-way to becoming objective creations. Dream-monsters or dream-children, one might say, incompletely detached from their parent yet showing often disquieting characteristics of their own. They belong at once to a psychological underworld and to a spiritual over-world – the second only as a result of Valéry's conscious efforts. To say that they are part of a private menagerie which is threatening to get out of control – the orang-outang in the self-contained flat – would be to go slightly further than is justified. But they have the fascination of that possibility. In their mixture of the human, the animal and the purely intellectual they are unique in French poetry while at the same time typifying the French genius, and they are undoubtedly the greatest and subtlest product of Valéry's mind. In Valéry's Serpent, for example, there is a touch of the physical as it might have been perceived by Leconte de Lisle, but the Serpent also clothes an *idea* of Satan and the two together form a perfect unity:

> Parmi l'arbre, la brise berce
> La vipère que je vêtis;
> Un sourire, que la dent perce
> Et qu'elle éclaire d'appétits,
> Sur le Jardin se risque et rôde,
> Et mon triangle d'émeraude
> Tire sa langue à double fil . . .
> Bête je suis, mais bête aiguë,
> De qui le venin quoique vil
> Laisse loin la sage ciguë!

In less mobile vein there is the palm-tree, passive and unproductive

---

[1] Narcissus cannot attain his own beauty except by destroying it: he is drowned in the pool while attempting to join his own reflection. Valéry treated this subject briefly in *Narcisse parle* (*Album de vers anciens*), at length in the *Fragments du Narcisse* (*Charmes*), and in more popular 'operatic' form in in the *Cantate du Narcisse* (1938).

in appearance, yet patiently storing up in itself sap and moisture (through its roots) which are necessary to the world outside it:

> Ces jours qui te semblent vides
> Et perdus pour l'univers
> Ont des racines avides
> Qui travaillent les déserts.
> La substance chevelue
> Par les ténèbres élue
> Ne peut s'arrêter jamais
> Jusqu'aux entrailles du monde,
> De poursuivre l'eau profonde
> Que demandent les sommets.

In this poem, which Valéry printed as the final piece in *Charmes*, there is a parallel between the tree's function and the poet's function, with a probable allusion to the long years during which Valéry was quietly storing up his poetic potential and the First World War was being fought:

> Qu'un peuple à présent s'écroule,
> Palme! . . . Irrésistiblement!
> Dans la poudre qu'il se roule
> Sur les fruits du firmament!
> Tu n'as pas perdu ces heures
> Si légère tu demeures
> Après ces beaux abandons;
> Pareille à celui qui pense
> Et dont l'âme se dépense
> A s'accroître de ses dons![1]

Only once, rejecting metempsychosis, does Valéry speak out in his own person. The result is the comparatively direct and vigorous poem which has won him more readers than any other. *Le Cimetière marin* is a meditation in a graveyard overlooking the Mediterranean at Sète. The physical scene, dominated by 'the three or four incontestable deities – the Sea, the Sky, the Sun', is evoked in all its glittering clarity. The poet moves carefully among the tombs, wondering at his own nature and destiny, but wondering also at the perfection of the noonday hour. Flawless and changeless in itself, it has only him, a living

---

[1] For the subject of this poem, as for the rhyme-scheme, cf. Lamartine's *Le Chêne*, a stanza of which is quoted on p. 107. Lamartine uses octosyllabic lines, while Valéry's lines are of seven syllables. In *La Pythie* and in part of *Ébauche d'un serpent*, however, Valéry's rhyme-scheme and metre are identical with Lamartine's. This rhyme-pattern is that of the old *dizain* as practised by Ronsard (Marot and Scève followed a different pattern).

human consciousness, both to stain its perfection and to realize its existence at all:[1]

> Midi là-haut, Midi sans mouvement
> En soi se pense et convient à soi-même . . .
> Tête complète et parfait diadème,
> Je suis en toi le secret changement.
>
> Tu n'as que moi pour contenir tes craintes!
> Mes repentirs, mes doutes, mes contraintes
> Sont le défaut de ton grand diamant . . .

The dead have already 'changed sides' to become part of the great anonymous universe. All that was human and personal in them has returned to the earth:

> Ils ont fondu dans une absence épaisse,
> L'argile rouge a bu la blanche espèce,
> Le don de vivre a passé dans les fleurs!
> Où sont des morts les phrases familières,
> L'art personnel, les âmes singulières?
> La larve file où se formaient des pleurs.

The immortality of the soul is a fiction, kept up by funeral monuments and pious imagery:

> Maigre immortalité noire et dorée,
> Consolatrice affreusement laurée,
> Qui de la mort fais un sein maternel,
> Le beau mensonge et la pieuse ruse!
> Qui ne connaît, et qui ne les refuse,
> Ce crâne vide et ce rire éternel!

[1] This part of the poem happens, perhaps fortuitously, to give the humanist's reply to Leconte de Lisle's much simpler poem, *Midi*. Having painted a sun-drenched landscape L. de Lisle concluded:

> Homme, si, le cœur plein de joie ou d'amertume,
> Tu passais vers midi dans les champs radieux,
> Fuis! La nature est vide et le soleil consume:
> Rien n'est vivant ici, rien n'est triste ou joyeux.
>
> Mais si, désabusé des larmes et du rire,
> Altéré de l'oubli de ce monde agité,
> Tu veux, ne sachant plus pardonner ou maudire,
> Goûter une suprême et morne volupté,
>
> Viens! Le soleil te parle en paroles sublimes;
> Dans sa flamme implacable absorbe-toi sans fin;
> Et retourne à pas lents vers les cités infimes,
> Le cœur trempé sept fois dans le néant divin.

Other sophisms are rejected and finally the poet, seeing the sea suddenly whipped into activity by the wind and feeling the response in his own living body, turns towards the element which had also spelt life for the Young Fate and shakes off his meditation in a burst of physical lyricism not unworthy of Rimbaud:

> Oui! Grande mer de délires douée,
> Peau de panthère et chlamyde trouée
> De mille et mille idoles du soleil,
> Hydre absolue, ivre de ta chair bleue,
> Qui te remords l'étincelante queue
> Dans un tumulte au silence pareil,
>
> Le vent se lève! . . . il faut tenter de vivre!
> L'air immense ouvre et referme mon livre,
> La vague en poudre ose jaillir des rocs!
> Envolez-vous, pages tout éblouies,
> Rompez, vagues! Rompez d'eaux réjouies
> Ce toit tranquille où picoraient des focs![1]

In this poem Valéry writes at last in the first person of some of the great commonplaces of experience. He does so with typical subtlety and the detail of some of his conceptions is exceedingly complex. Yet one cannot help feeling that he has rejoined in his general intention the great Romantic tradition of poetry as represented by Lamartine and Vigny, and to that extent has rejected Mallarmé. From Mallarmé, however, he had inherited a love of verbal precision coming at times near to *préciosité*, and this alone would be enough to obscure his affiliations with the Romantic spirit. If *Le Cimetière marin* is not his most typical poem, nor – for the reader prepared to 'specialize' in Valéry – his most interesting, it shows an extension of range which greatly increases his stature.

v

Valéry was the last of a type of poets which seems, at least temporarily, to have become extinct. It is not only for the element of nineteenth-century Symbolism in his make-up, nor for his exacting theory of 'poetic' language, that he appears dated. It is for his conception of the poet as a conscious and conscientious artist working tirelessly on verbal nuances and sound-patterns as an essential process

---

[1] In this much-commented line, the 'calm roof' is the sea before the wind struck it. The white foresails (*focs*) of boats appeared like birds pecking at it as they dipped up and down.

in his trade: within the framework, moreover, of the traditional metres and verse-forms. It was worth doing, most younger poets would agree, but it is not worth doing again. And it is not the way to express what the younger poets have to say. His verse still gives great pleasure, but who would dream of imitating it?

Yet beneath this intricate richness of form, much of the thought belongs fully to the twentieth century. The nature of the self, its sub-divisions, its oscillations between the conscious and the unconscious, still preoccupy contemporaries as they preoccupied Valéry. For the modern psychologist he is not writing beautiful nonsense, like Maeterlinck or – too often in this one respect – Yeats. It is true that he avoids public themes. Party, nation and religion are as absent from his verse as the motor-car. Although unusual in an age of *engagement*, this is not an essential lack. Like the palm-tree, the poet does not need to be 'engaged' in detail in order to belong inescapably to this world. One can rig up that tired scarecrow, the modern sensibility, and say, truly but somewhat flatly, that Valéry perceived the same things as we do, but in a different and broader way. But in the end one comes back to the question of form, 'music' and the artistic conscience. Not the conception but the execution is the dividing-line. Saint Valéry has ascended too perpendicularly into his Paradise of language, where no one of any consequence dares or cares to follow him.

He is still greatly revered. He was and remains a true poet. But meanwhile poets of lesser gifts have set the tone for modern poetry. Whatever its virtues and objectives, the cultivation of language in a perfectionist sense is not one of them.

Chapter 22

The Impact of Surrealism

FRENCH poetry during the past half-century has diverged so sharply from its older ways that it may seriously be asked whether it should not be approached as an entirely new study. Certainly, features familiar to the reader of earlier poetry persist in it. The spirit of Hugo, Rimbaud and Mallarmé, as well as of Claudel and Apollinaire, is by no means dead. Several lesser poets than these, who belonged essentially to the pre-1920 world, have with some justification been claimed as forerunners by the Surrealists. But, although the influence of this earlier poetry can often be recognized, it appears in such unfamiliar contexts, such novel transformations, that the reader whose responses are attuned to nineteenth-century verse, up to and including the Symbolists, may well feel that he must go to school all over again when confronted with the work of modern poets.

If he has this feeling, he will be in the right frame of mind to appreciate a phase of literature whose quality and importance are now beyond question and which, moreover, expresses the world in which he lives. If it is possible, and in our opinion justified, to regard much that Apollinaire wrote as *faux moderne*, such an attitude could not be maintained with any semblance of justification before the mass of excellent poetry which has been written during the past forty years. To refuse it serious consideration because of its obscurity or because certain small sectors of it appear wantonly meretricious is unreasonable. Every important movement has its lunatic fringe, made up about equally of stragglers and of scouts who have outrun the range of their communication-equipment, but the strength of the main body cannot be estimated by a stray prisoner captured from among these.

Because of the richness of modern poetry, no less than its closeness to us, the next two chapters do not attempt to show it in the same perspective as the poetry of earlier periods. The scale, as compared to the past, is not yet apparent. Trends are engaged of which, short of prophecy, it is impossible to say whether they are in a rising or a declining phase. Good poets are writing whose work is fortunately still not complete. Even some who can write no more, like Éluard, are not yet ready to be seen in a true relationship to their contemporaries and predecessors. For such reasons, and because the criteria by which they ought to be judged have not yet fully defined themselves, it is not proposed here to measure their importance as we have attempted to do with the poets of the nineteenth century. We shall be more concerned with recording and with tracing possible lines along which future distinctions and even classifications might be made. But it would be misleading, and it is not intended, to imply that there are no poets now writing of the stature of, say, Verlaine or Chénier, to whom chapters have been devoted earlier in this book.

II

The movement which most radically affected French poetry in the second quarter of this century was the Surrealist movement. By an odd coincidence it took shape just at the time when Valéry was perfecting his version of Symbolism. Its history is well known and can be described briefly.

During the First World War, a group of young exiles of various nationalities living temporarily in Switzerland launched the movement known as Dada. The name has been variously explained. By one of the founders, the Alsatian Hans Arp, in these words:

> I hereby declare that Tristan Tzara found the word Dada on 8 February 1916, at 6 p.m. I was present with my twelve children when Tzara for the first time uttered this word ... This occurred at the Café de la Terrasse in Zürich and I was wearing a brioche in my left nostril.[1]

According to a second account, perhaps less apocryphal, the name was produced by a random consultation of the dictionary. In French, *dada* is the equivalent of *gee-gee*, and means also *hobby-horse*. In any case, it served its purpose admirably, suggesting at once the movement's infantilism, its preference for words nearer to the incoherent cry than to rational speech, and its determination to take over nothing to which an existing mystique could be attached. Reacting against the first of the mass slaughters of the century, and also influenced by pre-war movements like Cubism and Futurism, the Dadaists approached the arts as revolutionary nihilists, convinced at least that whatever had been established before was bad, and ready to experiment in any direction whatever provided that it was new. Dadaism had repercussions in

[1] Hans Arp, *Dada-au-grand-air* (1921).

politics and in art, but the branch of it brought to Paris in 1919 was predominantly literary. It soon triggered the much more serious movement of French Surrealism, from which Tzara broke away, leaving André Breton and other young writers such as Aragon, Éluard and Soupault in possession of the field.

Breton, who became the leader and principal spokesman, was a trained psychiatrist, with experience in war hospitals. He was able to found on good Freudian reasons his doctrine that 'higher reality' exists only in the unconscious. Unlike the Dadaists, who were concerned mainly with breaking down, he and his friends could claim an impressive constructive philosophy for Surrealism. They did so, in a number of pronouncements of which the chief was Breton's first *Manifeste du surréalisme* (1924). Surrealism aimed at expressing more of the true personality than had ever been attempted before. Freud seemed to have placed a wonderful new key to human nature in the investigator's hand. It was simply necessary to liberate the unconscious in all the activities of daily life. Of these activities, literature was only one, and not necessarily the chief. Its role in the early history of the movement was limited to the transcribing of dreams and to writing 'automatically' in a dazed or trance-like state.

Thus Surrealism, viewed historically, was the third great step in a hundred years towards the 'liberation' of art. The first had been taken by the Romantics, the second by the Symbolists – who had come very near to the discovery of the unconscious, even if they did not name it. Each movement aimed at giving fuller and therefore truer expressions to the human psyche, and each has achieved a progressive relaxation in form, so that with the Surrealists this aspect of 'liberation' comes near to dissolution. As a consequence of their doctrine, the Surrealists discarded all concern with form, since such a concern implies a conscious preoccupation with the means of expression, to the detriment or distortion of the spontaneous thing expressed. Prose, then, written without premeditation, or the loosest kind of free verse, were used because they seemed the most convenient media and, naturally, no stress was laid on a distinction between verse and prose.

At this point a detached observer might remark: 'Surrealism makes poetry very easy. You simply have to shut your eyes and write.' And he envisages an idle, effortless process, empty of all the qualities associated with the exertion of the will. Yet the words which most often recurred under the pens of French critics writing of Surrealist and allied poetry were, first, *revolution*, which is understandable in both the social and the literary contexts; and, equally, *adventure, risks, dangers* and even *hero-poets*. What was heroic or even risky in drifting with the stream of the unconscious? Briefly, from the Surrealist point of view, it meant a plunge into the unknown and so spelt a dangerous adventure similar to the kind that Rimbaud attempted. But for the Freudian Surrealist the unknown was to be found entirely within the self and it was not the contacting of it (as for Rimbaud) which was either dangerous or arduous. It was rather that, *after contact*, the whole of the self was laid bare and committed. The writer's psyche *is* his work and for the pure Surrealist it was impossible to cheat on this score. For better or worse, he laid everything that he had on the table; and the 'danger' presumably (though it is impossible to find a specific statement on the point) was that which has always been associated with meeting one's true image face to face.

A hostile commentator would indeed pity the poet delivered to his own unconscious and deliberately stripped of the armour of his trade. Limitations of quality and of depth become immediately visible and the heroic adventure may end all too easily in the shallows of triviality. The situation is indeed irremediable if the labour of the artist to amend, or at least reorder, his fundamental shortcomings is forbidden. If an infinite capacity for taking pains never was, as the nineteenth century tended to believe, a condition of genius, at least it could, suitably directed, become the basis of mildly interesting work. On the other hand, the personality of authentic depth and interest should emerge from the Surrealist process enhanced. Genuine simplicity, no less than genuine complexity, can do without the trappings of art – but it is very rare.

But the austerest canons of Surrealism have been observed by very few except for a short time. Perhaps by none except André Breton, who should be classed as a prose-writer rather than as a poet. It would be irrelevant to say that none of even the temporary *purs* was a great artist in the traditional sense (in which art includes craftsmanship but transcends it), since it was their declared intention not to be. But if not great artist, great what? What was the ultimate Surrealist aim in using means of expression at all? To this the truest short answer would be: To reveal hitherto hidden associations in the faith that something must come of it. And sometimes it does.

Now that time has clarified the perspective, the Surrealist movement can be seen to bear comparison with the Pléiade movement of the sixteenth century. Both were founded on trends already in existence before them which they confirmed and defined in manifestos and in practice. This open definition, with the arguments it threw up, was influential in itself. It stressed, sometimes at the expense of distortion, features in earlier writers not always representative of their work as a whole, but which came to be looked upon as alone significant, and so worthy of imitation. Surrealism in particular could claim fore-runners in Lautréamont, Rimbaud, Jarry, as well as in Apollinaire, Max Jacob and Fargue. Excepting these, the main stress in Breton's movement, as in Ronsard's, was on a violent break with the past and a contempt for those who did not share his ideas. Both groups assem-bled young and highly gifted writers who acquired in association a consciousness of aims which, left to themselves, they might never have realized. In short, just as one can say that the Pléiade grouping represents and synthesizes the main innovations of French Renaissance poetry, so one can claim for the Surrealists a comparable role in this century.

There is a further parallel. Though Breton, considered as an original writer, was no Ronsard, as a *chef d'école* he faced similar problems. Ronsard's various listings of his adherents remind one of Breton's more violent expulsions of former disciples or sympathizers from the Surrealist Pantheon. The reasons were sometimes personal, but usually principles were also at stake, ideological and often political. Many more writers passed through the Surrealist movement than remained in it, yet in nearly every case it had contributed something to their formation, even when they explicitly repudiated it. Other poets who never belonged to the movement, including some too young to have done so, can best be characterized in relation to it. There is an obvious analogy here with the post-Pléiade generation.

The poets considered briefly in the following pages were Surrealists in differing degrees. It is pointless to try to identify them exactly with a doctrine which cannot itself be exactly defined, or to show precisely where they diverge from it. Surrealism was a watershed from which many streams began to flow and, to complete the metaphor, they flowed in various directions.

III

Éluard, Char, Aragon

As a poet, Paul Éluard (1895–1952) was born with Surrealism. He had, it is true, published some early poems under the influence of Unanimism – the 'mass-soul' movement launched early in the century by Jules Romains and others. But little change was necessary for him to find his true affinities in André Breton's young group. Surrealism merely brought an increased mystery and depth to his fundamentally simple songs inspired by emotional experience. Human love is the *motif* of nearly all his poetry, keeping him perpetually aware of the sensual aspect of things, whether they are the physical person, or the objects which surround us: trees and fruit, light and shade, sky, clouds and sea:

> L'éventail de sa bouche, le reflet de ses yeux,
> Je suis le seul à en parler,
> Je suis le seul qui soit cerné
> Par ce miroir si nul où l'air circule à travers moi
> Et l'air a un visage, un visage aimé,
> Un visage aimant, ton visage . . .[1]

All his experience, even when it is not erotic, is rendered in terms of sensations, the feel and appearance of tangible things:

> Je sors des caves de l'angoisse
> Des courbes lentes de la peur
> Je tombe dans un puits de plumes
> Pavots je vous retrouve
> Sans y songer
> Dans un miroir fermé
> Vous êtes aussi beau que des fruits
> Et si lourds ô mes maîtres
> Qu'il vous faut des ailes pour vivre
> Ou mes rêves.[2]

Love, troubled or, more usually, serene, brings to life a universe without a hierarchy. Sun and stars are on the same orbit as bird, table and bed – all familiarly equidistant from the humanity at the centre. In other words, Éluard is the happy man who has no conscious religion, no sense of the absolute. Yet his poetry has been called metaphysical. This is tenable when one remembers that one characteristic of the metaphysical poet is that he mixes up the different orders of the physical and the spiritual, ignoring the established distinctions and cutting his peculiar cross-section through them. Although such words as 'God' and 'spirit' are never used by Éluard, neither are they intellectually excluded and there is nothing to prevent a reader to whom such concepts are essential to his view of life from supplying them tacitly. Because of this further dimension created or suggested by the

---

[1] In *Capitale de la douleur* (1926).   [2] From *L'Amour la poésie* (1929).

most authentic handling of poetry – the use of ordinary, simple words by a man who gives them their literal meaning as he himself conceives it and whose attention is not diverted by prosodic rules – Éluard is more than the poet of physical impressions: more than, or at least different from, Verlaine. He is probably our Lamartine, with virtues well beyond those immediately apparent at a first reading, and flaws also.

If Éluard had no expressed religion, he had other kinds of shared belief. Surrealism itself had been a kind of church for its inner circle of writers. In 1938 Éluard broke with Breton. He was beginning to move towards Communism, but the war and the German occupation supervened and his first militant act of faith was resistance to the enemy as a Frenchman. He 'resisted' as a writer, composing, editing and helping in the distribution of clandestine literature. Early in 1942 he joined the Communist Party, a move which then seemed a natural corollary to resistance, and to which he was also drawn by his intensely human feeling for the solidarity of mankind. From 1946 until his death his activities on committees and at congresses, as well as some of his poems, certainly justified seeing him as a Communist writer. What attracted him was the theoretical purity of the doctrine, when contrasted with the corruption of democracy and the menace of those forces which can loosely be called fascist. Beyond this, he idealized fraternity in exactly the same way as the pre-1914 Socialists, and could rightly claim that his belief in it was a simple extension of his feeling for the human individual. His more 'public' poems, whether of Resistance or for Communism, tend to be flat and even platitudinous. Éluard had more to lose than most poets in writing of the moment and for the mass.

But it must not be thought that, even in his last years, the 'private' poet was entirely lost in the propagandist. The most famous and moving of his Resistance poems, *Liberté*, is purely a long enumeration of the familiar things which surround the poet physically and spiritually, while at the end of each verse, as a refrain, comes the reminder that freedom must be among them:

> Sur mes cahiers d'écolier
> Sur mon pupitre et les arbres
> Sur le sable sur la neige
> J'écris ton nom
>
> ... Sur la jungle et le désert
> Sur les nids sur les genêts

Sur l'écho de mon enfance
J'écris ton nom

... Sur l'absence sans désir
Sur la solitude nue
Sur les marches de la mort
J'écris ton nom ...

Liberté.[1]

How different is this treatment from the rhetorical *Liberté, liberté chérie* of the *Marseillaise*.

And as late as 1946 he wrote *Poésie ininterrompue*, his greatest and longest single poem, which testifies to his delight in the physical life of the individual and to its validity as the only true basis of society:

De l'océan à la source
De la montagne à la plaine
Court le fantôme de la vie
L'ombre sordide de la mort
Mais entre nous
Une aube naît de chair ardente
Et bien précise
Qui remet la terre en état
Nous avançons d'un pas tranquille
Et la nature nous salue
Le jour incarne nos couleurs
Le feu nos yeux et la mer notre union

Et tous les vivants nous ressemblent
Tous les vivants que nous aimons

Les autres sont imaginaires
Faux et cernés de leur néant ...

Éluard will remain, not as a political poet, but as a writer who restored, after Symbolism, simplicity to poetry and reintroduced reality without becoming prosaic. For that last quality, as for the 'mystery' which hangs over his apparently ordinary themes, what we have to thank is Surrealism.

With Éluard may be considered René Char, who was born twelve years later (1907) and in certain respects is his successor. He joined the

---

[1] In *Poésie et vérité* (1942).

Surrealist group at the age of twenty-two and left it at about the same time as Éluard. He fought with great distinction in the Resistance movement – but without embracing Communism – and published the poems arising from that experience in *Seuls demeurent* (1945), followed by a poetic diary, *Feuillets d'Hypnos* (1946). These works first brought his name before a wide public. Before then he had published comparatively little and was hardly known outside the Surrealist inner circle. Through his forties he continued to write with increasing independence and authority which were affirmed over the next twenty years with no decline in poetic quality – rather the opposite. Unprovincial because he has shared in the main national experiences of his generation, he has nevertheless retained deep roots in his native Provence, which supplies a physical environment, palpable but not 'colourful' in the Romantic sense, for all his best poetry. This has a specifically rustic foundation which Éluard's lacks and it is possible to make a first approach to him as a nature poet of the same order as Robert Frost. When Frost wrote of the tree outside his window:

> Vague dream-head lifted out of the ground,
> And thing next most diffuse to cloud,
> Not all your light tongues talking aloud
> Could be profound.

> But tree, I have seen you taken and tossed,
> And if you have seen me when I slept,
> You have seen me when I was taken and swept,
> And all but lost.

> That day she put our heads together,
> Fate had her imagination about her.
> Your head so much concerned with outer,
> Mine with inner weather . . .

he was saying more explicitly what Char constantly says also. For each poet the natural object serves as more than a simile or a symbol. It is identified with the human sensibility to a point at which the two become indistinguishable, as in Char's:

> Rivière trop tôt partie, d'une traite, sans compagnon,
> Donne aux enfants de mon pays le visage de ta passion.

> Rivière où l'éclair finit et où commence ma maison,
> Qui roules aux marches d'oubli la rocaille de ma raison.

Rivière, en toi terre est frisson, soleil anxiété.
Que chaque pauvre dans sa nuit fasse son pain de ta moisson.
Rivière souvent punie, rivière à l'abandon. . .[1]

As with Éluard, Char's use of imagery in his mature work might be said to derive from Surrealism. But it is no longer fortuitous and the associations, spontaneously 'natural' though they may have been in their origin, are organized by an intelligence working above the level of consciousness. It is the intellectual process, complex but far from irrational, which makes Char's poetry appear difficult (as was Mallarmé's in a very different way), yet highly rewarding when read closely.

This strongly cerebral element has enabled critics to discern in his work a moralizing tendency, which finds its expression in aphoristic form. A poetic La Rochefoucauld, it has been suggested. And why not, extrapolating this one tendency, go further and draw the comparison with actual poets: La Fontaine the fabulist or, much nearer in time, Sully-Prudhomme, now completely despised and neglected, but the most popular 'philosophical' French poet of the late nineteenth century, Nobel prize-winner in 1901, and author of the once universally quoted *Le Vase brisé*:

> Le vase où meurt cette verveine
> D'un coup d'éventail fut fêlé;
> Le coup dut l'effleurer à peine,
> Aucun bruit ne l'a révélé.

> . . . Souvent aussi la main qu'on aime,
> Effleurant le cœur, le meurtrit;
> Puis le cœur se fend de lui-même,
> La fleur de son amour périt. . .

With Sully-Prudhomme's simile of the heart as a cracked vase one might compare Char's simile of the swift – free, elusive and terribly fragile – in his poem *Le Martinet*:

> Martinet aux ailes trop larges, qui vire et crie sa joie autour de la maison. Tel est le cœur.
> Il dessèche le tonnerre. Il sème dans le ciel serein. S'il touche au sol, il se déchire.
> Sa repartie est l'hirondelle. Il déteste la familière. Que vaut dentelle de la tour?

[1] From *Chanson pour Yvonne* (*La Sorgue*).

No doubt quite accidentally, this poem is written in the metre of J.-A. de Baïf's fifteen-syllable line (see p. 35 above), used with slightly greater freedom.

> Sa pause est au creux le plus sombre. Nul n'est plus à l'étroit que lui.
> L'été de la longue clarté, il filera dans les ténèbres, par les persiennes de
> minuit.
> Il n'est pas d'yeux pour le tenir. Il crie, c'est toute sa présence. Un
> mince fusil va l'abattre. Tel est le cœur.[1]

The conceptual basis of the two poems, if defined in general terms,
is the same. The obvious difference in impact may be attributed partly
to fresher powers of observation and to a profounder or subtler sensibility. But above all it is a question of poetic idiom, conditioned no
doubt by Surrealism and capable of expressing perceptions which
Sully-Prudhomme's generation may well have possessed but which
they had no artistic means of either realizing or communicating –
though Rimbaud and Mallarmé were already creating these. Char's
compressed moralizations become more evocative because of their
apparent obscurity, as in general do all his metaphors, which are fundamentally pictorial. In the third line above, *dentelle de la tour* suggests
the undulating flight of the swallow as it weaves a delicate lace-pattern
round the tower. (Compare a more familiar English metaphor, 'to
weave arabesques', or, for another poem on a bird's flight, at once
descriptive, metaphorical and symbolic, *The Windhover* of Gerard
Manley Hopkins.) All this is indeed 'nature poetry', but when written
sensitively in an elliptical and disciplined style it acquires wider potentialities and can become an expression of the human condition rather
than just a comment upon it.

In the following extract from a typical prose-poem, the mill is
associated with past memories of human presences (joyous and exuberant, it appears) to a point of almost complete identification. This can
be classed as animism, but with absolutely none of the mystic overtones which occur in Hopkins and such French poets as Jouve:

> Le Moulin du Calavon. Deux années durant, une ferme de cigales, un
> château de martinets. Ici tout parlait torrent tantôt par le rire, tantôt par
> les poings de la jeunesse. Aujourd'hui, le vieux réfractaire faiblit au milieu
> de ses pierres, la plupart mortes de gel, de solitude et de chaleur. A leur
> tour, les visages se sont assoupis dans le silence des fleurs.[2]

A third poet played an important part in the early history of Surrealism. Like Éluard, Louis Aragon (b. 1897) was a member of Breton's
original group and by his works in prose contributed notably to the
building-up of the movement. After a visit to Russia in 1930 he broke

---

[1] From *La Fontaine narrative*.
[2] From *Affres détonation silence* in *Le Poème pulvérisé* (1947).

with Surrealism and became an active Communist. (The true Surrealists, when not apolitical, have felt naturally drawn to either anarchism or Trotskyism.) His early poems were little more than half-playful fantasies, as might be expected of a writer who has expressed himself more naturally and much more prolifically in the essay and the novel. His great moment as a poet came in 1939–40, when the Phoney War and then the fall of France inspired those simple, rhythmic and nostalgically emotional pieces which brought him fame (*Le Crève-cœur*, 1941) and at the same time quickened his private feelings into sincerely felt love-poetry (*Les Yeux d'Elsa*, 1942). Further volumes reflected the growing pride of the French in Resistance, the iniquities of Vichy and the invader and, after the war, the struggle of the Marxist-led proletariat.

Le Crève-cœur is still Aragon's most interesting book of verse. It caught what appeared to be the voice of France at a particularly poignant moment of confusion and defeat:

> O mois des floraisons mois des métamorphoses
> Mai qui fut sans nuage et Juin poignardé
> Je n'oublierai jamais les lilas et les roses
> Ni ceux que le printemps dans ses plis a gardés. . .

It seemed the voice of France because it evoked some of the more romantic aspects of her past and carried echoes of other poets – Verlaine, Péguy, Apollinaire. Looking back, it is easy to class this verse of Aragon's as facile and imitative and to realize that it never deserved serious consideration as war-poetry.[1] At the time it came as a lonely affirmation, when the future appeared completely dark, of national qualities which could be universally appreciated, and which it seemed might easily be lost for ever. On that level its appeal went deep, though for a generation which has not shared the same experience it may well be no more evocative than *Lili Marlene*, and of about the same quality. More critically, it is surprising that a poet who had passed through Surrealism and embraced Russian Communism should have anchored himself so firmly in tradition, both emotionally and technically. His aim, and no doubt his historic importance, was to create a popular poetry accessible to everyone in the same way as ballad-poetry and this

---

[1] For a rather cruel contrast, compare these lines referring to the earlier war of 1914–18:

> I have seen a green country, useful to the race,
> Knocked silly with guns and mines, its villages vanished,
> Even the last rat and last kestrel banished –
> God bless us all, this was peculiar grace.
>
> Edmund Blunden, from *Report on Experience.*

aim was consistent with the doctrine of socialist realism towards which his Communism disposed him. But no such movement developed in French poetry and, after a brief period of fame, Aragon as a poet has remained on an isolated branch of a tree which is more vulnerable than vigorous. None of his later verse has seriously modified that position.

IV

Desnos, Michaux, Prévert, Queneau, Audiberti, Artaud

Several other poets of the Surrealist line obtained wider recognition in the 1940s, largely because of the influence of the war. War, which accelerates scientific and technical progress, can apparently have the same effect on literary developments. One of the most genuine of these poets was Robert Desnos (1900–45) who belonged to the original Surrealist group, played an active part in the Resistance, was arrested and died of typhus in a concentration camp exactly a month after the war in Europe came to an end. His early poetry was a good example of the Surrealist cult of dream-writing. His later poetry was simpler and included pieces directly concerned with the Resistance movement. Some of it was written in the traditional metres, with rhyme. Though this may suggest a parallel with Aragon, the content was very different. Desnos has been seen, like Char, as a poet determined to come to terms with life as it lies directly before him – and this involves a keen awareness of physical environment – with no attempt to escape into transcendentalism. His best poems are based on this sincere, if rather narrow, conception of humanism.

All this must imply acceptance, not indeed passive but perhaps arrived at after great suffering and difficulty and without recourse to religion. Detectable in Éluard, Desnos and Char, it is entirely lacking in other poets who find their world unacceptable or incomprehensible, or both at once. These include the protesters, the trouble-makers, the ironists and – in other periods but not this one – the reformers.

Foremost among this family of poets is Henri Michaux, who never adhered to the Surrealist movement or any other grouping, but who presents many features which can only be called surrealistic. Born in Belgium in 1899 but a self-adopted Frenchman, Michaux has travelled widely and led a life of experiments and explorations, principally internal. He has taken up painting with success and has passed through the mescalin experience, emerging disillusioned (*Misérable miracle*, 1956). There are signs here and there in his work of a specifically religious quest, equally fruitless. He has admitted an 'incapability to conform' – not, it appears, in a spirit of rebellion but because he honestly cannot see what to conform to. In his restlessness, his perplexities and his apprehensions he is a modern Baudelaire crossed with a Kafka. For him, the individual is oppressed both from without and within by irrational forces and his characteristic response has been to construct artificial worlds which (unlike the dream-worlds of the Surrealists) he knows to be artificial and to which therefore he brings the reservation of humour. Much of his work can be read as amusing, until on second thoughts one reflects that it is too near reality to be funny.

All his writing has been in prose or the loosest kinds of free verse. What is 'poetic' is the imagination and a great facility in verbal invention, particularly apparent in his books of the thirties.

Michaux does not lend himself to brief quotations. Many of his pieces are long and have to be read as wholes, since they usually reach a pointed conclusion. This opening of a long description of sick-bed fancies centred upon animals does, however, provide an example of Michaux's matter-of-fact juxtaposition of the real and the imaginary:

> Avec simplicité les animaux fantastiques sortent des angoisses et des obsessions et sont lancés au-dehors sur les murs des chambres où personne ne les aperçoit que leur créateur.
> La maladie accouche infatigablement d'une création animale inégalable.
> La fièvre fit plus d'animaux que les ovaires n'en firent jamais.
> Dès le premier malaise, ils sortent des tapisseries les plus simples, grimaçant à la moindre courbe, profitant d'une ligne verticale pour s'élancer, grossis de la force immense de la maladie et de l'effort pour en triompher; animaux qui donnent des inquiétudes, à qui on ne peut s'opposer efficacement, dont on ne peut deviner comment ils vont se mouvoir, qui ont des pattes et des appendices en tous sens. . .[1]

Nearer in form to a recognizable 'poem' is a piece such as *Immense voix* – the overpowering voice of a generalized father-figure, which nevertheless can be defied or ignored:

> . . . Immense voix qui boit nos voix
> Immense père reconstruit géant
> par le soin, par l'incurie des événements
>
> Immense toit qui couvre nos bois
> nos joies
> qui couvre chats et rats

[1] From *Animaux fantastiques*, in *Lointain intérieur* (1938).

Immense croix qui maudit nos radeaux
qui défait nos esprits
qui prépare nos tombeaux

Immense voix pour rien
pour le linceul
pour s'écrouler nos colonnes

Immense 'doit' 'devoir'
devoir devoir devoir
Immense impérieux empois[1]

. . . Suffit! ici on ne chante pas
Tu n'auras pas ma voix, grande voix
Tu n'auras pas ma voix, grande voix

Tu t'en passeras, grande voix
Toi aussi tu passeras
– Tu passeras, grande voix.[2]

Michaux's work gives an impression of innocent perplexity in a
nightmare world which he is conscientiously attempting to map.
Sometimes it has the 'nonsense' quality of Edward Lear's poems, but
the nonsense goes deep and one can be virtually sure that Michaux
is not playing about.

That is not wholly true of two other poets, both of whom belonged
for a time to the Surrealist movement proper. Jacques Prévert (b.
1900), who had made a name as writer of film-scripts in the thirties,
scored an immediate success in 1946 with *Paroles*, his first book of
collected poems, some of which had been written as much as fifteen
years earlier. He now appeared as a satirist of great destructive power,
skilled at deflating pomp and pretension and the conventional values
(especially religious and nationalistic) of bourgeois morality. His
satire preferably takes the form of *naïveté* – a *fausse naïveté* of course,
but for the purpose it does not matter, witness his well-known piece
Familiale:

La mère fait du tricot
Le fils fait la guerre
Elle trouve ça tout naturel la mère
Et le père qu'est-ce qu'il fait le père?
Il fait des affaires
Sa femme fait du tricot

[1] *empois*: starch.   [2] *Immense voix*, from *Épreuves, exorcismes* (1945).

Son fils la guerre
Lui des affaires
Il trouve ça tout naturel le père
Et le fils le fils
Qu'est-ce qu'il trouve le fils?
Il ne trouve rien absolument rien le fils
Le fils sa mère fait du tricot son père des affaires lui la guerre
Quand il aura fini la guerre
Il fera des affaires avec son père
La guerre continue la mère continue elle tricote
Le père continue il fait des affaires
Le fils est tué il ne continue plus
Le père et la mère vont au cimetière
Ils trouvent ça tout naturel le père et la mère
La vie continue la vie avec le tricot la guerre les affaires
Les affaires la guerre le tricot la guerre
Les affaires les affaires et les affaires
La vie avec le cimetière.

This deadpan kind of humour is immediately comprehensible and it helped to make Prévert a widely popular poet. Sometimes he is a little more difficult to follow, but his work is never truly obscure or profound and the Surrealism back to which it can be traced has lost its mystery to retain only its incongruity. This can often be preserved even in English, which is a measure of its accessibility:

'The noblest conquest of man is the horse,' says the President, 'and if only one is left, I shall be that one.'
That ends his speech. Like a rotten orange hurled hard against a wall by a bad-mannered youngster, the *Marseillaise* bursts out. . . .

Paroles established Prévert's position and manner and these have not changed significantly in the work he has published since. Topical events have given him new occasions for his satire, which has tended to become broader and even more popular. He has also written verse of a sentimental character, which has an immediate appeal but must be considered as lightweight.

Raymond Queneau (b. 1903) is also suspect on the grounds of depth and durability. He has written a number of novels, including the very successful *Zazie dans le Métro* (1959). His first volume of verse, *Les Ziaux* (1943), is characteristic and contains poems as good as any he has written since. Many of them are written in the traditional metres with rhymes, used freely, and contain displays of a linguistic virtuosity which tends to defeat its own ends. The general theme is pessimistic, but the execution is exuberant, with a slight suspicion of self-conscious cleverness. This may be unfair: that old figure of the clown whose heart is breaking was after all a genuine sufferer. And Queneau is much less a clown than a verbal conjurer. One cannot help responding seriously to such a poem as *Je crains pas ça tellment*, in which Queneau minimizes his fear of death and of which these are three stanzas from a poem which runs to eight in all:

> Je crains pas ça tellment la mort de mes entrailles
> et la mort de mon nez et celle de mes os
> Je crains pas ça tellment moi cette moustiquaille
> qu'on baptisa Raymond d'un père dit Queneau

> . . . Je crains bien le malheur le deuil et la souffrance
> et l'angoisse et la guigne et l'excès de l'absense
> Je crains l'abîme obèse où gît la maladie
> et le temps et l'espace et les torts de l'esprit

> Mais je crains pas tellment ce lugubre imbécile
> qui viendra me cueillir au bout de son curdent
> lorsque vaincu j'aurai d'un œil vague et placide
> cédé tout mon courage aux rongeurs du présent. . .[1]

A few lines from *Trains dans la banlieue ouest* illustrate even better the typical mixture of popular unliterary speech and verbal invention of this essentially urban poet:

> . . . Le train court court court court court court
> sur les mignonnes railles nues
> seins d'acier cuisses de satin
> bras étendus sur les traverses

> cadavre exquis tu boive' encore
> tu boive' encore le vin mousseux
> la co la como la motive
> te tire encor par les cheveux

> Voici passer auprès de toi
> la douce enfant migne cervelle
> c'est ton grand train ton autocar
> ton camion lourd ton omnibelle. . .[2]

The point at which verbal virtuosity becomes verbal intoxication is often imprecise, and this was the case with Audiberti (Jacques Audiberti, 1899–1965). Though he worked for many years in Parisian

[1] From *Les Ziaux*.   [2] From *L'Instant fatal* (1948).

THE IMPACT OF SURREALISM

journalism, he was born at Antibes and possessed in full the southern loquacity which brings to French literature an element not unlike the Irish element in English literature. Like Queneau, he wrote a number of remarkable novels. He was also a dramatist, whose later plays, tending to farce, enjoyed considerable commercial success. Though never a nominal Surrealist, he appeared often to write in a state of delirium, using – again like Queneau – traditional metres in a new way. His torrential outpourings of rhymed alexandrines make one wonder whether the established poetic forms need be considered incompatible with Breton's concept of psychic automatism. A rhythmic habit, so thoroughly assimilated that it operates without effort, can provide the ideal 'vehicle' for the images and associations of the subconscious. The question of form is then solved, not by attempted abolition but by the facility with which it appears to take care of itself.[1]

As a spinner of words Audiberti is inexhaustible and the effect, temporarily at least, is very exhilarating. This appears in his long *Stèle aux mots*, of which these are two stanzas:

> ... Les mots, chaussés de plomb sournois, l'ongle buté,
> jumelés d'isthme entre leurs cous pleins de carottes,
> avec des scions à la pointure des marottes
> je les chéris cessant de nous déconcerter.

> Les mots, souvent bouvreuils, risibles de mélange,
> mère, mer, tue et tu, vend, vent, van, puits, poix, pou,
> par la voix refusés permettront tout à coup
> des jardins de cristal pour dissoudre l'Archange.[2]

Such poets write for the immediate impact. When one tries to analyse the thought-line or to follow the poet in his intricate associations of images and sounds one is often disappointed. What is a rewarding effort with Mallarmé or Valéry sometimes ends here with the realization that one has simply been retracing mental doodlings, however originally expressed. This is the weak point of all writing, Surrealist or other, which attempts innovations in language – or, at the lower end of the scale, plays tricks with it. In English, Dylan Thomas and even Joyce are not always above suspicion in this respect.

---

[1] Cf. what has been written above (p. 110) on Lamartine's 'wordless harmonies'.

[2] From *Toujours* (1944). Translated literally: 'Words, shod with stealthy lead, their claws stubborn, isthmus-paired between their necks full of carrots, with shoots made to fit the jester's fancies [one possible meaning], I cherish them ceasing to disconcert us.

'Words, often bullfinches, laughably intermingled, *mère, mer, tue* and *tu, vend, vent, van, puits, poix, pou*, refused by the voice will suddenly allow gardens of crystal to dissolve the Archangel.'

The last three French poets considered have a certain kinship with
the *fantaisistes* of Apollinaire's generation, who were openly whimsical
and whose principal aim was to amuse, sometimes by a light-hearted
verbal juggling. Whimsy and a sense of humour have never conquered
a place in serious poetry and this is where Surrealism and all that stems
from it is most vulnerable. It can so easily merge into playfulness,
which is generally taken to assume either a superficial approach or
a conscious technique.

One writer who was an early Surrealist before breaking with the
movement can be cleared of such associations. Antonin Artaud (1896–
1948), now famous for his work in the theatre and his theories about
it, including his conception of the 'Theatre of Cruelty', published two
early books of poetry.[1] They reflect the nightmare world of a man
who was later to spend nine years in a lunatic asylum. Madness is the
other frontier of Surrealism, where it perhaps touches something
deeper than itself, as Romanticism did in Nerval. Antonin does not
figure prominently among the poets, but his work is a proof, more
convincing even than that of Michaux, of the disquieting power of
unexpected associations of words and images:

> Avec moi dieu-le-chien, et sa langue
> qui comme un trait perce la croûte
> de la double calotte en voûte
> de la terre qui le démange. . .[2]

---

[1] *L'Ombilic des limbes* and *Le Pèse-nerfs* (both 1925).
[2] From *l'Ombilic des limbes*. 'With me god-the-dog, and his tongue which like an arrow
pierces the crust of the double-vaulted canopy of the earth which itches him.'

Chapter 23

Some Other Modern Poets

A NUMBER of important modern poets have been unaffected and unattracted by Surrealism. If, as suggested in the previous chapter, Surrealism is the modern equivalent of the Pléiade movement, perhaps some future Lanson will dismiss these as twentieth-century *attardés et égarés*, leaving it to a future post-Lanson to rehabilitate them, as has been done with the 'baroque' poets. It is an interesting prospect, though the analogy cannot be pressed too far. It is even more difficult to discern common features among the modern independents than among the so-called baroque writers of the sixteenth and seventeenth centuries. Several tend to employ the old regular metres with more frequency than the Surrealists and in that respect stay nearer to tradition, but there are too many exceptions to this – even within the work of the same poet – to allow of a classification on grounds of literary form. Ideological classifications also break down, but one partial grouping is possible. A few of these poets draw their inspiration from religion (as did nearly all the old poets who escaped the main Pléiade influences). It is not the inverted or tortured religion of certain Surrealists, or of Baudelaire, but a Christian faith rooted in Catholicism and comparable to that of Claudel and Francis Jammes.

II

Jouve, Pierre Emmanuel, La Tour du Pin and others

Pierre Jean Jouve was born in 1887. He published several early volumes of poetry and, like Éluard, was in contact with the Unanimist group of writers, but in 1924 he experienced a deep religious crisis and renounced all his previous work. His true career as a writer began with *Les Mystérieuses Noces* (1925) and continued almost uninterruptedly until the 1960s. Besides numerous volumes of poems, his work includes several novels with symbolical and religious implications, essays on literature and music (in particular Mozart's *Don*

Giovanni and Alban Berg's *Woẓẓek*) and translations of Shakespeare's *Sonnets* and of three Shakespearian tragedies.

Nearly all Jouve's poetry has an erotic basis which furnishes the symbolism for his religious concepts; or alternately one can say that sexuality and religion are intimately related, as in the Song of Songs and the writings of some of the great mystics; the relationship is found also in religious 'baroque' poets such as La Ceppède.[1] Jouve's interpretation of the Don Juan legend in his essay on the Mozartian opera is a typical illustration of his angle of approach. He has, however, introduced a fresh element into the old and relatively uncomplicated religious eroticism because of his knowledge of Freudian psychology. This is the influence which might appear to link him with Surrealism, but it reached him quite independently. It fills his work with a similar obscurity, arrived at by a different route and in some poems owing a considerable debt to Mallarmé. There is a curious merging of Surrealist and Mallarmean theory in Jouve's claim that the function of poetry is 'to force greater reality into existence (*forcer le plus réel à exister*)'. But whereas with Mallarmé it was indeed a question of 'force' or effort, classic Surrealism could hardly admit this.

Jouve's poetry is not easy to understand without considerable study, which it usually repays. The following short poem, *Hélène dit*, is typical of his work of the thirties:

> Conduis-moi dans ce couloir de nuit
> Amant pur amant ténébreux
> Près des palais ensevelis par la nostalgie
> Sous les forêts de chair d'odeur et de suave
> Entrecoupées par le marbre des eaux
> Les plus terribles que l'on ait vues! Et qui es-tu
> Inexprimable fils et pur plaisir
> Qui caches le membre rouge sous ton manteau
> Que veux-tu prendre sur mon sein qui fut vivant
> Dedans mon pli chargé des ombres de la mort
> Pourquoi viens-tu à l'épaisseur de mes vallées de pierre?[2]

Jouve's Hélène, who appears in other poems and in one of his novels, appears to have been a composite figure suggested by three actual women in the same way as Gérard de Nerval's lost and idealized love. Hélène dies, showing the close relationship between love and death, and also between love and the sense of sin, both of which accompany Jouve's eroticism and without which any description of that persistent obsession would be incomplete. The poems which

---

[1] See above, pp. 43–4.   [2] From *Matière céleste* (1937).

Jouve went on to write in his seventies express, very naturally, a stronger preoccupation with the idea of death, a certain taming of the erotic content but no renunciation, and some signs that he had achieved a psychological synthesis which made his world acceptable and explicable to him. This poem, from his latest book of poetry (*Ténèbre*, 1965) can be seen to contain all these things:

> Qu'un sursaut, le plus fort de mes anciens sursauts
> Saisisse encor mon âme à l'heure avant-dernière
> Et que ma voix perdant la bouche des amours
> Vers plus d'amour atteigne à la phrase angélique,
>
> Baise à la frange une Présence de haut ciel
> Indulgente et sacrée à laquelle est soumise
> La dure humeur de vivre; et prononce le mot
> Enfantin et vieillard dans l'éternelle fuite:
>
> Rien! le parfait état, adorateur de Vie,
> Où nos cœurs flamboyants connaissent la survie.

Jouve can now be seen as a poet hardly less interesting than Mallarmé and Valéry, and his work is sufficiently rich and complex to call for as detailed an exploration as theirs at the hands of future critics. He belongs to the same line and, though the fact has not so far been generally recognized, can be classed as a late Symbolist.

Christianity, with its themes and myths sometimes profoundly reinterpreted, lies at the root of all the work of Pierre Emmanuel (b. 1916), the most impressive of the openly religious poets of the century. Though strongly influenced by Jouve, he is much less addicted to sexual imagery, but has instead a tremendous rhetorical vigour which Jouve lacked and which indeed would have been foreign to him. Pierre Emmanuel has been criticized for this verbal energy and the criticism might be justified if it produced mechanical flows of words with insufficient content, but this is far from the case. His verse is full of meanings which can only be expressed in this particular poet's characteristic language. He is rhetorical in the same way as d'Aubigné, of whom he is sometimes reminiscent, or Du Bartas, or even Milton. The sweep or *souffle* of his longer poems is not a device but a natural mode of expression.

His first volumes of note were *Tombeau d'Orphée* (1941) and *Le Poète et son Christ* (1942), followed closely by collections of poems inspired by the German occupation of France and the Resistance,

L

whose moral aspects they explored. His most ambitious single volume
no doubt grew from meditation on this war-experience and took as its
theme the rejection of God and the rise of a man who was eagerly
accepted as a substitute God and became the tyrant-king of humanity,
only to collapse finally into nothingness. This work, *Babel* (1951),
centres upon the building of a new Tower of Babel, constructed not
so much of stones as of blood, skulls and human aspirations, of which
last it becomes the prison:

> Monte, Babel, tordant de ta clameur la pierre!
> Nous aurons des carriers pour équarrir les fronts.
> Nous crépirons notre tombeau de notre haleine
> Nous dallerons de crânes creux notre prison.
> Nos cœurs, ces vieux lions endormis dans leur cendre
> En rêvant grifferont les voûtes, n'ayant plus
> Assez d'air pour rugir . . . Écrase-les, Babel!
> Monte, épaissis toujours tes pompeuses murailles
> Rends l'ombre impénétrable entre le ciel et nous.
> Cette race de courtilières[1] ne désire
> Rien d'autre que d'enfouir sa peur au plus épais,
> Et la crinière des lions, la force mâle
> S'est éteinte avec le soleil. Monte, Babel!
> Les lions sont mangés par les termites, l'homme
> Par le nœud de serpents que son ventre a nourris.
>   . . . Nul ne sait
> Ce qu'il pense. L'esprit vidé par les narines
> Ainsi que la cervelle inerte des momies,
> Les vivants étagés serrent les flancs, paroi
> D'yeux fixes et que l'œil du tyran illumine
> Tous ensemble, d'un reflet sec. . .

1984, but worse in this ideology, in which the loss of God is added
to, or identified with, Orwell's loss of personal human qualities. The
unrhymed alexandrines in which this passage and much of *Babel* is
written, as well as other poems of Pierre Emmanuel's (though he sometimes uses the same metre with rhyme or assonance), may be responsible for the impression of over-emphatic eloquence which his work
has made. They are certainly not 'd'ordre lisse et coulant', like the
alexandrines of Racine and Lamartine.[2] In nearly every line certain
words demand to be strongly stressed and it is impossible to read
them aloud without hammering them out, again as in d'Aubigné.
Perhaps this gives them an old-fashioned quality, but this idiom is not

---

[1] *Courtilière*: 'mole-cricket', a burrowing insect.   [2] See above, pp. 110–11.

pastiche and since it is entirely appropriate to the poet's view of the world and his response to it, he must be allowed to express this in his own powerful way.

Pierre Emmanuel also uses shorter, less insistent metres, as well as free verse and the *verset* (*Chansons du dé à coudre*, 1947; *Evangéliaire*, 1961). He is frequently less successful with them and many of the meditations on New Testament subjects and various aspects of the Crucifixion which appear in his later poems will appeal mainly to the conventional Christian. All this is entirely consistent, but it makes one regret the fire and fury of his other work. The words which Blake put in the mouth of the prophet Isaiah might be applied to him at his best: 'My senses discovered the infinite in everything, and as I was then persuaded, and remained confirmed, that the voice of honest indignation is the voice of God, I cared not for consequences, but wrote.'

The profoundly religious poetry of Jean Cayrol (b. 1911) has a quieter note, more immediately personal, and avoiding the epic theme and manner. Cayrol is a rare example of the writer who passed with no violent volte-face from open Surrealism (*Le Hollandais volant*, 1936) to equally open Christian poetry (*Les Phénomènes célestes*, 1939; *Miroir de la rédemption*, 1944). He suffered during the war in a German concentration camp, an experience which gave *Poèmes de la nuit et du brouillard* (1945) and later poems on the theme of Lazarus risen from the grave and confronting a new life (as in *Pour tous les temps*, 1955). He has turned increasingly to the novel. Like Emmanuel, Cayrol often uses a free, unrhymed alexandrine, mingled with other lines of various lengths. Another Catholic poet, Luc Estang (b. 1911) uses quite regular versification, including full rhymes. His only prosodic development is to have abandoned the alexandrine of his earlier work in favour of an eleven-syllable line. Though this may be regarded as a truncated alexandrine, it is hardly an innovation, since it goes back to the *impair* prescribed by Verlaine. Luc Estang's books of verse include *Trans-humances* (1939), *Puissance du malin* (1941), *Les Béatitudes* (1948), *Les Quatre Éléments* (1955), *D'une nuit noire et blanche* (1962). He also has expressed his strong religious and theological preoccupations in novels and essays.

A fourth poet of the same generation, with a comparable Catholic outlook and background, is Patrice de La Tour du Pin (b. 1911). On publishing *La Quête de joie* in 1933 he was acclaimed as a young poet who might renew the old tradition just then reeling under the heaviest pressure from the Surrealists. His first published single poem, *Les Enfants de septembre*, described the passage of migratory waterfowl over the marshes of his native Sologne where, in the family château, he was growing up in that environment peculiar to the old French aristocracy. The life is that of the country gentleman, familiar from childhood with the woods and their fauna, and soaked mentally in the values and legends of the past, with the nostalgic and magic aura which these possess. Clearly, it has little in common with the life of a Parisian journalist. Wounded and taken prisoner in the war, La Tour du Pin embarked on *Une Somme de poésie*, a huge work of which the first volume appeared in 1946 and which is still incomplete. His aim was to create a whole symbolic world, with its own legends and characters, reproducing on a poetic plane the religious and natural worlds with which he was familiar. There are echoes of the Arthurian romances, but the general conception, as well as the style, reminds one of the great Romantic poets of the nineteenth century. Regular alexandrines are used to comparable effect, interspersed with free verse and prose. As time went on La Tour du Pin seemed to get lost in his own work. Fine separate poems can be detached from the *Somme*, but the whole is unwieldy and amorphous.

III

Supervielle, Saint-John Perse, Ponge

Two poets of very considerable stature refuse to be placed in any general scheme. Surrealism has nothing to do with their work, yet they cannot be satisfactorily described as traditionalists. They have nothing in common with each other except their independence. Each has steadily gone his own way, amassing an enviable reputation as he did so.

Jules Supervielle (1884–1960) was the elder by a few years. Born in Montevideo of French parents and educated in France, like Lautréamont and Laforgue before him, he differed from those tubercular poets in living long enough to return and settle for a time in his birthplace. But he remained in close touch with France, served there in the 1914 war, and never felt himself an expatriate. Yet he appeared detached from his contemporaries in a way which is not easy to define. His work might seem to derive from Symbolism but, if so, it has taken an unusual road. The difference has been ascribed to physical environment; the landscape and skies of South America, of which he has often written, are not those of France, and neither is the vital tempo. But the difference might be explained more profitably by the influence of modern South American poets, some of whom have qualities very similar to Supervielle's. They in their turn have been influenced indirectly by the French Symbolists, beginning with Verlaine, and this factor operating at one or two removes through a different racial temperament could account for the unfamiliar form which Symbolism or symbolism takes in Supervielle. While not ceasing to be thoroughly French, his work has a freshness and simplicity not matched elsewhere in recent French poetry – except, evidently quite by chance, occasionally in Éluard. In his lighter poems there is a play of fantasy which brings him dangerously near to the whimsical. But such is his sincerity and the seriousness of the underlying thought that the danger is nearly always averted.

Like Char in this respect, Supervielle found all his images and symbols in 'nature' – the sea, the sky, trees, plants and animals. Particularly animals and birds with which, together with children, he felt a fraternal sympathy. This poem, though by no means one of his best, expresses as well as anything he has written his sense of the identification of the human personality with the rest of the physical universe, and also his basic optimism:

> Ce peu d'océan, arrivant de loin,
> Mais c'est moi, c'est moi qui suis de ce monde,
> Ce navire errant, rempli de marins,
> Mais c'est moi, glissant sur la mappemonde,
> Ce bleu oublié, cette ardeur connue,
> Et ce chuchotis au bord de la nue,
> Mais c'est moi, c'est moi qui commence ici,
> Ce cœur de silence étouffant ses cris,
> Ces ailes d'oiseaux près d'oiseaux sans ailes
> Volant, malgré tout, comme à tire d'ailes,
> Mais c'est moi, c'est moi dans l'humain souci.
> Courage partout, il faut vivre encore
> Sous un ciel qui n'a plus mémoire de l'aurore![1]

Supervielle's first notable poetry was in *Débarcadères* (1922), published after the First World War when he was thirty-eight. He continued writing almost until the year of his death, producing books of poems as well as novels and stories which have the same qualities of fantasy and grave charm. His principal individual volumes of poems were: *Gravitations* (1925), *Le Forçat innocent* (1930), *La Fable du*

[1] *Ce peu* ... from *Ciel et terre* (1942).

monde (1938), *Poèmes de la France malheureuse* (1941–2), *Oublieuse mémoire* (1949), *Le Corps tragique* (1959). But he can be read most easily in the collected volumes which he also published.

Saint-John Perse (the pseudonym of Alexis Léger) has spent much of his life outside France, but with that biographical fact all possible resemblance with Supervielle ends. His work is difficult, hermetic, and written for the most part in a kind of poetic prose. He was born in the French West Indies in 1887, educated in France, and entered the diplomatic service. He served for some years in Peking before being posted to the Quai d'Orsay. Here he attained high rank as an expert on international affairs until he was exiled by the Vichy Government in 1940. He was appointed adviser to the Library of Congress and has remained in the United States. While his poetry has been the private indulgence of a high civil servant, it shows nothing of the amateurishness which such a description might suggest. At most there are traces of the aestheticism of the 1890s in his work – the fastidious search for the rare and perfect word – but this feature is a means, not an end as in minor writers. After *Éloges* (1911), he published *Anabase* (1924), the description of a symbolical journey to a high plateau whose features are vaguely Asian – perhaps Mongolian. Like Claudel, whom he knew personally and whom he followed in the same career and some of the same places, he used the *verset* in these works, but without the same impetuously emotional flow. In him, it was denser and suggested a man of more carefully disciplined culture and with minuter powers of observation:

> Nous n'habiterons pas toujours ces terres jaunes, notre délice. . .
> L'Été plus vaste que l'Empire suspend aux tables de l'espace plusieurs étages de climats. La terre vaste sur son aire roule à pleins bords sa braise pâle sous les cendres – Couleur de soufre, de miel, couleur de choses immortelles, toute la terre aux herbes s'allumant aux pailles de l'autre hiver – et de l'éponge verte d'un seul arbre le ciel tire son sucre violet.
> Un lieu de pierres à mica! Pas une graine pure dans les barbes du vent! Et la lumière comme une huile.[1]

After *Anabase*, Saint-John Perse published nothing for eighteen years, but the experience of being driven from France and of watching his country's plight helplessly from a distance shocked him again into poetry and caused him to emerge, at the age of nearly sixty, as still a contemporary.

[1] From *Anabase*. An English translation by T. S. Eliot was published in 1930.

In *Exil* (1942, reprinted in 1946 with *Pluies* and *Neiges*) and *Vents* (1947) he used the same form as before, but with a certain loosening due to the pressure of personal emotion. His concern with human destiny was more openly stated and there were more biblical turns of language, so that his kinship with Claudel appeared somewhat closer in this later verse. Passages such as this from *Exil* are pure Claudel and could be fitted without difficulty, as to the language, into the latter's *Grande Ode IV* (*La Muse qui est la Grâce*):

Je vous connais, ô monstre! Nous voici de nouveau face à face. Nous reprenons ce long débat où nous l'avions laissé.

Et vous pouvez pousser vos arguments comme des mufles bas sur l'eau: je ne vous laisserai point de pause ni répit.

. . . Que voulez-vous encore de moi, ô souffle originel? Et vous, que pensez-vous encore tirer de ma lèvre vivante,

O force errante sur mon seuil, ô Mendiante dans nos voies et sur les traces du Prodigue?

Le vent nous conte sa vieillesse, le vent nous conte sa jeunesse. . . Honore, ô Prince, ton exil!

Et soudain tout m'est force et présence, où fume encore le thème du néant.

These tendencies were accentuated in *Amers*, published in 1960 – the year in which the poet received the Nobel Prize – and which was followed in 1963 by *Oiseaux*. Here, the human feeling sometimes breaks through in a sensual emotionalism which one regrets. Lacking Claudel's Catholic fervour with its spiritual driving-power, Saint-John Perse is left in the end with himself and nature (as was Supervielle, but so differently) and the two things do not perfectly coalesce. Certainly his rains, winds, snows and seas[1] are symbolical of human experience, but they are not absorbed into the personality. The poet's virtuosity, his immense and patient skill in finding the right and evocative word in every instance, becomes a barrier. There is too much premeditation.

Yet it is for this quality that he most deserves reading. He is a poet for other poets and connoisseurs. To follow him in his intellectually controlled imagery, his never capricious (as in a poet such as Audiberti) choice of nouns and adjectives may not give immediate pleasure, but it is an experience and an object-lesson. One might begin by reading some of his best descriptive passages purely as descriptions, then come to realize afterwards how much else the poet has put in in the way of suggestions and associations. In these few lines from *Neiges*, morning

[1] The literal meaning of *Amers* is 'sea-marks'.

brings the realization that snow has fallen unexpectedly during the night, softly and heavily, covering and transforming the town:

> ... Nul n'a surpris, nul n'a connu, au plus haut front de pierre, le premier affleurement de cette heure soyeuse, le premier attouchement de cette chose fragile et très futile, somme un frôlement de cils. Sur les revêtements de bronze et sur les élancements d'acier chromé, sur les moellons de sourde porcelaine et sur les tuiles de gros verre, sur la fusée de marbre noir et sur l'éperon de metal blanc, nul n'a surpris, nul n'a terni

> cette buée d'un souffle à sa naissance, comme la première transe d'une lame mise à nu. . . Il neigeait, et voici, nous en dirons merveilles: l'aube muette dans sa plume, comme une grande chouette fabuleuse en proie aux souffles de l'esprit, enflait son corps de dahlia blanc. Et de tous les côtés il nous était prodige et fête. Et le salut soit sur la face des terrasses, où l'Architecte, l'autre été, nous a montré des œufs d'engoulevent.[1]

Another prose-poet who might appear to possess some of the same qualities is Francis Ponge (b. 1899). He became known with *Le Parti pris des choses* (1942) and followed it with *Proèmes* (1948), *Le Lézard* (1953), *Le Savon* (1967) and other volumes. In theory he describes natural objects – 'things' or beasts – and meditates upon their essence independently of their human associations. Man, with his emotions, is either ignored or placed on the same level as the rest of the animal, vegetable and mineral kingdoms, which the poet finds more interesting. (This has a general similarity with the cult of the *object* in the New Novel of the fifties, particularly the novels of Robbe-Grillet, which emphasized 'things' before people. In a different order of literature it invites comparison with Rémy Belleau's sixteenth-century poems on the essences of precious stones and natural objects.[2]) This 'mineral poetry', as some French critics have called it, produces such results as this description of pebbles on the beach:

> ... Apporté un jour par l'une des innombrables charrettes du flot, qui depuis lors, semble-t-il, ne déchargent plus que pour les oreilles leur vaine cargaison, chaque galet repose sur l'amoncellement des formes de son antique état, et des formes de son futur.

> Non loin des lieux où une couche de terre végétale recouvre encore ses énormes aïeux, au bas du banc rocheux où s'opère l'acte d'amour de ses parents immédiats, il a son siège au sol formé du grain des mêmes où le flot terrassier le recherche et le perd. . .[3]

But the theory hardly works. Even in this passage 'les charrettes du flot' must suggest man-made carts discharging their loads in a

---

[1] *Engoulevent*: 'nightjar'.   [2] See above, p. 34.
[3] From *Le Galet* in *Le Parti pris des choses*.

human-organized operation. More seriously still, the erosion of the rocks which produces the pebble is forced into an inappropriate context when called 'l'acte d'amour de ses parents immédiats'. To suggest that rocks couple is a flight of fantasy no less extreme than to invent a speaking cat or tree, which belong to the world of the fairy-tale. What Ponge practises is in fact an inverted anthropomorphism, with the supposed essence of the object projected back on the human consciousness, instead of the more usual reverse process. Neither is he a detached observer. In most of his work he constantly comments and even moralizes, creating a new, if pessimistic and materialistic, didacticism.

Nevertheless, the intention is plain and the example is there of a tendency for other writers to develop if they can. The human reaction is to be played down. The unhuman physical environment – or, in Existentialist philosophy, the phenomenal – is to be instated in its own right, and words must be found (but this is the almost insuperable difficulty) to define that right in a language free of extraneous associations.

IV

The poets considered in this and the previous chapter had completed all, or most of, their best work by the 1950s. The oldest of them, Saint-John Perse, Supervielle and Jouve, were born in the same decade as T. S. Eliot and Ezra Pound; the youngest, Pierre Emmanuel and La Tour du Pin, are only a few years younger than Auden. Who, it might be asked, are their successors?

One reason why this question cannot be answered satisfactorily, at least at present, is to be found in a change in the standing and function of poetry itself. After a renewal of vigour arising from the war of 1939–45, French poetry ceased fairly rapidly to be a main medium of expression for the national sensibility, as happened in England also. 'Poetry', of course, still flourished elsewhere, in the novel and the drama and sometimes in the popular and mass media, but in the narrower definition of poetry as a literary form with something at least approaching a recognizable structure it was no longer widely read.

Yet it continued to be written. As far as can be judged there has been no decline in the number of poets or in the quality of their work, published often in ephemeral 'little reviews'. From this poetic activity of a high average level, few names stand out prominently. That of Yves Bonnefoy is one of the most notable, but he was born as early as

1923 and cannot be considered a young poet. Nevertheless his work is typical of much modern French poetry, which possesses certain general characteristics.

Negatively, it is not based on any established religious, philosophical or metaphysical systems and lacks the strong convictions associated with these; as another consequence, it does not reflect the mythologies connected with such systems, although it still contains occasional references, usually oblique, to aspects of Greek and even Christian mythology. Neither is it political. Though deep issues of national conscience have occupied French intellectuals, French poetry since Aragon and Prévert has not been *engagée*, either idealistically or satirically. No notable 'public poetry' has emerged. Equally, the 'private poetry' has been remarkably restrained in the open expression of emotion. The tendency to subordinate this to a contemplation of the objective world, which we have observed in Saint-John Perse and Ponge, has been very strong. Love, particularly in its erotic aspect, is probably still the main theme, but the treatment tends to be symbolical and even, in a discreet way, metaphysical, and these developments sometimes give it a new significance. While attempting to confine himself to sex, shell-fish and stones, the poet is led to indulge in the old human weakness of speculating on the meaning of life, though he can only do this very indirectly.

The result is an esoteric poetry. The popular forms have failed. No true poet can command a large audience, nor does he seek to do so. Most modern French poetry is either apparently casual and uninsistent (an extreme development of Verlaine and Apollinaire), or it demands the closest attention and study by readers who are prepared to become initiates (in this respect only developing the tradition of Mallarmé) and in any period such readers cannot be numerous. Given the historical moment, this is the form in which poetry has the best chance of survival, addressed to the happy few. Poetry sung in night-clubs or recited in pubs is fun, but the more difficult kind has greater staying-power and in the end, in spite of its restricted appeal, much greater influence.

Bibliography

Works concerning more than one poet
(The titles marked † are anthologies, the rest studies.)

General

†BOASE, A. M. *The Poetry of France.* 4 vols. Methuen, 1964–73.
†MANSELL JONES, P. *The Oxford Book of French Verse.* Oxford University Press, 1957.
GUTMANN, R. A. *Introduction à la lecture des poètes français.* Flammarion, 1946.
GRAMMONT, M. *Petit traité de versification française.* A. Colin, 1965.

Sixteenth to eighteenth centuries

†AURY, D. *Anthologie de la poésie religieuse française.* Gallimard, 1943.
CHAMARD, H. *Histoire de la Pléiade.* 4 vols. Didier, 1939–40.
†GRAHAM, V. E. *Sixteenth-Century French Poetry.* University of Toronto Press and O.U.P., 1965.
†GRAY, F. *Anthologie de la poésie française du 16e siècle.* Appleton-Century-Crofts, 1967.
LEBÈGUE, R. *La Poésie française de 1560 à 1630.* 2 vols. Société d'édition d'enseignement supérieur, 1951.
†MOURGUES, O. DE. *An Anthology of French Seventeenth-Century Lyric Poetry.* O.U.P., 1966.
— *Metaphysical, Baroque and Précieux Poetry.* O.U.P., 1953.
PEYRE, H. *Qu'est-ce que le classicisme?* Rev. ed. Nizet, 1965.
RAYMOND, M. *Baroque et Renaissance poétique.* Corti, 1955.
†ROUSSET, J. *Anthologie de la poésie baroque française.* 2 vols. A. Colin, 1961.
— *La Littérature de l'âge baroque en France.* Corti, 1961.
SCHMIDT, A.-M. *La Poésie scientifique en France au seizième siècle.* A. Michel, 1939.
†— *Poètes du seizième siècle.* Pléiade, 1953.
†STEELE, A. J. *Three Centuries of French Verse, 1511–1819.* Edinburgh University Press, 1956.
WINEGARTEN, R. *French Lyric Poetry in the Age of Malherbe.* Manchester University Press, 1954.

Nineteenth and twentieth centuries

†BÉDOUIN, J.-L. *La Poésie surréaliste.* Seghers, 1964.
BERNARD, S. *Le Poème en prose de Baudelaire jusqu'à nos jours.* Nizet, 1959.

†CLANCIER, G.-E. *Panorama critique de Rimbaud au surréalisme*. Seghers, 1953.

DUPLESSIS, Y. *Le Surréalisme*. Presses Universitaires de France, 1964.

FOWLIE, W. *Age of Surrealism*. University of Indiana Press, 1960.

GIBSON, R. *Modern French Poets on Poetry*. Cambridge University Press, 1961.

†HACKETT, C. A. *Anthology of Modern French Poetry*. Blackwell, 1964.

MARTINO, P. *Parnasse et symbolisme*. A. Colin, 1925.

†MATTHEWS, J. H. *French Surrealist Poetry*. University of London Press, 1966.

MICHAUD, G. *Le Message poétique du symbolisme*. 4 vols. Nizet, 1947.

NADEAU, M. *Histoire du surréalisme*. Club des Éditeurs, 1957.

†PARMÉE, D. *Twelve French Poets, 1820–1900*. Longmans, 1957.

RAYMOND, M. *De Baudelaire au surréalisme*. Corti, 1952.

RICHARD, J.-P. *Poésie et profondeur*. Éditions du Seuil, 1955. (On Nerval, Baudelaire, Verlaine, Rimbaud.)

— *Onze études sur la poésie moderne*. Éditions du Seuil, 1964. (On Char, Ponge, Bonnefoy, etc.)

ROUSSELOT, J. *Dictionnaire de la poésie française contemporaine*. Larousse, 1968.

†— *Panorama critique des nouveaux poètes français*. Seghers, 1953.

SCHMIDT, A.-M. *La Littérature symboliste*. P.U.F., 1947.

Individual Poets

The chief poetical works only of each poet are listed, with dates of first publication, unless otherwise stated (wr. = written, with publication later). Then follow particulars of modern editions, with selected studies for further reading.

Chapter 1

François Villon (b. Paris, 1431 (?); trace lost after January 1463)

Les Lais (wr. 1456), *Le Testament* (wr. 1461). First printed edition 1489. *Œuvres*. Ed. A. Longnon, rev. L. Foulet. Champion, 1923.
  Ed. A. Mary. Garnier, 1951.
  Ed. A. Pauphilet in *Poètes et romanciers du moyen age*. Pléiade, 1952.
Le Testament et poésies diverses. Ed. B. Nelson Sargent. Appleton-Century-Crofts, 1967.

DESONAY, F. *François Villon*. Droz, 1947.

SICILIANO, I. *F. Villon et les thèmes poétiques du moyen age*. Nizet, 1934; reprinted 1967.

Chapter 2

Pierre de Ronsard (1524–85)

Odes (1550–2), *Amours de Cassandre* (1552–3), *Amours de Marie* (1555–6), *Hymnes* (1555–6), *Discours* (1560–3), *Sonnets pour Hélène* (1578).

Édition critique des œuvres de Ronsard. Ed. P. Laumonier *et al.* S.T.F.M., 1914 etc. (For specialists.)

Œuvres complètes. Ed. G. Cohen. 2 vols. Pléiade, 1938.

Les Amours. Ed. H. W. and C. Weber. Garnier, 1963.

Sonnets pour Hélène. Ed. M. Smith. Droz, 1970.

LEBÈGUE, R. *Ronsard, l'homme et l'œuvre.* Rev. ed. Boivin, 1966.

GADOFFRE, G. *Ronsard par lui-même.* Éditions du Seuil, 1960.

SILVER, I. *The Intellectual Evolution of Ronsard,* Vol. I. Washington University Press, 1969.

Chapter 3

Joachim Du Bellay (1522–60)

L'Olive (1549–50), [*Deffence et illustration de la langue françoise* (1549)] *Jeux rustiques* (1558), *Les Antiquités de Rome* (1558), *Les Regrets* (1558).

Œuvres. Ed. H. Chamard, 7 vols. Droz, 1908–31.

Ed. E. Courbet. 2 vols. Garnier, 1918.

Les Antiquités de Rome et Les Regrets. Ed. E. Droz. Droz, 1945.

In *Poètes du 16e siècle.* Ed. A.-M. Schmidt. Pléiade, 1953.

Jeux rustiques. Ed. V.-L. Saulnier. Droz, 1947.

Selection in *Poems.* Ed. H. W. Lawton. Blackwell, 1961.

SAULNIER, V.-L. *Du Bellay, l'homme et l'œuvre.* Boivin, 1951.

Chapter 4

(1) Clément Marot (1496–1544)

Épîtres, Épigrammes, Élégies, Chansons, Rondeaux, Oraisons (all wr. c. 1514–1544), collected in *L'Adolescence Clémentine* (1532–4) and *Œuvres* (1538 and 1542); *Psaumes* (1541–3).

Critical edition of complete poetic works by C. A. Mayer. 4 vols. University of London, Athlone Press, 1958–70.

Œuvres complètes. Ed. A. Grenier. 2 vols. Garnier, 1938.

JOURDA, P. *Marot, l'homme et l'œuvre.* Boivin, 1940.

(2) Maurice Scève (1501?–63?)

Délie (1544), *La Saulsaye* (1547), *Microcosme* (1562).

Poésies complètes. Ed. P. Guégan. Garnier, 1927.

Délie. Ed. I. D. McFarlane. C.U.P., 1966.

In *Poètes du 16e siècle.* Ed. A.-M. Schmidt. Pléiade, 1953.

SAULNIER, V.-L. *Maurice Scève.* 2 vols. Klincksieck, 1948.

(3) Guillaume de Salluste Du Bartas (1544–90)

La Semaine (1578), *Seconde Semaine* (1584).
Works. Ed. U. T. Holmes *et al.* 3 vols. O.U.P., 1935–40.
Selections in M. Braspart, *Du Bartas, poète chrétien.* Delachaux et Niestlé,
   1947.
In *Poètes du 16e siècle.* Ed. A.-M. Schmidt. Pléiade, 1953.

(4) Agrippa d'Aubigné (1551–1630)

Le Printemps (wr. *c.* 1570–4), *Les Tragiques* (1616).
Le Printemps. Ed. B. Gagnebin and F. Desonay. 2 vols. Droz, 1948–52.
Les Tragiques. Ed. A. Garnier and J. Plattard. 4 vols. Didier, 1932–3.
   Ed. J. Bailbé. Garnier-Flammarion, 1968.
   Selections ed. I. D. McFarlane. Athlone Press, 1970.
PLATTARD, J. *A. d'Aubigné.* Hatier, 1935.
BUFFUM, I. *A. d'Aubigné's 'Les Tragiques'.* Yale University Press, 1951.
BAILBÉ, J. *A. d'Aubigné, poète des 'Tragiques'.* University of Caen, 1968.

(5) Jean de Sponde (1557–95)

Essai de quelques poèmes chrétiens (1588).
Poésies. Ed. A. M. Boase and F. Ruchon. Cailler, 1949.
Méditations. Ed. A. M. Boase. Corti, 1954.

(6) Jean de La Ceppède (*c.* 1550–1622)

Théorèmes sur le sacré mystère de notre rédemption (1613–21).
Selection in F. Ruchon, *Essai sur la vie et l'œuvre de J. de La Ceppède.* Droz,
   1953.

Chapter 5

François Malherbe (1555–1628)

Les Larmes de Saint Pierre (1587), *Odes* and versions of Psalms (1600–27),
   Œuvres (1630).
Poésies. Ed. J. Lavaud. 2 vols. Droz, 1936–7.
Œuvres poétiques. Ed. R. Fromilhague and R. Lebègue. Les Textes français,
   1968.
FROMILHAGUE, R. *Malherbe, technique et création poétique.* A. Colin, 1954.
— *La Vie de Malherbe.* A. Colin, 1954.

Chapter 6

(1) Théophile de Viau (1590–1626)

Œuvres (1621–6)
Œuvres poétiques. Ed. J. Streicher. 2 vols. Droz, 1951–8.

(2) Antoine-Girard de Saint-Amant (1594–1661)

Œuvres (1629–32, 1642, 1649), *Moïse sauvé* (1653), *Dernier recueil de diverses poésies* (1658)
Œuvres complètes. Ed. J. Bailbé. 5 vols. S.T.F.M., 1970 etc.
Œuvres poétiques. Ed. L. Verane. Garnier, 1930. (Selection.)
LAGNY, J. *Le Poète Saint-Amant*. Nizet, 1964.

(3) Tristan L'Hermite (*c*. 1601–55)

Les Plaintes d'Acante (1633), *Les Amours* (1638), *La Lyre* (1641), *Vers héroïques* (1648), *L'Office de la Sainte-Vierge* (1646).
Les Amours et autres poésies choisies. Ed. P. Camo. Garnier, 1925.
Poésies choisies. Ed. P. A. Wadsworth. Seghers, 1962.

Chapter 7

Jean Racine (1639–99)

Plays listed on p. 69, footnote. Non-dramatic verse: *Paysage de Port-Royal* (juvenile), *Hymnes du Bréviaire romain* (1687), *Cantiques spirituels* (1694).

Œuvres complètes. Ed. R. Picard. 2 vols. Pléiade, 1951–2.
MOREAU, P. *Racine, l'homme et l'œuvre*. Hatier, 1952.
VINAVER, E. *Racine and Poetic Tragedy*. Manchester University Press, 1955.
GIRAUDOUX, J. *Racine*. Grasset, 1930.
KNIGHT, R. C. (ed.). *Racine*. Macmillan, 1969. (Modern critical essays with good bibliography.)

Chapter 8

Jean de La Fontaine (1621–95)

Adonis (wr. before 1657), *Le Songe de Vaux* (wr. 1658–61), *Élégies* (1661–1671), *Contes et nouvelles en vers* (1665–74), *Fables* (1668–94).

Fables, contes et nouvelles. Ed. R. Groos *et al*. Pléiade, 1933.
    Ed. G. Couton. 2 vols. Garnier, 1961–2.
Œuvres diverses. Ed. P. Clarac. Pléiade, 1942.
CLARAC, P. *La Fontaine, l'homme et l'œuvre*. Boivin, 1947.
GUITON, M. *La Fontaine, Poet and Counterpoet*. Rutgers University Press, 1961.
KOHN, R. *Le Goût de La Fontaine*. P.U.F., 1962.
MOURGUES, O. DE. *O Muse, fuyante proie*. Corti, 1962.

Chapter 9

André Chénier (1762–94)

Bucoliques, Élégies, Odes (wr. *c*. 1780–94), *Iambes* (wr. 1794). First published edition, 1819.

Œuvres complètes. Ed. G. Walter. Pléiade, 1950.
Poems. Ed. F. Scarfe. Blackwell, 1961. (Selection.)
FABRE, J. *Chénier, l'homme et l'œuvre.* Hatier-Boivin, 1955.
SCARFE, F. *A. Chénier, his Life and Work.* O.U.P., 1965.

Chapter 10

Alphonse de Lamartine (1790–1869)

Méditations poétiques (1820), *Les Nouvelles Méditations* (1823), *Les Har-
monies* (1830), *La Chute d'un ange* (1838), *Recueillements poétiques*
(1839).
Œuvres poétiques complètes. Ed. M.-F. Guyard. Pléiade, 1963.
Méditations. Ed. F. Letessier. Garnier, 1968.
GUILLEMIN, H. *Lamartine, l'homme et l'œuvre.* Boivin, 1940.
GUYARD, M.-F. *A. de Lamartine.* Éditions Universitaires, 1956.

Chapter 11

Alfred de Vigny (1797–1863)

Poèmes antiques et modernes (1826), *Les Destinées* (1864).
Œuvres complètes. Ed. F. Baldensperger. 2 vols. Pléiade, 1948–9.
Poésies complètes. Ed. A. Dorchain. Garnier, 1948.
Les Destinées. Ed. V.-L. Saulnier. Droz, 1947.
CASTEX, P.-G. *A. de Vigny, l'homme et l'œuvre.* Boivin, 1952.

Chapter 12

Victor Hugo (1802–85)

For chief works, including verse collections, see above, p. 125, footnote.
Œuvres complètes. Ed. P. Meurice and G. Simon. 45 vols. Imprimerie
Nationale, 1904–52. (For specialists.)
Les Contemplations. Ed. A. Dumas. Garnier, 1962.
La Légende des siècles, etc. Ed. J. Truchet. Pléiade, 1950.
BARRÈRE, J.-B. *V. Hugo, l'homme et l'œuvre.* Boivin, 1952.
— *La Fantaisie de V. Hugo.* 3 vols. Corti, 1949–60.
GUILLEMIN, H. *V. Hugo par lui-même.* Éditions du Seuil, 1951.

Chapter 13

Alfred de Musset (1810–57)

Namouna (1832), *Rolla* (1833), *Les Nuits* (wr. 1835–7).
Poésies complètes. Ed. M. Allem. Pléiade, 1957.
Premières poésies and *Poésies nouvelles.* Ed. G. Bulli. Livre de Poche, 1966.
Selection in P. Soupault, *A. de Musset.* Seghers, 1957.
TIEGHEM, P. VAN. *Musset, l'homme et l'œuvre.* Boivin, 1945.

Chapter 14

Charles Baudelaire (1821–67)

Les Fleurs du mal (1857), *Petits poèmes en prose* (1869).
Œuvres complètes. Ed. Y.-G. Le Dantec. Pléiade, 1952.
    Ed. M. Ruff. Éditions du Seuil, 1968.
Les Fleurs du mal. Ed. J. Crépet and G. Blin. Rev. ed. Corti, 1968.
    Ed. A. Adam. Garnier, 1959.
Petits poèmes en prose. Ed. R. Kopp. Corti, 1969.
PEYRE, H. *Connaissance de Baudelaire*. Corti, 1951.
RUFF, M. *Baudelaire, l'homme et l'œuvre*. Boivin, 1955.
STARKIE, E. *Baudelaire*. Faber and Faber, 1957.
AUSTIN, L. J. *L'Univers poétique de Baudelaire*. Mercure de France, 1956.
FAIRLIE, A. *Baudelaire, 'Les Fleurs du mal'*. Arnold, 1960.
SARTRE, J.-P. *Baudelaire*. Gallimard, 1947. (The Existentialist interpretation.)

Chapter 15

(1) Charles-Marie René Leconte de Lisle (1818–94)

Poèmes antiques (1852), *Poèmes barbares* (1862), *Poèmes tragiques* (1884),
    Derniers poèmes (1895).
Poésies complètes. 4 vols. Lemerre, 1927–8.
Choix de poésies. Lemerre, 1933.
ESTÈVE, E. *L. de Lisle, l'homme et l'œuvre*. Boivin, 1923.
FLOTTES, P. *L. de Lisle*. Connaissance des Lettres, 1954.
VIANEY, J. *Les 'Poèmes barbares' de L. de Lisle*. E. Malfère, 1933.

(2) José-Maria de Heredia (1842–1905)

Les Trophées (1893). Repub. Lemerre, 1933.
IBROVAC, M. *J.-M. de Heredia*. 2 vols. Nizet, 1923.

Chapter 16

Paul Verlaine (1844–96)

Poèmes saturniens (1866), *Fêtes galantes* (1869), *La Bonne Chanson* (1870),
    Romances sans paroles (1874), *Sagesse* (1881), *Jadis et naguère* (1884),
    Amour (1888), *Parallèlement* (1889). For later volumes see above, p.
    180, footnote.
Œuvres poétiques complètes. Ed. Y.-G. Le Dantec. Pléiade, 1938.
Œuvres poétiques. Ed. J. Robichez. Garnier, 1969. (1866–89 only.)
ADAM, A. *Verlaine, l'homme et l'œuvre*. Boivin, 1953.
MARTINO, P. *Verlaine*. Boivin, 1924.
RICHARDSON, J. *Verlaine*. Weidenfeld and Nicolson, 1971.

Chapter 17

Arthur Rimbaud (1854–91)

Verse poems (wr. *c*. 1870–2), *Une Saison en enfer* (1873), *Les Illuminations* (1886),[1] *Poésies complètes* (1895).
Œuvres complètes. Ed. R. de Renéville and J. Mouquet. Pléiade, 1963.
Œuvres. Ed. S. Bernard. Garnier, 1960.
STARKIE, E. *Arthur Rimbaud*. Hamish Hamilton, 1961.
ÉTIEMBLE, R., and GAUCLÈRE, Y. *Rimbaud*. Gallimard, 1950.
HACKETT, C. A. *Rimbaud*. Bowes and Bowes, 1957.

Chapter 18

Stéphane Mallarmé (1842–98)

L'Après-midi d'un faune (1876), *Poésies* (1887), *Un Coup de dés* (1897).
Œuvres complètes. Ed. H. Mondor and G. Jean-Aubry. Pléiade, 1951.
MICHAUD, G. *Mallarmé, l'homme et l'œuvre*. Boivin, 1953.
VALÉRY, P. *Écrits divers sur S. Mallarmé*. Gallimard, 1950.
RICHARD, J.-P. *L'Univers imaginaire de Mallarmé*. Éditions du Seuil, 1961.
CHISHOLM, A. R. *Mallarmé's 'Grand Œuvre'*. Manchester University Press, 1962.
CHADWICK, C. *Mallarmé: sa pensée dans sa poésie*. Corti, 1962.

Chapter 19

(1) Gérard de Nerval (1808–55)
Les Chimères (1854). Ed. J. Moulin. Droz, 1949.
Œuvres. Ed. A. Béguin and J. Richer. 3 vols. Pléiade, 1952.
Les Filles du feu, Les Chimères. Ed. L. Cellier. Garnier-Flammarion, 1965.
BÉGUIN, A. *G. de Nerval*. Corti, 1945.
CELLIER, L. *G. de Nerval, l'homme et l'œuvre*. Boivin, 1952.

(2) Théophile Gautier (1811–72)
Albertus (1832), *La Comédie de la mort* (1838), *España* (1845), *Émaux et camées* (1852).
Poésies complètes. Ed. R. Jasinski. 3 vols. F. Didot, 1932.
Émaux et camées. Ed. J. Pommier and G. Matoré. Droz, 1947.
LARGUIER, L. *Th. Gautier*. Tallandier, 1948.
RICHARDSON, J. *Th. Gautier*. Reinhardt, 1958.

(3) Tristan Corbière (1845–75)
Les Amours jaunes (1873). Ed. Y.-G. Le Dantec. Gallimard, 1953.
Selection in J. Rousselot, *Tristan Corbière*. Seghers, 1952.
SONNENFELD, A. *L'Œuvre poétique de Tristan Corbière*. Princeton University Press and P.U.F., 1960.

[1] See above pp. 203–4.

(4) Jules Laforgue (1860–87)

Les Complaintes (1885), *L'Imitation de Notre-Dame la Lune* (1886), *Derniers vers* (1890).

Poésies. Ed. G. Jean-Aubry. 2 vols. Mercure de France, 1922.

Derniers vers. Ed. M. Collie and J. M. L'Heureux. University of Toronto Press and O.U.P., 1966.

Selection in M.-J. Durry, *Jules Laforgue*. Seghers, 1952.

GUICHARD, L. *J. Laforgue et ses poésies*. P.U.F., 1950.

RAMSAY, W. *J. Laforgue and the Ironic Inheritance*. O.U.P., 1953.

REBOUL, P. *Laforgue*. Hatier, 1960.

Chapter 20

(1) Paul Claudel (1868–1955)

Poetry: *Connaissance de l'Est* (prose poems, 1900), *Cinq grandes odes* (1910), *La Cantate à trois voix* (1914), *Poèmes de guerre* (1922), *Feuilles de saints* (1925).

Principal plays: *Tête d'or* (1890), *La Ville* (1893), *Partage de midi* (1906), *L'Otage* (1911), *L'Annonce faite à Marie* (1912), *Le Pain dur* (1918), *Le Père humilié* (1920), *Le Soulier de satin* (1930).

Œuvres. Ed. J. Madaule. *Théâtre*, 2 vols. *Œuvre poétique*, 1 vol. Pléiade, 1951–7.

Selections in L. Perche, *P. Claudel*. Seghers, 1949.

Separate titles published by Gallimard.

MADAULE, J. *Le Génie de P. Claudel*. Desclée de Brouwer, 1933.

CHONEZ, C. *Introduction à P. Claudel*. A. Michel, 1947.

FUMET, S. *Claudel*. Nouvelle Revue Française, 1959.

MAVROCORDATO, A. *L'Ode de P. Claudel*. Droz, 1955.

LESORT, P.-A. *P. Claudel par lui-même*. Éditions du Seuil, 1963.

(2) Guillaume Apollinaire (1880–1918)

Alcools (1913), *Calligrammes* (1918).

Œuvres poétiques complètes. Ed. M. Adéma and M. Décaudin. Pléiade, 1959.

Selections in A. Billy, *Apollinaire*. Seghers, 1947.

ADÉMA, M. *Apollinaire le mal-aimé*. Plon, 1952.

DURRY, M.-J. *G. Apollinaire: 'Alcools'*. Sedes, 1955.

DAVIES, M. *Apollinaire*. Oliver and Boyd, 1964.

Chapter 21

Paul Valéry (1871–1945)

La Jeune Parque (1917), *Charmes* (1922).

Both contained in *Poésies*. Gallimard, 1942.

Œuvres. Ed. J. Hytier. 2 vols. Pléiade, 1957–60.

BÉMOL, M. *P. Valéry*. Les Belles Lettres, 1949.

HYTIER, J. *La Poétique de Valéry*. A. Colin, 1953.
SCARFE, F. *The Art of P. Valéry*. Heinemann, 1954.
INCE, W. N. *The Poetic Theory of P. Valéry*. Leicester University Press, 1961.

Chapter 22

Titles of the principal poetic works of these poets are given in the text of the chapter. All, except Prévert and Audiberti, appear in the series *Poètes d'aujourd'hui* (Seghers): selections with introductions and bibliographies. See also the relevant anthologies and general critical works listed above under 'Nineteenth and twentieth centuries'. Additionally:

(1) Paul Éluard (1895–1952)

Œuvres. Ed. L. Schéler. Pléiade, 1968.
Choix de poèmes. Gallimard, 1951.
CARROUGES, M. *Éluard et Char*. Éditions du Seuil, 1945.

(2) René Char (b. 1907)

Collective volumes: *Fureur et mystère* (1948), *Recherche de la base et du sommet* (1965). Selections in *Commune présence*, preface by G. Blin (1964). All Gallimard.
RAU, G. *René Char*. Corti, 1957.

(3) Louis Aragon (b. 1897)

GARAUDY, R. *L'Itinéraire d'Aragon*. Gallimard, 1961.

(4) Robert Desnos (1900–45)

Collective edition: *Domaine public*. Gallimard, 1953.

(5) Henri Michaux (b. 1899)

Selections in *L'Espace du dedans* (1944), *La Vie dans les plis* (1949).
Selected writings of H. Michaux. With trans. by Robert Ellmann. New Directions. Routledge, 1952.
BRÉCHON, R. *Michaux*. Gallimard, 1959.

(6) Jacques Prévert (b. 1900)

QUÉVAL, J. *J. Prévert*. Mercure de France, 1955.

(7) Raymond Queneau (b. 1903)

BENS, J. *Queneau*. Gallimard, 1962.
BERGEN, A. *R. Queneau*. Droz, 1963.

(8) Jacques Audiberti (1899–1965)

DESLANDES, A. *Audiberti*. Gallimard, 1964.

(9) Antonin Artaud (1896–1948)

Œuvres complètes. Gallimard, 1956–67.

Chapter 23

See note heading previous chapter. Selections from all the following poets except Luc Estang, Cayrol and Bonnefoy appear in the series *Poètes d'aujourd'hui* (Seghers).

(1) Pierre Jean Jouve (b. 1887)

Œuvre poétique. 4 vols. Mercure de France, 1964–7.
STAROBINSKI, J., *et al. P. J. Jouve.* La Baconnière, 1946.
ROUSSELOT, J. *P. J. Jouve.* L'Esprit des Lettres, 1956.
CALLANDER, M. *The Poetry of P. J. Jouve.* Manchester University Press, 1965.
Special number of *La Nouvelle Revue Française.* 1 March 1968.

(2) Pierre Emmanuel (b. 1916)

Selected poems in *Ligne de Faîte.* Éditions du Seuil, 1966.

(3) Patrice de La Tour du Pin (b. 1911)

Une Somme de poésie. N.R.F., 1946.
Le Second Jeu. N.R.F., 1959.

(4) Luc Estang (b. 1911)

Earlier poems collected in *Les Quatre Éléments* (1955).

(5) Jean Cayrol (b. 1911)

OSTER, D. *J. Cayrol et son œuvre.* Éditions du Seuil, 1967.

(6) Jules Supervielle (1884–1960)

Poèmes. Gallimard, 1945.
Choix de poèmes. Gallimard, 1947.
GREENE, T. W. *J. Supervielle.* Droz, 1958.
Special number of *La Nouvelle Revue Française*, No. 94 (1960).
HIDDLESTON, J. A. *L'Univers de Supervielle.* Corti, 1965.

(7) Saint-John Perse (b. 1887)

CAILLOIS, R. *Poétique de Saint-John Perse.* Gallimard, 1954.
CHARPIER, J. *Saint-John Perse.* Gallimard, 1962.
LORANQUIN, A. *Saint-John Perse.* Gallimard, 1963.
KNODEL, A. *Saint-John Perse, a study of his poetry.* Edinburgh University Press, 1966.

(8) Francis Ponge (b. 1899)

Le Grand Recueil (1961), *Tome premier* (1965), *Le Nouveau Recueil* (1967).
THIBAUDEAU, J. *Ponge par lui-même*. Gallimard, 1967.

(9) Yves Bonnefoy (b. 1923)

Du mouvement et de l'immobilité de Douve (1953), *Hier régnant désert* (1956),
   Pierre écrite (1965).

Index

Principal references are shown in italics